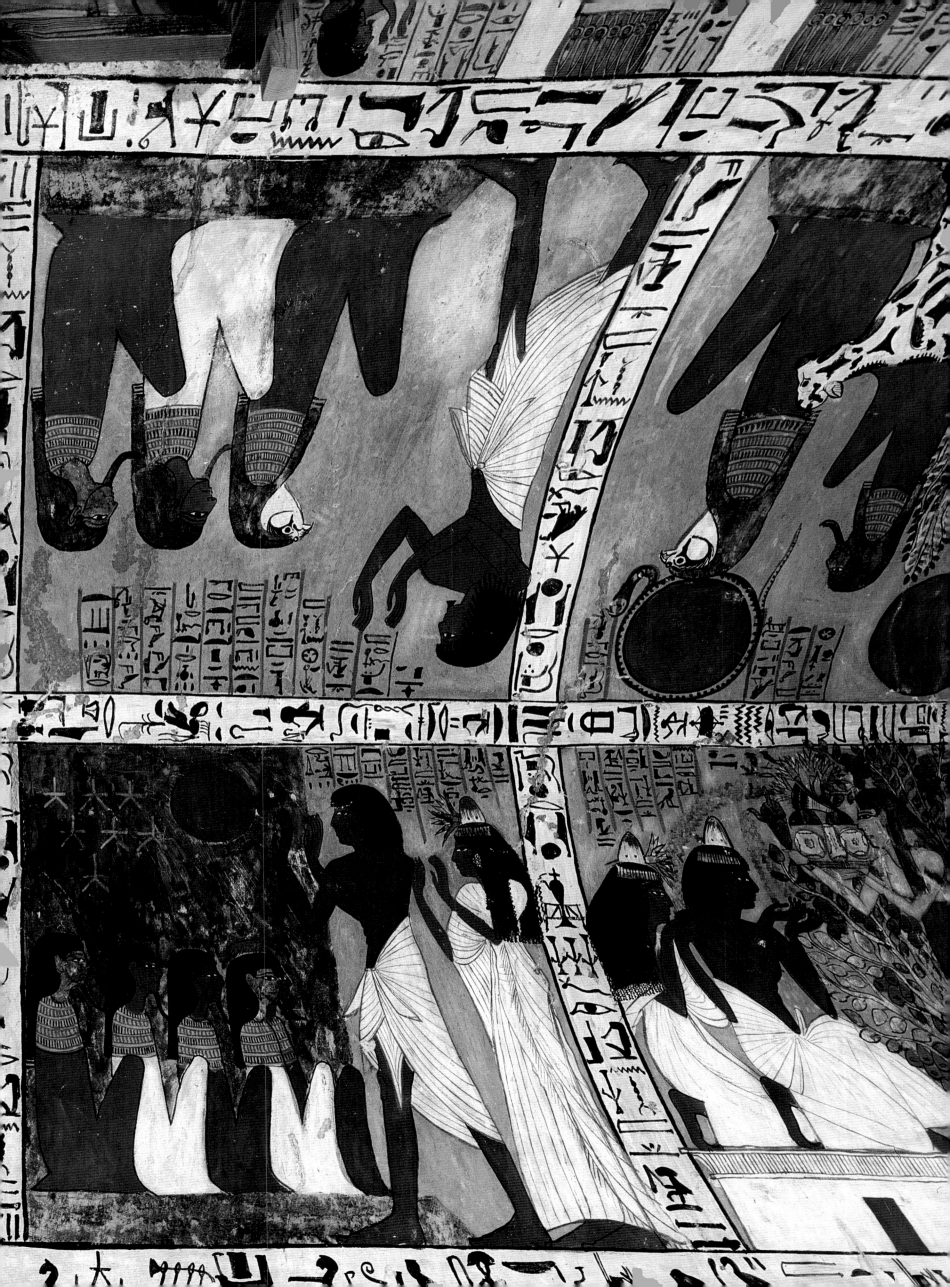

# The Hidden Treasures of Antiquity

E D I T E D   B Y   A L B E R T O   S I L I O T T I

## BARNES & NOBLE
### NEW YORK

| TEXTS | | EDITORS | TRANSLATION |
|---|---|---|---|
| | | Valeria Manferto De Fabianis | C.T.M., Milan |
| Marilia Albanese | Danila Piacentini | | GRAPHIC DESIGN |
| Walter Alva | Filippo Salviati | | Clara Zanotti |
| Furio Durando | Claudio Saporetti | EDITORAL COORDINATION | |
| Paola d'Amore | Alberto Siliotti | Fabio Bourbon | |
| Matos Moctezuma | Marcello Spanu | Bianca Filippone | |
| Emiliana Petrioli | Alberto Trombetta | Giulia Gaida | |

# CONTENTS

*1 A PHOENICIAN FUNERARY MASK INTENDED TO PROTECT AGAINST EVIL INFLUENCES.*

*2-3 SACRED FIGURES SURROUNDING THE TOMB OF ANTIOCHUS I AT NEMRUD DAG (TURKEY)..*

*4-5 ANGKOR WAT (CAMBODIA), ONE OF THE LARGEST FUNERARY MONUMENTS IN THE WORLD.*

*6-7 THE TOMB OF SENNEDJEM, A WORKER AT THE ROYAL NECROPOLIS IN THEBES (EGYPT).*

*8 ONE OF THE JAGUAR HEADS OF THE FUNERARY*

*ACCOUTREMENTS OF THE LORD OF SIPAN (PERU).*

*9 ONE OF THE GUARDS OF QIN SHI HUANGDI, FIRST EMPEROR OF CHINA.*

*10-11 AN ETRUSCAN MAN AND WIFE LYING ON A KLINE, OR DINING COUCH.*

*12-13 QIN SHI HUANGDI'S OFFICERS ALIGNED IN THE TOMB OF THE FIRST EMPEROR.*

*14-15 THE BATTLE OF KURUKSHETRA, NORTH OF DELHI, DEPICTED IN A LOW RELIEF AT ANGKOR WAT (CAMBODIA).*

© 2000 by White Star S.p.A.

This 2006 edition published by Barnes & Noble, Inc. by arrangement with White Star S.p.A.

ISBN-13: 978-076-078-881-3
ISBN-10: 076-078-881-2
Library of Congress Cataloging-in-Publication Data available
Printed and bound in China
1 3 5 7 9 10 8 6 4 2
Color separation by Fotomec, Turin

# PREFACE

Preface

Every civilization and culture in the history of man has paid particular attention to the fact of death and to the closely linked concept of a world beyond the grave.

Man's refutation of death as a part of life is reflected in the conviction, held unconsciously by every one of us, that we are in some way immortal. This persuasion, refuted by logic, is shown in the belief in an existence beyond life, an Afterlife, that has been variously represented by all cultures throughout the ages.

Since the Paleolithic era, man has believed in this supernatural reality and considered death – an ineluctable fact that not even the gods were able to avoid – as a passage to another world and the start of a long journey, sometimes considered to be filled with difficulties and danger, that would take the deceased to a parallel world in some way attached to the real one.

For prehistoric man, the natural world in which he lived was not a simple physical environment but a dimension pervaded by supernatural forces that were part and parcel of the world and contributed to events that occurred within it. As such, death did not represent the end of life but a passage to another existence that was imagined to be concretely and tangibly similar to earthly life in which the dead had the same prerogatives, the same desires and, above all, the same needs.

In other words, there was no proper boundary between the world of the living and the world of the dead but, on the contrary, a continuous interaction; this followed from prehistoric man's belief, demonstrated in many myths, that heaven and earth were originally one and the same and only divided at a later time.

This concept was also fundamental to other civilizations: in the Egyptian cosmogony, for example, the god of the air, Shu, separated the earth personified by the god Geb from the heaven personified by the goddess Nut. And the Sumerians believed that the god Enlil decreed the same separation and so created the world that we know.

The notion that the world beyond the grave could interact in some way with our world meant that the dead became objects of worship; at first in simple rituals but later in more complex cults that saw their tombs increase in size and elaborateness until they became "dwellings of eternity."

16 BOTTOM
*MAGNIFICENT ETRUSCAN*
*ORNAMENTS LIKE THESE*
*STUDS FROM TODI ARE*
*EVIDENCE OF THE*
*REFINEMENT THIS*
*CIVILIZATION ACHIEVED.*

16-17 *THIS FRESCO IN THE*
*TOMB OF THE DIVER AT*
*PAESTUM SHOWS A*
*BANQUET SCENE, A THEME*
*THAT WAS COMMON IN*
*ETRUSCAN FUNERARY*
*ICONOGRAPHY.*

In the region of the Near East now corresponding to Iraq, the custom of burying the dead following a precise ritual seems to have already been developed during the Middle Paleolithic era; this is indicated by the grave found at Shanidar, dated to about 70,000 BC, in which the skeleton of a Neanderthal man was found lying on a bed of flowers.

The earliest form of burial so far known in Africa was found at the site named Nazlet Khater-4 in Egypt and has been dated to circa 33,000 BC. In this grave, a man similar to the European Cro-Magnon was buried on his back with a stone axe near his head. This rudimentary grave shows the appearance of a new sensibility and a different attitude towards death and the Afterlife. It represents an embryonic form of the cult of the dead that was sometimes transformed into the cult of the ancestors which enabled an individual to affirm his identity as a member of a particular group or tribe.

Only when man abandoned his economy based on hunting, fishing and gathering that forced him to live a nomadic lifestyle, and passed to a life that centered on exploiting the agricultural resources of his land and domestication of animals, which required that he remained stationary, could he practice a real cult of the dead and build elaborate tombs.

Settlement also imposed the creation of organized structures with areas set aside for crafts, commerce and the first religious ceremonies. It also saw the creation of a leader who directed and regulated all the collective work necessary for the consolidation of a prevalently agricultural economy.

Other figures with specific responsibilities were soon collected around this emblematic individual, for example, the construction of defensive structures, the organization of social life and the performance of religious rituals. This step led to the development of social classes and prefigured the appearance of the warriors, the functionaries and the priests. The presence of a central leader and the existence of a hierarchical society made construction of the first monumental tombs possible, as such enormous constructions required a collective effort that transcended the

*18 bottom The tombs in the royal necropolises at Ur in Iraq date from the 3rd millennium BC. They contained grave goods of exquisite manufacture – like this small cosmetics container which belonged to Princess Pu-Abi – that demonstrate how far the art of the culture had developed.*

*19 The entrance to the burial chamber of Pashedu at Deir el-Medina in Egypt was decorated with passages from the Book of the Dead and watched over by the god Anubis with the head of a dog.*

*20-21 The deceased Horemheb, the pharaoh of obscure birth who concluded the XVIII Dynasty, offers wine to Isis and Harsiesis, the falcon-headed sun god.*

*18 top The splendid grave goods of Tutankhamon contained a great deal of jewelry, including this breastplate decorated with cloisonné inlays with the gold head of a vulture. It was found in the casket that lay in the treasure room.*

individual and with which the group was able to identify. In the fifth millennium BC in Europe, Neolithic man had turned to agriculture. He built the first large tumulus tombs and dolmens in the typical expressions of a megalithic culture that combined funerary, religious and magical rites.

At Jericho in the eastern Mediterranean, populations of the Natufian culture that had begun to practice rudimentary forms of agriculture from the 9th millennium BC, already

*22 TOP  THIS GOLD ORNAMENT IS IN THE SHAPE OF AN EAGLE'S HEAD AND WAS FOUND IN A MIXTEC TOMB AT MONTE ALBÁN.*

*22-23  THE BAS-RELIEFS AT ANGKOR WAT DISPLAY MYTHOLOGICAL SCENES ALONG THE FIRST PORTICO OF THE TEMPLE.  THIS SECTION SHOWS FANTASTIC*

*SEA CREATURES THAT REFER TO THE MYTH OF THE "CHURNING OF THE MILKY OCEAN" ASSOCIATED WITH THE CREATION OF THE UNIVERSE.*

*23  THE CHINESE TERRACOTTA FUNERARY STATUE WITH TRACES OF ITS ORIGINAL POLYCHROME COLORING IS OF A NOBLEWOMAN OF THE TANG*

*PERIOD.  THE ELABORATE HAIRSTYLES OF THE STATUES ARE A VALUABLE SOURCE OF INFORMATION ON THE FASHIONS AND CUSTOMS OF THE PERIOD.*

observed a cult of the dead in which they covered the skulls of the deceased with plaster and set sea-shells in the eye cavities to remodel their features to resemble the living.

In the same period in the Anatolian highlands and in the East, the first early urban centers were forming in which an increasingly marked diversification of sepulchers depending on class and social rank was becoming apparent. The result was the construction of tombs with structures above ground. In northern Luristan

in the Iranian highlands, dozens of small villages arose, one of which, named Choga Mish, grew out of all proportion to cover a surface area of between 10-18 hectares and thus become one of the first urban centers in the history of man.

Early stable settlements with an economy based on hunting, fishing and gathering also appeared in Egypt between the sixth and fifth millennium BC. They too followed a precise ritual in the burial of the dead in which the bodies were wrapped in lengths of cloth and buried on their right side in the fetal position with the head pointing south and face towards the west. This last fact points to the existence of a connection between the world of the dead and the setting sun.

At Mehrgarh in the Indus valley during the same period, the dead were placed in shaft-tombs together with offerings of jewelry set with semi-precious stones. The tombs were then closed by a wall of bricks.

In China, where the domestication of plants was already a fact and the cultivation of rice practiced in huge paddies in the Yangtze delta, the dead were buried in accordance with a precise funerary ritual with the body lying north-south.

It was only in the third millennium BC, at the end of the Neolithic era and the start of the Bronze Age, that the first true examples of monumental tombs appeared containing grave goods: these were the megalithic mounds in Europe, the large proto-dynastic tombs in the necropolises of Abydos and Saqqarah in Egypt, the royal tombs at Ur, the sepulchres built by the Liangzhu culture in the region of Lake Tai in China, and even the earlier funerary mounds – the *kurgan* – raised by the nomadic peoples that lived on the Caucasian and Siberian steppes.

One fact seems to have bound all the different Neolithic civilizations and cultures on the planet together: the belief in a world beyond the grave. The cult of the dead became increasingly important and dwellings of eternity began to be endowed with the characteristics of monumentality and permanence that were to make certain works of funerary architecture some of the most beautiful fruits of the genius of man.

*24-25 LEAVING MYTHOLOGY ASIDE, THE HISTORIC VICTORY OF THE KHMER KING JAYAVARMAN VII (12TH-13TH CENTURY) OVER THE CHAM, HIS ARCHENEMIES, IS DEPICTED IN THE SOUTHERN GALLERY OF THE BAYON, IN CAMBODIA. THE IMAGES OF THIS COMPLEX ARE INVALUABLE FOR THE RECONSTRUCTION OF THE MATERIAL CULTURE OF THE KHMER PEOPLE.*

# EUROPE

## From dolmens to the treasures of Vergina

The first examples of tombs in Europe date from the Paleolithic period when a proper funerary ritual was formulated for the first time. It included fairly elaborate and complex practices which involved the burial of the deceased dressed in his best clothes and accompanied by his most precious objects and which demonstrate a belief in life beyond the grave and practices that permitted or aided passage to the Afterlife.

It was only during the Mesolithic period that the custom of burying the dead in precisely defined areas – the first necropolises – was developed, but it was necessary to wait until the Neolithic period for the construction of the first European "dwellings of eternity." The complexity and often the large dimensions of the structures promised protection and perpetuity to the dead and consequently lasted longer than the houses of the living.

Around 5000 BC, the first megalithic funerary structures began to appear and spread throughout Europe, reaching their highest splendor in Brittany, England, Ireland, and the Maltese archipelago. These solid structures were made using blocks of rock that were sometimes of enormous size and are typified by *dolmens* and by passage-tombs covered with large earthen mounds. The mound over the famous passage-tomb built at New Grange in Ireland in 3400 BC, nine hundred years before the pyramids at Giza, had a diameter of 90 meters and a height of 15 meters. Tombs of this nature, sometimes constructed with ornate funerary chambers, may be considered the first "dwellings of eternity" to be built in Europe. At least 200 of the 15,000 known megalithic tombs in Europe were decorated with high and low reliefs of concentric geometric motifs, such as circles or

*26  THIS 19TH CENTURY PRINT SHOWS A VIEW OF THE NECROPOLIS AT TARQUINIA. THE ETRUSCANS SETTLED IN ITALY FROM THE 8TH CENTURY BC IN THE AREAS NOW COVERED BY TUSCANY AND LAZIO. THEY WERE THE FIRST EUROPEANS TO BUILD ELABORATE TOMBS, AND THE DEGREE OF THEIR COMPLEXITY REFLECTS THE DEEP FAITH THEY HAD IN THE AFTERLIFE.*

**NEW GRANGE**

**EUROPE**

**ESSÉ**
**CARNAC**
**GAVRINIS**
**BARNENEZ**
**LOCMARIAQUER**

**CERVETERI**
**TARQUINIA**

**VERGINA**

**MYCENAE**

**XAGHRA**
**HAL SAFLIENI**

spirals of obscure significance and, more rarely, of anthropomorphic elements, which probably bore a symbolic meaning and were an expression of religious beliefs.

In some cases, the burial places were enormously extensive, for example, the mound at West Kennet in England, to the south of Avebury, in which a multiple chamber tomb was built over 100 meters long that contained at least 50 buried bodies. Similarly, the large underground tomb of Hal Saflieni on the Maltese island of Gozo was practically a maze of 33 chambers distributed across a surface area of 500 square meters.

The funerary rituals used during the Neolithic period remain mostly unknown even if in many cases a close link has been shown to exist between the cult of the dead and the cult of fertility – a well-known phenomenon in ancient Egypt – that developed out of the agrarian origins of Neolithic religion.

In addition, there is much evidence to suggest that the practice of the funerary banquet was already in use. The custom demonstrates the existence of a belief in an eternal life that represented an improvement on earthly life and was sometimes considered as a sort of reward for valorous or good behavior. The material, rock, used to build these tombs has always been associated with inalterability and permanence and so represented a promise of eternity for the dead who were buried together with tools, weapons, and precious objects, sometimes specially made, as necessities for a journey to the Underworld.

With the advance of technology and the introduction of metalworking (which initiated the Bronze Age), the grave goods became richer and more elaborate and included precious objects of various typologies decorated with artistic refinement. The objects also acquired a symbolic value in that they were supposed to represent the wealth, status, and power of the deceased in the world beyond the grave.

The royal tombs in the necropolis of Mycenae in Greece date from the second millennium BC and were contemporaneous with those of the 18th dynasty in Egypt. They combined the monumental aspect of megalithic tombs (the architrave over the entrance to the "Treasury of

Atreus" weighs about 120 tons) with the more elegant characteristics of Bronze Age sepulchers. The rulers of Mycenae were buried with embossed gold-leaf funerary masks in shaft-tombs with vast underground chambers or in tombs with corbel domes (the so-called *thòlos*) in which concentric rows of stone slabs could exceed 12 meters in height.

During the Iron Age that followed, the Etruscans in the Italian peninsula interred their dead in large subterranean chamber-tombs decorated with bas-reliefs that generally depicted scenes from daily life. The artistic and stylistic perfection of these tombs reached its apex between the seventh and the fifth century BC. The tombs were grouped in large necropolises of which the most interesting are at Tarquinia in Lazio and Cerveteri in Tuscany. They could not boast the magnificent architecture of the megalithic or Mycenaean tombs, but the refinement and elegance of their wall paintings shows a love of earthly life as well as the status and wealth of the deceased and his family. It is probable that these wall paintings were not simply evocations of a past life but magically represented a sort of backdrop for the new existence in the Afterlife.

The range of decorative themes in the Etruscan tombs was an expression of an aristocratic and oligarchic society. The widespread theme of the banquet was a proper reproduction of those organized during the lifetime of the dead in which musicians and dancers accompanied the event. The portrayal extended to real objects of value such as gold cups, drinking containers and wine jugs used on special occasions that were placed beside the body of the deceased along with personal objects and splendid jewelry.

Study of these grave goods has shown that the Etruscans were not only highly artistic but had reached a level of technology that permitted the manufacture of complex and sophisticated gold jewelry using techniques such as granulation and filigree.

Like the Egyptians, the Etruscans imagined that the dead set off on a long journey to the world beyond the tomb that had little in common with the paradisiacal Fields of Iaru painted in the

Theban tombs of the New Kingdom. For the Etruscans, the Underworld was a dark and sad place dominated by frightening deities. This metaphysical conception was profoundly affected by the influx of Greek culture and explains the Etruscans' deep attachment to terrestrial life and their need to represent it in funerary art.

Constructed shortly after the Etruscan tombs, the royal tombs in the necropolis of Aigaì near Vergina in Macedonia date from the start of the fourth century BC. Discovered during the 1980s, they were based on large underground chambers decorated with wall paintings but were given monumental façades and covered with earthen mounds.

The particularly elaborate structure of two of these tombs, found intact and identified as those of Philip II of Macedonia, killed at Aigaì in 335 BC, and his father Amyntas III, uses a barrel-vault for the first time in a burial chamber and demonstrates the existence of an indigenous funerary architecture that was developed in Greece from the fourth to the second century BC.

The extraordinary grave goods placed in Philip II's tomb (also known as Tomb II at Vergina) included weapons, jewelry and other objects made from gold and silver, in addition to two stone sarcophaguses containing two beautifully embossed gold urns holding the remains of the king and his wife. Their bodies had been incinerated in accordance with the ancient practice recorded during the age of Homer by which Greek heroes freed themselves from their mortal bodies to journey down the dark and gloomy pathways of Hades.

Ireland

NEW GRANGE

ESSÉ
CARNAC
GAVRINIS
BARNENEZ
LOCMARIAQUER

France

# Megalithic tombs in

# BRITTANY AND

Brittany and Ireland

# IRELAND

From the earliest times in its history, humankind has felt the need to protect the bodies of the dead in single or collective tombs; the latter have sometimes been constructed using a very simple structure, but others are so complex as to appear monumental in nature. The earliest voluntary examples of inhumation – the great majority of which were simple trenches – date from the Middle Paleolithic (100,000 – 40,000 BC). Megalithic construction, however, originated during the Mesolithic period (ca. 10,000 BC) when several communities in Brittany (France) and near the estuary of the river Tagus (Portugal) used large stone slabs to form a boundary around collective tombs. During the Neolithic period, burial places underwent gradual change, becoming more complex and imposing and characterized by decorative motifs that often held a symbolic

*32  THIS IS A PICTURE OF THE MENHIR OF LOCMARIAQUER IN FRANCE. IT IS THE LARGEST MENHIR SO FAR FOUND IN EUROPE BUT LIES ON THE GROUND BROKEN IN FOUR PARTS.*

*32-33  THE AERIAL PHOTOGRAPH SHOWS THE ALIGNMENT AT LE MENÉE IN CARNAC. THE HEIGHTS OF THE MENHIRS VARY GRADUALLY; THOSE AT THE START (WEST) STAND ABOUT 3.6 METERS HIGH BUT SHORTEN TO ABOUT 50 CM IN THE EASTERN SECTION.*

value. It was during this stage of prehistory that humanity settled, founded the first villages and dedicated much of its time to the building of structures used to worship the Mother Goddess (responsible for the cycles of nature) and the cult of the dead. It was also during the Neolithic period that the macroscopic development of megalithic architecture took place, the origin of which cannot be traced to one particular center. The opinion expressed by V. Gordon Childe in 1925, that this cultural and constructive

phenomenon originated in the East from whence it spread to Europe, has been rebutted by the "dendochronology" dating method devised by Hans E. Suess in 1967 based on Carbon-14 calibration. This method has shown that the European megalithic structures are older than those in the eastern Mediterranean.

The term "megalithic," coined by Algernon Herbert in 1849, is derived from the Greek words *mégas* (large) and *lithos* (stone) and refers to the extraordinary structures to be found in

various regions around the world. To judge by the large number of such structures on its territory, it seems certain that megalithic construction was mostly developed in France around 5000 BC and then it spread into Portugal (3900 BC), Spain (3600 BC), and the British Isles. It is not known if the megalithic phenomenon had an indigenous origin in the Maltese archipelago (4100-2500 BC), as it was only on these small Mediterranean islands that temples were built next to underground structures. The role played by the impressive megalithic complexes is more easily understood if one considers the symbolic importance of stone in prehistory, as the seemingly permanent nature of lithic materials made them a symbol of eternity and often of fertility as well.

The principal megalithic structures are *menhirs*, alignments, *cromlechs* and *dolmens*. Mainly found in France and dating from the Neolithic period, *menhirs* are also found in various regions of western Europe; the etymology of the term comes from the Breton words *men* (stone) and *hir* (long). These are stones that stand on end in the ground, ranging from 1-12 meters in height. The imposing menhir of Locmariaquer (Morbihan) in France is an exception, with a height of 23.5 meters and weighing around 300 tons, but which now lies on the ground broken into four parts. It is difficult to understand the real function of *menhirs*. Some were perhaps phallic symbols; penetrating the bowels of the Mother Earth, they expressed the act of fertilization. In other cases, their proximity to burial monuments or

places of worship indicated the holiness of the place. The fact that anthropomorphic figures were carved on some monoliths suggests that these *menhirs* (or better, statue-*menhirs*) were considered the incorruptible seat of the soul of the dead and therefore guaranteed immortality.

*Menhirs* set out in parallel lines form what are known as "alignments." The most striking example is at Carnac (Brittany) which was originally formed by 3000 *menhirs* over 3 kilometers in 10 parallel rows. The purpose of the alignments is not known, although various hypotheses have been put forward: some scholars consider that the complex was used as an astronomic observatory, others that the stones had a connection with the cult of the sun (the generator of all forms of life) and of the dead; this second theory is based on the nearby presence of *dolmens* and chambered tombs.

Arrangements of *menhirs* in circles or

*34-35 THE GIGANTIC TOPPLED MENHIR AND TOMB KNOWN AS THE "MERCHANTS' TABLE" WERE FOUND ON THE COAST NEAR LOCMARIAQUER.*

*34 BOTTOM LEFT THE GALLERY-GRAVE DOLMEN OF MOUGAU-BIHAN NEAR COMMANA, FINISTÉRE IS NEARLY 13 METERS LONG WITH UPRIGHTS TOPPED BY LARGE STONE SLABS.*

*34 BOTTOM RIGHT THE DOLMEN IN THE PHOTOGRAPH IS SITUATED ON THE FRENCH NORTH COAST. THE PHOTOGRAPH GIVES A PARTIAL VIEW OF THE INTERIOR.*

*35 TOP THIS IS PERHAPS THE LARGEST OF THE MANY GIGANTIC DOLMENS FOUND IN THE COUNTRYSIDE AT CARNAC. THE COVERING SLAB CONFERS A "MAJESTIC" APPEARANCE ON THE STRUCTURE*

*35 BOTTOM THE USE OF SMALLER AND THINNER SLABS THAN THOSE NORMALLY USED GIVES THIS DOLMEN AT GALLERIA AN ELEGANT APPEARANCE.*

ground were covered by enormous mounds of earth suggests that European Neolithic peoples attempted to reproduce the characteristics of underground tombs that were well suited to housing the dead. This type of grave – known as "chambered tombs" – is divided into "gallery graves" and "passage graves." The first were formed by a long narrow room covered by stone slabs in which the dead were laid; the second comprised a megalithic passage, with a roof made from stone slabs, that led into a large sepulchral chamber covered by a huge slab or by a *tholos* – a false dome formed by arranging gradually projecting stones in circles. This second, peculiar method of construction is seen throughout the Mediterranean areas with unvarying continuity up until the age of the Etruscan civilization.

These megalithic tombs were for the most part collective and were characterized by fine

# Megalithic Tombs

semicircles form *cromlechs*, the name of which once more comes from the Breton language: *crom* (circle) and *lech* (place). Their diameters vary remarkably: the smallest are the Sardinian circles at Li Muri-Arzachena which measure between 5 and 8 meters while the largest, at Avebury in England, has a diameter of 427 meters. The functions of the megalithic circles, mostly concentrated in the British Isles, were related to burial and worship, although some of them were indisputably astronomical observatories.

The term *dolmen* is taken from the Breton words *dol* (table) and *men* (stone). These are

burial monuments consisting of one or more horizontal slabs resting on vertical stones (uprights). Some of these structures had a chamber preceded by an entrance passage and others were covered by a mound of earth. These two types of construction form the most conspicuous forms of Neolithic inhumation and represent the roots of the architectural development of complex funerary monuments spread across France (Brittany) and Ireland. The custom of exploiting natural ravines as burial-places, common in other areas, was not widespread in western Europe; however, the fact that most of the megalithic tombs built above

tomb goods such as domestic, agricultural and ornamental objects. It seems that the dead were provided with everything that was considered useful for their journey to the world beyond the grave. The walls of the tombs were occasionally decorated with carved motifs of the Mother Goddess, the greatest of the protective deities, who was also represented in stylized statuettes. The presence of the Mother Goddess confirms the connection between the cult of the dead and the fertility cult typical of Neolithic peoples. It was probably thought that once the dead were laid in the earth, they acquired the vital energy necessary for the renewal of the seasonal cycles.

# Brittany's monuments

Another complex *dolmen*-type structure worthy of note is the extraordinary monument at Barnenez on the tip of the Kernéléhen en Plouézoc'h (Finistére) peninsula, containing 11 "passage-type" *dolmen* structures that vary in layout and size, which can be reached via corridors that are all entered through the same side of the mound that covers them.

The mound stretches for 75 meters in length and varies in width from 20-25 meters and 6-8 meters in height. In addition to the 9

*dolmens* with burial chamber covered by a false dome of projecting stones, there is a traditionally shaped *dolmen* (with a round chamber covered by a large stone slab) and another that has an antechamber covered in the style of a *tholos* in the area between the chamber and the passage.

The decorations on the stone slabs of some of the monuments merit description; for example, an axe with handle and a wavy arabesque appear on one of the supporting stones of a chamber, both frequent motifs in megalithic art. The mound that covers the sepulchral structures was bounded by an almost rectangular wall. It is thought that the Barnenez monument is one of the oldest in Brittany and was built over two periods during the Middle Neolithic because a date has been provided (3800 BC, C-14 non-calibrated) for one of the monuments located in the eastern section of the mound, and another date (3500 BC, C-14 non-calibrated) for one of the structures in the western section. As has already been noted, the origin of the technique for building a false dome using projecting stones is lost in the mists of

time, perhaps as long as 6000 years ago.

The structure was mainly built using stones found *in situ*, but the passages were covered using granite slabs that were transported a distance of two kilometers.

Another huge megalithic construction is the gallery-grave at Essé known as Roche-aux-Fées, which means Fairy Rock, that was probably intended as a collective burial site. It may also have been used as a shrine during the Late Neolithic, although we do not know what ceremonies would have been performed there.

The monument, roughly 20 meters in length, is made up of about 40 Cambrian red schist slabs of which 7 large covering stones each weigh from 30-40 tons. The material used was dragged more than 4 kilometers using means that must have included sloping surfaces, levers and rollers. The structure is characterized by a monumental entrance followed by a low passage 1 meter high divided into 4 sections by 3 pillars, and by a large chamber with high walls that measure 14.3l x 4w x 2h meters.

On occasion, the splendor of the megalithic tombs was accompanied by elegant patterned decorations that gave the monuments an air of refinement.

An example is the *dolmen* known as the "Merchants' Table" at Locmariaquer (3500-3000 BC) in which the inside of one of the uprights displays a semicircular motif with four rows of axes illuminated by a figure in the center of the composition that seems to represent the sun. Lower down there are unidentifiable markings.

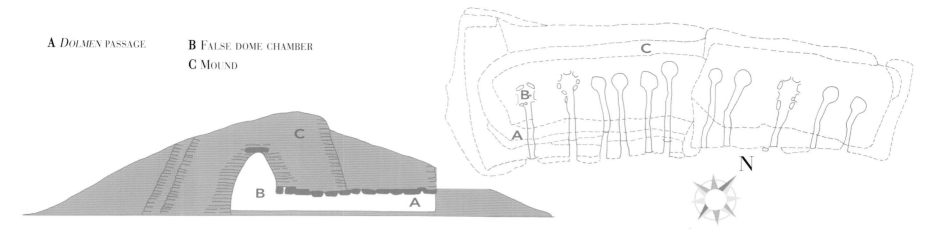

**A** *DOLMEN* PASSAGE  **B** FALSE DOME CHAMBER
**C** MOUND

N

# Brittany's monuments

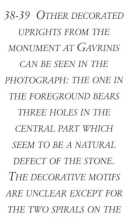

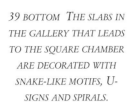

*38 TOP SOME UPRIGHTS ARE DECORATED: THE SLAB IN THE CENTER BEARS THE REPRESENTATION OF A FOUR-SIDED SHIELD, THE ONE ON THE RIGHT TWO SHIELDS, ONE ABOVE THE OTHER, AND THE ONE ON THE LEFT, A PAIR OF AXES.*

*38-39 OTHER DECORATED UPRIGHTS FROM THE MONUMENT AT GAVRINIS CAN BE SEEN IN THE PHOTOGRAPH: THE ONE IN THE FOREGROUND BEARS THREE HOLES IN THE CENTRAL PART WHICH SEEM TO BE A NATURAL DEFECT OF THE STONE. THE DECORATIVE MOTIFS ARE UNCLEAR EXCEPT FOR THE TWO SPIRALS ON THE BASE.*

*38 BOTTOM THIS STONE TUMULUS COVERS ONE OF THE MOST INTERESTING MONUMENTS IN BRITTANY: THE GALLERY-GRAVE ON THE ISLAND OF GAVRINIS.*

*39 BOTTOM THE SLABS IN THE GALLERY THAT LEADS TO THE SQUARE CHAMBER ARE DECORATED WITH SNAKE-LIKE MOTIFS, U-SIGNS AND SPIRALS.*

**A** BURIAL CHAMBER
**B** DOLMEN PASSAGE

Another of Brittany's megalithic structures that stands out is on the island of Gavrinis in Larmor-Barden; the carvings on the extraordinary *dolmen* were so beautiful it was considered one of the wonders of the world. An enormous cairn covers the Late Neolithic gallery-type *dolmen* (3500-3000 BC calibrated date) at Gavrinis. It was formed by a 14-meter-long corridor, made of large slabs with uprights decorated with symbolic motifs, that led into a small square chamber. The use to which this monument was put also seems to have been exceptional, as its function was largely based on worship. It is known that the function of various megalithic constructions had altered over

time and "funerary" structures evolved into "cult" structures.

An important point is that Gavrinis was oriented towards a solstice.

The monument is especially distinguished from other megalithic structures by the conspicuous decorations on its uprights (23 of the 29 uprights in the passage were decorated). The range of iconographic representations includes symbolic figures whose meaning cannot always be understood. The motifs in the form of a wave and concentric arcs are interesting. The concentric semicircle surrounded by multiple wavy lines is the main symbol but the axes, common in megalithic art, should also be mentioned. One of the

uprights at Gavrinis was decorated with 3 rows of carved axes, mostly in pairs, surrounded by multiple wavy lines, while an engraving on another upright shows an enormous axe and long-horned bulls. It is difficult to offer any interpretation of these symbolic motifs, though they were sometimes connected with the fertility cult as can be deduced from the figures of the bull and the spiral. The latter was often believed to be a symbol of water but also of the snake, and a snake was important in its symbolism of the underworld, the world of the dead and, through the annual shedding of its skin, also of eternal rebirth.

The refined and elegant decorations at

Gavrinis combined with those on other monuments – though fewer in number and simpler in design – demonstrate that Neolithic peoples had reached a fairly developed intellectual level. After all, their constructions were not simply built for utilitarian purposes (burial) but also aesthetic reasons, as shown by the embellishment of the megalithic monuments with ornamental as well as symbolic motifs.

It appears that the axe, the bow, the snake, and the horn were representations of masculinity while motifs of eyes and breasts were those of femininity. The Mother Goddess was often represented in anthropomorphic form in the megalithic tombs.

# The extraordinary tomb
# at New Grange

The British Isles are home to an amazing number of megalithic monuments, but very few equal the complex typology of the architectural structure at New Grange in Ireland. It is highly probable that the Neolithic settlements in Ireland were established before those in other zones of the British archipelago, i.e. around 4700 BC (calibrated date), but the megalithic structures do not seem to have been built before ca. 3700 BC.

Together with the three enormous mounds at Knowth, New Grange, and Dowth, which all contain a chamber of large size, the valley of the river Boyne is home to many other small mounds, standing stones, ruined circles, and megalithic structures that have induced scholars to advance the hypothesis that, for a long period of time, the valley was considered "sacred."

Although the tomb at New Grange was located near two large mounds, it stands out for the refinement and impressiveness of its ornamental motifs. The monument, built around 3400 BC (calibrated date), takes the form of an oval mound 15 meters high with a diameter of over 90 meters. Inside there is a long passage-type *dolmen* that leads to a chamber in the shape of a transept with a false vault ceiling made using large slabs that weigh more than a ton each. The base of the mound is marked by 97 stones, mostly decorated, and surrounded by an enormous circle of *menhirs*.

The orientation of the tomb at New Grange allows the rays of the rising sun to enter through an opening in the passage so that the chamber is lit up on the winter solstice (21 December).

Of the many slabs decorated with ornamental motifs at New Grange, first should be mentioned the one positioned in front of the tomb's entrance passage; it is embellished with spiral motifs that are similar to those incised on the slabs of the roughly contemporaneous megalithic temples in Malta. Similarities with the Maltese designs can be seen in the double spiral, in the double spiral that denotes an "eye-type" motif, in the simple circular motifs, and in plant motifs. The plant motifs on the stone slabs in the Maltese temples represent the vital force of plants – perfectly suited to civilizations in which agriculture formed the

*40 TOP AND 40-41 THE MOUND AT NEW GRANGE IS ONE OF THE LARGEST SO FAR DISCOVERED IN EUROPE. THE LARGE PHOTOGRAPH SHOWS THE ENTRANCE THAT LEADS TO THE INTERNAL CHAMBER CONTAINING 3 CELLS. THE FRONT SECTION IS MADE FROM WHITE STONE, WHILE THE BASE OF THE MOUND IS BOUNDED BY SLABS. A CIRCLE OF MENHIRS, OF WHICH ONLY 12 REMAIN, SURROUNDS THE STRUCTURE.*

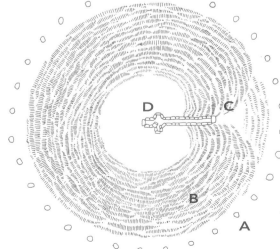

## LEGEND

**A** CIRCLE OF *MENHIRS*
**B** MOUND
**C** *DOLMEN* PASSAGE
**D** BURIAL CHAMBER

# The extraordinary tomb at New Grange

42 TOP AND BOTTOM LEFT
THE CENTRAL CHAMBER AT
NEW GRANGE IS
CHARACTERIZED BY THREE
SIDE CELLS WITH LARGE
BUT SHALLOW BOWLS ON
THE FLOOR, AS IT IS SHOWN
BY THESE PICTURES. THE
WALLS AND THE CEILING
ARE DECORATED WITH
SPIRAL MOTIFS.

basis of life; besides being present in Ireland and Malta, the plant motif is also seen in France. The spiral patterns on the slabs at New Grange are often associated with triangular or diamond-shaped motifs; sometimes isolated carvings of triple spirals appear or triangles on the walls or on blocks enclosing the tomb.

The meanings of the iconography on the

42 RIGHT THE LOW-
VAULTED CEILING OF THE
CENTRAL CHAMBER AT
NEW GRANGE HAS BEEN
KEPT IN EXCELLENT
CONDITION. IT REACHES A
HEIGHT OF 6 METERS FROM
THE FLOOR.

stone monuments are unknown, but it seems that the common features of megalithic art, including the art found in Malta, can only be explained by a common philosophy and similar magical-religious thoughts connected with the rite of collective burial.

It should be pointed out that the splendor of the Irish monument can still be admired because the wall made from quartz and granite that surrounds and supports the mound has recently been restored.

43 THIS VIEW OF THE
CORRIDOR IN THE LARGE
MOUND AT NEW GRANGE
SHOWS THE ARRANGEMENT
OF THE LARGE STONE SLABS
THAT ALMOST GIVE THE
INTERIOR AN AIR OF
"HOLINESS." THIS IS THE
PASSAGE THAT LEADS TO
THE INTERNAL CHAMBER.

# The Cult of the Dead in the ETRUSCAN territories IN LAZIO

*Italy*

**CERVETERI**
**TARQUINIA**

*44 TOP THE LOVELY AND BEAUTIFULLY DRESSED VELIA SPURINNA APPEARS ON A WALL IN THE FAMILY TOMB AT TARQUINIA (TOMB OF THE ORCUS I) WITH A DELICATELY SAD EXPRESSION IN HER EYES.*

*44 CENTER AND 44-45 THE TERRACOTTA CINERARY URN FROM CERVETERI (CA. 520 BC) IS ONE OF THE MASTERPIECES OF ETRUSCAN POTTERY FROM THE LAST DECADES OF THE 6TH CENTURY BC. A BRIDAL COUPLE IS SHOWN HALF-LYING ON AN ELEGANT KLINE AS THE MAN, WITH HIS UPPER BODY UNCLOTHED, EMBRACES HIS WIFE. THIS POT IS PART OF THE COLLECTION IN THE LOUVRE BUT A SIMILAR URN CAN BE SEEN IN THE VILLA GIULIA NATIONAL MUSEUM IN ROME.*

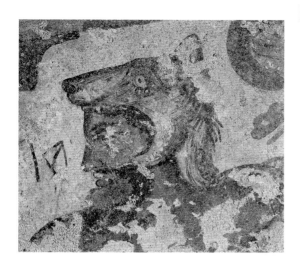

The beliefs and rituals linked to the destiny of man make up a large part of the complex spirituality of the Etruscan civilization. A written tradition that has been handed down to modern times portrays the Etruscans as a deeply religious people strongly linked to the cult of the dead. This was recorded by the Latin historian Titus Livius (V, 1, 6) and confirmed by the Christian apologist Arnobius (*Adv. Gentes*, VII, 26), who defined Etruria as "the generator and mother of every superstition," referring to the Etruscans'

scrupulous observance of cult practices.

This tradition states that the immense wealth of religious doctrines and rules was collected at the end of the Etruscan civilization into a series of sacred books in which all the information that had been passed orally down the generations was codified, as though in an authentic *summa*.

Unfortunately, the loss of the original religious literature, defined by the Latins as the *etrusca disciplina*, has meant our knowledge of this particular aspect of their civilization is

*45 TOP ON THE FAR WALL OF THE TOMB OF THE ORCUS II AT TARQUINIA (320-300 BC), HADES, DRESSED IN HIS CHARACTERISTIC WOLF-SKIN, IS PRESENT AT THE SAD PROCESSION OF HOMERIC HEROES IN THE UNDERWORLD.*

incomplete and indirect. Some references in classical sources speak of the existence of *Libri Haruspicini* dedicated to the art of divination through the reading of animal livers, *Libri Fulgurales*, the practice of divination linked to lightning, and *Libri Rituales* in which the rules to be followed in the practices of the cult of the dead were collected. A particular section of the *Libri Rituales*, the *Libri Acherontici*, was dedicated to the world beyond the grave and to the rites necessary to ensure that the individuality of the deceased was able to survive the anguish of death.

The few items in our possession seem to confirm the contents of the literary sources: the bronze model of a sheep's liver found near Piacenza was a basic tool for the divinatory practices of an Etruscan soothsayer; a liturgical text was written on the bandages of the mummy of Zagabria in a sort of extract from the *Libri Rituales* that contained special ritual prescriptions in the form of a calendar; finally, the *Tegola* (i.e., terracotta tile) from Capua bears a transcription of a funerary ritual mentioning offerings, libations, and sacrifices in an extraordinary confirmation of the existence of cult practices dedicated to divination related to the underworld.

The extreme ritualism of Etruscan religion was derived from its concept of divinity, which was understood as an obscure entity that imposes itself on the will of man, depriving him of all autonomy. It was therefore incumbent upon him to act in accordance with his lowly station, to try to read and interpret every divine manifestation and to placate the anger of the gods with ceremonies and sacrifices.

The exterior aspects of religion were the responsibility of the priests who were entrusted with overseeing a vast protocol. One of the most important figures was the *haruspex* or soothsayer, whose duty it was to interpret the

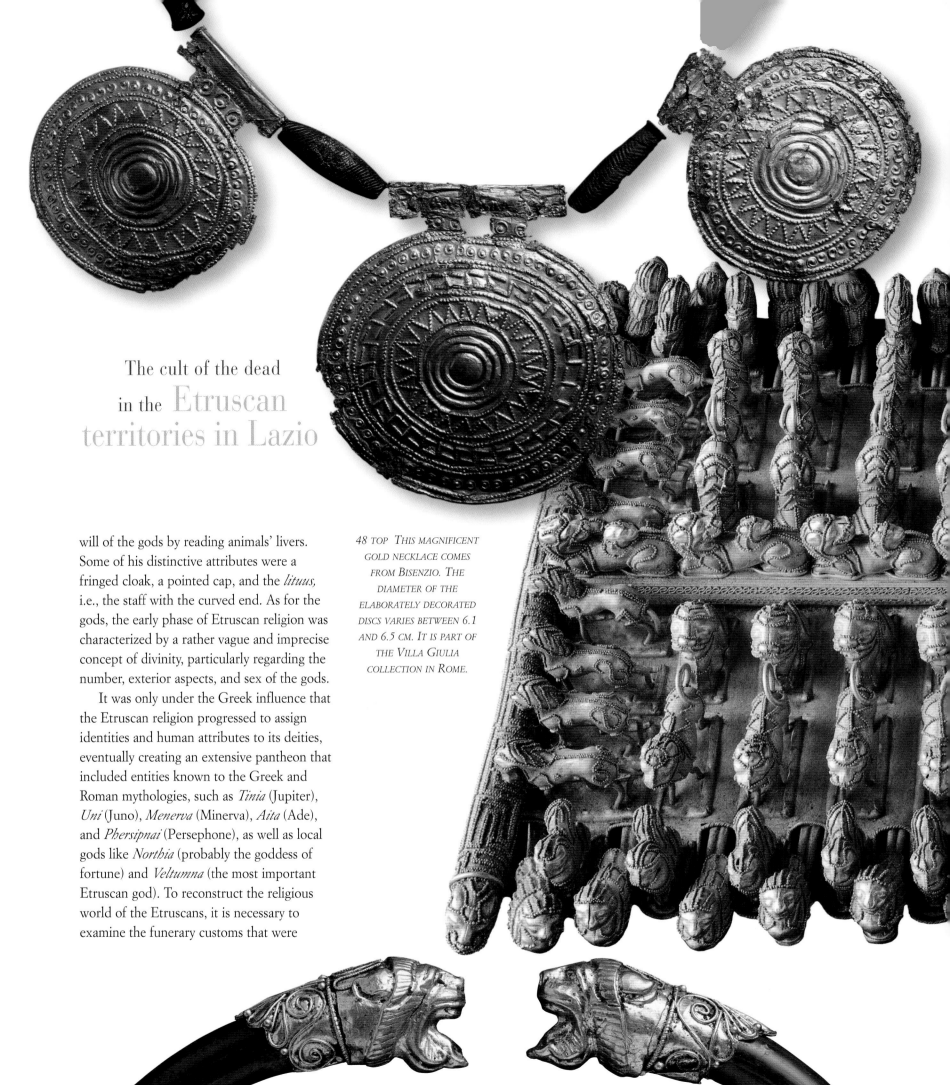

## The cult of the dead in the Etruscan territories in Lazio

will of the gods by reading animals' livers. Some of his distinctive attributes were a fringed cloak, a pointed cap, and the *lituus,* i.e., the staff with the curved end. As for the gods, the early phase of Etruscan religion was characterized by a rather vague and imprecise concept of divinity, particularly regarding the number, exterior aspects, and sex of the gods.

It was only under the Greek influence that the Etruscan religion progressed to assign identities and human attributes to its deities, eventually creating an extensive pantheon that included entities known to the Greek and Roman mythologies, such as *Tinia* (Jupiter), *Uni* (Juno), *Menerva* (Minerva), *Aita* (Ade), and *Phersipnai* (Persephone), as well as local gods like *Northia* (probably the goddess of fortune) and *Veltumna* (the most important Etruscan god). To reconstruct the religious world of the Etruscans, it is necessary to examine the funerary customs that were

*48 TOP THIS MAGNIFICENT GOLD NECKLACE COMES FROM BISENZIO. THE DIAMETER OF THE ELABORATELY DECORATED DISCS VARIES BETWEEN 6.1 AND 6.5 CM. IT IS PART OF THE VILLA GIULIA COLLECTION IN ROME.*

*48-49 THIS GOLD PLATE COMES FROM THE TOMB OF THE BERNARDINI FAMILY FROM PALESTRINA (680-660 BC) AND WAS WITHOUT DOUBT AN ORNAMENT ON THE CLOTHES OF THE*

*DECEASED. IT IS DECORATED WITH 131 FIGURES INCLUDING CHIMERAS, LIONS, HORSES, AND SIRENS. TWO LARGE PINS ATTACHED IT TO THE MATERIAL.*

*48 BOTTOM THE TIPS OF THIS BLUE GLASS PASTE BRACELET ARE OF TWO LIONS DECORATED WITH FILIGREE PALMETTES. THE ORNAMENT IS ROUGHLY 9 CM IN*

*DIAMETER AND WAS MANUFACTURED AT THE END OF THE 6TH CENTURY BC. IT WAS FOUND AT VULCI AND IS HELD AT THE VILLA GIULIA MUSEUM IN ROME.*

determined by the conception of the ultimate fate of man.

During the earliest phase, it seems that the conviction that the individuality of the dead could survive in the burial place was dominant. This was the basis for the need to supply the body with food, drinks, weapons, and various articles in accordance with a rituality that was already present during the Villanovan period (9th-8th century BC). However, the widespread custom of cremating the body and placing the ashes in an urn (then placed in a hole in the ground) would seem, at least on the surface, to contradict this ideology by liberating the "spirit" from the restrictions of the body. On the contrary, the custom of using urns in the form of a house or vases that reproduced the features of the deceased demonstrated the desire for a return to normality after suffering the anguish of death and preparation of the deceased for the new phase of his existence.

This concept seems reinforced by the progressive shift towards interment that spread through southern and coastal Etruria from the 8th century BC. The new rite meant the dead were no longer cremated but placed in a tomb that bore the appearance of real rooms but, as a

result of space restrictions, below ground. From this moment on, the chamber tomb became the typical sepulcher of Etruria and spread even into the northern areas traditionally associated with cremation.

The chamber tomb also became the preferred place where members of the deceased's family would pour out all the joys and worries, victories and defeats of terrestrial life, not just as an act of love due to the dead, but also as a confirmation of the identity and high social rank of the family. This was the reason, in addition to the belief in the survival of the dead, why the tomb was modeled on the house and why so many objects were placed in it – not everyday objects, but the most beautiful, used only on grand occasions – and why the walls of the tomb were decorated with scenes of banquets, dances, and games.

It is above all through the representation of a banquet – the real occasion of which required substantial financial and organizational resources – that the family wished to reaffirm their political and economic power. The scenes are a clear allusion to banquets organized by the master of the house on his own property where particular importance was given to the display of valuable personal ornaments and the furniture used for the party. The same happened inside the tombs with marvelous gold objects, drinking pots (*kylikes*), pouring jugs (*oinòchoai*), and other large containers for liquids such as jars and amphoras, either made locally or imported, all of which were magnificent service objects used to support the ideology that conditioned the life of the aristocracy.

One object in particular became the symbol of the symposium: the *kantharos*, a characteristic attribute of Dionysus, that alluded to the presence of the symposiarch. Its purely symbolic value is confirmed by its widespread diffusion in tombs despite its rarity among objects in domestic use.

Other status symbols, in addition to articles related to banquets, were personal ornaments and metal plate; likewise armbands, earrings, clasps, and chest plates made from gold leaf and decorated with elegant techniques like dusting or granulation.

dead, a dark, anguished world dominated by the presence of terrifying demons like the goddess *Vanth* (perhaps the Greek Moira) with her enormous wings and torch that symbolized implacable fate; *Charum* (Charon) with the features of a beast and armed with a hammer to ward off the members of the deceased's family; and *Tuchulcha*, with the face of a vulture, the ears of a donkey, and armed with snakes.

Analysis of later monuments suggests it was believed that all the dead were destined to suffer the same fate: it could not be avoided by

even the most illustrious for, whom the only consolation was to continue trumpeting their terrestrial superiority through the display of status symbols and proclamation of their achievements in public life. A thin ray of light, however, seems to have illuminated this dark and obscure destiny. Several literary sources seem to make explicit reference to the existence of doctrines of salvation according to which the spirit of the deceased could achieve states of blessedness and deification consequent upon precise ceremonies performed for the souls of the dead in an expression of genuine Etruscan spirituality.

Buckles for both men and women were sometimes made in such enormous sizes that it was clear their use was decorative rather than practical.

From the fifth century BC, the influx of Greek culture produced important changes in Etruscan eschatology that progressively weakened the oldest religious beliefs. Under the influence of Greek mythology and religion, the idea was gradually established of transmigration of the soul towards a world beyond the tomb on the basis of the Homeric underworld.

The destiny of man was then symbolized by the journey towards the kingdom of the

50 BOTTOM THIS DIADEM WAS FOUND IN TARQUINIA. IT IS MADE OF THREE ROWS OF MOULDED IVY LEAVES ALTERNATED WITH TWO ROWS OF BERRIES DECORATED WITH AN ENGRAVED SURFACE

51 THIS ENORMOUS GOLD CLASP ADORNED THE CLOTHING OF THE DECEASED BURIED IN THE CELL OF THE REGOLINI-GALASSI TOMB. FIVE LIONS IN PROFILE FRAMED BY PLANT MOTIFS ARE SHOWN IN THE CENTER OF THE OVAL DISC. THE ARC OF THE OVAL, IN THE SHAPE OF A LEAF, HAS ROWS OF GOSLINGS AND WINGED LIONS.

# The necropolises of Tarquinia

*52 BOTTOM LEFT AND RIGHT ON THE SIDE WALLS OF THE TRICLINIUM TOMB AT TARQUINIA (480-470 BC) MUSICIANS PLAYING A LYRE AND A DOUBLE FLUTE PRECEDE TWO GROUPS OF FIGURES ADVANCING TOWARDS THREE COUPLES AT BANQUET ON THE BACK WALL.*

*52-53 THE SARCOPHAGUS OF THE "MAGNATE" (LAST QUARTER OF THE 4TH CENTURY BC) BELONGED TO MAGISTRATE VELTHUR PARTUNUS. THE DECEASED HOLDS A PATERA IN HIS RIGHT HAND AS HE BANQUETS.*

*54 AND 55 WARRIORS SUCCUMB IN THE BATTLE SCENES DECORATING THE AMAZON SARCOPHAGUS, FOUND AT TARQUINIA.*

The necropolises at Tarquinia and Cerveteri have played a role of great importance in reconstructing the social life, the customs, the eschatology, and the religious world of the Etruscans. In ancient literary tradition, the name Tarquinia is linked to Tagete, the boy who issued from a clod of earth and revealed the *Etruscan discipline* to Tarconte, the founder of the city. From the middle of the 8th century BC, the city was one of the most prosperous centers in Etruria: its position close to the sea gave it a particularly favorable trading location and brought it cultural influences from

civilizations further afield.

The number of its burial grounds was already substantial: besides those at Poggio Selciatello and Poggio Selciatello di Sopra, there were also cemeteries at Poggio dell'Impiccato, Civitucola, Poggio Gallinaro, Poggio Quarto degli Archi, and at the necropolises in the San Savino valley.

The most famous and important of the city's burial areas is at Monterozzi, which was to become the main city cemetery from the beginning of the sixth century BC. This is the site where an extraordinary series of roughly

150 painted tombs was discovered, nearly all in recent years thanks to new research techniques, most of the tombs were dated to the period from the mid-sixth – mid-fifth century BC.

The internal structure of the tombs consists of a small, more or less rectangular chamber dug out of the rock that is generally reached via a stepped corridor.

More complex layouts exist, like the one at the Tomb of the Bulls, in which a main chamber opens onto two smaller rooms.

Decoration of the tombs is not limited to the walls but also covers the ceilings.

56-57 *The occupant,
a magistrate, appears
in his full dignity of
public figure on the lid
of this sarcophagus
from Tarquinia
(5th century BC).*

*56 TOP  A SMALL STAG LIES ALONGSIDE THE OCCUPANT OF THE ANCIENT TOMB KNOWN AS THE BOCCHORIS TOMB, FROM TARQUINIA, WHICH DATES BACK TO THE 7TH CENTURY BC.*

*56 BOTTOM  THE FAMOUS TERRACOTTA WINGED HORSES OF TARQUINIA ADORNED THE QUEEN'S ALTAR, THE LARGEST ETRUSCAN TEMPLE KNOWN TO SCHOLARS (5TH-6TH CENTURY BC).*

*58  A PHERSU, A MASKED PRIEST-AUGUR (THE LATIN WORD PERSONA, "MASK", MAY BE DERIVED FROM THIS TERM) DANCES ON A WALL OF THE TOMB OF THE AUGURS, MORE CORRECTLY KNOWN AS THE "TEMPLE OF THE PHERSU," WHICH DATES BACK TO 530 BC.*

*59  A DANCER PERFORMS FOR GUESTS ON A WALL OF THE TOMB OF THE TRICLINIUM, FROM TARQUINIA, WHICH DATES BACK TO THE 5TH CENTURY BC. AS MUCH ETRUSCAN ART REVEALS, THE ARISTOCRATIC BANQUET HAD AN IMPORTANT SOCIAL ROLE.*

In general, several of the structural elements of a roof are reproduced, such as a central strip painted in red to imitate the ridge-pole, while the two sloping sides are often decorated with multi-colored rosettes or four-sided motifs laid out like a chessboard in imitation of the tent under which the deceased was laid out to the public gaze (*pròthesis*).

A central bracket imitating the support for the large beam represented on the ceiling occupies the gable sections (the highest parts) of the entrance wall and back wall. Two animals, generally feline, face one another on either side of it and often give the tomb its name. The most interesting element in the decoration, however, is the figured frieze that fills the middle section of the walls. The subjects in the frieze represent

scenes from the life of the royal family, moments of aristocratic relaxation, and ceremonies performed on the death of a member of the family to celebrate his social and economic status. This is the purpose of the representation of the banquet scenes in which family members are entertained by musicians (generally a flute player and a *cithara* player) and dancers and served by a great many busy attendants.

This can be seen in the Tomb of the Lionesses, so called for the paintings of two feline animals difficult to identify on the gable section of the back wall. The side walls depict

the most important scene: four male figures reclining on beds in the typical banqueting position. The size they have been painted – larger than the others present – indicates the high social standing of the family to which they belonged. Games are also commonly represented: one important example can be seen in the Tomb of the Jugglers in which the ceremonies to honor the deceased are portrayed. In this case, the person for whom the tomb was built may be the figure sitting on the extreme right of the back wall, resting on a long stick and dressed in purple, the color that signifies high rank. A woman in front of him

balances a candlestick on her head while a young man throws rings. The scene takes place to the sound of a flute and under the gaze of several spectators, while four dancers moving to the rhythm of Pan pipes on the right wall complete the scene. On the left wall, an old man, perhaps the priest and organizer of the games, advances with slaves and attendants, and next to him is a character who appears interested in what is taking place on the entrance wall where, despite the precarious state of conservation of the scene, it is possible to identify two figures covered by a skin imitating the movements of an animal.

Besides the representations of banquets, dances and games, sports contests can also be seen. The examples in the tombs offer a wide panorama of the disciplines practiced during sporting occasions, festivals, or funerary ceremonies. There were walking and running races, chariot races, discus and javelin throwing, boxing and wrestling, and the long jump.

In the Tomb of the Augurs, a small rectangular chamber, the pictorial decoration covers the four walls and ceiling based on a schema already seen in other tombs of the sixth and fifth century BC. A false door is shown in the center of the back wall representing the door of Hades, while two figures mourn the deceased on either side. Two inscriptions indicate that the figures are priests or individuals responsible for organizing the funeral ceremonies. The side walls are decorated with the contests that have been held in honor of the deceased. On the right wall two wrestlers with the low-caste names *Teitu* and *Latithe* face one another on either side of three metal containers which probably represent the prize for the winner. On the left wall, a flute player is shown with two boxers. The decoration is completed by another scene which, for its violent and cruel subject, cannot be classified as a sporting discipline. A hooded man holding a stick attempts to defend himself against the attacks of a dog held on a leash but incited by a figure wearing a pointed head-dress and bearded mask, which an inscription informs us represents *Phersu*. The term has been related to the Latin word *persona*, i.e., mask, and the scene has been compared to Roman gladiatorial fights, which are traditionally considered to have been derived from the Etruscans. It is not the hooded figure who comes off worse, however. On the left wall, in

The Tomb of the
Augurs

what seems to be the next stage of the fight, *Phersu* runs off followed by his adversary who seems to have vanquished the ferocious animal.

Whoever painted this picture is considered one of the most important artists in Tarquinian painting which, by that stage, was open to the Ionian artistic influence that dominated Etruscan figurative painting for the second half of the sixth century BC. He is, therefore, regarded as a leader of his art who appears to have trained other important painters responsible for the Tomb of the Jugglers and the Tomb of the Olympics.

63 TOP *THE SMALL TOMB OF THE AUGURS (CA. 530 BC) WAS THE MASTERPIECE OF THE NEW WAVE OF IONIC ARTISTS DURING THE LAST DECADES OF THE 6TH CENTURY BC. THE MASTER ARTIST WHO PAINTED THESE DECORATIONS WAS ONE OF THE MOST ILLUSTRIOUS FIGURES IN TARQUINIAN PAINTING.*

Sports contests were shown on the walls of another masterpiece of Tarquinian wall painting, the Tomb of the Chariots, but the frescoes from this tomb have been detached by the Central Restoration Institute and displayed in the city museum to prevent further deterioration in their condition. The decoration in this small chamber was somewhat complex, starting with the projection of the large central beam and the supporting bracket in the center of the gable section. The ceiling is decorated in a polychrome chessboard pattern of white, blue and red squares. Two semi-reclining figures are shown on the tympanum drinking. The pictorial decoration is organized into two registers: the lower strip shows banqueting scenes and dances that refer to the ceremony that took place around the *pròthesis* tent.

The banquet stretches as far as the back wall and includes three male couples reclining on beds attended by servants and a flute player. The upper register depicts sports contests with a crowd awaiting the start of the events on two wooden platforms painted in the corners where the back wall meets the side walls. Various sportsmen await: charioteers with their chariots, pancratists, wrestlers, boxers, and discus throwers. The painter of this scene is without doubt the greatest painter who ever practiced in Etruria.

64-65 *THE FOWLING AND FISHING TOMB IS SPLIT INTO TWO CHAMBERS LAID END TO END. ON THE FAR WALL OF THE SECOND CHAMBER, FOUR FIGURES IN A BOAT ARE FISHING IN A SEA FILLED WITH FISH; NEXT TO THEM, A YOUNG MAN ARMED WITH A SLING TRIES TO HIT DUCKS FROM THE TOP OF A ROCK (CA. 530 BC).*

The Tomb of the Bulls

whose task it was to flush out the prey and head them towards the hunters. Hunting hares, shown here, was particularly risky and required great personal skills. Being a noble pastime, it must have required great organizational effort and extensive resources of people and equipment. The representation of this subject in a tomb is therefore indicative not so much of the skill of the deceased as a hunter but of his wealth and high social rank.

The decoration of the second room in the Fowling and Fishing Tomb is based on two levels. Below, a greenish base with a wavy upper line represents the sea on which several dolphins are playing; above, in boats, figures fish using lines, nets and harpoons while, on the rocks, others attempt to catch flocks of birds.

The theme of the banquet is limited to the gable section of the back wall in this tomb. A couple of newlyweds dressed in their finest and attended by cup-bearers, maids, and a flute

His technical skills can be seen not only in the ability with which he prepared the thin layer of plaster on which he painted the picture, but above all in the naturalness of the gestures and movements of the characters. In order to achieve this, he abandoned the rigid conventionality of the patterns normally used and attempted to make optimal use of the spaces in the great Attic tradition of the end of the sixth century BC.

An interest in nature is shown in the Fowling and Fishing Tomb split into two chambers that lie end to end. On the walls of the first chamber, a series of half-naked dancing figures are alternated with slender trees on which headbands and crowns hang. Two riders return from the day's hunting on the tympanum of the back wall. The scenes show how hunting was an activity reserved exclusively for the nobles, who were usually depicted in large groups. The high-ranking hunters were accompanied by numerous beaters and by dogs

player are shown on a *kline* in the center of the picture.

Honoring the deceased was done not only by the portrayal of episodes from his life or that of his family, but also through the representation of important subjects taken directly from Greek mythology. An example is the Tomb of the Bulls, the earliest painted funerary monument in Tarquinia. The tomb belonged to *Aranth Spurianas*, an ancestor perhaps of the noble Tarquinian family, the *Spurinas*.

66 ONE OF THE MOST HIGHLY REGARDED TOMBS, THE DECORATION IN THE TOMB OF THE BARON (CA. 510 BC) WAS INSPIRED BY THE LATER IONIC ARTISTIC TRADITION. THIS PHOTOGRAPH SHOWS A DETAIL OF A FRESCO IN WHICH THE DECEASED GOES TOWARDS HIS BRIDE RAISING A CUP IN HIS LEFT HAND.

On the back wall of the first chamber, in the space between the two doors that lead to the smaller chambers, we see the theme dear to Greek pottery of Achilles' ambush of Troilus, one of the sons of Priam. Troilus rides his horse towards a fountain behind which Achilles is hiding. This scene is the only mythological subject in 6th and 5th century BC tombs. The uncertainties in the execution of the scene reveal the difficulties the painter

respects to the deceased three times. In the center of the back wall, a bearded figure between two young horsemen and accompanied by a flute player approaches a woman holding a cup in one hand. The man, probably the deceased, receives the homage of his wife and children. The scene is repeated on the left wall but, this time, the two children have dismounted and salute the woman. On the other wall, the two riders salute one

67 TOP THE SCENES IN THE TOMB OF THE BARON, IN PARTICULAR THIS ONE ON THE LEFT WALL, ARE STRIKING FOR THE ELEGANCE AND BALANCE OF THE COMPOSITION AND FOR THE SYMMETRICAL USE OF THE COLORS.

67 BOTTOM THIS DETAIL IS ALSO FROM THE LEFT WALL OF THE TOMB OF THE BARON. IT SHOWS TWO YOUNG RIDERS SAYING THEIR LAST GOODBYE TO THE DECEASED BELOW.

encountered in attempting a subject of such vast dimensions. His technical ability is best shown in the small figures in the frieze and the gables where his skills as a pottery decorator are evident.

A scene more closely linked to the sorrow of the deceased's family is shown on the walls of the Tomb of the Baron, the masterpiece of late Ionic art. A broad red strip on the ceiling of the little chamber reproduces the ridge-pole resting on a bracket shown in the center of the gable section. A cornice of parallel bands forms the upper limit of the figured frieze where the family is shown paying their

another. These three wall scenes were arranged with care. Moving the center of the composition from the side walls to the back wall, the painter succeeded in merging the three episodes into a single story which can be appreciated in its entirety as the spectator enters the small chamber.

The arrangement of the figures in each scene and the choice of colors – never too bright nor too strongly contrasting – demonstrate a skilful ability to create balance. The artist's preference for slender, elongated forms reflects the widespread influence of Ionic art at the end of the 6th century BC,

which had replaced the more solid and vigorous forms of the previous decades seen in the Tomb of the Leopards and the Tomb of the Augurs.

At the start of the 5th century BC, Tarquinian wall painting settled on certain decorative schemas and compositional formulas that remained the preferred taste of the aristocratic clients for more than a century. One of the most important innovations was the positioning of the banquet scene with three *klinai* on the back wall of the tomb so that representations of dances or games were limited to the side walls.

The Tomb of the Baron

*68-69  THE RIGHT WALL OF
THE TOMB OF THE
LEOPARDS SHOWS A MAN
WITH A LARGE CUP (KYLIX)*

*IN HIS HAND. HE HEADS
TOWARDS THE BANQUET,
OPENING A PATH THROUGH
A GROUP OF DANCERS.*

The new layout was adopted for the first time by the painter of the Tomb of the Chariots but soon became a constant feature of all tombs during the 5th century BC. On the back wall of the Tomb of the Triclinium, three couples of men and women recline on their beds attended by various slaves. The delicate profiles of the figures, the grace and stateliness of their gestures, belie the Attic models from the start of the century by which they were inspired. Similar stylistically to these frescoes are those in the Tomb of the Funeral Bed in which the decoration depicts the last honors paid to the deceased during the *pròthesis* ceremony.

Another eloquent example is offered by the Tomb of the Leopard, which unfortunately now suffers badly from saltpeter rot. Nevertheless, it is still possible to appreciate

the lively polychrome coloring that extends from the geometrical patterns on the ceiling to the figured scenes on the walls. The central space on the ceiling is occupied by the ridge-pole adorned by variously sized circular decorations. The projections are ornamented with a chessboard pattern of white, red, green and blue squares. The supporting bracket of the column does not appear on the tympanum, which has been replaced by two leopards facing each other on a background decorated with plant motifs. The figured frieze occupies most of the wall space. The pattern is shown on the back wall with three couples attended by two servants. The pattern is completed by a procession of figures on the right wall and six servants on the left wall.

Tarquinian painting suffered a serious setback between the mid-5th and start of the

4th century BC due to a cultural regression resulting from defeat at the battle of Cuma; the battle was the outcome of an increase in Syracusan power and the Etruscan loss of naval supremacy in the Tyrrhenian sea. But Tarquinia returned to being a powerful city in the early decades of the 4th century BC, and its necropolises were enriched with new tombs in which the individual married couple was no longer portrayed, but rather a larger group of characters from the same family clan.

The dead were still honored in the tombs but with an explicit statement of political titles and religious responsibilities, or through the recording of deeds performed during their earthly life. There were also important novelties in the choice of figurative subjects linked, above all, to the world beyond the grave.

69 top  A group of
figures on the left
wall of the Tomb of
the Leopards advances
towards the table
guests holding objects
for use in the banquet.

69 bottom
The scenes on the
walls of the Tomb of
the Leopards are
typical of the
funerary iconography
of the 5th century BC:
the banquet occupies
all the space on the
far wall.

## The Tomb of the Leopards

70 TOP  THE TUMULUS OF THE MOULDINGS HAS INTERESTING FEATURES: IT IS SMALL BUT THE HEIGHT OF THE DRUM IS ACCENTUATED, IN PART DUG OUT OF THE ROCK, IN PART INTEGRATED WITH ROWS MADE FROM TUFA OR MACCO (A LOCAL STONE).

70-71  DARK PASSAGES LEAD INTO THE BURIAL MOUNDS OF THE BANDITACCIA NECROPOLIS IN CERVETERI. THIS UNINTERRUPTED SERIES OF TOMBS ON A CIRCULAR BASE CONSTITUTES ONE OF THE MOST EVOCATIVE ARCHAEOLOGICAL LANDSCAPES OF THE ENTIRE ETRUSCAN AREA.

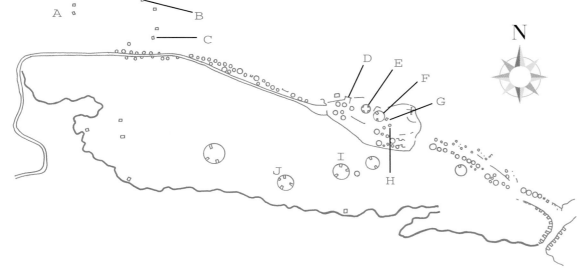

## LEGEND

**A** TOMB OF THE FIVE SEATS
**B** TOMB OF THE ALCOVE
**C** TOMB OF THE TRICLINIUM
**D** TOMB OF THE CAPITALS
**E** MOUND II
**F** MOUND I
**G** TOMB OF THE RELIEFS
**H** TOMB OF THE SMALL HOUSE
**I** MOUNDS OF THE SHIELDS AND THE SEATS
**J** MOUND OF THE PAINTED ANIMALS

71 TOP LEFT  TUMULUS II OF THE BANDITACCIA NECROPOLIS HOUSES: THE CAPANNA TOMB (1), THE TOMB OF THE DOLII (2), THE TOMB OF THE BEDS AND SARCOPHAGUSES (3) AND THE TOMB OF THE GREEK VASES (4).

71 TOP RIGHT  A LONG CORRIDOR, THE DROMOS, GIVES ACCESS TO THE TOMB.

# The monumental necropolis of Cerveteri

*71 BOTTOM LEFT
THE LARGE VASE (MID-7TH
CENTURY BC) FROM ONE
OF THE SEPULCHERS AT
CERVETERI BEARS THE
SIGNATURE OF THE FAMOUS
POTTER FROM CHALCIDICE,
ARISTONOPHOS, WHO
EMIGRATED TO SICILY AND
THEN MOVED ON TO
ETRURIA. THE VASE SHOWS
A NAVAL BATTLE BETWEEN
THE GREEKS AND THE
ETRUSCANS AND THE
BLINDING OF POLYPHEMUS.*

While the importance of the tombs in Tarquinia lies in their marvelous wall paintings, the significance of the graves at Cerveteri derives from the fact that the slow development of their structure must have reflected changes in the construction of their civil buildings.

The ancient town stood on a steep-sided tableland shaped by the watercourses named the Fosso del Manganello and the Fosso della Mola. Little remains of the Etruscan city, but there is much to be seen in its necropolises at Monte Abatone, Sorbo, and Banditaccia.

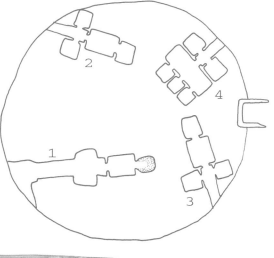

The earliest tombs were underground chambers cut in the tufa and topped by a protective earth mound; the edges of the mound were marked and supported by a circular drum of tufa slabs or simply hewn from the rock.

The necropolises were fairly irregularly laid out along roads that led to the city. The size of the mounds varied widely, perhaps in relation to the economic resources of the families. The Capanna tomb in the necropolis at Banditaccia is the oldest of this method of burial, followed shortly after by what is probably Cerveteri's best-known tomb, the Regolini-Galassi tomb named after the archpriest, Alessandro Regolini, and the general, Vincenzo Galassi, who discovered it on 21 April 1836 near Sorbo, south of the city, along the road that leads to the sea. The tomb consists of two long, narrow chambers lying end to end and two small chambers to the sides of the first long chamber. This reflects the most common model of the houses of the Cerveteri aristocracy, in which the two main rooms were the living room and bedroom. The remains of three people were found inside the tomb, one cremated and the other two interred, which indicates how the family had accepted the gradual and untraumatic change in practice.

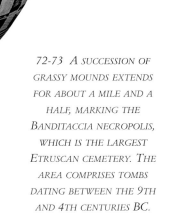

*72-73 A SUCCESSION OF
GRASSY MOUNDS EXTENDS
FOR ABOUT A MILE AND A
HALF, MARKING THE
BANDITACCIA NECROPOLIS,
WHICH IS THE LARGEST
ETRUSCAN CEMETERY. THE
AREA COMPRISES TOMBS
DATING BETWEEN THE 9TH
AND 4TH CENTURIES BC.*

*74-75 Dug out of the tufa at the top of the hill, this road crosses all of Banditaccia necropolis.*

*74 bottom left The façade of the famous twin tomb at Cerveteri imitates coeval examples of civilian construction (end of the 4th century BC).*

*74 bottom right From the mid-6th century BC, the adoption of a new structure broke the centuries-old tradition of the mound. Tombs appeared looking like a cube which were entered via a door from the necropolis road.*

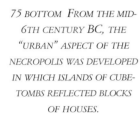

75 TOP  THE BURIAL
CHAMBER WAS TURNED INTO
A HOUSE: TWO SEATS STAND
AT THE SIDES OF THE
ENTRANCE IN AN ALLUSION
TO THE PLACES OCCUPIED
BY THE MALE AND FEMALE
HEADS OF THE FAMILY IN
THE ATRIUM OF THE FAMILY
HOME.

75 BOTTOM  FROM THE MID-
6TH CENTURY BC, THE
"URBAN" ASPECT OF THE
NECROPOLIS WAS DEVELOPED
IN WHICH ISLANDS OF CUBE-
TOMBS REFLECTED BLOCKS
OF HOUSES.

The body in the far room was probably that of a woman; she was surrounded by a much richer set of grave goods than the others. Many of the items reveal the wealth of the family, for example, her personal gold ornaments, bronze and bucchero plates, and the many articles made from ivory and amber. Some, like the bucchero statuettes known as "the weepers," symbolize the eternal sorrow felt by family members on the passing of their relatives.

The family's wealth was linked to the prosperity of Cerveteri during the 7th century BC when the city controlled the iron mines in the Tolfa mountains and maritime commerce flourished. [a]

Like Tarquinia, the Cerveteri nobility invested their tombs with the function of displaying the prestige of the dead and their families. Similarly, their grave goods were linked to the concept of the banquet, which was one of the preferred means of glorifying their social status. The aim of displaying their wealth was to legitimize the power that they exercised, an objective they pursued with the exhibition of marvelous ornamental objects made from precious metal and numerous weapons, often simply made for parade purposes.

From about 670 BC, new construction techniques brought a radical transformation in building and marked the definitive transition from the tomb built in the form of a hut to the tomb representing a house.

They seem to reproduce the domestic environment in all details, particularly the execution of the ceilings. Full relief representations of beams demonstrate the adoption of heavy roofs in civil architecture based on a framework of beams to support roof tiles. A new type of internal tomb layout became popular at the end of the century that was to continue through the following period: the ground plan of the new tomb was based on a large rectangular chamber and three smaller cells reached through the back wall of the large room. This layout is well represented in the

76-77 THE MOST
REPRESENTATIVE OF THE
4TH-CENTURY TOMBS IS
THE TOMB OF RELIEFS IN
BANDITACCIA NECROPOLIS.
IT BELONGED TO THE
MATUNA FAMILY, MEMBERS
OF THE CAEREAN
NOBILITY.

76 BOTTOM THE CAPANNA
TOMB IN MOUND II IS THE
EARLIEST EXAMPLE OF A
CHAMBER-TOMB AT
CERVETERI. IT CONSISTS OF
A CHAMBER WITH A LOW

BENCH THAT RUNS ALONG
THE WALLS AND A SECOND,
SMALLER AND LOWER
ROOM.

77 TOP THE TOMB OF THE
SHIELDS AND THE SEATS IN
BANDITACCIA NECROPOLIS
HAS A CENTRAL ROOM
DECORATED WITH LARGE
ROUND COPPER SHIELDS IN
RELIEF; TWO THRONES
WERE ALSO CARVED IN AN
ALLUSION TO THE
PRESENCE OF THE PATER
AND MATER FAMILIAS.

77 BOTTOM HIGH-
QUALITY POTTERY HAS
BEEN FOUND AMONG THE
OBJECTS THAT MAKE UP
THE GRAVE GOODS IN THE
UNDERGROUND TOMBS AT
CAERE (CERVETERI).
THESE TWO KYLIXES
WERE IMPORTED DIRECTLY
FROM GREECE, WHERE
THEY WERE
MANUFACTURED DURING
THE FIRST HALF OF THE
6TH CENTURY BC.

Tomb of the Capitals built in Banditaccia necropolis at the end of the 7th century BC. The tomb has a short access corridor onto which three doors open: the two at the sides give onto small cells, and the central door leads into the nucleus of the tomb. The first room is a reproduction of the atrium of an Etruscan house and is adorned with a couple of octagonal pillars with Aeolian capitals; three doors in the back wall lead into small rooms lit by two small windows in the vestibule.

The Tomb of the Shields or the Seats is a demonstration of how this new layout continued to be used at least until the beginning of the 6th century BC. A corridor leads to a rectangular atrium without pillars, covered by a flat roof and decorated with nine projecting beams. Three small rooms lead off from the atrium.

From the middle of the 6th century BC, a new design of sepulcher began to appear in Banditaccia necropolis. This was the "cube tomb," a quadrangular construction that imitated the outside of a house with an inner chamber in which the bodies were laid. It is probable that the concept of this structure was prompted by the need to create a sepulcher able to make best use of the ever smaller space available. The adoption of cube-tombs initiated a cycle of restructuring work in the necropolises in which a grid pattern of roads separated the tombs into blocks.

It may well be that the diffusion of the new type of tomb received a significant impetus from the determined spirit of a new class of middleclass of citizens whose aim it was to curb the unlimited political and economic power of the nobles expressed, on a funerary

long stairway that leads into the four-sided chamber with a two-sided sloping roof supported by two sturdy pillars. Thirty-three niches along the walls were used for depositions while one in the center of the back wall was reserved for the pater and mater familias; this niche differed from the others in the careful representation of the feet, cushions, and front panel of the *kline*

level, in gigantic mounds. But from the 5th century BC, these class conflicts seem to have subsided and even the layout of the necropolis seems to have lost the importance of the century before.

Most of the tombs were dug at great depth in the tufa and consisted of a single four-sided chamber, completely free of any decoration, with long benches on which the bodies were deposed. There were more elaborate tombs, however, belonging to a new class of nobility that had risen from the class conflicts of the previous century. These were vaulted tombs decorated with false rock façades made from blocks of tufa or simply four-sided chambers supported by pillars with benches for the less important burials and a four-sided bay dug out of the back wall for the most important couple.

The best-known of this last category is the Tomb of the Reliefs. This is reached via a

where the figures of Typhon and Cerberus were portrayed. The walls and pillars are decorated with extraordinary stucchi (plaster models) of furniture and furnishings typical of a wealthy household, as well as articles of war, hunting, and play.

*78 TOP LEFT  IN THE LEFT CHAMBER IN THE TOMB OF THE FIVE SEATS IN CERVETERI (SECOND HALF OF THE 7TH CENTURY BC), FIVE SEATS WERE SCULPTED IN THE ROCK TO HOLD THE TERRACOTTA IMAGES OF THE FAMILY'S ANCESTORS.*

*78 TOP RIGHT THE CAMPANA MOUND CONTAINS TWO TOMBS. CAMPANA 1 HAS A LONG CORRIDOR, A CENTRAL CHAMBER AND TWO LATERAL CHAMBERS. A BED AND THREE BASKETS WERE CARVED OUT OF THE ROCK IN THE CHAMBER ON THE LEFT.*

78 BOTTOM THE
TORLONIA TOMB IN THE
NECROPOLIS OF MONTE
ABATONE COMPRISES AN
ANTE-CHAMBER FOR THE
LESS IMPORTANT BURIALS
AND AN ALCOVE IN WHICH
A KLINE WITH MILLED
FEET HELD THE REMAINS
OF THE MALE AND FEMALE
HEADS OF THE FAMILY.

78-79 THE TOMB OF THE
ALCOVE BELONGING TO
THE TARNAS FAMILY HAS A
SINGLE ROOM DIVIDED
INTO THREE SECTIONS BY
TWO LARGE FLUTED
PILLARS. NEAR THE FAR
WALL, THREE SMALL STEPS
LEAD TO A FOUR-SIDED
BAY RESERVED FOR THE
DEPOSITION OF THE PATER
AND MATERFAMILIAS.

79 BOTTOM THE TOMB
OF THE CAPITALS IN
BANDITACCIA NECROPOLIS
(START OF THE 6TH
CENTURY BC) CONTAINS
FUNERARY BEDS CARVED
IN THE ROCK AGAINST THE
WALLS OF THE MAIN ROOM
ON WHICH THE BODIES OF
THE DECEASED WERE LAID.

# The underground tomb of
# HAL SAFLIENI and the
# BROCHTORFF circle
## IN THE ISLANDS OF THE MALTESE ARCHIPELAGO

Gozo Island

XAGHRA

Malta Island

HAL SAFLIENI

I n the context of megalithic structures, the temple and underground structures of the islands of the Maltese archipelago are of particular importance. Attributed to the Neolithic period (4100-2500 BC calibrated dates), they are still unique for both the typology of their architectural structure and for the iconography of their art. The latter does not consist merely of ornamental patterns similar to those in French and Irish megalithic tombs, but also statuary intended to represent the figure of the Mother Goddess that played a leading role in the Maltese agrarian civilization of the Neolithic period.

The concentration of megalithic structures in the Maltese archipelago is surprising where, so far, 30 temple complexes and 2 underground complexes have been discovered; the subterranean structures were used for collective burials. In all probability, the extraordinary development of megalithic construction can be ascribed to the technical ability of the

inhabitants and to the local presence of easily worked materials such as coralline limestone and globigerina limestone which the builders could use in the production of monuments.

It should be noted that the custom of digging tombs out of the rock was widespread in the archipelago and that the tombs in the earliest period of Neolithic civilization had very simple forms but, in later stages, given the close connection between the fertility cult and the cult of the dead, they took on a complex funerary appearance characterized by elements typical of temple architecture. Further confirmation is given by the fact that the underground structures of Hal Safleini (Malta) and of Brochtorff (Gozo) were located near temples. Objects found in the Brochtorff circle provide eloquent evidence of the fertility worship of the Mother Goddess that was practiced there; in addition to the statuettes

of female figures with exaggerated features related to fecundity (breasts and buttocks), a surprisingly tall statue from the Tarxien complex measuring 3 meters, should also be mentioned.

Also worthy of discussion is the labyrinthine structure of Hal Saflieni which, despite presenting analogies with the contemporaneous Brochtorff circle on the island of Gozo, appears to be a unique example for its size – it covers a surface area of roughly 500 square meters and reaches a depth of 11 meters – for the complexity of its architecture and for the finds that have been made there. The Hal Saflieni underground tomb was gouged out of the soft globigerina limestone using wedges and digging sticks and its walls were smoothed with flint scrapers and blades; the structure is dated to the Neolithic period (4100-2500 BC, calibrated dates). Given that it was created over a period of more than a millennium, it seems permissible to think that the 3 levels that it comprises may have been used for different purposes over time. The complex comprises 33 sections that were used for funerary and cult functions; worship was mainly performed on the second level where the rooms were built in a similar architectural style to those in surface temples. The rooms on the first level, dated to the first-second Middle Neolithic (4100-3600 BC), have recently been completely excavated following demolition of houses that stood above the complex. The discovery of the complex in 1902 took place quite by chance when workers constructing houses dug a well for rainwater and discovered the rooms on the first level. Making use of these as a dump, they caused serious damage. After the houses had been completed, the Director of the Archaeological

Museum was informed of the existence of the underground Neolithic cult-funerary complex.

The three levels showed a gradual architectural development. The shape of the three-stone entrance and the appearance of the unsmoothed walls of the chambers that still show abundant traces of red ochre (red ochre seemed to be the symbol of blood, life, and rebirth and can be linked to the cult of the dead) are evidence that the first floor dated from the earliest phase. The presence of the remains of burials, bones, and fragments of pottery suggests that this level was used for functions primarily associated with burial

to which worship was also linked. It seems undeniable that there was a cult dedicated to the Mother Goddess: this is shown by the presence of a headless limestone statuette and two small heads that, in all probability, were inserted into the neck of such statuettes (found also in Maltese temples) in spring, when addition of the vital principle (the head) recreated the Goddess responsible for the growth of natural world.

The development of cult worship was only in its embryonic stage on the first level but evolved until it had taken on better defined characteristics on the second. As already noted,

the architecture of the chambers that reproduced the megalithic structure of surface temples, combined with archaeological finds having clear religious implications, implies that the second level was used as an "underground temple."

The large rooms on the second level, whose walls were finely decorated using red ochre among other materials, can be dated to the first-third Late Neolithic (the Gigantija phases 3600-3300/3000 BC and Saflieni-Tarxien 3300/3000-2500 BC), the period during which large megalithic temples were built on the Maltese archipelago in honor of the Mother Goddess.

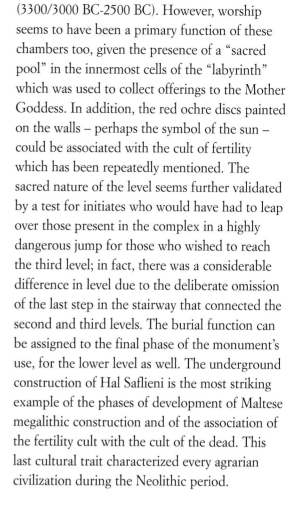

(3300/3000 BC-2500 BC). However, worship seems to have been a primary function of these chambers too, given the presence of a "sacred pool" in the innermost cells of the "labyrinth" which was used to collect offerings to the Mother Goddess. In addition, the red ochre discs painted on the walls – perhaps the symbol of the sun – could be associated with the cult of fertility which has been repeatedly mentioned. The sacred nature of the level seems further validated by a test for initiates who would have had to leap over those present in the complex in a highly dangerous jump for those who wished to reach the third level; in fact, there was a considerable difference in level due to the deliberate omission of the last step in the stairway that connected the second and third levels. The burial function can be assigned to the final phase of the monument's use, for the lower level as well. The underground construction of Hal Saflieni is the most striking example of the phases of development of Maltese megalithic construction and of the association of the fertility cult with the cult of the dead. This last cultural trait characterized every agrarian civilization during the Neolithic period.

These rooms perfectly represented the surface temples including a *sancta sanctorum*. This was very probably where the ceremony of hierogamy took place in which the priest and priestess, as representatives of the god and goddess, were joined in holy union. This rite, intended to ensure the continuance of the agrarian cycles and associated with the cult of the Mother Goddess, seemed proven by the discovery of naked female statuettes and a phallic symbol that were similar to finds made in temple structures elsewhere in the archipelago.

The burial function of the second level can be attributed to the final phase of its use; the absence of architectural structures to separate the areas used for worship from those reserved for the deposition of bodies may have excluded contemporaneous use of the two functions, since the air at different depths would have been unbreathable for the worshippers. The rooms on the third floor show no similarity to elements of megalithic temple architecture and have been dated to the third Late Neolithic

*82-83 THE PHOTOGRAPH SHOWS ONE OF THE ROOMS AT HAL SAFLIENI. IT IS MADE FROM PILLARS, COLUMNS AND BURIAL NICHES CARVED PERFECTLY FROM THE ROCK WITH STONE TOOLS.*

*83 CENTER A CELL AND A NICHE FOR THE ORACLE OPEN IN A WALL IN THE ORACLE ROOM ON THE SECOND FLOOR. THE CEILING IS DECORATED WITH SPIRALS IN RED OCHRE.*

*83 TOP THE ARCHITECTURAL STRUCTURE OF HAL SAFLIENI RESEMBLES THAT OF SURFACE TEMPLES.*

*83 BOTTOM LEFT THIS ALABASTER STATUETTE IS HEADLESS AND HAS AN ASYMMETRIC HOLE IN HER NECK.*

*83 BOTTOM RIGHT THIS FIGURE IS ALSO MADE FROM ALABASTER. IT HAS A COLLAR (OF FLESH) AROUND ITS NECK. THE TWO STATUETTES ABOUT 6 CM HIGH WERE FOUND IN HAL SAFLIENI AND CAN BE SEEN TODAY IN THE VALLETTA MUSEUM.*

# The Brochtorff circle

Following the discovery of the Brochtorff circle on Gozo during a research project backed by scholars of renown, the spread of the use of collective burial customs during the Neolithic period was confirmed. The mortuary, comprising a series of natural grottoes used for burial, was identified for the first time in 1820 in the locality of Xaghra on the island of Gozo and was gradually cleared from 1987 on. The circle shares clear similarities with the

meters in diameter. It is very likely, in our assessment, that prehistoric man on the Maltese archipelago had tried to protect the temple structures and the funerary-cult complex with stone circles intended to mark the boundary between the sacred and profane areas.

Marked by two large stones, the entrance to the Brochtorff circle is located near the Gigantija temples. It led to an area

contemporaneous (4100-2500 BC) underground complex of Hal Saflieni on the island of Malta, for example, in its undeniable likeness to temple architecture (although the Brochtorff circle was somewhat simpler) for purposes of worship and burial as well as its physical proximity to temples. It is known that the Hal Saflieni complex lies near the temples at Tarxien and the Brochtorff circle near those of Gigantija; the objects found inside the structures share common characteristics that are unquestionably linked to the fertility cult.

The funerary-cult complex on Gozo was bounded by a stone circle 45

*84 TOP THE PAINTING WAS PRODUCED BY CH. BROCHTORFF IN 1894 FOLLOWING THE FIRST DISCOVERY OF THE MONUMENT IN 1820. IT SHOWS THE MEGALITHIC CIRCLE OF XAGHRA THAT WAS LATER RENAMED THE "BROCHTORFF CIRCLE".*

*84 BOTTOM LEFT STATUETTES OF MOTHER GODDESSES WERE FOUND IN THE BROCHTORFF CIRCLE. THIS IS AN UNUSUAL EXAMPLE IN THAT IT SHOWS TWO FEMALE FIGURES: ONE HOLDS A BOWL IN HER HAND, THE OTHER A BABY.*

CHARACTERIZED BY TRILITHIC STRUCTURES, A LARGE (PROBABLY CEREMONIAL) BOWL, AND SMALL CELLS IN THE ROCK.

84-85 THIS PICTURE SHOWS SOME OF THE FINDS MADE DURING EXCAVATIONS OF THE BROCHTORFF CIRCLE.

85 BOTTOM THE AERIAL PHOTOGRAPH SHOWS GIGANTIJA TEMPLE NEAR THE BROCHTORFF CIRCLE. NOTE HOW THE TEMPLE STRUCTURE IS SIMILAR TO

THAT OF THE FUNERARY MONUMENT. IT IS BOUNDED BY A CIRCLE OF STONES THAT PROBABLY HAD A "SACRED" PROTECTIVE PURPOSE.

connection is further borne out by the presence in these rooms of a stone jar the shape of which bears clear similarities to the one found in the Tarxien temples which was used for offerings in the fertility cult. A highly stylized group of statuettes (height 16 cm) in the shape of a stick were found among the iconographic array in the Brochtorff circle; they too seem to be unique and it is difficult to hypothesize any function for them. The archaeologists responsible for excavation of the site have emphasized that these statues may have been specifically linked with ceremonies associated with death.

The funerary-cult aspects of the Brochtorff circle – characterized by the skeletons of inhumed bodies, temple-like architectural design, and objects irrefutably connected with the fertility cult – confirm the hypothesis advanced several times, that the use of collective burial in grottoes, which had its roots in the first phases of the Neolithic period and gradually evolved until it reached the height of its development in the underground structure at Hal Saflieni, was widespread throughout the Maltese archipelago. And this funerary practice was closely linked to worship of an agrarian nature that had characterized the Neolithic civilizations of western Europe.

characterized by a "megalithic threshold" bounded by architectural elements linked to the fertility cult (bethels) and by small burial trenches, some of which date from the Zebbug phase (4100 BC). Note, however, that the grottoes used for burial on this site were natural and that the temple-like structures were built in this pre-existing "sacred" spot.

Steps lead from this area used predominantly for burial to a lower level, some 4-5 meters below the surface. The archaeologists who cleared the site have expressed the hypothesis that further excavation may reveal more levels, as at Hal Saflieni.

The Brochtorff structure contained small rooms used for worship, no larger than 4x6 meters, where terracotta statues of obese

females related to the fertility cult and of great interest were found. A pair of female figures, one of which seems to be holding a child in her arms, is yet another unique find. That statues linked to the fertility cult were found in a funerary context is not incomprehensible given the close connection with the cult of the dead, as has been previously mentioned more than once. It is our opinion that this

Although the monument on Gozo is simpler in structure than that at Hal Saflieni, the two can be equated from a "functional" point of view.

To sum up, it can be stated that the Maltese structures seem to constitute the most complete phase of western megalithic construction from an architectural and iconographic viewpoint.

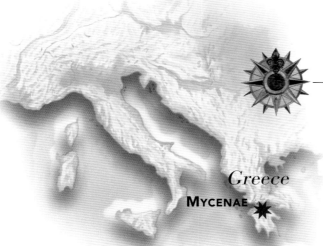

*Greece*
**MYCENAE**

# The tombs and treasures of the kings of
# MYCENAE
Mycenae

From the 17th-12th century BC across most of Aeneolithic Greece and, from at least the 14th century BC, in Crete, there flourished the most important pre-classical western civilization in the Mediterranean, universally called "Mycenaean" after the city Mycenae in Argolis. Excavations begun in the 1870s by Heinrich Schliemann, and still in progress, have uncovered the imposing ruins of one of its most important political and economic centers.

Mycenae rose during the 17th century BC on a steep hill in view of the fertile plain of Argos and the gulf of Nàfplion, protected by Mount Sàra and Mount Aghios Ilìas on the one hand, and by the steep gorges of Chàvos and Kokorètsa on the other. Its huge defensive wall was built using the "Cyclopean" polygonal technique with later inserts in pseudo-isodome style (i.e., in almost regular rows of parallelepiped blocks). Its uneven perimeter runs for roughly a kilometer around the excavated remains of the palace and the town, following the shape of the hill. We do not, however, know the original height or any specific details of the

defensive structures, but its dating is more certain: the system built in the middle of the 14th century BC was more strictly related to the defense of the royal palace; this was followed by significant amplification of the walls in the mid-thirteenth century BC and by a further, smaller expansion to the east almost a century later.

It was this last development of the walls that is

related to the theme of this book, as its purpose was to incorporate Circle A, the royal necropolis from the 16th century BC, which was transformed into a funerary sanctuary that bore very close resemblances to the cult characteristics of a *heròon*. Here, Heinrich Schliemann and his successors (1876) discovered and excavated 6 shaft-tombs.

The funerary architecture of Mycenaean centers had been based on monumental forms since the 17th century BC, when the first simple burial chambers were entirely dug out of the rock bed. They normally consisted of a short entrance corridor (*dròmos*) and frequently stood opposite "chapels" used for the funerary ritual. Adoption of this burial chamber design, according to the experts, is evidence of Egyptian and Cretan influences, which were probably known to the Mycenaeans as a result of their close relations with the land of the pharaohs and the island of Minos. During the same period, the use of the shaft-tomb appeared and started to spread; it consisted of a vast underground chamber with pebble floor, walls built with small stones, and a ceiling made from wooden planks and earth or from joists supporting thin stone slabs.

*86 TOP LEFT THE FUNERARY CIRCLE A AT MYCENAE THAT HEINRICH SCHLIEMANN BEGAN TO EXCAVATE IN 1876 CONTAINED SIX LARGE SHAFT-TOMBS, ALL DATED TO THE 16TH CENTURY BC. THEY BELONGED TO MEMBERS OF THE CITY'S RULING DYNASTY.*

*86 BOTTOM LEFT THE LAST SECTION OF THE RAMP OF THE ANCIENT MYCENAEAN ROAD THAT LEADS TO THE ENTRANCE OF THE CITY IS STILL FLANKED ON BOTH SIDES BY THE REMAINS OF SOLID "CYCLOPEAN" WALLS BUILT DURING THE 13TH CENTURY BC IN THE TYPICAL SCEE DEFENSIVE LAYOUT.*

*86 TOP RIGHT THE FAMOUS RELIEF THAT ADORNS THE RELIEVING TRIANGLE OF THE LION GATE DEPICTS TWO LIONS (OR LIONESSES) FACING ONE ANOTHER ON EITHER SIDE OF A COLUMN WITH A MINOAN SHAFT AND CAPITAL THAT STANDS ON A TALL PLINTH.*

### LEGEND
**A** MYCENAE
**B** CIRCLE A
**C** CIRCLE B
**D** TREASURY OF ATREUS
**E** TOMB OF CLYTEMNESTRA
**F** TOMB OF AEGISTHUS
**G** TOMB OF THE LIONS

86-87 THIS OVERALL VIEW OF CIRCLE A SHOWS HOW THE 16TH CENTURY BC MOUND WAS INCORPORATED WITHIN THE WALLS BUILT DURING THE 14TH-13TH CENTURY BC. ALSO VISIBLE ARE THE CONTAINING WALLS THAT MARK THE EDGE OF THE FUNERARY AREA, AND THE CIRCULAR ENCLOSURE FORMED BY TWO RINGS OF VERTICAL SLABS STILL COVERED, HERE AND THERE, BY HORIZONTAL SLABS. THESE ARE SIGNS OF THE CONVERSION OF THE SITE INTO A "HEROIC" SANCTUARY.

87 BOTTOM TOMB IV IN FUNERARY CIRCLE A CONTAINED THIS PRECIOUS RHYTON IN THE SHAPE OF A LION HEAD LINED WITH THICK GOLD LEAF WHICH MAY HAVE BEEN USED IN THE FUNERAL CEREMONY.

88 MOUNT SÀRA, SOUTHEAST OF THE CITADEL, DOMINATES THE BARE LANDSCAPE OF MYCENAE, WITH FUNERARY CIRCLE A AND THE LION GATE CLEARLY VISIBLE IN THE FOREGROUND. THE RUINS OF THE "PALACE", EMPHASIZED BY THE ROSY LIGHT, CAN BE SEEN IN THE CENTER OF THE VIEW, ARRANGED ON TERRACES SLOPING TOWARDS THE SOUTH. THE WALLS DATE BACK TO THE HEIGHT OF THE CITY'S SPLENDOR, BETWEEN THE 14TH AND 13TH CENTURIES BC.

89 A FRESCO FOUND IN THE PALACE AT MYCENAE DEPICTS THE FAMOUS "DANCER," WHO WAS PROBABLY A NOBLEWOMAN. THE FULL AND SINUOUS FIGURE CLEARLY SHOWS THE MINOAN INFLUENCE ON MYCENAEAN ART. SHE IS SHOWN HOLDING A SNAKE, WHICH WAS A VERY WIDESPREAD APOTROPAIC SYMBOL IN THE ANCIENT MEDITERRANEAN WORLD.

90 TOP  IN 1876, FIVE YEARS AFTER THE INCREDIBLE DISCOVERY OF TROY, SCHLIEMANN ACHIEVED ANOTHER EXTRAORDINARY FEAT, UNEARTHING MYCENAE.

90-91  LATE 19TH-CENTURY VISITORS ADMIRE THE RECENTLY EXCAVATED FUNERARY CIRCLE A. THE DISCOVERY OF THE "CITY OF AGAMEMNON" HAD A HUGE RESONANCE IN EUROPE.

*92 TOP  SOME OF THE FAMOUS GOLD-LINED DEATH MASKS COME FROM TOMB IV IN CIRCLE A. THIS ONE IS FROM THE TYPOLOGY OF THE CONVEX, ROUND FACE WITH ROUND, PROTRUDING EYES. CLEARLY IT WAS NOT SUPPOSED TO REPRESENT THE DECEASED WHOSE FACE IT COVERED.*

*92 CENTER  VERY SIMILAR TO THE PREVIOUS MASK IN TYPOLOGY, STYLE, AND AESTHETICS, THIS MASK ALSO FOUND IN TOMB IV IN CIRCLE A WAS ALSO DECORATED USING EMBOSSING AND ENGRAVING TECHNIQUES.*

*92 BOTTOM  THIS EXTREMELY FINE GOLD-SHEET DIADEM WAS FOUND IN TOMB III OF CIRCLE A. THE STYLIZED FLORAL DECORATIONS ARE TYPICAL OF MYCENAEAN ART.*

The most impressive examples of this type of funeral chamber are the 6 tombs dug up by Schliemann and Stamatàkis in Circle A, the oldest royal necropolis circled by the walls of the citadel and clearly converted into a "heroic" sanctuary by consolidation of the earthworks with massive buttresses made using small blocks. An enclosure formed by a *dròmos* built using two uprights crowned by a lintel marked the boundary of the funerary area on which 11 stele, some decorated, others not, indicated the locations of the shafts that were reopened and closed on the occasion of each new deposition.

In these tombs 19 bodies were found (8 men, 9 women, and 2 children) with the magnificent grave goods today displayed in the National Archaeological Museum in Athens, including the most famous and beautiful works of gold produced by the Mycenaean civilization: the unusual funerary masks made from gold sheet that, according to Demargne, were worked directly on the faces of the bodies, plus the ceremonial containers, personal ornaments, and weapons both for practical use and for show. The magnificence of the objects that demonstrate the wealth of the *wànakes* ("lords") of Mycenae and the ostentation of the ceremony preceding the burial – a solemn procession accompanied the deceased to the last resting place and carried the precious objects that were to be buried with the dead – have induced archaeologists to wonder where the Mycenaeans obtained their gold, given the scarcity of deposits in Greek soil. The semitic origin of the Mycenaean word for the metal, "*ku-ru-so*", widely documented on pottery tablets in Linear B (the writing used by this people) and evidently similar to the more recent classical Greek word "*chrysòs*," have suggested to many that Egypt or the Near or Middle East may have been the source, given that there were important economic, trading, and cultural relationships between them created by the establishment of ports of call by the Mycenaeans along the coasts of southern Anatolia, Syria, and Palestine. Revelation of the interest of the Achaeans in the Dardanelles strait and the Black Sea also suggests there may have been a Pontic connection to the gold from the distant "hyperborean" regions, nor can the possibility be excluded that the metal may have come from the southern Iberian peninsula, where it seems relations between the Mycenaeans and the Tartessians were close.

## The treasures of the kings of Mycenae

In any case, Mycenaean jewelry was constantly affected by Cretan art stylistically, figuratively, and thematically, initially through the purchase of luxury products from Minos, and later more interactively following the conquest of the island (15th century BC). The formal indigenous art of Mycenae tended towards abstract and geometrical decorations, but this was enriched and stimulated by the figurative naturalism of the Minoans. The influence would have been felt through importation of Minoan products but also through the probable, though as yet unproved, presence of Cretan artists in Mycenaean cities. The 6 embossed and engraved gold-sheet masks were typically Mycenaean. The one imaginatively attributed by Schliemann to Agamemnon, king of Mycenae and commander of the Achaean expedition in the Trojan War narrated in the *Iliad*, has justly achieved renown. The name is utterly misleading as it was placed on the face of a dead *wànax* around the mid-16^th century BC, at least 300 years before the birth of the son of Atreus.

Paradoxically, the value of such magnificence

has not increased with being consigned to the darkness of a tomb; the significance of these objects does not seem to be limited to the simple wish to perpetuate the face of the deceased – only schematically delineated at that – in precious metal. The most original funerary constructions in the Mycenaean world made their first appearance in the first half of the 14th century BC. These were enormous corbel domed tombs (*thòlos*) built to house the bodies of members of the royal family. They were probably developed from a Cretan archetype that had evolved since the 16th century BC in Messenia. From there the design had arrived in Argolis just where the loveliest and most famous examples can be seen in Mycenae.

The most celebrated corbel domed tomb is undoubtedly the one known as the "Treasury of Atreus" dated to approximately 1250 BC. The characteristics developed over the centuries in this spectacular typology are represented definitively in this tomb. The large circular chamber with the false dome is entered from an uncovered *dròmos* measuring 36 x 6 meters (117' x 19'6") lined by sloping walls made with enormous parallelepiped blocks arranged in regular rows. Access is through an enormous doorway measuring 5 x 3 meters closed by a stone slab – discovered broken into pieces as the probable result of tomb robbers and of the absolute, derisive negligence that the Turkish authorities tolerated during their domination of Greece – decorated and framed by smooth, green marble columns marked with typically Mycenaean zigzag motifs. The relieving triangle above was filled by a screening stone decorated with geometrical and "architectural" motifs which, in turn, was framed by small green marble columns. The lintel is particularly impressive, weighing roughly 120 tons. The huge circular room rose more than 13.5 meters on a diameter of 14.5 meters. Concentric rows of stone blocks shaped and plastered to create a perfectly curved false dome rose layer upon layer, gently projecting until the capstone sealed the structure at the top. The small burial chamber was dug to

one side out of the rock bed, from which the earth-covered dome emerged above, sloping down onto the sides of the *dròmos*.

Closer to the west side of the walls of the acropolis, not far from the famous Lion Gate, lie the shaft-tombs of Circle B (1650-1550 BC), a small royal necropolis in which less impressive grave goods than those in Circle A have been found. The funerary structure built using the polygonal technique was 28 meters in diameter and contained 14 tombs similar in style to those within the walls, all marked by stele. In addition there were 12 interments which appear to have been reserved for individuals of a lower social rank. Tomb R was reused in the 15th century BC and was provided with an access corridor in a typology similar to Mycenaean cities on the coasts of Cyprus and Syria.

The tomb known as the "*Thòlos* of Aegisthus" is very old (ca. 1550 BC). Its corbel dome, now partially collapsed, was around 12 meters high and had a diameter of roughly 14 meters. The 22 meter access corridor was cut straight out of the rock, as was a part of the circular funerary chamber. The entrance was embellished at a date later than its first construction. Close by, more for reasons related to mythology than philology, lies the "*Thòlos* of Clytemnestra," which dates from about 1250 BC and is reached through a *dròmos* 37 meters long. It was plundered in ancient times and during the final phase of Ottoman domination of Greece. Its façade and relieving triangle were constructed with half-columns and slabs of decorated and painted plaster. The perfectly round funerary chamber is 13.50 meters across.

Other corbel domed tombs around Mycenae normally date from 1400-1250 BC. Interesting and easily entered is the so-called "*Thòlos* of the Lions" with dimensions equal to that of Aegisthus but with a collapsed dome. Visits to other corbel domed tombs on the west side of the hill in the royal necropolis are less easy.

The Mycenae of the living also offers an insight into the civilization that has taken its name from the city. Mycenaean society was based on a social pyramid with the *wànax* at its head and its backbone

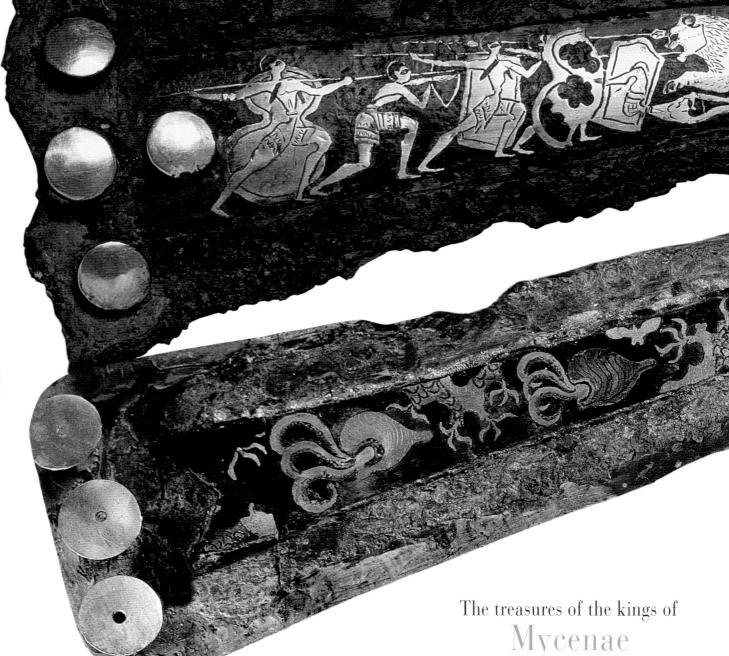

The treasures of the kings of
# Mycenae

represented by the warrior nobles, the owners of the land and its resources, who were proficient at promoting, developing, and coordinating the activities of a busy crafts and trading class that covered a wide range of economic pursuits.

The economic power of the Mycenaeans during the Bronze Age is confirmed by the many products of Mycenaean origin found in the lands encircling the Mediterranean from the Near East to the southern tip of the Iberian peninsula. In Italy they have been found from the lower reaches of the river Po and river Adige right down to Puglia and Sicily. Lovely pottery, finely worked metal articles, and high-quality cloth were diffused from various cities able to rely on a network of decentralized trading centers which were probably responsible for distribution of exports and organizing the importation of raw materials from various regions.

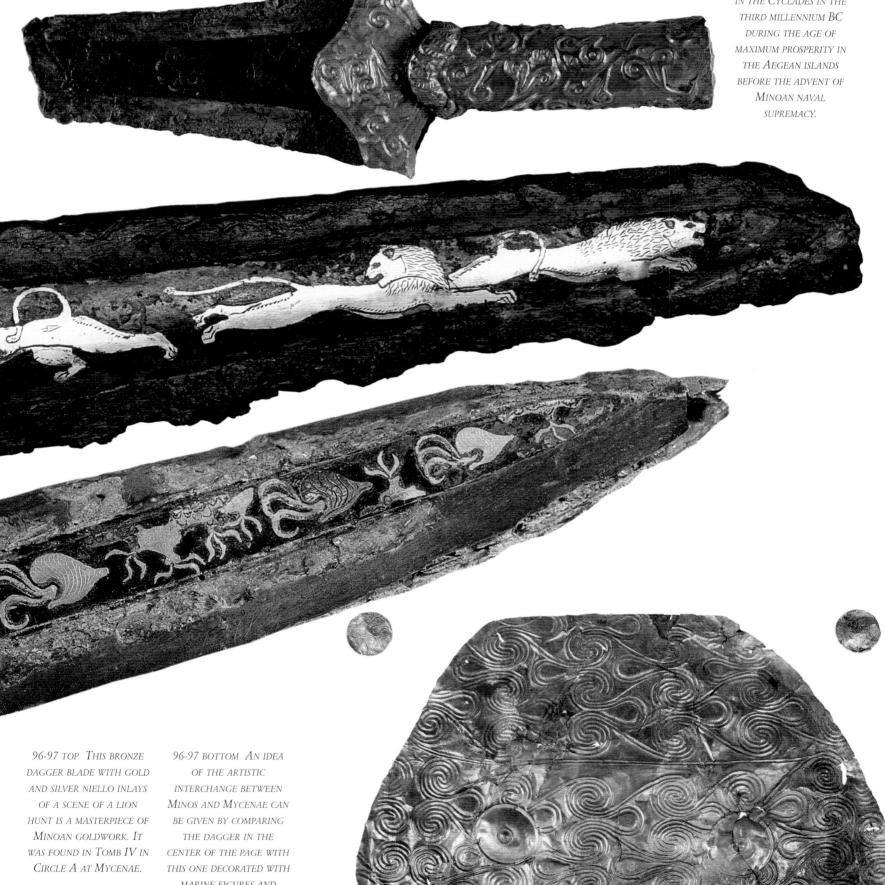

The route around the base of the massive defensive walls on the south side from the famous Lion Gate or, if you prefer to follow a more circuitous path, from the more modest North Gate, is truly stimulating.

The Lion Gate was built using the ancient three-stone technique that was especially widely used by the Mycenaean civilization; it had two vertical elements, the piers, and a massive lintel that was thickest in the middle. A typical contrivance of Mycenaean "Cyclopean" architecture was adopted above the lintel: this was the "relieving triangle." To prevent the lintel from being overloaded by the weight of the masonry above the aperture of the gateway, shaped blocks were laid on top of one another, progressively projecting so as to deflect the weight towards the ends of the lintel that rested directly above the piers. The triangular space so created was, as always, filled with decorative reliefs,

in this case with a screening slab much thinner than the rest of the wall.

The visual impact of the Lion Gate and its bastions is very strong: the relief above the colossal monolithic lintel displays clear stylistic references to Middle Eastern art and all the symbolic force of the art of this warlike monocracy. The screening stone is fairly typical of Mycenaean art with its figurative naturalism but it does not have the lively emphasis of color and gentleness of the chiaroscuro of Minoan art; consequently, it was a sparer, leaner art, as is corroborated in examples of their pictorial art.

Ramps lead to the top of the natural acropolis where the ruins of the royal palace lie. It was built between ca. 1350 and 1330 BC around a typically Mycenaean feature, the *mègaron*, and organized on several floors with propylaea, courtyards, and service and residential

areas spread over two stories accessible via stairways. This is all that remains of the palace that witnessed the events, sometimes glorious, sometimes tragic, in the history of the House of Atreus. One spot in particular makes a powerful impression, as the floor paintings on a red background in one of the bathrooms relate to the assassination of Agamemnon, the destroyer of Troy, by his wife Clytemnestra and her lover, Aegisthus, the story of which is recounted in the tragedy *Agamemnon* by Aeschylus. Here too, wide use must have been made of wood and plaster in addition to stone, the primary function of which was load-bearing.

There are several houses of interest in the acropolis of Mycenae that probably belonged to families of the warrior nobles who served the *wànax*. Inside the walls on the south side of the hill, the "House of Warriors," higher up the

The treasures of
the kings of
Mycenae

"House of Columns" and, outside the walls, the "House of the Oil Merchant" are examples of rich town residences built close to the palace.

A secret postern with a corbel dome stands in the northeastern section of the town; it is easily visible to the inhabitants but hardly noticeable to those who approach the city from outside. From an open space below the postern, it is still possible to walk down the first section of a covered stepped ramp to a depth of 18 meters where a combination well and water tank provided water to the inhabitants in times of siege.

Now it is time to return to the ramp that leads down from the Lion Gate and to take a last look at the valley below lined with citrus trees and vineyards at the foot of the ancient fortress of the House of Atreus, and to reflect: Mycenae has spoken to us from the silence.

# The tomb of Philip II of Macedonia at
# VERGINA

Vergina

From 1977 to 1980 Greek archaeologist Manòlis Andronìkos worked on excavations of the necropolis in Aigaì, the ancient capital of the kingdom of Macedonia, situated near the modern village of Vergina. It was here that members of the Macedonian royal family and nobility were buried after the capital was transferred to Pèlla at the end of the fifth – start of the sixth century BC. Andronìkos made a series of exceptional discoveries in the area of the "Great Tumulus," a modest earthen mound created artificially that bore a close

*100 BOTTOM LEFT THIS AXONOMETRIC RECONSTRUCTION OF THE TOMB OF PHILIP II AT VERGINA SHOWS THE LAYOUT OF THE STRUCTURE: TWO ROOMS WERE LAID END TO END COVERED BY THE CHARACTERISTIC VAULTED CEILING, AN INGENIOUS INVENTION BY MACEDONIAN ARCHITECTS.*

*100 BOTTOM RIGHT THE HANDSOME AND ELEGANT FAÇADE OF THE TOMB OF PHILIP II, ADORNED WITH THE FAMOUS PAINTED FRIEZE DEPICTING A WINTER HUNT, IS WORTHY OF A ROYAL "DWELLING OF ETERNITY."*

*100-101 THIS SPLENDID GOLDEN CROWN DECORATED WITH MYRTLE LEAVES AND NO LESS THAN 112 GOLDEN FLOWERS, IS A WONDROUS MASTERPIECE OF MACEDONIAN JEWELRY. IT WAS FOUND IN THE VESTIBULE OF THE ROYAL TOMB AND BELONGED TO CLEOPATRA, THE SECOND WIFE OF PHILIP II*

VERGINA

*Greece*

*101 TOP NOT FAR FROM THE ROYAL TUMULUS IS ANOTHER ROYAL TOMB, THAT OF RHOMAIOS, WHICH DATES BACK TO 250 BC.*

*101 BOTTOM THE PERFORATED SIDES OF THIS BRONZE LAMP HOLDER, FOUND IN THE BURIAL CHAMBER, ALLOWED THE DIFFUSION OF THE LIGHT OF THE LAMP PLACED ON ITS FLOOR.*

*102-103 THE PALACE OF PHILIP II, BUILT IN THE MID-4TH CENTURY BC, OCCUPIED A HUGE AREA ARRANGED AROUND A PERISTYLE.*

a politically dominant aristrocratic family who was worshipped as a hero. It seemed that this tomb had been broken into and robbed of its valuable grave goods by Galatian mercenaries in the pay of Pyrrhus, the king of Epirus, around 280 BC. Although it only measured 2.90 x 4.30 x 3 meters, it was immediately recognized as being the tomb of a high-ranking person who was buried here during the first half of the fourth century BC. Splendid frescoes covered 3 of the inner walls of the chamber: the north wall bears one of the oldest and most important examples of Greek wall painting, *The Abduction of Persephone*, attributed by Andronìkos to the famous painter Nikòmachos. The archaeologist also presumed that this was the tomb of king Amyntas III, the father of Philip II.

The most important discovery, however, was Tomb II: Philip's tomb is in fact one of the largest monumental Macedonian-style tombs, measuring 9.10 x 5.60 x 5.30 meters. The walls were made using large blocks of *pòros* carefully plastered. The layout was based on two chambers placed end to end, with a monumental architectural façade that created the illusion of a blind portico. The entrance was flanked by elegant Doric columns framing double doors made from marble and decorated with bronze studs. A colored architrave rested on the columns with a painted relief frieze of a hunting scene depicting men on foot and horseback and wild animals in a forest in winter. The two chambers were covered by a single barrel vault, which was an important structural innovation introduced by Macedonian architects in the fourth century BC. Studies carried out by Andronìkos have shown that this is the first example of a barrel vault in a Greek tomb; it can be dated to much earlier than the end of the fourth century BC, the date normally put forward by scholars to justify the theory that this typology of tomb had been introduced to the west from the Near East following Alexander the Great's expedition. But this theory suggests that the Greeks had not had the opportunity in their history to absorb Oriental architectural models before the formation of the Macedonian empire or, more probably, that they were unable to create the structures of the arch and the barrel vault with the funerary pictorial decoration.

visual relationship with the nearby remains of the royal palace: four royal tombs in "Macedonian" style, i.e., with an underground chamber with a monumental architectural façade and a barrel vault, were discovered and brought to light. One of these, Tomb II (which, like Tomb III, had miraculously remained intact), was later identified with certainty as being the burial place of Philip II of Macedonia, the man who ended the independence of the Greek city-states and was father to the famous Alexander the Great. Tomb I, known as "Persephone's Tomb," was built in the "chamber tomb" style which was a direct development of the "cist tomb," i.e., without a monumental architectural façade or barrel vault; it lay near a structure identified as a *heròon* and was therefore linked to the cult of the forefather of

The Grave Goods of
Philip II

104 TOP  THIS OTHER
GOLD CROWN OF
UNEQUALED BEAUTY IS
BASED ON A DESIGN OF OAK
LEAVES AND ACORNS. IT WAS
WORN BY PHILIP II.

104 BOTTOM  THE
MAGNIFICENT IRON ARMOR
BELONGING TO PHILIP II
WAS UNDOUBTEDLY WORN
ON STATE OCCASIONS. IT IS
DECORATED WITH GOLD
LION-HEAD STUDS.

104-105  THE SPLENDID
GOLD LINING OF PHILIP II'S
QUIVER FOR DRESS
OCCASIONS STILL DISPLAYS
THE EMBOSSED
DECORATION OF SCENES OF
THE CONQUEST OF TROY.

105 TOP RIGHT  THIS TINY
IVORY HEAD OF PHILIP II
MEASURES ONLY 3 CM. IT IS
A REPLICA OF A FAMOUS
BRONZE STATUE OF THE
KING MADE BY LEOCHÀRES
FOR THE PHILIPPEUM IN
OLYMPIA.

The hypothesis continues that, having enlarged the size of cist-tombs to create monumental forms during the middle of the fourth century BC, Macedonian architects made use of barrel vaults to deal with the static problems created by such large structures, which they decorated with sculpted and painted façades.

Tomb II at Vergina contained a rich set of grave goods. Right from his first analysis of the objects, Andronìkos believed he had discovered the tomb of Philip II, who was assassinated in the Aigaì theatre in 335 BC. The abundance of gold, silver, and bronze articles was truly worthy of a king: they could all be dated to between 350-330 BC and included a quiver made from gilded silver, gold crowns (one based on a design of oak leaves), diadems made from solid silver then gilded, small plates, a breastplate, gold studs depicting the "starred" sun of Macedonia, the remains of a leather and fabric cuirass trimmed with gold-lined squares and strips, and a decorative shield comparable to the one borne by Achilles for the variety of scenes and themes with which it was embellished. An important indicator was given when five miniature ivory heads were found that probably decorated a bed; they portrayed members of the royal family from the age of Philip

II and Alexander the Great. The five heads were recognized as bearing a direct iconographic relation to the portraits of the Argead dynasty produced by the sculptor Leochàres for the Philippeum in Olympia, the ex-voto temple built by Philip in the great pan-Hellenic sanctuary after his victory at Chaeronea against the Greeks (338 BC). If all this were not enough, the tomb also contained two glittering box-shaped urns/ossuaries decorated with embossed gold and settings. The urns were placed inside simple stone boxes, one in the funeral chamber, the other in the vestibule. Bearing in mind the dates provided by historical sources, Andronìkos conjectured that the cremated remains in the urns (belonging to a man and a woman wrapped in a royal garment of purple and blue embroidered with gold, of which fragments remain) were of Philip II and his second wife, Cleopatra. The hypothesis aroused enormous interest in the scientific world but also some uncertainties: some experts agreed that such magnificent grave goods might belong to members of the Macedonian royal family but believed it was more probable that the two bodies had belonged to Philip III Arrhidaeus, who succeeded his half-brother Alexander the Great to the throne in 323 BC, and his wife Eurydice;

they were both assassinated by Olympias, Alexander's mother, and buried with royal honors by the powerful Cassander, who took the crown in 317 BC. A series of paleo-anthropological and paleo-pathological analyses was then performed on the male skeleton by a group of English specialists. The results were of exceptional importance in resolving the question. Historical sources from the age of Philip II state that the king had lost his right eye and his face had been disfigured by an arrow fired at him during the siege of Methòne in Chalcidice (354 BC). Prag, Musgrave, and Neave

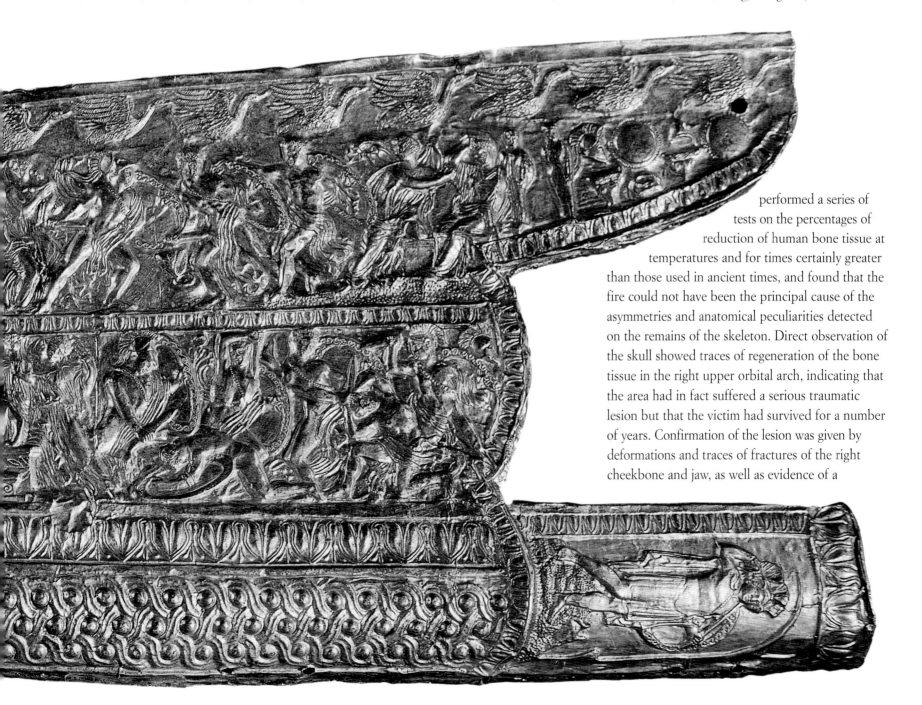

performed a series of tests on the percentages of reduction of human bone tissue at temperatures and for times certainly greater than those used in ancient times, and found that the fire could not have been the principal cause of the asymmetries and anatomical peculiarities detected on the remains of the skeleton. Direct observation of the skull showed traces of regeneration of the bone tissue in the right upper orbital arch, indicating that the area had in fact suffered a serious traumatic lesion but that the victim had survived for a number of years. Confirmation of the lesion was given by deformations and traces of fractures of the right cheekbone and jaw, as well as evidence of a spontaneous adjustment of the jaw to allow food to be chewed. At this point, refusing to look at ancient portraits of Philip II so as to remain uninfluenced during their studies, Prag and his colleagues began to work with fragments of the skull to make a plaster reconstruction. To no little surprise, the skull of the deceased appeared disfigured and partially deformed by a devastating wound to the right eye and surrounding area caused by violent penetration of a blunt object. Careful reconstruction of the face based on the mould of the skull reproduced the most probable appearance of the man during the last years of his life: as a photograph published in the *Journal of Hellenic Studies* in 1984 shows, a hideous scar must have run right across the lost eye and covered much of the orbital area and cheekbone. Following assessment of the profile of the nose and the addition of hair and a beard in the style of Macedonian kings before the beardless Alexander the Great, a portrait was produced that bears an extraordinary similarity to all the images of Philip II that still exist on statues, coins and medallions. The skeleton of Vergina, then, really is of Philip II of Macedonia, since it testfies to the serious injury he suffered in 354 BC that caused the loss of his right eye and the disfigurement of the

surrounding face. And, therefore, it was the bones of Philip II that were placed in the splendid gold-sheet parallelepiped *làrnax*. The symbol of the kingdom of Macedonia, the star with 16 rays, was embossed on the cover of the urn, while the sides were decorated with rows of rosettes created with particles of gold and blue glass paste and framed by friezes showing lotus buds, acanthus volutes, and palmettes. Smaller rosettes adorned the supports created in the shape of lion's paws.

Tomb III at Vergina, known as the "Prince's tomb," had a simpler façade but contained a rich set of royal grave goods in which a silver *hydria* held the remains of an adolescent male of about 14 years of age wrapped in a purple sheet. A gold crown on the neck of the vase indicated that the boy had to have been a king. Once again basing his deductions on the chronology of the grave goods and the age of the deceased, Andronìkos suggested that the body belonged to Alexander IV, the son of Alexander the Great and Roxana, who was assassinated with his mother in 310 BC by Cassander. The mystery remains, however, of identification of the body buried in Tomb IV, also characterized by a Doric entrance.

The Grave Goods of Philip II

# Pyramids, buried treasure and rock tombs

NEMRUD DAGH

PALMYRA

UR

GIZA

PETRA

BAHARIYA

VALLEY OF THE KINGS
DEIR EL-MEDINA
SHEIKH ABD EL-QURNA

AFRICA

# AFRICA AND THE NEAR AND MIDDLE EAST

It was during the third dynasty in ancient Egypt, during first half of the third millennium BC, that the first real monumental tombs in the history of man were seen.

Although royal tombs were closely linked to a statement of earthly power in the proto-dynastic era, it was during the third dynasty that "dwellings of eternity" also developed into a symbol of the divinity of the pharaoh and of his heavenly power that went beyond death and which could benefit the entire country. To express these new ideas, Imhotep, chief minister and architect to the pharaoh Neterikhet Djoser, designed the first stepped pyramid at Saqqarah which symbolised either a stairway to heaven from earth, or thrown down from heaven to earth, for the pharaoh to ascend. This idea was expressed several times in the formulas and invocations carved in the stone of the pyramids from the fifth dynasty onwards that were to evolve into the *Texts of the Sarcophaguses* and the *Book of the Dead*.

Djoser's successors also adopted the concept of the tomb-pyramid which, in the reign of Snefru, the first pharaoh of the fourth dynasty, assumed its definitive form as an expression of the increasing importance of the solar cult in association with the cult of the pharaoh.

The evolution of religious thought meant that a stairway to heaven was no longer necessary and the smooth sides of the pyramid – a stone rendition of the rays of the sun – equally permitted the soul of the pharaoh to ascend to heaven. From the age of Snefru, the pyramid itself was associated with other structures like the

*108-109 This drawing by David Roberts shows the pyramids at Giza. Built towards the middle of the 3rd millennium BC, they were the first true dwellings of eternity with monumental architecture and the only one of the Seven Wonders of the ancient world to have survived to the modern day.*

temple in the valley and the processional ramp that were to be given their definitive form in the pyramid of Cheops, the largest dwelling of eternity in the ancient world.

At around the same time, towards the middle of the third millennium BC, the Sumerians created the first city-state in the region between the Tigris and the Euphrates, called Mesopotamia by the Greeks, where the kings were buried in tombs together with magnificent grave goods. Of the 1,840 tombs found in the necropolis of Ur, 16 belonged to members of royalty and were of particular importance. The underground tombs were of simple design with undecorated burial chambers and vaulted ceilings reached via a ramp. Some of these tombs, for instance the one belonging to Queen Pu-abi discovered in 1938, had never been broken into.

During excavation, the bodies of dozens of courtiers, soldiers and women were found on the tombs' access ramps, each of which held a cup in their hands that in all probability had once contained a deadly poison. We do not know if these were sacrificial victims or voluntary suicides (the latter hypothesis is more likely) but it is certain that, having shared their ruler's fate, these individuals were expected to serve him in the afterlife. This practice was seen at Ur for the first time, no trace of it ever having been discovered in Egypt.

The royal tombs of Ur contained gold and silver musical instruments, statuettes of animals made from gold and lapis lazuli, weapons, gold helmets like the one belonging to Prince Meskalamdug decorated with very fine embossing, and jewellery set with semi-precious stones like agate, carnelian and lapis lazuli. These objects demonstrate the high level of refinement achieved by Sumerian goldsmiths, their mastery of the "lost wax" method, and knowledge of granulation and filigree techniques that were used at Ur for the first time. The extensive use of gold and silver (metals that probably came from Persia or Arabia) and stones like lapis lazuli (that originated in the highlands of Afghanistan) are evidence that as early as the third millennium BC, an extensive trading network already existed.

The royal tombs at Ur contained the largest and most precious sets of grave goods so far discovered from the third millennium BC and it is highly probable that they would have rivalled those of the Egyptian pharaohs during the age of the pyramids.

As far as we are aware, throughout the entire area of the Near and Middle East, only the tombs of the Theban rulers of the New Kingdom (1550-1076 BC) boasted grave goods comparable to those of the kings of Ur from a thousand years earlier. Having abandoned the concept of the royal tomb, the Egyptian rulers of the New Kingdom built enormous tombs dug out of the rock, decorated with texts of magical and religious symbolism. Knowledge of these texts was supposed to allow the dead pharaoh to overcome the thousand obstacles that would beset him on his journey beyond the grave that would culminate in his being reunited with Ra, the Sun god, whom was believed to be his father. All these splendid underground tombs, broken into and plundered since ancient times, contained fabulously rich sets of grave goods as was shown by the discovery of the tomb of Tutankhamon, the only sepulchre from ancient Egypt to have survived until modern times intact.

A large and rich tomb was not just the privilege of members of royalty but also of important dignitaries and even simple artists or craftsmen. These too were buried in tombs with magnificent wall paintings though based on different pictorial themes, for instance, scenes from everyday life rather than those linked to the mysterious journey to the Underworld. One of the most beautiful is the tomb of Sennefer, the "Mayor of Thebes", who lived during the 18th dynasty in the second half of the 16th century BC. The paintings on the walls of this tomb demonstrate the highest levels of Egyptian art. But what differs the ancient Egyptian civilisations from all the others that arose around the Mediterranean and in the Near East was the preservation of the mortal remains of the dead. This custom resulted in the development of embalming techniques from rather rudimentary practices during the fourth dynasty to an elaborate procedure that reached its peak during the New Kingdom.

Referred to in detail by Herodotus, the funerary ritual of embalming continued to be practised in simpler forms even up to the Greco-Roman period. Evidence of this is given by the immense necropolis discovered in 1997 in the Bahariya oasis situated in the Libyan Desert in Egypt. Excavation of this site began in 1999 and is bringing to light large hypogean tombs, though devoid of architectural structures, containing dozens of perfectly preserved mummies.

The contrary is true at Petra in the Jordanian desert where the Nabateans settled around the first century BC. These were originally a nomadic people that controlled the routes across the Arabian Desert and consequently the entire trading network of the Near East. They settled in a hidden valley surrounded by mountains where they built Petra, a monarchical state. Here they dug dozens of superb tombs out of the rock, all embellished with monumental façades sculpted from the multi-colored sandstone that is the primary geological feature of the site. Being so easily prey to tomb robbers, the tombs have survived but without the bodies of the dead or their grave goods.

The only large Near Eastern tomb that has remained secret until the present day, despite being easily located, was that of Antiochus I, king of Commagene, a region of strategic importance between the Taurus mountains and the Euphrates in what is today Turkey. Here, on the peak of a mountain over 2000 meters high called Nemrud Dagh, Antiochus built an enormous tumulus-tomb decorated outside with two large altars still in excellent condition. Protected by thousands of cubic meters of stones, his burial chamber has remained inviolate despite all the efforts made over recent decades not only by tomb robbers, but also archaeologists.

110 *THE EXPRESSION ON THE FACE OF THE YOUNG PHARAOH TUTANKHAMON IS SERENE. THE IMAGE WAS REPRODUCED ON THE THIRD SARCOPHAGUS MADE FROM SOLID GOLD. HE WEARS A NEMES HEAD-DRESS AND A CEREMONIAL BEARD.*

112-113 *THE DECEASED NEFERTITI, THE GREAT ROYAL BRIDE OF RAMSES II (12TH CENTURY BC), IS WELCOMED AND REASSURED IN THE AFTERLIFE BY THE GODDESS HATHOR.*

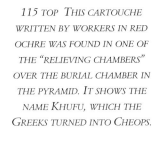

GIZA
*Egypt*

# The Pyramid of
# CHEOPS

Cheops

Cheops

It was in Egypt during the first half of the third millennium BC that the earliest examples of monumental funerary architecture appeared, representing the first true dwellings of eternity in history: the pyramids.

The word "pyramid" is derived from the Greek word *pyramis* which, in turn, seems to come from the word *pyramos*, meaning pointed loaves of bread; the ancient Egyptians, on the other hand, referred to these monuments as *mer*, expressed by a hieroglyphic illustrating their shape and which meant "place of [heavenly] ascension."

The biblical story of Joseph in Egypt suggested to European travelers, merchants, and Crusaders who visited the pyramids during the Middle Ages that these strange monuments were the granaries Joseph had built for the pharaoh to stave off famine. Not until the start of the 17th century did the idea that the pyramids had been built as tombs – as stated by classical authors – begin to make headway.

The pyramids at Giza were preceded chronologically by the large, mud-brick tombs of first dynasty rulers erected at Abydos, whose shape and decoration were strictly related to the center of royal power on earth, i.e., the pharaoh's palace. Pyramids are the symbolic expression of the divine character of the king and of his link with the sun god, whose son he became on death. As a mediator between the heavens and the earth, the pharaoh was able to extend the benefits he derived from his divine birth to the people and to the country that he governed, so ensuring them well-being and prosperity.

Pyramids developed out of *mastaba*, an Arabic word that means "bench," used by Egyptian workers to mean the raised, table-shaped structures that covered a deep well destined to contain the royal sarcophagus; the *mastaba* represented one of the first expressions of funerary architecture during the early dynastic period.

During the reign of Neterikhet Djoser at the start of the third dynasty (2630-2611 BC), the

115 TOP THIS CARTOUCHE WRITTEN BY WORKERS IN RED OCHRE WAS FOUND IN ONE OF THE "RELIEVING CHAMBERS" OVER THE BURIAL CHAMBER IN THE PYRAMID. IT SHOWS THE NAME KHUFU, WHICH THE GREEKS TURNED INTO CHEOPS.

114 CHEOPS, THE SON OF SNEFRU AND SECOND RULER OF THE 4TH DYNASTY, WAS THE BUILDER OF THE LARGEST PYRAMID IN EGYPT, BUT WE ONLY KNOW WHAT HE LOOKS LIKE FROM THIS IVORY STATUETTE FOUND AT ABYDOS. IT IS A LITTLE OVER 7 CM TALL AND KEPT IN THE CAIRO MUSEUM.

114-115 THE PYRAMIDS AT GIZA WERE BUILT BETWEEN 2560-2460 BC AND ARE THE ONLY ONE OF THE SEVEN WONDERS OF THE ANCIENT WORLD STILL IN EXISTENCE.

royal architect Imhotep (later deified and assimilated by the Greeks with the god of medicine, Asclepius) designed the first pyramid on the plateau at Saqqarah. Designed as a series of raised sections over a *mastaba*, this construction was "stepped" so that the soul of the pharaoh could ascend to heaven.

In this way, the pyramid expressed the newly stated concept of royalty as the point of contact between the heavens and earth, between man and god. Imhotep's creation met with great success; Djoser's successors adopted the form of the pyramid to be their eternal abodes, but with a series of architectural and structural alterations

that led to the construction of the first true pyramid in the fourth dynasty during the reign of Snefru in the necropolis of Dahshur some kilometers to the south of Saqqarah. Development of the stepped structure to the true pyramid reflected an analogous evolution in religious thought whereby the straight sides that diverge from a point down to the ground represented the materialization in stone of the sun's rays that allowed the soul of the pharaoh to ascend to heaven. The geometrical form of the pyramid reflected the point of union of the three axes of the world: the vertical one that united the earth with the heavens, i.e., with the

solar body personified by the god Ra; the terrestrial axis that ran north-south parallel to the Nile and which was connected with the royal function; and the celestial axis that joined east to west and symbolized the daily course of the sun on earth that was regenerated each day.

Both the terrestrial and the celestial axes are represented by precise structures in a pyramid: the first is identified in the corridor that descends from the entrance to the burial chamber and, ideally, to the outside at a point sometimes marked by a small structure (known as a satellite pyramid) that also served as a royal cenotaph, in that the pharaoh was also king of the south of Egypt.

construction caused such amazement in ancient history that it was included in the Seven Wonders of the World compiled in the second century BC by Philon of Byzantium.

Flanked to the east and west by two large groups of tombs of dignitaries who had been given the privilege of being buried near their pharaoh and, therefore, of sharing his divine nature, the immense pyramid of Khufu (referred to by the Greeks as Cheops) deeply struck the imagination of all travelers of antiquity, starting with Herodotus who traveled through Egypt in the sixth century BC and who dedicated space to the pyramids of Giza in the second book of his *History*, with particular emphasis on that of Cheops.

It is to Herodotus' account that we owe the idea – as false as it is well-established – that the pyramids were built by slaves whose lives were risked to satisfy the ambition of a despotic pharaoh.

Originally 146.6 meters high, the pyramid was built using just under 2.5 million blocks of limestone weighing on average 2.5 tons each, and the surface area it covers is almost 6 hectares.

As none of the many bas-reliefs which decorate the tombs of the Old Kingdom and which illustrate the main activities of the period make even the smallest reference to the construction of a pyramid, and as we also lack information from epigraphic sources, we cannot know with certainty the technique the Egyptians used to build these structures. The only account we have is the one handed down to us by Herodotus, in which true information is often mixed with elements of fantasy: "Cheops ordered all Egyptians to work for him. Some, accordingly, were appointed to drag blocks of stone from the quarries in the Arabian mountains down to the Nile, others he ordered to receive the stones when transported in vessels across the river and haul them to the Libyan mountains. And they worked to the number of a hundred thousand men at a time, each shift for three months. The time during

The second axis was linked to the concept of resurrection and was symbolized by the processional ramp that connected the temple in the valley to the mortuary temple, one of the principal structures linked with the pyramid. The axis evoked the passage of the body of the pharaoh from the world of the living, represented by the east, to the afterlife, represented by the west.

Usually, the mortuary temple was located to the east of the pyramid: it was here that the dead and deified pharaoh was worshipped by the living because he reflected cosmic order and therefore guaranteed order on earth.

The temple in the valley was built on the edge of a (probably rectangular) pool that was connected directly with the Nile and was used to hold the body of the pharaoh at the start of the funeral ceremony.

The lack of inscriptions prevents us from knowing the actual funerary ritual used during the epoch of the pyramids; however, we do know that there was already a form, if only a simple one, of mummification. This ceremony probably took place in temporary structures called *uabet* (purification tent) or *per nefer* (place of regeneration) near the valley temple where the body of the ruler was washed and mummified.

The largest of the necropolises belonging to nearby Memphis, the capital of the Old Kingdom of Egypt, stood on the plateau at Giza, and it was here that the art and science of the construction of the pyramids reached its apex with the pyramid of Cheops, the third sovereign of the fourth dynasty. This

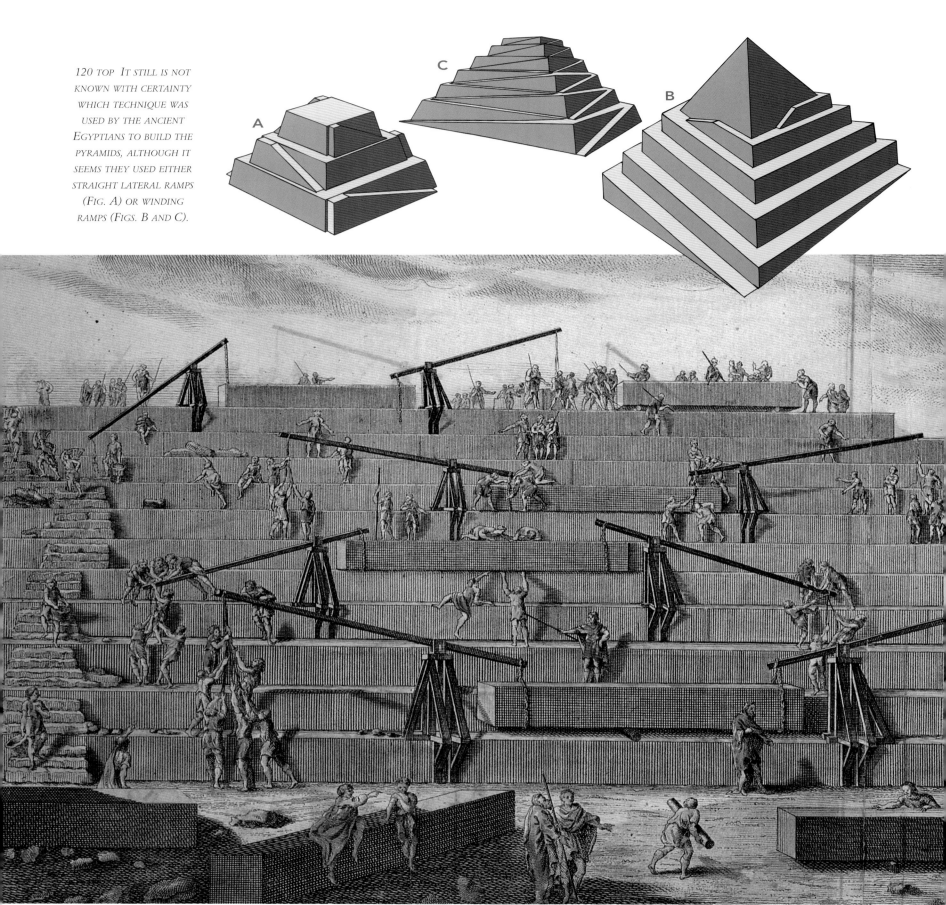

120 TOP IT STILL IS NOT KNOWN WITH CERTAINTY WHICH TECHNIQUE WAS USED BY THE ANCIENT EGYPTIANS TO BUILD THE PYRAMIDS, ALTHOUGH IT SEEMS THEY USED EITHER STRAIGHT LATERAL RAMPS (FIG. A) OR WINDING RAMPS (FIGS. B AND C).

which the people were thus oppressed by toil lasted ten years on the road which they constructed, and along which they hauled the blocks; a work, in my opinion, not much less than the Pyramids … It took ten years to build this road and the underground rooms on the rise where the pyramids stand, rooms that Cheops had built as his tomb on an island which was created by digging a channel for the Nile. To build the pyramid, it took 20 years: it is square, each side measures 800 feet and it is of almost equal height, and it is made with polished stones perfectly fitted; no stone measures less than 30 feet. This pyramid was built in steps, some of which were called *krossai* and others *bomides*. After building the first layer so, they raised the

remaining stones using machines made of short timbers, raising them from the ground onto the first set of steps. When the stone had been raised onto the first set of steps, it was placed on another, similar machine positioned there and dragged onto the second set and so on. There were as many machines as there were tiers of steps, or they moved the machines, which were easy to carry, onto the next tier each time they moved the stone" (Herodotus, Book II).

We know that Cheops reigned for 23 years and that his first act as pharaoh was to begin the construction of his tomb, so therefore work on the pyramid could not have lasted more than twenty years or so – a fact that agrees with Herodotus' account – but it is difficult to

believe that 100,000 men were used if only because of the logistical problems resulting from managing so many people. Recent calculations, though difficult to quantify exactly, suggest that the labor force required would have ranged between 6,000 and 17,000 men.

The workforce that built the pyramid probably consisted of professionals with various levels of specialization who were supported by a multitude of simple laborers enlisted from the farmers during the annual Nile flood (June-September), when all work in the fields was suspended. It is probable that this employment was a duty impossible to escape but, in any case, the work would have been paid for with food. The engineers and the laborers lived in camps

close to the work place referred to as "Pyramid City," the necropolis of which has recently been discovered just a few hundred meters from the pyramid of Cheops.

Herodotus' account does not explain well how the gigantic blocks of limestone were raised and positioned. Various theories suggest the use of large ramps made from mud bricks reinforced with the trunks of palm trees. There are two main hypotheses about the form of these ramps: one suggests there was a straight perpendicular ramp to one side of the pyramid, the other, spiral ramps around the construction.

Both theories have obvious weak points: the theory of the straight ramp does not take into account that, calculating the gigantic size required, the work necessary to build it beforehand and

then demolish it after would have been more than that needed for construction of the pyramid itself. The theory of the spiral ramp does not account for the extreme difficulty the workers would have had in moving the blocks of stone round right-angle corners. Wall-paintings in private tombs have told us, however, that the blocks of stone were dragged after being raised onto wooden sleds whose runners were lubricated with water or oil to diminish the friction. Herodotus tells us in very general terms that "machines made of short timbers" were used and, to indicate the blocks of stone, he uses the words "*krossai*" and "*bomides*," which are usually not translated. It is possible that the two types of blocks were named for their position and that the pyramids were built from a central nucleus outwards.

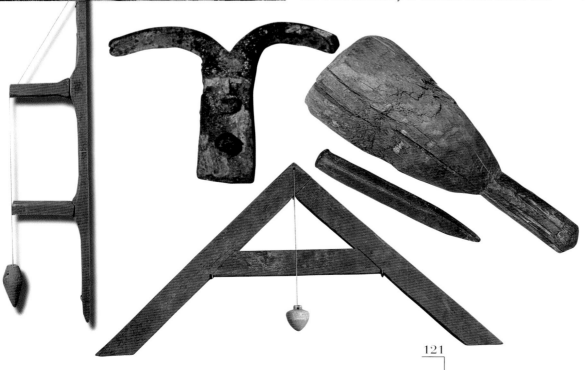

The precision of the astronomical orientation of the pyramids suggests that the technical and scientific knowledge of the Egyptians during the mid-third millennium BC was already very advanced: for example, the deviation of the pyramid of Cheops from north is just 3'6" compared to the best measurement available to us today, and the maximum disparity in length of the sides is less than 5 cm. The architects of the period used simple but extremely effective instruments like the square, the plumb line and the *merket*, made from a wooden stick topped by a fork that, in combination with the plumb line, could sight distant objects and determine their height and inclination precisely. It is known for certain that all geometrical calculations were based on a unit of measure called the "royal cubit" (equal to 52.4 cm) which was divided into 7 hands, and that each hand (7.5 cm) was subdivided into 4 fingers (1.87 cm); the finger was the smallest unit.

The Egyptians' extensive knowledge of geometry and mathematical sciences is proven by

which already stated the fundamental measurements of the structure: its height, the length of each side, the inclination of the faces, its topographical position and orientation – all decisions that would have taken into account factors such as alignment with places of worship, existing pyramids, and heavenly bodies or constellations.

The land chosen for the construction, on which the positions of the corners of the future pyramid were marked with extreme precision, was carefully leveled and marked with wooden stakes. Next, the important foundation ceremony took place, during which the pharaoh held a cord that connected the stakes and, after ritual purification of the site, placed some amulets in a small trench as the "foundation deposit." Construction proper began only then, with teams of workers carrying out different specific and precise tasks. First, a pool connected to the Nile was dug out to allow the boats used to transport the materials to tie up; then a sloping surface was created that would

the *Rhind papyrus* which has been dated to the Second Middle Period but is probably a copy of an older document; the papyrus shows many problems of applied geometry relating to pyramids.

The many tools found, such as wooden clubs, copper or bronze chisels, and picks leave no doubt about the instruments used by the builders of the pyramids who, curiously, although knowing of the wheel, made almost no use of it.

Construction began after the king's approval of the design submitted to him by his architects,

become the ramp along which the great blocks of stone for the base of the pyramid would be dragged. At the same time, teams in the quarries at the nearest possible site to Giza were preparing coarse blocks of limestone that would form the center of the pyramid. Other teams were working on the opposite bank of the Nile in the large quarries of Tura – the "Arabian mountains" as described by Herodotus – where light-colored limestone cut into slabs would be used for the final lining of the pyramid. Next began the work of positioning the corner stones,

the raising of the first perimeter layers, and construction of the mortuary apartments inside the pyramid, later to be lined with other stones. The structure of these internal chambers differs between pyramids although they share nearly the same layout of basic elements: the entrance, the descending corridor and the chamber for the sarcophagus.

When the pyramid was finished, a cusp called a *pyramidion* was placed on its tip. The pyramidion was coated with electron, a special alloy of gold and silver, which was designed to

124-125 *The Giza pyramids were built on the left bank of the Nile about 10 kilometers from modern Cairo's city center on a limestone plateau now surrounded by modern buildings.*

125 top *The "Rhind Papyrus" contains a series of geometric problems and demonstrates the high level of scientific knowledge of the ancient Egyptians.*

125 bottom left *To build the pyramid of Cheops, 2.3 million blocks of stone were used, having an average measurement of a cubic meter. The pyramid was originally covered with a casing of light-colored limestone, but this has since been removed.*

125 bottom right *The fine sculpted limestone pyramidion that once crowned the Pyramid of Cheops is displayed at the foot of the monument.*

126-127 *The Pyramid of Chefren (2520-2494 BC) is the only one of the three main monuments at Giza to have preserved part of its limestone facing.*

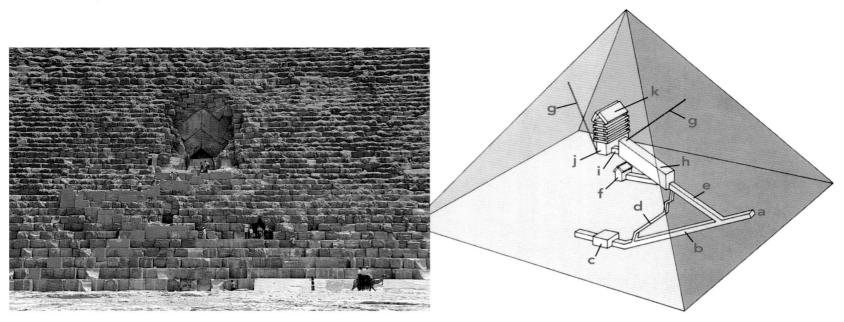

128 TOP THE CURRENT ENTRANCE TO CHEOPS' PYRAMID IS SITUATED ABOUT TEN METERS LOWER THAN THE ORIGINAL ENTRANCE. IT WAS PROBABLY OPENED BY CALIPH AL-MAMUN IN 820 BC, WHO ENTERED THE PYRAMID AND, ACCORDING TO THE HISTORIAN AL-MASSUDI, FOUND SEVERAL PRECIOUS OBJECTS THERE.

128-129 THE PYRAMID OF CHEOPS, ALSO KNOWN AS THE GREAT PYRAMID, WAS CALLED "AKHET KHUFU" IN ANCIENT TIMES, MEANING "THE HORIZON OF CHEOPS." EACH SIDE MEASURED 230.37 METERS AND THE TIP WAS 146.6 METERS HIGH.

129 LEFT THE BURIAL CHAMBER IS MADE FROM ENORMOUS RED GRANITE BLOCKS FROM ASWAN AND CONTAINS AN UNDECORATED SARCOPHAGUS MADE FROM THE SAME MATERIAL. THE SIZE OF THE SARCOPHAGUS IS LARGER THAN THE ENTRANCE DOOR.

## LEGEND

a ENTRANCE
b DESCENDING CORRIDOR
c UNDERGROUND CHAMBER
d SERVICE CORRIDOR
e ASCENDING CORRIDOR
f QUEEN'S CHAMBER
g VENTILATION SHAFTS
h GREAT GALLERY
i ANTE-CHAMBER
j KING'S CHAMBER
k RELIEVING CHAMBERS

## LEGEND

A KING'S CHAMBER
B ANTE-CHAMBER
C CORRIDOR BLOCKS
(GRANITE SHUTTERS)
D RELIEVING
CHAMBERS

reflect the sun's rays into the desert and Nile valley below. Each pyramid was given a name that evoked the glorious destiny of the king and the pyramid's function as the seat of the mysterious transformation that concluded with the divine rebirth of the ruler.

The pyramid of Cheops was named the "horizon of Cheops" and is distinguished not just for its extraordinary size but also for the complexity of its internal structures. These have

*129 TOP RIGHT THE BLOCKS OF THE GREAT GALLERY PROJECT BY 2.3 INCHES ON EACH LEVEL.*

*130-131 THE RECTANGULAR PITS AT THE FOOT OF THE PYRAMID OF CHEOPS CONTAINED THE PHARAOH'S SACRED SHIPS, WHICH HAVE NOW BEEN RESTORED.*

given rise to many interpretations and attracted so much attention from pyramidologists that the neighbouring pyramids of Chefren and Mycerinus have been almost ignored.

The original entrance to the pyramid is located at a height of about 15 meters on the north side. It opens into a descending corridor that, after a passage of about 18 meters, forks on the one hand into an ascending corridor that leads into the Great Gallery and then heads towards the burial chamber, or King's Chamber, and, on the other hand, into a second descending corridor that leads to an underground rock chamber in the heart of the pyramid whose function is not yet perfectly understood but which seems to evoke the

dwelling of Sokar, the god of the Hereafter.

The pyramid also contains a third burial chamber, or Queen's Chamber, positioned in alignment with the vertical axis of the pyramid and reached via a horizontal corridor that begins at the entrance to the Great Gallery. Very probably this room was built to hold a large statue portraying the royal *ka*, or immaterial element that incarnated the character of the dead pharaoh in a kind of "double."

One theory holds that the construction of three chambers above one another corresponds to three alterations in the design during construction, but recent research prefers the theory that these structures were part of the initial design and were built to fulfil ritual requirements. Every constructional detail in the pyramid of Cheops seems to meet precise needs and at the same time demonstrate the extraordinary technical level achieved by the Egyptians in the middle of the third millennium BC. Construction of the Great Gallery with projecting blocks arranged with millimetric precision, and the King's Chamber, the ceiling of which is formed by nine granite slabs weighing 400 tons, are the most evident examples of this high technological level.

One particular detail seen only in the pyramid of Cheops and never reused in other similar structures is a sophisticated system of five compartments placed one over the other above the King's Chamber which perhaps were designed to lighten the pressure on the chamber ceiling and prevent its possible collapse.

Other structures still not fully understood are two square ventilation shafts approximately 20 cm across that pass from the King's Chamber and exit the pyramid on the north and south sides at heights of 71 m and 53 m.

The Pyramid of Cheops

The inclination and position of the two shafts, also present in the Queen's Chamber, were designed in accordance with a precise astronomic orientation: the shafts on the north side point towards the circumpolar stars while those on the south side are aimed at the constellation of Orion. Probably the shafts had a purely ceremonial function and were created to facilitate the ascent of the pharaoh's soul to the heavens. Outside, the eastern side of the pyramid is flanked by three subsidiary pyramids attributed to queen Henutsen, the half-sister of Cheops, to queen Meritetis, and to the king's mother, Hetepheres.Recent excavation work directed by Egyptian archaeologist, Zahi Hawass, has discovered a satellite pyramid near the south-west corner. The structures of the mortuary temple have nearly all disappeared, as have the materials used to build the processional ramp 825 meters long and the valley temple, whose foundation and part of the original flooring were discovered by Hawass in 1990.

The existence of huge boat-shaped ditches on the eastern side of the pyramid are evidence that boats were provided as part of the pharaoh's funerary goods. This custom was confirmed in 1954 when two other ditches were discovered on the south side of the pyramid that had been covered with limestone blocks weighing between 17 and 20 tons. One of the two ditches was excavated and opened: inside, there was a perfectly whole wooden boat disassembled into 1224 pieces which was given back its original shape after 14 years of patient restoration work. This extraordinarily elegant boat with tapering lines and a raised prow and stern, was 43.5 meters long and 5.6 meters wide. Its wooden planking was made from Lebanese cedar and was assembled using an ingenious system of joints and cord without having recourse to nails or metallic parts. The royal boat was designed for river navigation as is shown by its rather shallow draught (approx. 1.5 meters). It had no sail but was powered by ten sets of oars and steered by a

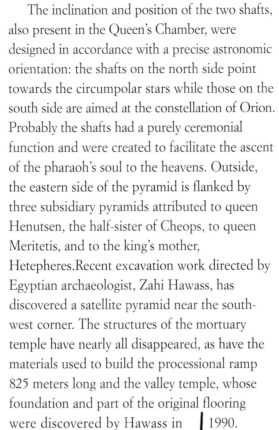

pair of rudders on the stern. What was the purpose of these boats arranged around the pyramid of Cheops? Did the pharaoh's boat ever sail down the Nile? Was it a ceremonial boat used to carry the body of the pharaoh to the pyramid or did it just have ritual and symbolic value?

These questions do not currently have a certain answer but it seems probable that the last hypothesis is the correct one. Boats had an extremely important function in a country like Egypt in which they were the only means of transport. The sun god Ra was imagined to cross the sky each day in a boat on his unchanging route from East to West, and the *Texts of the Pyramids* found carved inside the fifth dynasty pyramids at Saqqarah – the earliest religious texts known – make frequent reference to the heavenly navigation of the pharaoh. It is therefore probable that, according to the beliefs of the period, these boats were used by the soul of the pharaoh to reach his father Ra in the sky and to navigate with him for eternity.

*133 TOP RIGHT FIVE MORE TRENCHES THAT CONTAINED BARKS.*

*134-135 THE PYRAMID OF CHEFREN DOMINATES THE ADJOINING FUNERARY TEMPLE.*

*136-137 THE FALCON GOD HORUS PROTECTS THE BACK OF THE PHARAOH'S NECK.*

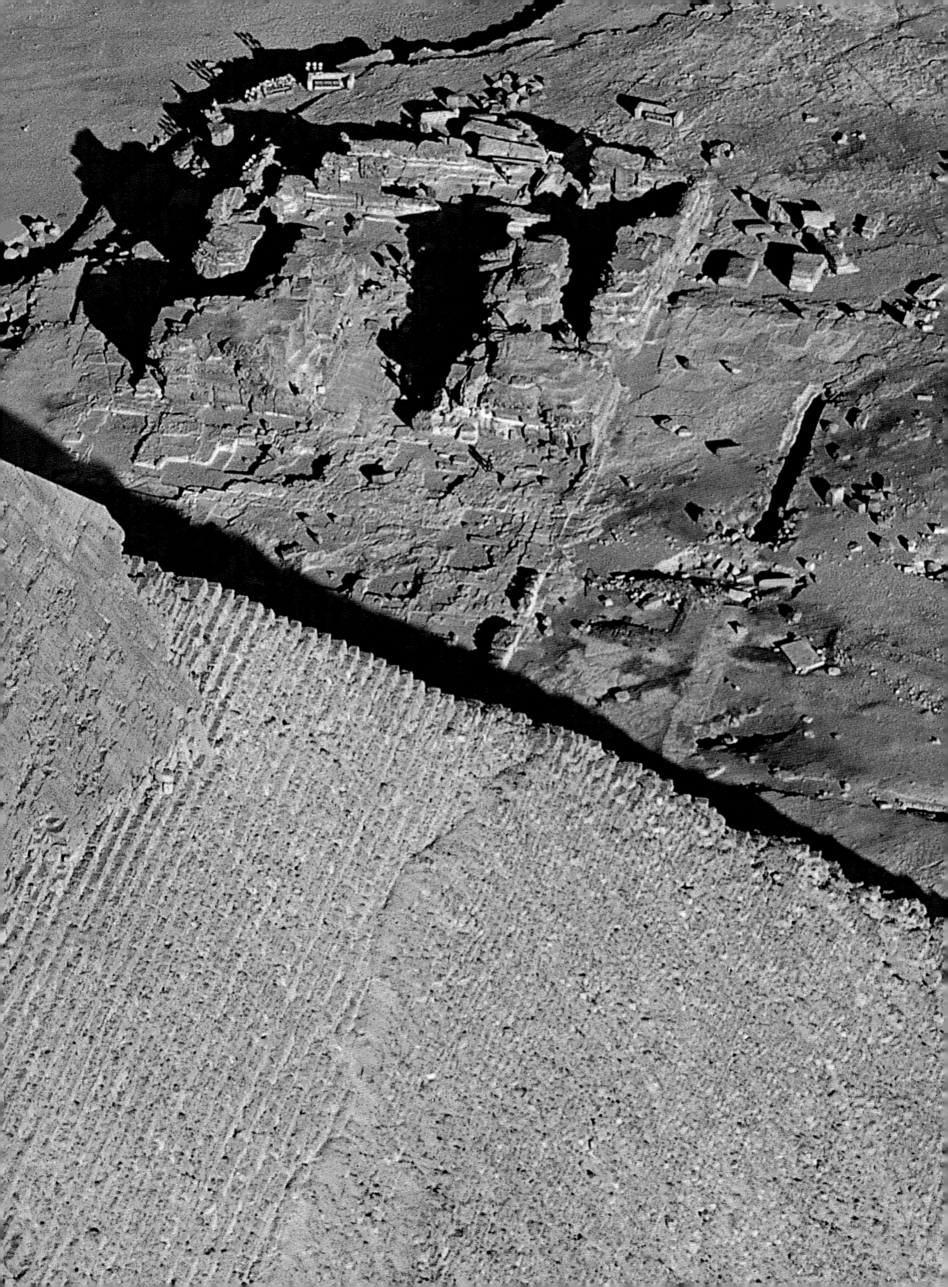

The age of the pyramids lasted for more than eight centuries until the end of the Middle Kingdom when, after several decades of political disorder during the Second Intermediate Period and the invasion of the Hyksos, power was regained by members of Theban families. Ahmosis expelled the Hyksos and founded the 18th dynasty. He transferred the capital to the city of *Uaset*, better known by its Greek name of Thebes, which lies on the east bank of the Nile, 500 kilometers south of ancient Memphis: these events marked the beginning of the New Kingdom. It was during this period that the pharaohs abandoned the concept of the pyramid as a royal tomb, preferring graves dug out of the rock of the mountains that lie along the west bank of the river. Here Ra, the Sun god, ended his daily passage across the sky and began his journey through the depths of the underworld on his divine bark. On the slopes of the mountains, which in this region lie some miles from the river banks, lay the silent kingdom of Osiris, "Lord of the Underworld," and of Anubis, the "Embalmer."

The priests long searched for the most suitable site for a royal necropolis. In the end, their choice

fell upon a remote valley in which the bed of an ancient river had gouged out the rocks of the mountain deeply. The fact that the valley was accessed with difficulty and was easily controlled was important for reasons of security, but the determining factor in its selection was that it had a very particular characteristic: it was overlooked by a mountain, known as the "Theban Peak," similar in shape to a pyramid. Thus the pyramid was no longer the tomb of a king but a symbol that emanated its magical protective power over the entire valley known to the ancient Egyptians as *ta sekhet aat*, "the great prairie."

Like the kings of the Old Kingdom, the Theban kings also began the construction of their abodes of eternity as soon as they ascended the throne. The high priests and royal architects drew up highly detailed plans in which all the features of the sepulcher, its layout and choice of decorative elements were set down. The plan of the royal tombs always included several essential features: the stairway, a descending corridor which might open onto side chambers, a vestibule and the chamber where the

## Legend

| | | | |
|---|---|---|---|
| 1 | KV n° 62 Tutankhamun | 26 | KV n° 56 |
| 2 | KV n° 9 Ramses VI/V | 27 | KV n° 58 |
| 3 | KV n° 8 Merneptah | 28 | KV n° 57 Horemheb |
| 4 | KV n° 7 Ramses II | 29 | KV n° 12 |
| 5 | KV n° 55 | 30 | KV n° 35 Amenhotep II |
| 6 | KV n° 6 Ramses IX | 31 | KV n° 49-52 |
| 7 | KV n° 5 | 32 | KV n° 53 |
| 8 | KV n° 3 | 33 | KV n° 36 |
| 9 | KV n° 46 | 34 | KV n° 61 |
| 10 | KV n° 4 Ramses XI | 35 | KV n° 29 |
| 11 | KV n° 45 | 36 | KV n° 47 Sptah |
| 12 | KV n° 44 | 37 | KV n° 13 |
| 13 | KV n° 28 | 38 | KV n° 14 Sethnakht/ Tauseret |
| 14 | KV n° 27 | | |
| 15 | KV n° 21 | 39 | KV n° 38 Thutmosis I |
| 16 | KV n° 60 | 40 | KV n° 15 Sethi II |
| 17 | KV n° 20 Hatshepsut | 41 | KV n° 40 |
| 18 | KV n° 19 Montu-Her- Kepeshef | 42 | KV n° 26 |
| | | 43 | KV n° 30 |
| 19 | KV n° 43 Thutmosis IV | 44 | KV n° 59 |
| 20 | KV n° 54 | 45 | KV n° 31 |
| 21 | KV n° 18 Ramses X | 46 | KV n° 32 |
| 22 | KV n° 17 Sethi I | 47 | KV n° 37 |
| 23 | KV n° 16 Ramses I | 48 | KV n° 42 |
| 24 | KV n° 10 Amenemhet | 49 | KV n° 33 |
| 25 | KV n° 11 Ramses III | 50 | KV n° 34 Thutmosis III |

*Egypt*
**VALLEY OF THE KINGS**

# The Valley of the Kings
# and the treasure of TUTANKHAMUN

Tutankhamun

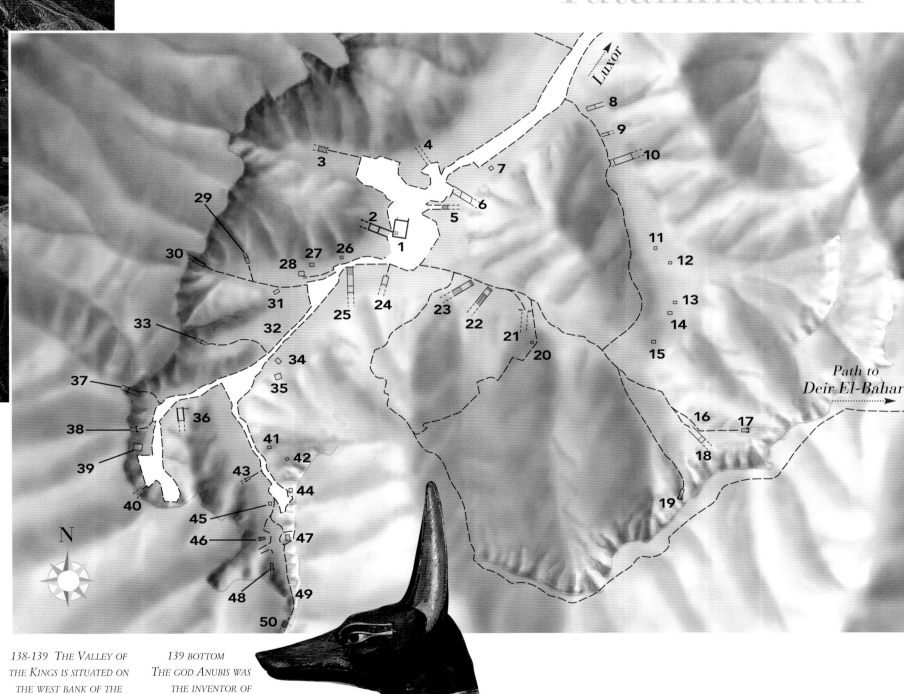

*Luxor*

*Path to*
*Deir El-Bahar*

N

*138-139 THE VALLEY OF THE KINGS IS SITUATED ON THE WEST BANK OF THE NILE OPPOSITE THE MODERN-DAY CITY OF LUXOR. IT IS OVERLOOKED BY A PYRAMID-SHAPED MOUNTAIN CALLED THE THEBAN PEAK AND WAS CHOSEN BY THE RULERS OF THE NEW KINGDOM (18TH-20TH DYNASTIES) AS THE LOCATION FOR THEIR DWELLINGS OF ETERNITY.*

*139 BOTTOM THE GOD ANUBIS WAS THE INVENTOR OF EMBALMING. HE IS ILLUSTRATED BOTH AS A BLACK DOG CROUCHED ON A SMALL NAOS AND AS A MAN WITH A DOG'S HEAD. HE WAS THE "GUARDIAN OF THE NECROPOLIS."*

140-141 *THE CEILING OF THE BURIAL CHAMBER IN MANY TOMBS REPRESENTS THE UNIVERSE WITH STARS*

*AND CONSTELLATIONS OR, AS IN THE TOMB OF RAMSES VI (KV NO. 9), THE GODDESS NUT, LADY OF THE SKY.*

141 TOP LEFT *THE GODDESS ISIS RECEIVES AN OFFERING IN THE TOMB OF HORAMED (KV NO. 57). ISIS WEARS A SOLAR DISC ON HER HEAD.*

141 TOP RIGHT *THE WALLS OF THE ROYAL TOMBS WERE DECORATED WITH PASSAGES TAKEN FROM IMPORTANT MAGICAL-RELIGIOUS TEXTS IN USE AT THE TIME; FOR*

*EXAMPLE, THE* BOOK OF THE AMDUAT *(THE* BOOK OF THAT WHICH IS IN THE UNDERWORLD*) IN THE TOMB OF AMENHOTEP II (KV NO. 35).*

sarcophagus of the pharaoh would lie, known as the "gold room" because this metal was the symbol of the incorruptible flesh of the gods.

Great attention was paid to the elements that would decorate the walls of the tomb; they included passages from the most important magical and religious texts in use at the time, accompanied by their illustrations. The general theme to which all royal tombs adhered was not so much the earthly life of the king or his military exploits – which were celebrated on the walls of temples – but the great underworld journey the

pharaoh would make. It is these decorative elements, the reflections of new theological and religious conceptions, that represent the major difference between the royal tombs of the New and Old Kingdoms. While the funerary apartments of the great pyramids of the fourth dynasty were completely bare of inscription or decoration, passages from the "Texts of the Pyramids" were carved on the walls of the burial chambers and antechambers from the reign of Unas at the start of the fifth dynasty. The texts were essentially magic formulas that had the

function of helping the dead king overcome the many obstacles he was to meet on his journey through the nether regions. They underwent a long evolution and in the New Kingdom were collected in various works: the *Book of Gates*, the *Book of Breaths*, the *Book of the Amduat*, the *Book of the Earth*, the *Book of Caves*, the *Litanies of Ra*, and the better known *Book of the Dead*. The choice of magical texts to be used for wall decoration was of the greatest importance, as the theological notions of the epoch believed that the soul of the king would follow a long and difficult

represented by a curved ceiling on which the goddess Nut, "Lady of the sky," was painted – to mingle with Ra.

The size of the tomb and the complexity of the decorative elements were, within certain limits, related to the duration of the reign; for example, the tomb of Ramses I, who reigned for only 16 months, is 29 meters long while that of his son, Sethi I, who reigned for 13 years, is 108 meters long.

When the plans for the sepulcher had received the pharaoh's approval, the workers and artists that lived in the village of Deir el-Medina close to the Valley of the Kings began their work.

A group of 60 or so men were divided into two teams, each working on one side of the tomb. Every ten days, they were allowed to rest for 24 hours. The skills of the men were specialized and complementary: stonecutters, plasterers, sculptors, designers, and decorators worked side by side in a sort of production line. First, the stonecutters set to work to dig a hole in the rock; the plasterers

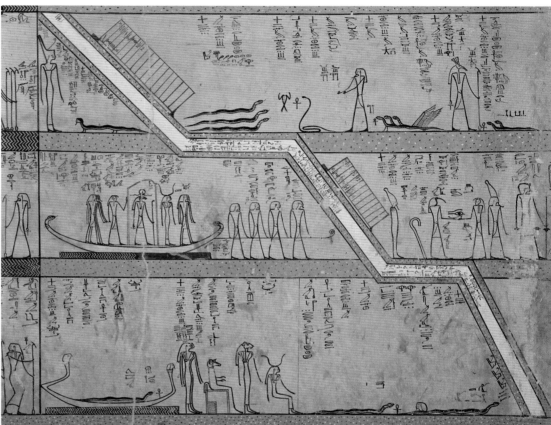

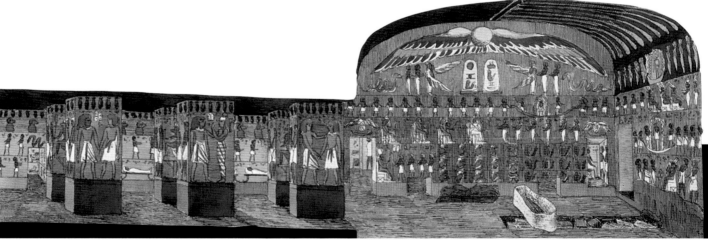

wandering that would conclude in his "solarization," i.e., his identification and fusion with the Sun god, Ra. The presence of these texts – initially painted and later carved – on the walls provided the dead king with the magic formulas needed to overcome the difficulties encountered on his journey through the underworld.

The burial chamber was therefore the place in which the mysterious process of regeneration and transformation of the pharaoh into a divine entity was performed. His soul would rise to heaven – which in the time of Ramses was symbolically

followed behind them applying a layer of clay, limestone, and crumbled straw over which a lighter layer of plaster was added, whitened with chalk. The decorations chosen by the high priests and the king were traced out using red ochre by the designers, who first divided up the space into squares using a string attached to a stick so that the figures and the texts would be properly placed, respecting the very precise rules of proportion. The designers were monitored by a supervisor who would correct any mistake with charcoal. Then it was the turn of the sculptors

who carved bas-reliefs in the rock that were later painted. Deeper in the tomb, the stonecutters continued excavating while the outer sections were almost brought to completion. This rational organization of the work allowed them to continue at an extraordinary speed so that a royal tomb could be prepared in just a few months despite the use of rudimentary tools. On the other hand, the largest and most complex tombs would require between six and ten years.

The form the royal funerary ceremony took remains unknown to us, but we do know that great

144 TOP THE GOD ANUBIS,
THE "DIVINE EMBALMER,"
PRACTICES HIS ART ON THE
BODY OF THE DECEASED.
THE IMAGE WAS PAINTED ON
THE WOODEN SARCOPHAGUS
OF DJEDHOREFANKH (22ND
DYNASTY).

144-145 LUNGS, LIVER,
STOMACH, AND INTESTINES
WERE EXTRACTED FROM THE
BODY OF THE DECEASED AND
PLACED IN FOUR SPECIAL
RECIPIENTS KNOWN AS
CANOPIC JARS. EACH OF
THESE ORGANS WAS PLACED
UNDER THE PROTECTION OF
A GOD WHOSE IMAGE WAS
SHOWN ON THE LID OF THE
VASE.

145 TOP THE FUNERAL
PROCESSION ACCOMPANYING
THE DECEASED TO HIS TOMB
WAS FOLLOWED BY GROUPS
OF WOMEN IN MOURNING
WHOSE HAIR HUNG LOOSE IN
A SIGN OF BEREAVEMENT
(TOMB OF RAMOSE TT
NO. 55).

advances in embalming took place during the
New Kingdom compared to the simple and
primitive techniques used at the times of the
pyramids, and that the body of the king
underwent long and complex treatment. The
embalming process was carried out in a separate
area called *uabet*, "the pure place," or *per-nefer*,
"the house of regeneration," and was preceded,
accompanied, and followed by the recitation of
prayers and magic rites. First the brain was
extracted through the nostrils using hooked
instruments. Then an incision was made on the
left side of the abdomen and the lungs, kidneys,
stomach, and intestines were removed; the
heart, considered the seat of thought and the
soul, was left in the thorax. The internal organs
extracted were placed in four canopic vases
placed under the protection of the four Sons of
Horus (Imset, Duamutef, Hapi, and Qebesenhuf)
and the gods Isis, Nefti, Neith, and Selkis. The
abdominal cavity was filled with myrrh and other
aromatic substances and sewn up.

The body was then covered with *natron*, a
special substance composed of sodium salts that
included carbonates, bicarbonates, chlorides,
and sulfates. After 70 days, when the
process of dehydration caused by the
*natron* had finished, the remains of the king

were washed and the final stage of the process was begun. A number of amulets was placed on the body, including the "scarab of the heart" engraved with Chapter XXX B of the *Book of the Dead*, entitled "Chapter to prevent the heart of Osiris (the name of the deceased followed) from being kept far away." After being wrapped in light linen bandages, the body of the pharaoh was taken to the royal palace. At this point, the real funeral ceremonies began: the body of the king was laid upon a draped platform that was pulled towards the tomb by the dignitaries of the kingdom accompanied by a large procession. Bearers followed carrying the king's grave goods, groups of women would shriek and cry, and priests with shaved heads burned incense and rattled percussion instruments called sistrums. The procession headed towards the "great and august necropolis of the millions of years of Pharaoh Life Strength Health in the West of Thebes" where the tomb had been built. This was where the fundamentally important ceremony of the "Opening of the Mouth" took place, which signified that the deceased would magically be able to use his mouth, eyes, and senses again in the Afterlife and therefore be

able to speak, drink, eat, and see once more. Then the royal remains were carried into the burial chamber where a monumental sarcophagus lay ready, finely sculpted with passages of religious texts and images of protective deities and covered by a heavy lid, often decorated with the effigy of the king in high-relief. The grave goods were arranged around the sarcophagus and in surrounding rooms, including objects of everyday use which the deceased would need in the afterlife and a papyrus on which the *Book of the Dead* was transcribed. Finally, several statuettes (*ushabti*) were placed in the tomb. The king could bring them to life by pronouncing the magic formula in Chapter VI of the *Book of the Dead* entitled "Chapter to make an *ushabti* do his work in the necropolis." The king was therefore able to order the *ushabti* (an ancient Egyptian word meaning "the respondents") to perform the most arduous of tasks in the Underworld just as in earthly life, and the *ushabti* would promptly reply, "I'll do it. Here I am!"

When all the grave goods had been positioned, the workers hermetically closed the entrance to the tomb, the seals of the necropolis were attached, and members of the royal family,

dignitaries and friends began the funerary banquet.

Once the tomb had been closed and sealed, no one could enter. The valley was also considered a forbidden area that no one except workers and guards could enter; nor did the cult of the dead king require visits to the burial place, since rites were performed on the edge of the Nile plateau in the memorial temples called "Castles of the millions of years."

Normally the entrance to the tomb was left showing, especially from the 19th dynasty onwards, and the guards of the necropolis would regularly inspect the seals to check that they had not been broken and would make out detailed reports. However, all the precautions taken to ensure that the tombs remained undisturbed turned out to be useless, as papyruses exist that

## The valley of the
# Kings

describe the tombs as being raided and plundered from as early as the 20th dynasty. The security of the tombs became so inadequate that the priests secretly decided to transfer the remains of the most important pharaohs to a place in the Theban mountains near the temple of Deir el-Bahari. Here the pharaohs remained hidden and protected for more than 2000 years until a local band of thieves of antiquities discovered the site in 1881. The sudden appearance on the Egyptian and European art markets of objects belonging to royal grave goods sparked the suspicion of Gaston Maspero, then Head of the Egyptian Antiquities Department, who subsequently found the site himself.

It is certain that by the end of the pharaonic age all the royal tombs had been broken into and plundered. It was only in 1922 that the excavation project headed by the English Egyptologist Howard Carter and financed by Lord Carnarvon discovered the only intact royal tomb in the whole of the Valley of the Kings. It belonged to a young pharaoh whose reign lasted only nine years and who had been almost unknown at the time of the discovery. Thanks to the discovery of the tomb of Tutankhamun, today we know the contents of the grave goods that accompanied a king on his underworld journey and what the abodes of eternity of the Theban rulers would have contained. If the small tomb of Tutankhamun contained more than 3500 objects – which alone account for a large part of the contents of the Cairo Museum – it is difficult to imagine the extent of the funeral trappings in gigantic tombs like those of Sethi I or Ramses II who, for the importance and the duration of their reigns, are not remotely comparable to the young king.

The tomb of Tutankhamun has disclosed new and important information on many aspects of royal funerary rites in use during the New Kingdom and gives us a better understanding of how the tomb of a Theban pharaoh was organized. Before Carter's discovery, Tutankhamun was little known. The ancestry of the royal prince, who spent his first years in the court of Amarna, is still not known with certainty.

It is probable he was the son of Amenhotep IV-Akhenaton and one of the king's secondary wives, named Kiya. His original name was Tutankhaton which means "the living image of Aton" but he changed this for reasons of political expediency to Tutankhamun or "the living image of Amon." The name was completed by the epithet *heqaiunushema*, "Lord of Heliopolis in Upper Egypt." Tutankhaton married his half-sister Ankhesenpaaton, "She that lives for Aton," the daughter of Akhenaton and his principal wife Nefertiti. During the period prior to his ascent to the throne, the decline of the court at Amarna and its worship dedicated to the god Aton had begun. Tutankhaton lived there under the influence of three important and authoritative figures, two of whom were destined to succeed him to the throne: the high priest, Ay, the head of the army, Horemheb, and the treasurer, Maya. The tomb of Maya was found in 1986 in the necropolis at Saqqara near that of Horemheb.

Tutankhaton inherited the throne at the age of nine after the death of Semenkhkare, either brother or son of Akhenaton, who had only reigned for two years and much of that as co-regent with Akhenaton. The young king took the enthronement name of *Nebkheperura*, "Lord of the manifestations of Ra," and moved the capital back from Amarna to Thebes. In year 2 of his reign, Tutankhaton changed his name to Tutankhamun as a symbol of the religious and political shift he had put into motion, which was completed after his

*148 TOP THE TOMB OF TUTANKHAMUN (KV NO. 62), OF WHOM WE SEE THE CARTOUCHE BEARING HIS ENTHRONEMENT NAME, NEBKHEPERURA, WAS THE ONLY ROYAL TOMB DISCOVERED WITH A NEARLY COMPLETE SET OF GRAVE GOODS.*

*148 BOTTOM THE OBJECTS IN THE ROYAL GRAVE GOODS WERE OFTEN EXQUISITELY MANUFACTURED, LIKE THIS DECORATION ON A WOODEN CASKET IN WHICH THE KING IS SHOWN DESTROYING HIS ENEMIES.*

*149 THE FUNERARY MASK MADE FROM GOLD, POLYCHROME GLASS PASTE AND SEMIPRECIOUS STONES IS ONE OF THE MASTERPIECES OF THE GOLDSMITH'S ART IN ALL OF HISTORY. IT WAS FOUND ON THE FACE OF THE MUMMY OF THE KING INSIDE THREE ANTHROPOID SARCOPHAGUSES WHICH IN TURN WERE PLACED INSIDE A QUARTZITE SARCOPHAGUS.*

The Valley of the Kings
and the treasure of
Tutankhamun

death by Ay and, more particularly, by Horemheb. The ascent to the throne of the new king meant the opening of the large Theban temples and the start of great works of construction, many of which were completed and also usurped by Horemheb.

Tutankhamun probably died during year 9 of his reign at the age of 18 in 1343 BC. The cause of his death is unknown but the presence of a sliver in his skull discovered during a second autopsy of his mummy in 1968 suggests an accident or, as has been proposed, an assassination.

It seems clear that the tomb discovered by Carter and known by the number KV 62 was not initially constructed for Tutankhamun, who in all probability had decided to build his tomb in the more distant Valley of the West, an offshoot of the Valley of the Kings, where the tomb of his grandfather Amenhotep III lay. The tomb discovered in the Valley of the West by the Italian explorer Giovanni Battista Belzoni in 1816 was decorated almost identically to that of Tutankhamun although it was much longer. This tomb was subsequently used by Ay, for whom tomb KV 62 in the Valley of the Kings was probably reserved (there are several tombs belonging to high dignitaries in the Valley of the Kings). It is likely that the exchange was determined by the unexpected death of the king, as tomb KV 62 was in a more advanced state of preparation. It is also apparent that KV 62 was made ready in a great hurry, since only the small

# The Valley of the Kings
## and the treasure of Tutankhamun

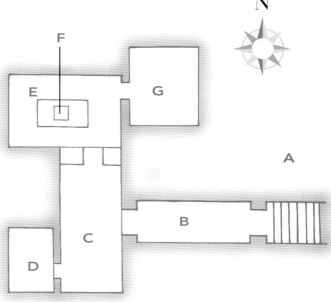

N

F

E

G

A

C

B

D

150 BOTTOM ONLY THE
WALLS IN THE BURIAL
CHAMBER WERE DECORATED
IN TUTANKHAMUN'S TOMB.
THE SCENE ILLUSTRATES A
PASSAGE FROM THE BOOK
OF THE AMDUAT AND THE
NIGHT-TIME NAVIGATION OF
THE BARK BELONGING TO
THE GOD KHEPRI.

150-151 IN THIS SCENE,
WHICH HAS NO EQUIVALENT
IN THE OTHER TOMBS IN
THE VALLEY OF THE KINGS,
AY, TUTANKHAMUN'S
SUCCESSOR, CELEBRATES THE
CEREMONY OF THE
OPENING OF THE MOUTH
BEFORE THE DEAD KING SO
THAT HE MIGHT MAGICALLY
HAVE THE USE OF SPEECH
AND HIS SENSES IN THE
UNDERWORLD.

151 BOTTOM ONLY THE
LARGE QUARTZITE
SARCOPHAGUS WAS LEFT IN
THE BURIAL CHAMBER IN
TUTANKHAMUN'S TOMB. IT
CONTAINED THE FIRST OF
THE THREE ANTHROPOID
SARCOPHAGUSES IN WHICH
THE MUMMY OF THE
PHARAOH WAS FOUND.

152-153
THE YOUNG KING, RIGHT, IS
WELCOMED BY THE GODDESS
NUT. IN THE CENTER, HIS
KA (SHOWN AS AN OLDER
MAN) ACCOMPANIES HIM
BEFORE THE MUMMIFIED
OSIRIS.

## LEGEND

**A** STAIRWAY
**B** CORRIDOR
**C** ANTE-CHAMBER
**D** ANNEX
**E** BURIAL CHAMBER
**F** SEPULCHER
**G** TREASURY

150 TOP THE TOMB OF
TUTANKHAMUN WAS SAVED
FROM TOMB ROBBERS BY
BEING COVERED WITH
RUBBLE THROWN DOWN
THE MOUNTAIN WHEN THE
LARGE TOMB OF RAMSES VI
(KV NO. 9) WAS BEING
EXCAVATED.

burial chamber has painted walls and that those decorations were quite unelaborate in nature.

The layout of the tomb is extremely simple, which indicates that it was originally intended for a private rather than royal burial. A stairway leads into a rectangular north-south antechamber called by Carter the "vestibule." A small opening in the west wall provided access to an annex while the door that led to the chamber containing the sarcophagus was in the north wall. The chamber also had a small annex on the east side which Carter named the "treasury."

It was the position of the tomb that prevented it from being plundered like all the others in the valley; lying immediately below the tomb of Ramses VI, it had been covered by

154 TOP TUTANKHAMUN'S TOMB WAS DISCOVERED ON 4 NOVEMBER 1922 BY THE ENGLISH ARCHAEOLOGIST HOWARD CARTER, WHO HAD BEEN WORKING ON IT FOR OVER 8 YEARS. THE LAST OBJECTS WERE REMOVED FROM THE TOMB ON 10 NOVEMBER 1930.

154 CENTER LEFT ACCOMPANIED BY LORD CARNARVON WHO FINANCED THE EXCAVATION, CARTER ENTERED THE FIRST ROOM IN THE TOMB (CALLED THE ANTECHAMBER) ON 26 NOVEMBER 1922. TWO AND A HALF MONTHS WERE REQUIRED TO EMPTY IT OF THE 700 OR SO OBJECTS IT CONTAINED.

## The jewels of
# Tutankhamun

154 CENTER RIGHT THE DOOR OF THE FOURTH AND LAST WOODEN SHRINE THAT ENCLOSED THE SARCOPHAGUSES, STILL SEALED, WAS SEEN BY CARTER FOR THE FIRST TIME IN 3247 YEARS.

MANY OBJECTS, IT CONTAINED THE LARGE GILDED WOODEN BOX THAT HELD THE KING'S CANOPIC JARS.

155 AFTER OPENING THE DOORS OF THE FOURTH GILDED WOODEN SHRINE, HOWARD CARTER ADMIRES THE QUARTZITE SARCOPHAGUS WITH HIS ASSISTANT ARTHUR CALLENDER.

154 BOTTOM THE SMALL ROOM ANNEXED TO THE BURIAL CHAMBER WAS NAMED THE "TREASURY" BY CARTER. AMONG ITS

a layer of rubble created during construction of the later and much larger tomb. In fact, Tutankhamun's tomb had been broken into prior to the construction of Ramses VI's tomb, but the thieves succeeded in making off with very little because they were probably disturbed. They took only objects of common use that could easily be disposed of, before they left the tomb without serious damage.

Having removed the debris that covered the narrow stairway, Carter found himself faced by a first walled doorway. Beyond that was a corridor partially blocked by sand and fragments of objects stolen from the tomb when it was broken into by the thieves. Among these objects was a splendid wooden head of Tutankhamun that rose out of a lotus flower, the symbol of the pharaoh's resurrection.

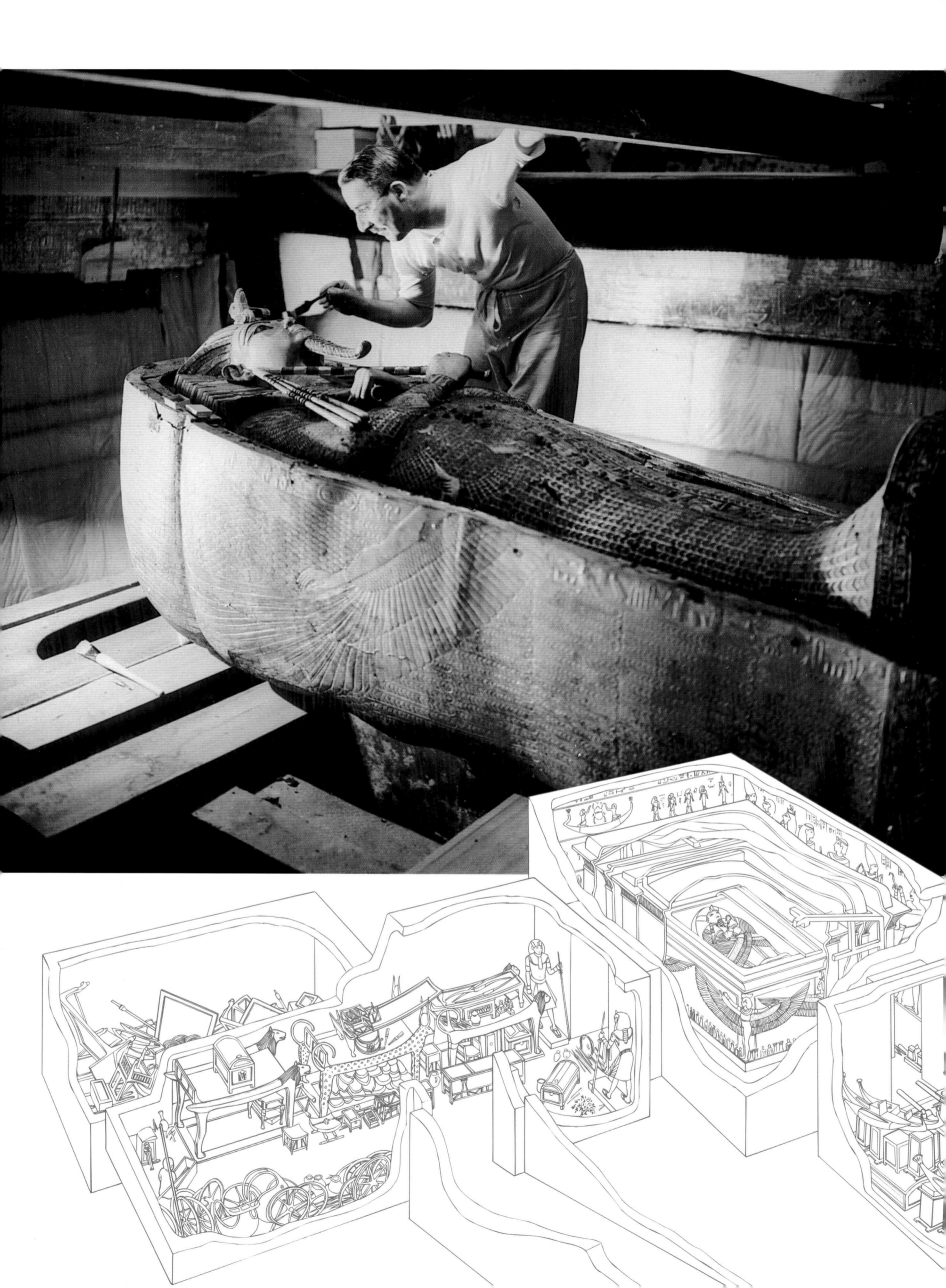

The corridor ended at a second walled doorway which, when opened, led into the antechamber. Here an extraordinary quantity of objects lined the walls, including three large ceremonial beds made from wood covered with gilded plaster.

Above, below, and to the sides of the beds lay many other objects from the king's grave goods, the most prominent of which were five large alabaster vases used to hold perfumes and

157 LEFT  TO EXTRACT THE WOODEN SHRINES THAT CONTAINED THE SARCOPHAGUSES, CARTER AND HIS HELPERS HAD TO REMOVE A PART OF THE STRUCTURE THAT SEPARATED THE ANTECHAMBER FROM THE BURIAL CHAMBER.

157 TOP RIGHT  TWO LARGE STATUES STOOD GUARD AT THE CORNERS OF THE NORTH WALL OF THE ANTECHAMBER. THEY PROTECTED THE DOOR (ORIGINALLY SEALED) THAT LED TO THE BURIAL CHAMBER.

157 BOTTOM RIGHT  THE TWO STATUES WERE CARVED IN WOOD BLACKENED WITH A COAT OF RESIN AND PARTIALLY GILDED. THEY BORE THE FACIAL FEATURES OF THE KING IN A REPRESENTATION OF HIS KA OR "DOUBLE." EACH STATUE STOOD 192 CM TALL.

ointments, wooden boxes, a wooden stool encrusted with ivory, and large wooden containers lined with whitish plaster that would have held all the various foods necessary for the afterlife of the king.

Standing in the antechamber was a small chair made from cedar with a splendidly carved backrest portraying the god Heb. Heb held two palm branches bearing the hieroglyph of the infinite at the bottom as a symbol of the eternity of time.

156-157 TOP  WHEN CARTER OPENED THE FIRST ANTHROPOID SARCOPHAGUS MADE FROM GILDED WOOD, HE FOUND A SECOND DECORATED WITH POLYCHROME GLASS PASTE.

156-157 BOTTOM  THIS 3D DRAWING SHOWS HOW TUTANKHAMUN'S TOMB APPEARED TO CARTER WITH ITS RICH SET OF GRAVE GOODS OF OVER 3000 OBJECTS, TODAY HELD IN THE CAIRO MUSEUM.

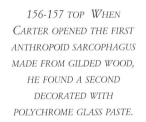

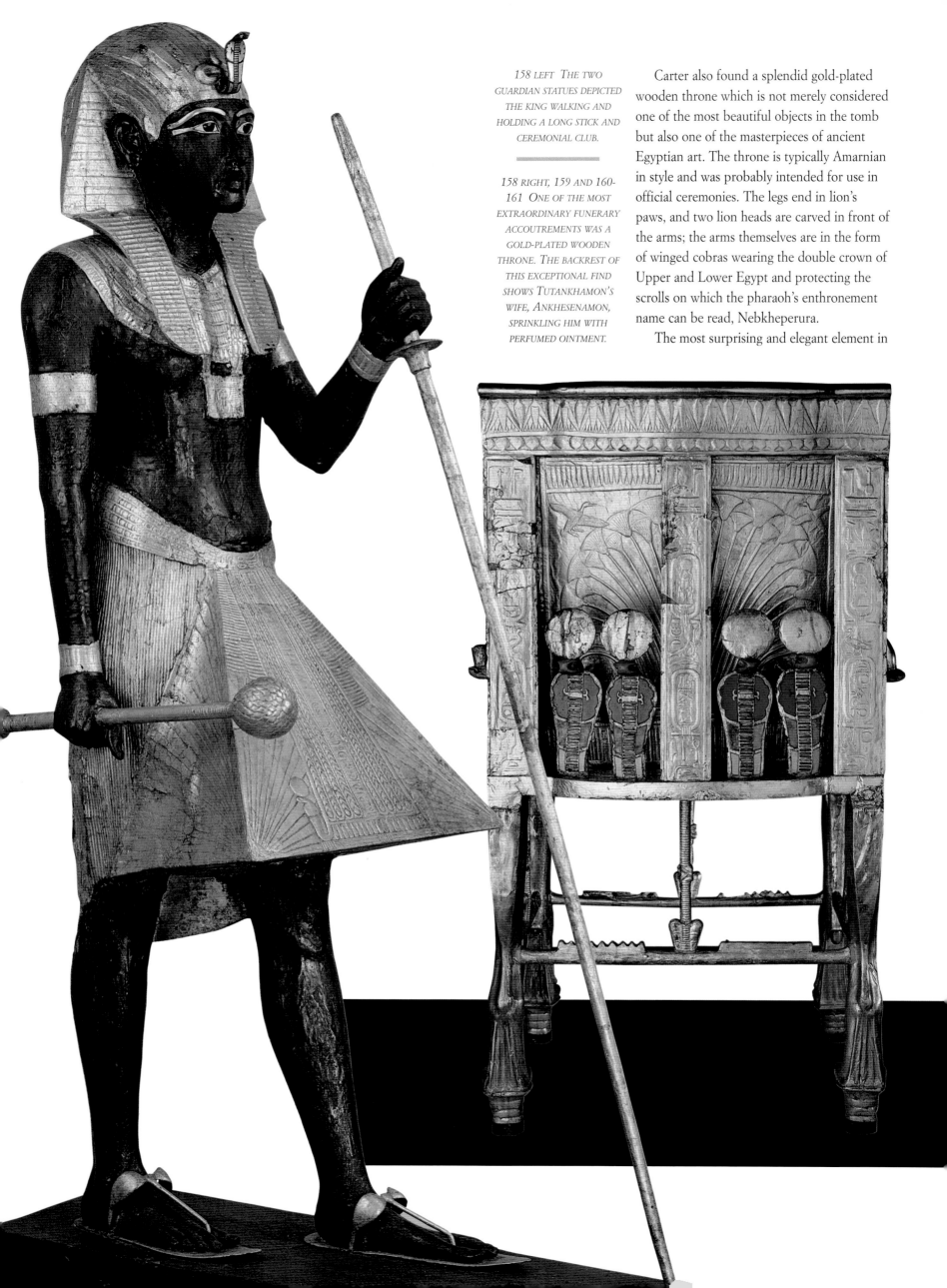

*158 LEFT THE TWO
GUARDIAN STATUES DEPICTED
THE KING WALKING AND
HOLDING A LONG STICK AND
CEREMONIAL CLUB.*

*158 RIGHT, 159 AND 160-
161 ONE OF THE MOST
EXTRAORDINARY FUNERARY
ACCOUTREMENTS WAS A
GOLD-PLATED WOODEN
THRONE. THE BACKREST OF
THIS EXCEPTIONAL FIND
SHOWS TUTANKHAMON'S
WIFE, ANKHESENAMON,
SPRINKLING HIM WITH
PERFUMED OINTMENT.*

Carter also found a splendid gold-plated
wooden throne which is not merely considered
one of the most beautiful objects in the tomb
but also one of the masterpieces of ancient
Egyptian art. The throne is typically Amarnian
in style and was probably intended for use in
official ceremonies. The legs end in lion's
paws, and two lion heads are carved in front of
the arms; the arms themselves are in the form
of winged cobras wearing the double crown of
Upper and Lower Egypt and protecting the
scrolls on which the pharaoh's enthronement
name can be read, Nebkheperura.

The most surprising and elegant element in

this splendid throne was, however, the backrest which portrayed Tutankhamun and his wife Ankhsenamon seated below a flowered pavilion. The portrait was made on embossed gold plate encrusted with glass paste and fragments of faïence. Wearing clothes made from silver, both wear blue *ibes*-wigs topped by elaborate crowns. The vivid scene is executed in pure Amarnian style; it shows the queen lovingly rubbing an ointment she had taken from a cup she holds in her left hand onto the arm of the king. Above the couple, the rays of the Sun god Aton radiate life to the royal couple.

The three large beds arranged against the

162-163 *THE WHOLE OF THE WEST WALL IN THE ANTECHAMBER WAS LINED WITH THREE LARGE RITUAL BEDS DECORATED WITH THE HEADS OF THREE DIFFERENT GODS: MEHET WITH THE HEAD OF A LION, MEHET-UERET, "THE GREAT FLOOD," WITH THE HEAD OF A COW, AND ANMUT WITH THE HEAD OF A HIPPOPOTAMUS. THE EXACT FUNCTION OF THE BEDS IS UNKNOWN, BUT A PASSAGE IN THE BOOK OF THE CELESTIAL COW SUGGESTS THAT THE BED OF MEHET-UERET WOULD TRANSPORT THE KING'S SOUL TO HEAVEN.*

162 TOP *The third of the three ritual beds was decorated with hippopotamus heads that evoke the goddess Anmut, "the Great Devouress," whose function in the Book of the Dead was to devour the souls of the dead who did not pass the Judgment of Osiris.*

162 CENTER *In addition to materials and clothing, the grave goods included 93 forms of footwear including a pair of gilded sandals.*

west wall of the vestibule are each 1.80 meters long and adorned with decorations of three different deities: Anmut, "She who devours the dead," with the head of a hippopotamus and the paws of a wild cat, Isis-Mehet with a lion's head, and Mehet-Ueret, the "Great Flood," with the head of a cow. We know that the beds were related to the resurrection of the king but not their actual function. We are aware that the bed with the image of Mehet-Ueret was similar to a solar bark that was supposed to transport the soul of the king; this information comes from some passages in the *Book of the Celestial Cow* engraved on the inner walls of the first shrine in the sarcophagus room.

Close to the bed decorated with the head of Anmut, the narrow passage opened by the thieves millennia ago, and never closed again by the guards of the necropolis, leads to the annexe from which the contents were not removed by Carter until five years after the discovery of the tomb. This little room, originally built to contain drinks, food, and ointments, held a multitude of different objects thrown in a pile almost 2 meters high.

It contained most of the king's weapons such as bows, arrows and spears, plus eight finely decorated shields, model boats, a hunting chariot probably used by the king and a gold-plated wooden throne encrusted with stones that was nicknamed the "ecclesiastical throne."

Among the other objects were an alabaster hand-basin that bore a model boat, also in alabaster, decorated at both bow and stern with steinboks' heads and carrying a sarcophagus

163 BOTTOM *This gold double box was found between the first and second shrines made from gilded wood. It was made in the form of two cartouches topped by atef-crowns and was used to hold unguents. The central figures in the box represent the king in different moments of his life and include Tutankhamun's enthronement name, Nebkheperura, in cryptographic form.*

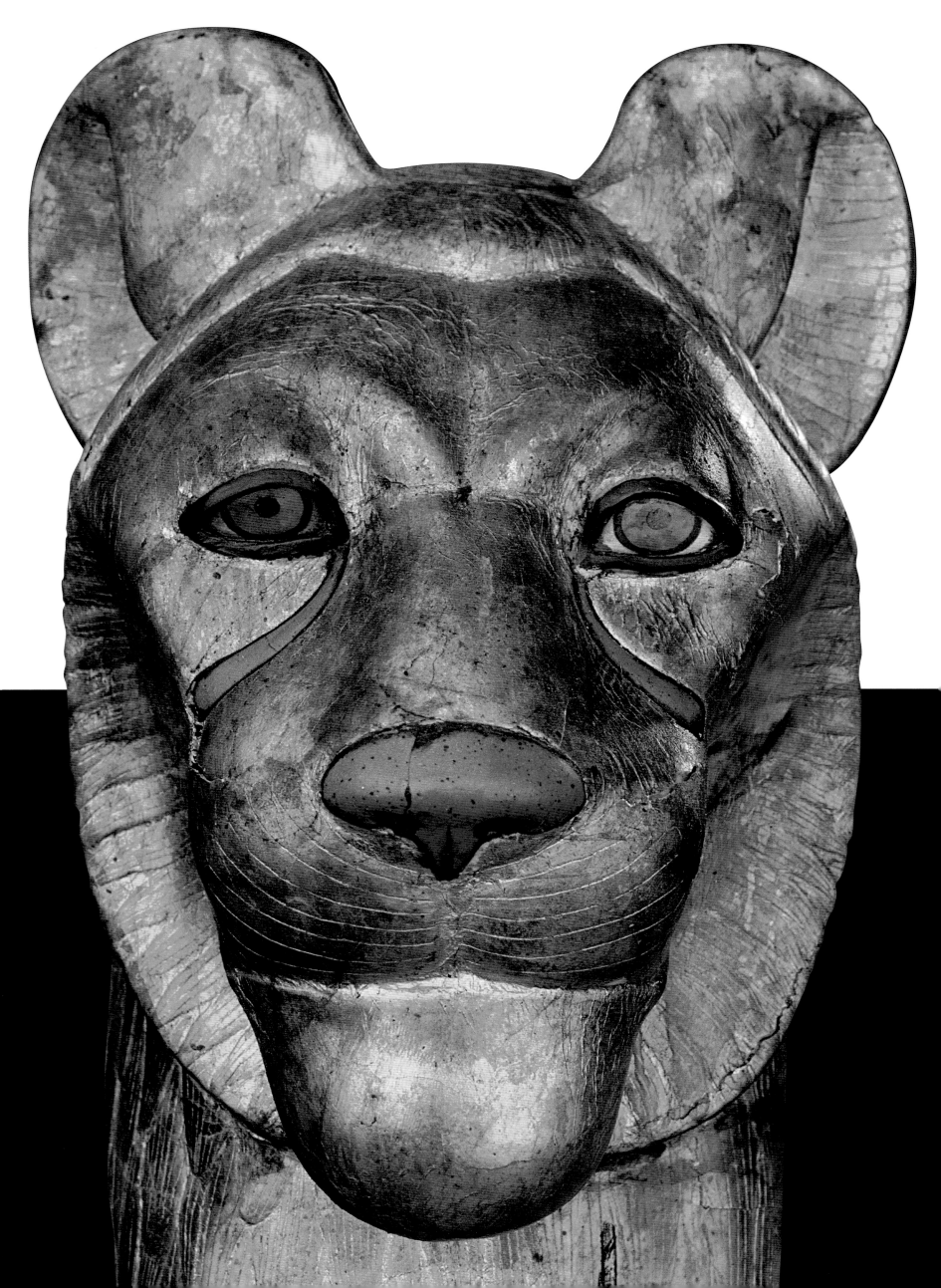

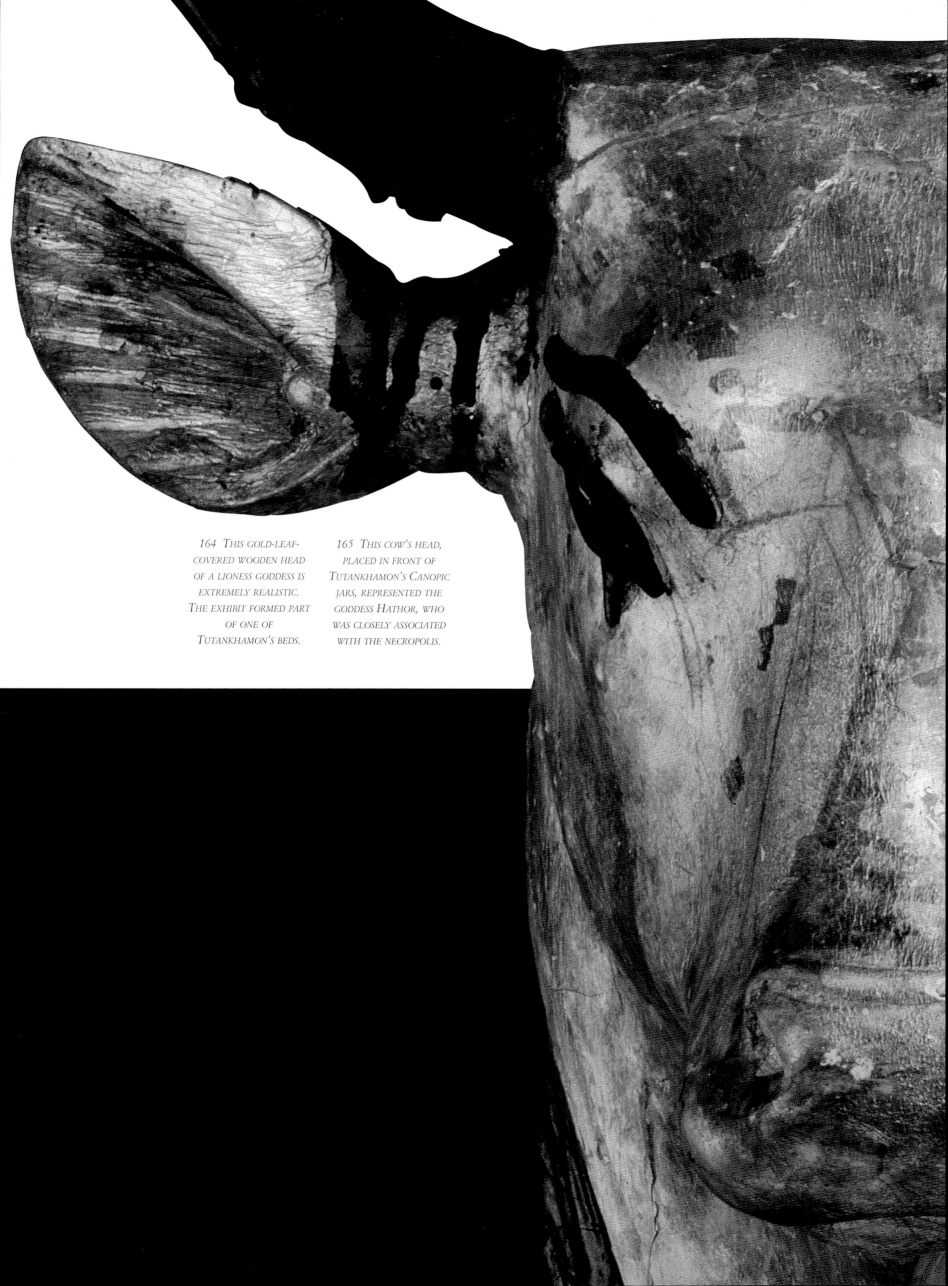

164 *This gold-leaf-covered wooden head of a lioness goddess is extremely realistic. The exhibit formed part of one of Tutankhamon's beds.*

165 *This cow's head, placed in front of Tutankhamon's Canopic jars, represented the goddess Hathor, who was closely associated with the necropolis.*

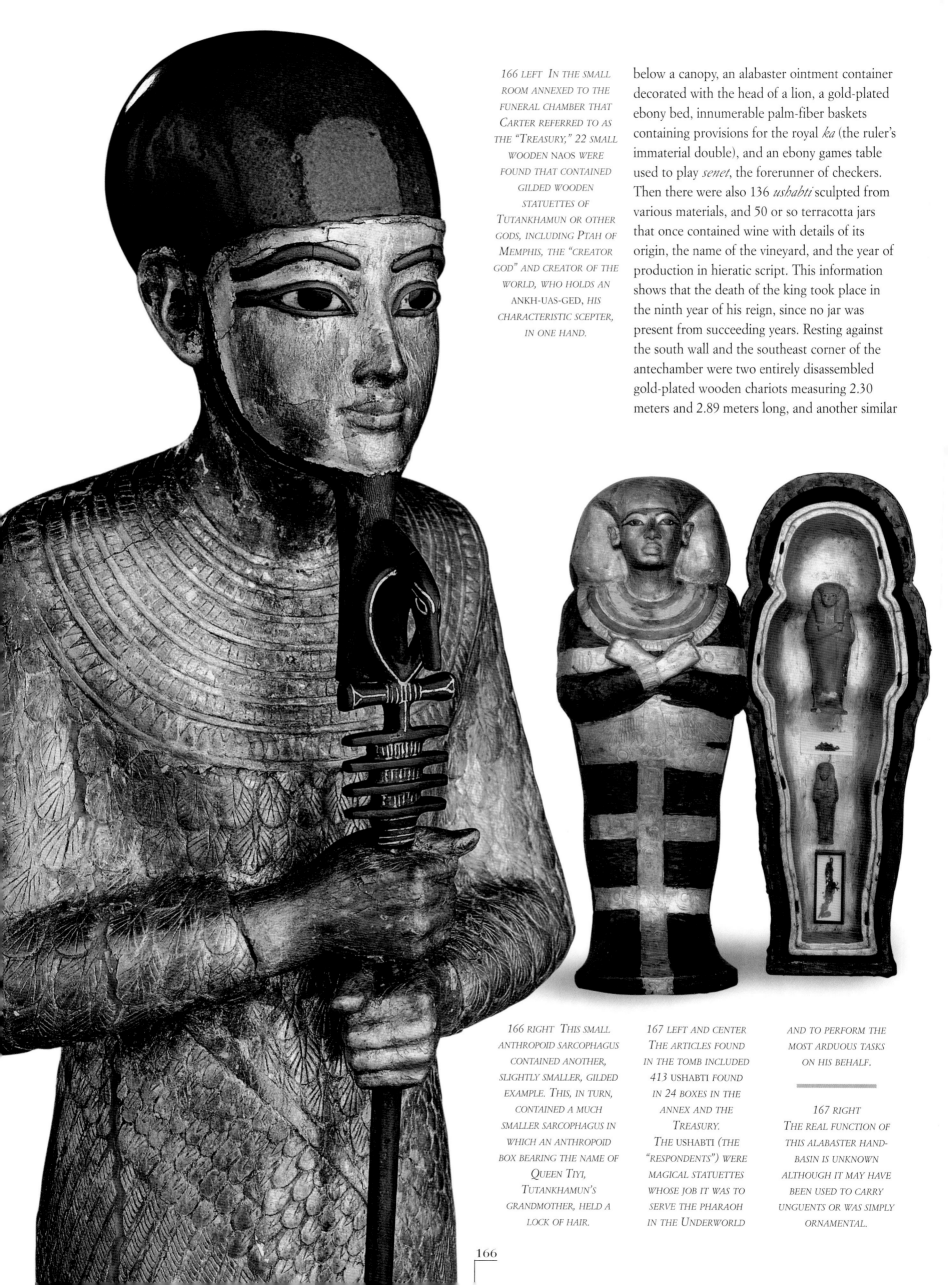

166 LEFT  IN THE SMALL
ROOM ANNEXED TO THE
FUNERAL CHAMBER THAT
CARTER REFERRED TO AS
THE "TREASURY," 22 SMALL
WOODEN NAOS WERE
FOUND THAT CONTAINED
GILDED WOODEN
STATUETTES OF
TUTANKHAMUN OR OTHER
GODS, INCLUDING PTAH OF
MEMPHIS, THE "CREATOR
GOD" AND CREATOR OF THE
WORLD, WHO HOLDS AN
ANKH-UAS-GED, HIS
CHARACTERISTIC SCEPTER,
IN ONE HAND.

below a canopy, an alabaster ointment container decorated with the head of a lion, a gold-plated ebony bed, innumerable palm-fiber baskets containing provisions for the royal *ka* (the ruler's immaterial double), and an ebony games table used to play *senet*, the forerunner of checkers. Then there were also 136 *ushabti* sculpted from various materials, and 50 or so terracotta jars that once contained wine with details of its origin, the name of the vineyard, and the year of production in hieratic script. This information shows that the death of the king took place in the ninth year of his reign, since no jar was present from succeeding years. Resting against the south wall and the southeast corner of the antechamber were two entirely disassembled gold-plated wooden chariots measuring 2.30 meters and 2.89 meters long, and another similar

166 RIGHT  THIS SMALL
ANTHROPOID SARCOPHAGUS
CONTAINED ANOTHER,
SLIGHTLY SMALLER, GILDED
EXAMPLE. THIS, IN TURN,
CONTAINED A MUCH
SMALLER SARCOPHAGUS IN
WHICH AN ANTHROPOID
BOX BEARING THE NAME OF
QUEEN TIYI,
TUTANKHAMUN'S
GRANDMOTHER, HELD A
LOCK OF HAIR.

167 LEFT AND CENTER
THE ARTICLES FOUND
IN THE TOMB INCLUDED
413 USHABTI FOUND
IN 24 BOXES IN THE
ANNEX AND THE
TREASURY.
THE USHABTI (THE
"RESPONDENTS") WERE
MAGICAL STATUETTES
WHOSE JOB IT WAS TO
SERVE THE PHARAOH
IN THE UNDERWORLD

AND TO PERFORM THE
MOST ARDUOUS TASKS
ON HIS BEHALF.

167 RIGHT
THE REAL FUNCTION OF
THIS ALABASTER HAND-
BASIN IS UNKNOWN
ALTHOUGH IT MAY HAVE
BEEN USED TO CARRY
UNGUENTS OR WAS SIMPLY
ORNAMENTAL.

but lighter model. The concept of the chariot had arrived with the Hyksos and from the 18th dynasty was used as a symbol of the power and strength of the king. Bas-reliefs and paintings of kings in battle always show them aboard chariots, sowing terror and destruction among their enemies.

Another extraordinary object found in the antechamber was a small gold-plated wooden *naos* that rested on a sled. This was a miniature reproduction of the ancient sanctuary of the vulture goddess Nekhbet, the protectress of Upper Egypt, as was indicated by the particular shape of the roof and the decorative bas-reliefs that showed 12 images of the goddess. The doors were held closed with silver chains but opened onto a bay in which there was a support for a small gold statue, probably removed by the

*168-169 DELICATE ALABASTER HEADS PORTRAYING THE SOVEREIGN ACTED AS STOPPERS FOR THE CANOPIC JARS THAT HOUSED THE DEAD KING'S INTERNAL ORGANS, EXCEPT FOR HIS HEART.*

thieves, and a pearl necklace with a pendant depicting the goddess Uerethekau, the "Great magician," suckling the king.

The walls at the sides were carved with bas-reliefs in the style of Amarna showing the royal couple at various moments of their family life. Two large wooden statues sprinkled with black resin and decorated with gilded elements stood near the north wall of the antechamber; a wooden box entirely painted with battle scenes shows the king on his chariot fighting Nubians and Asiatics and cutting down innumerable victims. The cover of the box – which contained the king's sandals and various articles of clothing – was painted with animals that were common at the time in Egypt: antelope, felines, and ostriches. The two statues, standing 1.90 meters high, represented the royal *ka* and had a protective function. One stood in each corner; the one on the left wore a *khayt*-headdress while the other wore a *nemes*-headdress. Both were shown, walking holding a long reed in the left hand and a gilded club in the right. An examination of the statues showed two cavities that originally would have held papyruses but which had been emptied and roughly closed. The statues stood on either side of a walled doorway covered by a layer of stucco into which the royal seals were impressed. In a small area at the bottom were the seals of the necropolis guards, indicating that they had closed a hole made

170 TOP THIS SMALL GOLD-PLATED WOODEN NAOS WAS USED TO HOLD A GOLDEN STATUE OF THE KING. THE STATUE WAS PROBABLY STOLEN BY THIEVES DURING THE TWO BREAK-INS AROUND THE YEAR 1319 BC.

170 BOTTOM THE INTERNAL ORGANS OF TUTANKHAMUN WERE HELD IN FOUR MINIATURE SARCOPHAGUSES PLACED INSIDE THIS ALABASTER TABERNACLE. THE TABERNACLE WAS DIVIDED INTO FOUR COMPARTMENTS CLOSED WITH FOUR LIDS, EACH DECORATED WITH THE IMAGE OF THE KING.

171 THE ALABASTER TABERNACLE CONTAINING THE CANOPIC JARS WAS HOUSED IN THIS LARGE GILDED WOODEN SHRINE. THE PROTECTIVE STATUES OF THE GODS (NEITH) WITH OUTSTRETCHED ARMS WERE PLACED IN THE CENTER OF THE WALLS.

172-173 TUTANKHAMON AND HIS WIFE, ANKHESENAMON, ARE SHOWN HUNTING WATER BIRDS ON ONE SIDE OF THE GILDED WOODEN NAOS HOUSING THE STATUE OF THE KING, WHICH WAS STOLEN BY TOMB ROBBERS.

there by the thieves.

When Carter removed a part of the wall, he saw a burial chamber completely filled by a gilded wooden shrine 6 meters long and 3 wide, decorated with a series of *ged*-pilasters that alternated with representations of *tit*-knots (the emblems of Osiris and Isis) engraved in the wood on a background of blue faïence. A space of only 76 centimeters was left between the shrine, closed by a two-wing door, and the walls of the funerary chamber. The shrine was decorated inside with passages from the *Book of the Dead* and contained, like Russian dolls, three other shrines all made from gilded wood and decorated with images of the world beyond the grave towards which the king had started on his long journey. The shrines had been assembled in the tomb before construction of the wall that separated the burial chamber from the antechamber, and Carter had to follow the procedure in reverse to be able to empty the tomb and study its contents.

This took roughly three months of continuous work. The doors of the innermost shrine, on which the images of the goddesses Isis and Nefti had been carved with their winged arms open in an attitude of protection, still showed the seal of the necropolis intact, demonstrating that the most important part of the tomb had remained untouched. The seal portrayed a jackal, evoking the god Anubis, crouching over nine bound prisoners who represented the enemies of Egypt. Once the seals had been removed and the doors of the fourth shrine opened, the pink quartzite sarcophagus could be seen. The four protective goddesses – Isis, Nefti, Neith, and Selkis – were sculpted, one at each corner, with their winged arms outstretched to protect the royal mummy. When the lid of the quartzite sarcophagus was lifted, Carter could see an anthropoid sarcophagus made from gilded wood covered by a linen shroud on which the king was represented in the guise of Osiris, with his arms folded on his

chest and hands holding the curved *heqa*-scepter and *nekhakha*-whip, the symbols of royal power.

This first anthropoid sarcophagus contained a second one, likewise covered by a linen shroud and a garland of lotus flowers, olive leaves and papyrus ribbons. Similar to the outer sarcophagus, the second one was made from gold-plated wood and was encrusted with blue, red, and green glass paste decorations arranged to form a sort of plumage. The king was once more portrayed in the likeness of Osiris in a true work of art that constitutes the most beautiful known example of the technique known as Egyptian *cloisonné*. This consists of filling small cells formed by welded gold threads with polychrome glass paste in a procedure that requires absolute precision and skill. This second and intermediate sarcophagus contained a third made from solid gold in the same form as the other two, completely sprinkled with perfumed resin and once more covered by a linen shroud and floral necklace. This final sarcophagus was 1.85 meters

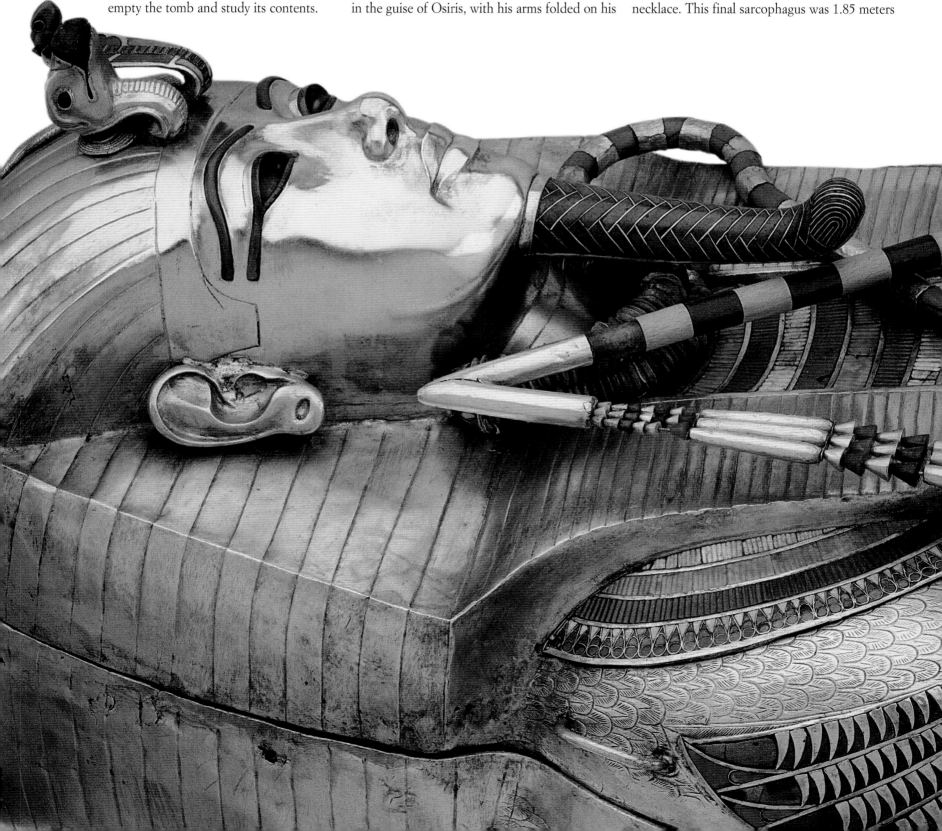

long and weighed 110.4 kilograms.

Once opened, the royal mummy could at last be seen covered with the famous mask, now one of the symbols of Egyptian civilization. Made from solid gold encrusted with semiprecious stones and polychrome glass paste, it is 54 centimeters tall, weighs a little more than 10 kg, and once again presents the king in the image of Osiris with his chin bearing a long ritual beard made from gold and encrusted with faïence. The forehead of the king, who wears the *nemes* headdress, is adorned with the heads of the vulture goddess Nekhbet and the cobra goddess Uaget, protectresses of Upper and Lower Egypt. Text engraved on the reverse of the mask cites Chapter 151b of the *Book of the Dead*, which places various parts of the king's body under the protection of different gods. The arms of the pharaoh were crossed and his hands covered with sheets of gold, holding the *heqa*-scepter and *nekhakha*-whip. The body of Tutankhamun, wrapped in linen bandages, was

*174-175 LIKE THE OTHERS, THE THIRD ANTHROPOID SARCOPHAGUS SHOWS THE PHARAOH WITH THE*

*FACIAL FEATURES OF THE GOD OSIRIS, BUT THIS SARCOPHAGUS WAS MADE FROM SOLID GOLD AND WEIGHS 110.4 KG.*

*175 TOP THIS BREASTPLATE IN THE FORM OF AN UGIAT EYE WAS FOUND AMONG THE MANY AMULETS FOUND ON THE MUMMY OF THE KING.*

*UGIAT MEANS "HEALED" IN THE SENSE THAT THIS WAS THE EYE OF HORUS WHO WAS INJURED BY SETH BUT HEALED BY THOT.*

*176 bottom left  As you can see in this section of a breastplate, the Egyptian goldsmiths were experts in the art of cloisonné. After creating a honeycomb on the surface to be decorated, they filled the holes with glass paste and semiprecious stones.*

*176 bottom right  The jewelry in the tomb contained many bracelets and armbands like this one, ornamented with a large* kheper-scarab *made from lapis lazuli in evocation of the Sun god Ra as he rises each morning on his journey across the sky.*

further protected by 143 amulets and precious objects, including a large chest-plate depicting the goddess Nekhbet in the form of a vulture with her wings spread, and two splendid ceremonial daggers a little over 30 centimeters long with finely decorated grips. The first, laid across the king's stomach, had a gold blade, while that of the second was made from iron, a metal from the Near East which at the time was very rare and precious. Other ornaments were 17 necklaces mostly made from gold, 24 bracelets, and 15 rings. The mummy measured 1.63 meters long but, despite the embalmers' skills, was in a mediocre state of preservation. An autopsy showed an incision 8.7 cm long had been made in the abdominal region to remove the internal organs and analysis of the epiphysial ossification allowed the age of the king to be estimated at between 17 and 19 years.

The king's hands were wrapped with sheets of gold and adorned by numerous rings bearing heraldic symbols. The top of his head had been completely shaven and covered by a linen bandage held in place by a gold band decorated with four cobras. Above these were spread the wings of the vulture of Nekhbet while the cobra of Uaget adorned the king's forehead.

Once the chamber had been emptied except for the quartzite sarcophagus, it was possible to examine the walls, the only paintings in the tomb. The decorations were very simple, particularly in comparison to the richness of the grave goods. Painted on a yellow background to symbolize gold, they showed fairly rare scenes and were notable for the absence of important religious texts. Three scenes were shown on the north wall: to the right is Tutankhamun's tutor and successor, Ay, wearing the skin of a wild cat typical of the *sem*-priest as he performs the ceremony of the "opening of the mouth" before the king portrayed in the guise of Osiris. In the center, the "Lord of the Two Lands, blessed with eternity," Tutankhamun, is shown in human form wearing the *ibes*-wig and standing in front of the goddess Nut, "Lady of the sky." To the left, the pharaoh is shown as a living ruler adorned with a *nemes*-headdress and followed by his *ka* as he embraces Osiris, the "Lord of the West."

On the west wall, we see a large scene inspired by the *Book of the Amduat* (the Book of that which is in the Underworld) in which 12 sacred baboons, in adoration of the sun, are set out on three horizontal registers. A fourth and higher register shows the bark of the Sun god Ra, shown in the guise of a *kheper*-scarab, which symbolizes the rising of the sun in the morning after completing its night-time journey and defeating the powers of darkness.

Only a small section of the south wall is decorated. It shows Tutankhamun in human form and wearing a white *khayt*-headdress; he is flanked by the god Anubis, who welcomes Tutankhamun with a gesture of his left arm, and

# The jewels of
# Tutankhamun

177 *THIS PENDANT IN THE
FORM OF A FALCON EVOKES
THE GOD RA-HARAKHTI
AND IS EVIDENCE OF THE
PERFECTION REACHED BY
THE ANCIENT EGYPTIANS IN
THE TECHNIQUE OF
CLOISONNÉ. THIS
TECHNIQUE PLACES GLASS
PASTE DECORATIONS AND
SEMIPRECIOUS STONES IN
HONEYCOMB SETTINGS.*

by the goddess Hathor-Imentet, "She that presides over the West," who attaches the symbol of eternal life, an *ankh*-cross, to his nose.

The east wall shows a funeral procession in which a group of 12 dignitaries, dressed in white and wearing the white band of mourning around their heads, drag the sarcophagus of Tutankhamun towards its eternal resting place. The sarcophagus lies inside a draped platform on a bark that in turn rests on a wooden sled. As the hieroglyphs proclaim above, the priests chant in loud voices, "O Nebkheperura, come in peace, o god, protector of the country!" Two figures with

shaven heads are probably Pentu e Usermontu, the vizier of Upper and Lower Egypt (similar to the role of a prime minister) and Horemheb, who was the person who held real power in the country.

A passageway through the east wall leads to a small side annex, referred to by Carter as the "treasury," in which a large gilded box that contained canopic jars was found on a sled. It was this box and its contents that turned out to be the most important find in the room. In front of the sanctuary, Carter found a gilded wooden head of the goddess Hathor in the form of a cow and a small *naos*, also of gilded wood, on which a black

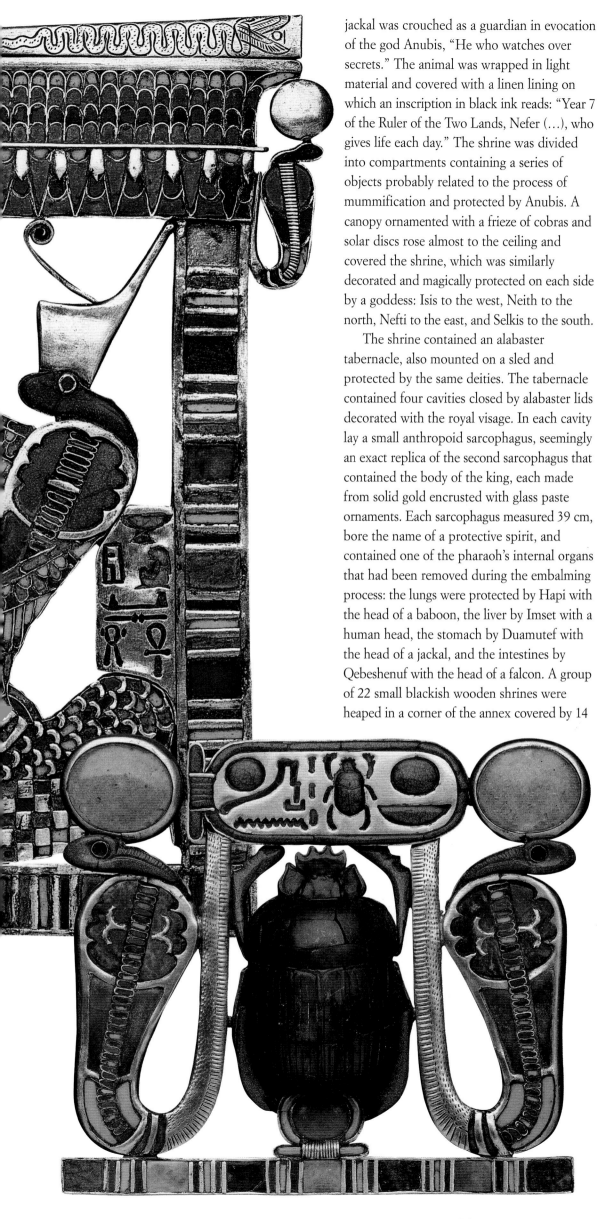

jackal was crouched as a guardian in evocation of the god Anubis, "He who watches over secrets." The animal was wrapped in light material and covered with a linen lining on which an inscription in black ink reads: "Year 7 of the Ruler of the Two Lands, Nefer (…), who gives life each day." The shrine was divided into compartments containing a series of objects probably related to the process of mummification and protected by Anubis. A canopy ornamented with a frieze of cobras and solar discs rose almost to the ceiling and covered the shrine, which was similarly decorated and magically protected on each side by a goddess: Isis to the west, Neith to the north, Nefti to the east, and Selkis to the south.

The shrine contained an alabaster tabernacle, also mounted on a sled and protected by the same deities. The tabernacle contained four cavities closed by alabaster lids decorated with the royal visage. In each cavity lay a small anthropoid sarcophagus, seemingly an exact replica of the second sarcophagus that contained the body of the king, each made from solid gold encrusted with glass paste ornaments. Each sarcophagus measured 39 cm, bore the name of a protective spirit, and contained one of the pharaoh's internal organs that had been removed during the embalming process: the lungs were protected by Hapi with the head of a baboon, the liver by Imset with a human head, the stomach by Duamutef with the head of a jackal, and the intestines by Qebeshenuf with the head of a falcon. A group of 22 small blackish wooden shrines were heaped in a corner of the annex covered by 14

model boats which were supposed to transport the dead king. Inside each shrine there were one or two ceremonial gilded wooden statues covered by small linen drapes: seven were of the king in various poses – hunting a hippopotamus with a harpoon, walking, riding on the back of a panther, etc. – the others represented a pantheon of 27 divinities. Ten wooden boxes contained 176 *ushabti* which, together with the 236 found in the annex and one in the antechamber, made 413 of these small statues in total equipped with 1866 various miniature farming tools. When the magic formulas were pronounced by the king, the *ushabti* would have come to life and been able to perform the arduous work required in the Underworld.

This brief examination of the tomb of Tutankhamun gives an idea of the complexity of the funerary rites of the ancient Egyptians. Terrestrial existence and the Underworld were two worlds linked by a concept of resurrection and immortality firmly rooted in the Egyptian soul that would only be equaled in Christianity 1300 years later.

182-183 IN THE TOMBS OF THE NECROPOLIS IN THE VILLAGE OF DEIR EL-MEDINA, WHERE THE CRAFTSMEN AND ARTISTS

WHO DUG AND DECORATED THE TOMBS OF THE NOBLES AND PHARAOHS LIVED, THE CULT CHAPELS WERE TOPPED BY SMALL ADOBE-

BRICK PYRAMIDS WITH A NICHE ON THE EASTERN SIDE WHERE THE STATUE OF THE DECEASED WAS PLACED.

183 TOP THE MORE THAN 500 PRIVATE TOMBS IN THEBES WERE GROUPED IN DIFFERENT NECROPOLISES BETWEEN THE VALLEY OF THE KINGS TO THE NORTH

AND THE VALLEY OF THE QUEENS TO THE SOUTH. THE LARGEST AND MOST IMPORTANT WAS THE ONE ON THE SLOPES OF THE HILL NAMED SHEIKH ABD EL-QURNA.

## LEGEND

a LARGE ENCLOSURE
b SMALL ENCLOSURE
c TEMPLE OF MENTUHOTEP
d TEMPLE OF HATSHEPSUT
e TOMBS OF THE NOBLES OF THE 11TH DYNASTY
f TEMPLE OF THUTMOSIS III
g TEMPLE OF AMENHOTEP II
h RAMESSEUM
i TEMPLE OF THUTMOSIS IV
l TEMPLE OF MERNEPTAH
m PTOLEMAIC TEMPLE

1 TT N 96 SENNEFER
2 TT N 100 REKHMIRE
3 TT N 69 MENNA
4 TT N 52 NAKHT
5 TT N 55 RAMOSE
6 TT N 1 SENNEGEM

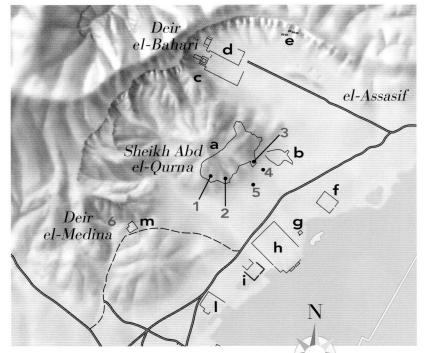

183 BOTTOM AN ENTIRE FUNERARY PROCESSION IS DEPICTED IN THE TOMB OF RAMOSE, "GOVERNOR OF THE CITY AND VIZIER" DURING THE TIME OF AMENOPHIS III/AMENOPHIS IV.

184-185 A MAGNIFICENT VIEW OF THE DEIR EL-MEDINA WORKERS' NECROPOLIS, WITH QUEEN HATSHEPSUT'S "TEMPLE OF MILLIONS OF YEARS" IN THE BACKGROUND.

186-187 DELICATE PLASTER RELIEFS SHOW THE VIZIER RAMOSE IN HIS TOMB.

# The tomb of SENNEFER

Sennefer

## and the tombs of the NOBLES IN THEBES

*Egypt*

DEIR EL-MEDINA
SHEIKH ABD EL-
QURNA

The private tombs that belonged to important figures, artists, and court dignitaries expressed the same theological and religious conceptions as the royal tombs but differed in their architecture and decorative themes. Whereas the funerary cult of the pharaohs was exclusively practiced in large memorial temples, the funerary cult of private individuals was celebrated in their actual tombs; but a tomb was more than simply the place where the body was buried, it included the area where the individual was worshipped.

### LEGEND

A ENTRANCE
B PYLON
C COURT
D STATUE OF THE DECEASED

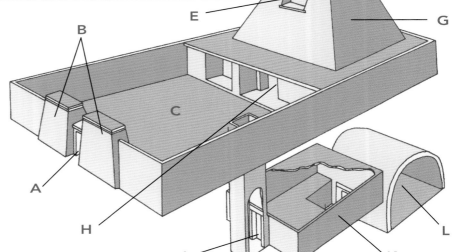

E STELE-DORMER    H CHAPEL    K VESTIBULE
F *PYRAMIDION*    I NICHE    L BURIAL
G ADOBE BRICK    J SHAFT    CHAMBER
PYRAMID

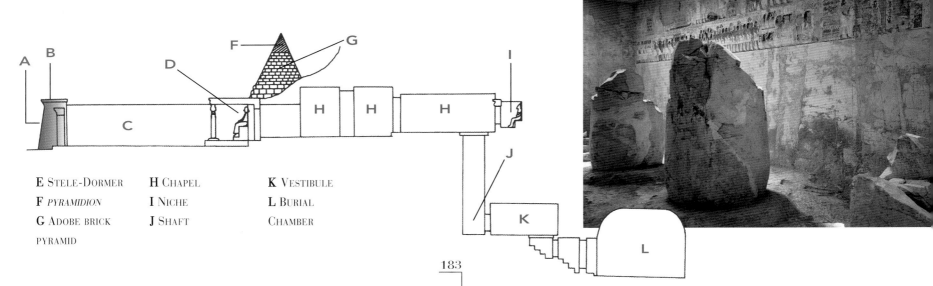

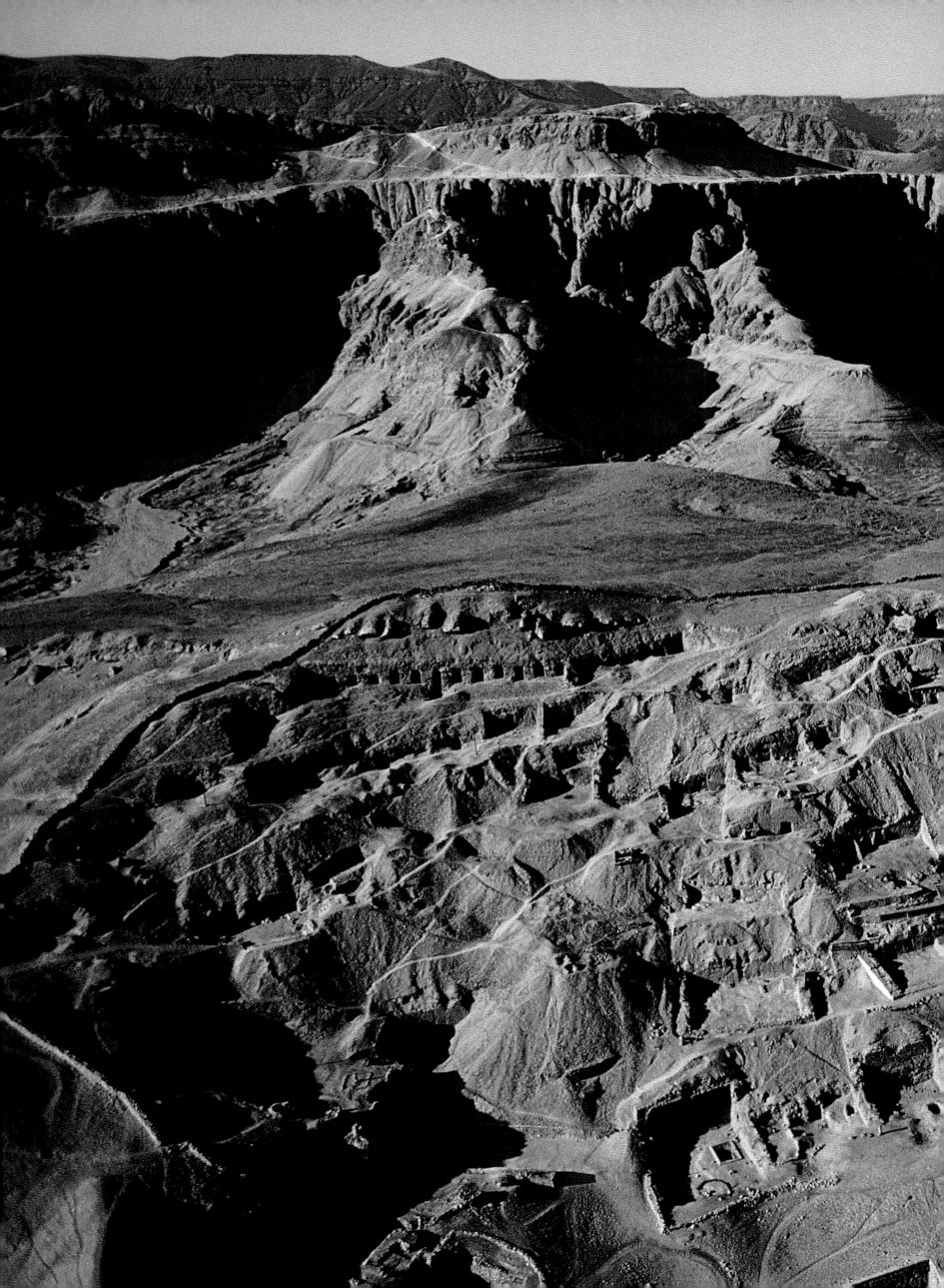

188 TOP  THE TOMB OF SENNEGEM WAS DISCOVERED INTACT IN 1886. THE WOODEN DOOR THAT CLOSED THE BURIAL CHAMBER WAS DECORATED WITH A SCENE IN WHICH THE DECEASED AND HIS WIFE INYFERTI PLAY AT SENET WHICH SYMBOLIZES THE "JUDGEMENT OF OSIRIS." THE OTHER SIDE OF THE DOOR (PICTURE ON THE RIGHT) SHOWS A SCENE AT THE TOP IN WHICH OSIRIS AND ISIS ARE WORSHIPPED AND, BELOW, PTAH-SOKARI-OSIRIS AND ISIS ARE WORSHIPPED.

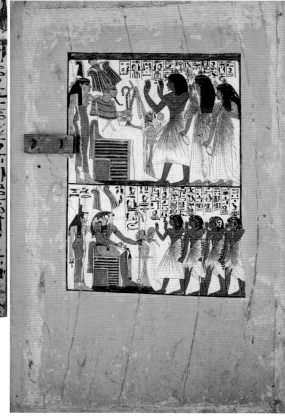

The architecture of private tombs expressed this double function by a clear separation of the area used for the interment of the body (an underground burial chamber generally reached via a vertical shaft that was sealed after the burial) and the chapel reserved for the cult of the deceased which, on a symbolic and functional level, corresponded to the royal memorial temples. The cult area generally consisted of a courtyard in front of the tomb entrance that may have been crowned by a small pyramid known as the *pyramidion*. The entrance led into a vestibule that lay transversal to the chapel, forming a ground plan in the shape of an upside-down T. The chapel was always decorated with polychrome wall-paintings and often contained a full-size statue of the deceased that was sometimes accompanied by statues of the man's wife and children.

A particular type of private tomb found in all the necropolises in the workers' village of Deir el-Medina was reserved for burial of the artists and workers who constructed and

188 BOTTOM  FOR THE ANCIENT EGYPTIANS, LIFE IN THE UNDERWORLD PASSED IN THE SAME MANNER AND WITH THE SAME RHYTHMS AS EARTHLY EXISTENCE. HERE, FOR EXAMPLE, WE SEE SENNEGEM SOWING SEEDS IN THE FIELDS OF IARU, AN IDYLLIC WORLD BEYOND THE GRAVE.

188-189  THE TOMB OF THE WORKER SENNEGEM IS DECORATED WITH SCENES OF LIFE AND WORK IN THE WORLD BEYOND THE GRAVE.

190-191  PASHEDU IS DEPICTED DRINKING WATER FROM A WELL ON THE WALL OF THE TOMB TO THE LEFT OF THE DOOR.

192-193  SENNEGEM AND HIS WIFE INYFERTI ARE PURIFIED BY A SEM-PRIEST, WHO CAN BE RECOGNIZED BY HIS LEOPARD SKIN.

decorated the large royal tombs. The entrance to the chapel in this model was always topped by an adobe pyramidion, and the part more richly decorated with paintings was, contrary to the normal design, the burial chamber. It was in this necropolis that the intact burial chambers of two tombs were discovered in 1886 and 1906 belonging to the workers' foreman, Sennegem, "Servant of the House of Truth," and the architect, Kha, "Head in the Great House," whose grave goods have shed much light on daily life in ancient Egypt. Kha's tomb contained five sarcophaguses belonging to himself and his wife Meryt; various sorts of furniture were arranged around the

sarcophaguses such as stools, small tables, a bed, boxes, caskets, and a wooden cabinet that contained Meryt's wig. There were also sheets of linen, various types of food and drinks, and even a crown made from flowers that could still be identified. A papyrus next to Kha's mummy contained practically the complete text of the *Book of the Dead*.

The other great difference between royal and private tombs was the contents of the scenes painted on the chapel walls, which in general depicted the daily life and earthly activities of the deceased rather than the Underworld.

Naturally passages and illustrations from the *Book of the Dead* and, in particular, the *Book of*

*Gates*, plus mythological and ritual scenes, the portraits of gods, offerings, and scenes of life in the Underworld were not completely ignored but were used in those rare cases in which wall-paintings decorated the burial chamber. However, themes of life beyond the grave were secondary to those depicting the earthly life of the deceased, who was the main character and inspirational theme of the entire decorative cycle. The link between these opposing iconographic motifs was the scenes portraying the funeral of the deceased which was nearly always shown; but, even in this case, the material, earthly scenes overshadowed the metaphysical ones.

The worldly part of the funeral ritual, generally not alluded to in the decorations of royal tombs with the exception of the tomb of Tutankhamun, is well documented in the private tombs where the paintings copiously describe, often with great artistic skill, the process and ritual of the embalming of the dead, the funeral procession with the servants carrying the funeral goods, the ceremonies relating to purification and entry into the tomb, the transportation of the sarcophagus into the burial chamber, and the large funerary banquet enlivened by musicians and dancers that was the final stage of the funeral ceremony. Our knowledge of the funerary ritual in use at the time of the Theban pharaohs comes very largely from these wall-paintings.

One of the commonest themes is the ritual pilgrimage of the deceased down the Nile to Abydos by boat. It was traditionally believed by ancient Egyptians that Abydos was the site of the tomb of Osiris, the god killed and dismembered by his wicked brother Seth. The body was pieced together again by Osiris' wife, Isis, who magically succeeded in bestowing life upon him once more and later gave birth to their son Horus. The body of the deceased was symbolically taken to Abydos (where the kings of the first dynasty were buried) to pay homage to Osiris, the symbol of resurrection and also Lord of the Underworld, in front of whose court the deceased was believed to present himself. Here, in the presence of 42 gods, the deceased was supposed to undergo the "Judgment of Osiris," in which his soul was weighed (*psychostasy*) as described in Chapter 125 of the *Book of the Dead*.

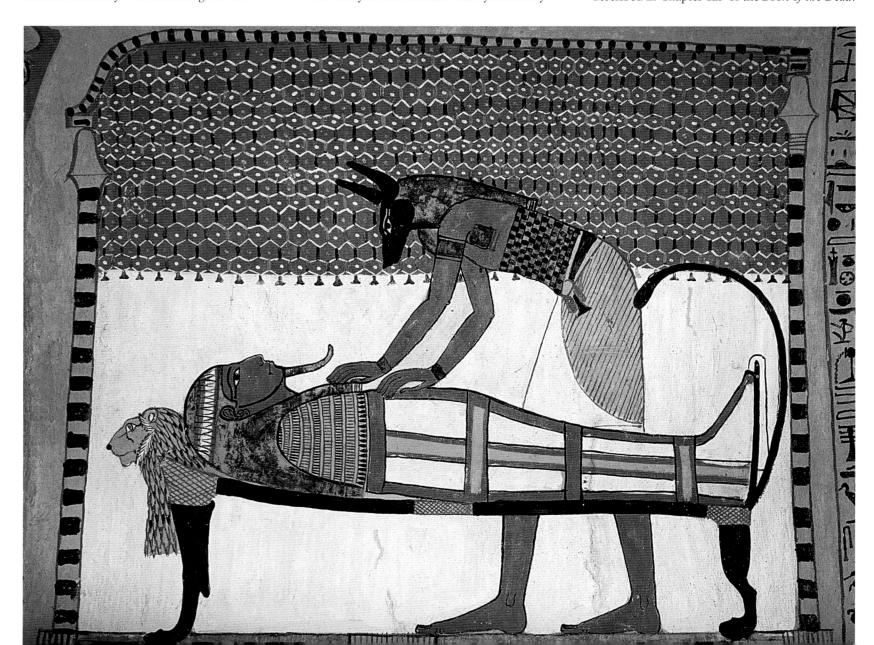

196-197 *In the tomb of Nakh (TT no. 52), the scribe and astronomer of Amon who lived during the reign of Thutmosis IV, the range of decorative elements is inspired by moments of daily life or the funeral ceremony of the deceased, as is shown by this splendid depiction of the funeral banquet that takes place to the music of a blind harpist.*

196 bottom
*This famous portrait of three young girls playing the harp, the lute and a flute of some kind is also taken from the banquet scene.*

197 bottom *In the tomb of Inerkhaou (TT no. 359), the "Foreman of the Lord of the Two Earths in the House of Truth" in the reign of Ramses II and Ramses IV (20th dynasty), the deceased is shown with his children and wife Waab before a priest who offers a container for ushabti.*

During this important stage of his underworld journey, the heart of the deceased (believed by the ancient Egyptians to be the seat of the soul and thought) was placed on the divine scale and its weight compared to that of the goddess Maat, the personification of cosmic order and sometimes represented by the hieroglyph of the ostrich feather that represents her name. The deceased would recite a "negative confession" before the divine assembly in which he declared the sins he had not committed during his earthly existence; the purpose of this was to purify himself and so allow the weight of his heart to be balanced against the weight of Maat. Only then could he be recognized as "justified" and be assimilated by Osiris himself.

Although emphasis was placed on the last stage of the deceased's earthly life, i.e., his death and funeral ceremony, the preferred and most often represented theme in tomb wall-paintings was unquestionably the deceased's daily activities. These were the inspiration for the most lyrical and loveliest paintings: agricultural activities from sowing to the harvest of the crops, fishing and bird-catching in the marshes, grape-picking and wine-making, preparation of foods, irrigation of gardens, and the manufacture of jewelry and articles to be used as grave goods were among the most widely

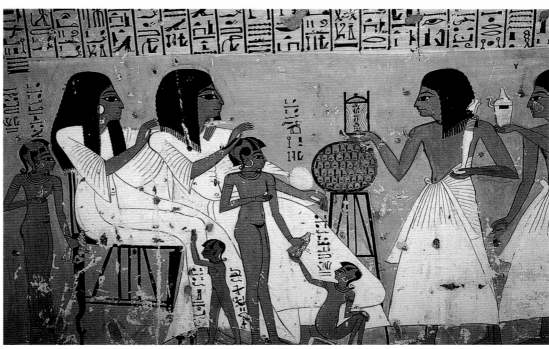

represented themes.

Often, many of the paintings were inspired by the public and private activities of the dead, who were generally important male court dignitaries. Scenes were often painted of the deceased during his official functions presiding over the collecting of taxes or the payment of tributes by foreign countries, checking agricultural work on the estates for which he was responsible, or inspecting workshops in which craftsmen are intent on their work.

In the scenes of everyday life, the deceased

was often shown together with his king during audiences with foreign delegations, during offerings of tributes or floral gifts, or perhaps worshipping the pharaoh in the form of a deity. Sometimes the pharaoh was shown alone in front of the other deities, or as a living being seated on his throne, or accompanied by his wife or children.

Frequent subjects in wall-paintings are the large religious festivals such as the feast of Montu, the Theban god of war, or the Festival of the Valley in which, once a year, the statues of Amon, his divine wife Mut, and their son Khonsu (the "Theban Triad") were transported by river from the temple of Karnak to the west bank from which a procession left directly for the temple of Deir el-Bahari.

On occasion, next to these solemn subjects, the paintings depicted small details of daily life that give us an idea of the actual experience of ancient Egyptians: for instance, a barber cutting the hair of a customer, a master beating a slave, or extraordinarily realistic paintings of small birds perching on branches, butterflies, locusts, birds' nests, and even a cat stalking possible prey in a papyrus bed.

Just as the royal tombs were grouped in the Valley of the Kings, the private tombs of important figures were concentrated in particular locations: on the slopes of the hill called Sheikh Abd el-Qurna halfway between the Valley of the Kings to the north and the Valley of the Queens to the south, in the workers' village of Deir el-Medina, and in other smaller necropolises situated near Sheikh Abd el-Qurna. Of the more than 400 private tombs in Theban

necropolises, perhaps the most representative from an artistic viewpoint is that of Sennefer, a powerful dignitary who took the title "Mayor of the City" and who lived during the reign of Amenhotep II (18th dynasty) in the second half of the 15th century BC.

The paintings in this dwelling of eternity are not only some of the most beautiful examples of Theban painting in the New Kingdom but also admirably illustrate the most important themes seen in the decoration of private tombs.

In addition, the paintings introduce important stylistic innovations. Sennefer's tomb was atypical architecturally and decoratively because the burial chamber was unusually large and completely covered with wall-paintings generally reserved for the public parts of the tomb, i.e., the chapel and vestibule. Also, the polychrome scenes were unusual in that the few paintings found in the burial chambers were inspired by the Underworld and contain passages from the *Book of the Dead* and the even older *Texts of the Pyramids*. Sennefer's tomb is dominated by the theme of the deceased and his wife Meryt, "the Beloved," united by a love that went beyond earthly life and was assimilated into the love that bound Osiris and Isis. In the paintings in the antechamber, Sennefer receives the offerings brought by a procession of priests headed by his daughter Mut-tuy, who offers her father an amulet in the form of a small heart made of lapis lazuli. A retinue of servants presents the grave goods and the ornaments that are to adorn the embalmed body of the deceased. The entire scene takes place below a pergola painted on the ceiling from which bunches of grapes hang in an evocation of the vine of Osiris that

200-201 *The ceiling of Sennefer's burial chamber is decorated with a grape-laden vine. A Sem-priest is shown purifying the deceased on the southern wall.*

200 bottom left *In the tomb of Sennefer, mayor of Thebes, the deceased is depicted beneath a sycomore tree with his wife.*

200 bottom right *Sennefer and Meryt are portrayed with a sekhem scepter and with lotus flowers.*

201 right *The pillars of the burial chamber are decorated with scenes of offerings made to Sennefer by Meryt – shown here handing her husband a cup with a drink – and amulets in the upper area.*

202-203 *At the foot of a sacred mountain, a falcon, a Ugiat eye and the deceased worker Pashedu are depicted worshipping the mummified Osiris, who receives a lighted brazier from a god facing him.*

represented the vital force of life and the god's regenerating power; the pergola was also responsible for the tomb being named the "Tomb of the Vines" by its first visitors. The unevenness of the rock in which the tomb was excavated was skilfully taken advantage of by the artists to give the decoration a three-dimensional effect previously unknown in Theban art.

The ceiling in the neighboring burial chamber is also partially decorated with the motif of the vine and in part with conventional geometric patterns; it is supported by four pillars entirely painted on each side. The paintings show 14 scenes of Sennefer receiving offerings from Meryt such as necklaces, lotus flowers, amulets, unguents, and balsams while

the decorations on two pillars illustrate the ritual of the Opening of the Mouth, also to be seen in the polychrome scenes on the east and south walls of the room. Another important theme shown in great detail is Sennefer's funeral in which his sarcophagus is carried to the necropolis, preceded by bearers of the grave goods and followed by friends and high court dignitaries. Other scenes on the north wall show Sennefer and his wife before tables heaped with offerings while hieroglyphic texts narrate that the scene depicts "Offerings that the king gives to Osiris, Lord of Eternity, so that he may procure bread and beer, meat and all things good and pure for the *ka* of Sennefer, justified." A large scene illustrates the ritual river pilgrimage to Abydos by

Sennefer and Meryt who sail a boat painted green to symbolize papyrus and, metaphorically, resurrection; this theme becomes prevalent in the last section of the decorations.

The tomb had a symbolic and ritual purpose that determined the entire decorative cycle in an evocation of the ritual journey through the Underworld of the deceased's soul which only concluded with its transformation and regeneration. Only then could the soul of the deceased "come out into the day." In the last of the scenes in the burial chamber, Sennefer and Meryt are shown standing as, now regenerated, they prepare to "come out into the day" and to see the "(solar) disc on its daily journey."

204 TOP LEFT  THE TEMPLE OF ALEXANDER THE GREAT WAS BUILT BY THE MACEDONIAN RULER WHEN HE PASSED THROUGH BAHARIYA ON HIS WAY BACK TO MEMPHIS HAVING CONSULTED THE ORACLE OF JUPITER AMON AT SIWA. IT IS ONE OF THE MOST IMPORTANT MONUMENTS IN THE OASIS AND IS SITUATED NEAR THE RECENTLY DISCOVERED NECROPOLIS.

204 TOP RIGHT  THE TOMBS FOUND IN THE GRAECO-ROMAN NECROPOLIS IN BAHARIYA OASIS IN THE LIBYAN DESERT IN EGYPT WERE DUG OUT OF THE LIMESTONE DEPOSITS OF THE SAHARA FORMED DURING THE TERTIARY ERA. EXCAVATION OF THE 13-SQUARE-MILE NECROPOLIS BEGAN IN 1999.

204-205 AND 205 BOTTOM  IN THE TOMBS OF BAHARIYA, DISCOVERED BY THE ARCHAEOLOGIST ZAHI HAWASS, THE DECEASED WERE ARRANGED NEXT TO EACH OTHER ACCORDING TO KINSHIP.

205 TOP  THE FACE OF ONE OF THE MUMMIES FOUND IN TOMB 54 IS ALMOST INTACT AND IS VIEWED BY THE ARCHAEOLOGISTS FOR THE FIRST TIME AFTER NEARLY 2000 YEARS.

# The golden mummies of

# BAHARIYA OASIS

Bahariya Oasis

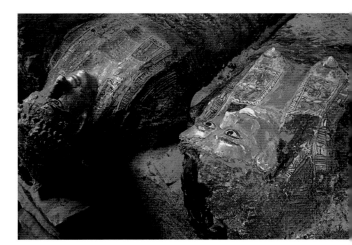

*206-207 LIKE THE TOMBS THAT IT HAS YIELDED, THE MODERN VILLAGE OF BAHARIYA IS CONSTANTLY THREATENED BY THE ADVANCING SANDS OF THE LIBYAN DESERT.*

Bahariya Oasis is the oasis furthest to the north of the four that lie in the easternmost section of the Sahara, the part of the Libyan Desert that lies in Egyptian territory. The origin of the name of the oasis is not certain, but it is quite probable that it is related to the Arab term *bahr,* which is commonly used to indicate the Mediterranean Sea (*el-bahr el-abiyad* = "the white sea"). As the Mediterranean marks Egypt's northern border, it is thought that the name "Bahariya" means "oasis of the north" as is cited in epigraphs dating from the Ptolemaic era.

Bahariya lies to the southwest of Cairo roughly 380 kilometers from the capital in a vast lens-shaped depression 94 kilometers long by 40 wide in which several limestone hills rise.

Egyptians have lived in this vast natural basin rich with thermal springs since the Middle Kingdom, the age during which the first important hydraulic works were

undertaken in the nearby region of Faiyum; the settlement grew especially at the time of the 18th dynasty when the oasis began to acquire a certain commercial and strategic importance. Its position allowed it to control the routes that connected the Nile valley with the western desert and Libya. This period saw the first funerary monuments in Bahariya, such as those a few kilometers from the modern village of el-Qasr.

They belonged to Amenhotep, called Huy, the governor of the oasis, and the bas-reliefs demonstrate that the region at that time was a center of wine and wheat production, which allowed the inhabitants to exist in a state of self-sufficiency.

During the 26th dynasty the oasis assumed a new level of importance. Following the disorders and uncertainties that characterized the Third Intermediate Period and the succeeding Ethiopian dynasties, the Saite rulers reorganized Egypt administratively and militarily while the Greeks took control of Cyrenaica, the region of Libya on the border of the Western Desert. During the reign of the pharaoh Amasi, Bahariya became the focal point of commerce between Libya and the Nile valley and consequently enjoyed a flourishing economy; the extent of its prosperity is shown by the four large tombs from this period that lie near the village of Bawiti, today considered the capital of the oasis. The

*208 TOP LEFT AND CENTER THE MUMMIES IN BAHARIYA OASIS WERE COVERED BY A LAYER OF*

*PLASTER THAT WAS THEN PAINTED WITH GOLD USING THE "CARTONNAGE" TECHNIQUE.*

*208 TOP RIGHT IN MANY CASES, THE MUMMIES WERE DECORATED WITH REPRESENTATIONS OF JEWELS AND THE HIEROGLYPHS OF FUNERARY TEXTS.*

*209 THE EYES AND EYEBROWS WERE PAINTED ON THE GILDED FACES OF THE BAHARIYA MUMMIES TO GIVE THE DEAD THE FEATURES OF THE LIVING.*

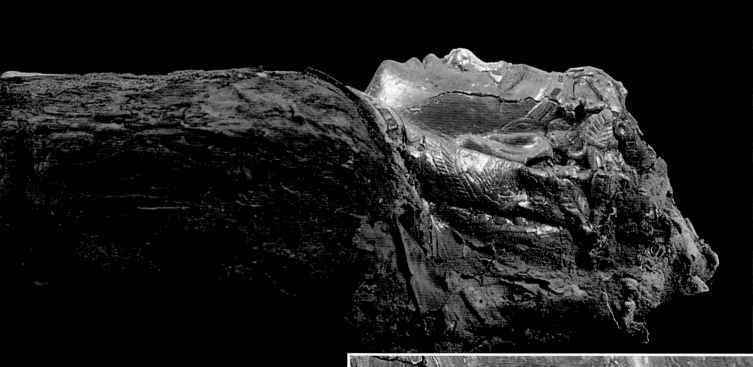

*208 BOTTOM THE CARTONNAGE ON ONE OF THE MUMMIES IN TOMB 54 REPRODUCED THE FEATURES OF A WOMAN VERY REALISTICALLY. THE IMAGE OF THE BA BETWEEN THE WOMAN'S BREASTS REPRESENTS THE SOUL OF THE DECEASED IN THE FORM OF A BIRD.*

# The golden mummies of Bahariya Oasis

210-211 *AFTER BEING CLEANED AND CONSOLIDATED, SOME OF THE MUMMIES FOUND IN TOMB 54 (ONE MAN, TWO WOMEN, AND TWO CHILDREN) WERE TAKEN TO THE INSPECTORATE OF ANTIQUITIES IN BAWITI, THE CAPITAL OF THE OASIS.*

210 *BOTTOM IT IS DIFFICULT TO ESTIMATE HOW MANY MUMMIES MAY BE BURIED IN THE NECROPOLIS, BUT ARCHAEOLOGISTS BELIEVE THERE MAY BE MORE THAN TEN THOUSAND.*

211 *TOP THE MUMMIFIED BODIES OF THE DEAD WERE LAID NEATLY IN NICHES EXCAVATED IN THE ROCK IN ACCORDANCE WITH A TYPICALLY GRAECO-ROMAN CUSTOM. AT THE TIME, THE POPULATION OF BAHARIYA OASIS NUMBERED APPROXIMATELY 30,000 PEOPLE.*

that was believed to be of such importance that it became a destination of pilgrimage.

Bahariya had become a center of importance when, in the second half of the fourth century BC, it was visited by Alexander the Great on his return from a trip to the Siwa oasis, the site of a temple where the famous oracle of Jupiter Amon practiced. The purpose of the Macedonian general's visit was to obtain divine confirmation of his direct claim to the Egyptian throne.

Alexander had a temple built at Bahariya which he dedicated to himself. It can still be seen in the locality of Qasr al-Megisbah and was until a few years ago the most famous monument in the oasis.

In 1996, the famous Egyptian archaeologist, Zahi Hawass, and his team discovered an

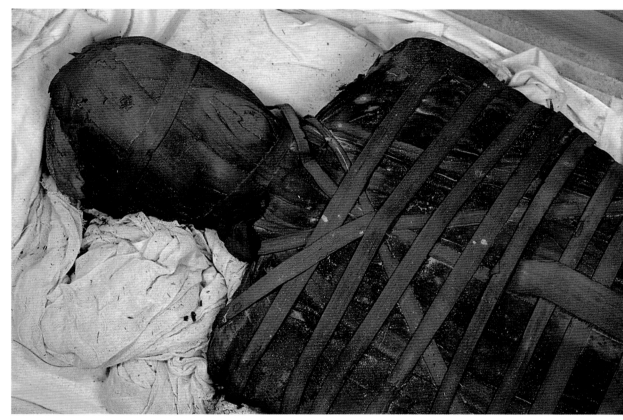

211 CENTER THE FACE OF THE DECEASED, A MAN OF ABOUT 35 WHOSE BODY WAS CAREFULLY WRAPPED IN THIN BANDAGES OF LINEN IMPREGNATED WITH RESIN, SHOWS NO TRACE OF DECORATION.

tombs belonged to two important state dignitaries named Petasthar and Thaty, who were responsible for the administration of the territory, and two rich merchants, Gedamonefankh and Bannentiu, who were father and son. The two latter tombs were dug underground just a few meters from one another and boast wall decorations of exceptional beauty based on Theban models. Also dating from this period is the first large common tomb discovered in Bahariya, situated roughly a kilometer further southwest in a site called Qarat al-Farargi ("the hill of the chicken seller"). This is an immense necropolis but not for humans; instead it was used to bury the bodies of the ibis, a bird that is no longer seen in Egypt today but which used to be considered the symbol of the god Thot. Thousands of mummified ibises have been found in a labyrinth of corridors and underground rooms

immense necropolis dating from the Roman era. Excavation began in 1999 and has already confirmed that it is the largest and most important burial site from this period ever found in Egypt. First estimates put the number of graves distributed over an area of 36 square kilometers at several hundred. This extraordinary find has been the subject of numerous articles and television reports by the world's press and has made the name of Bahariya famous in just a few months.

The four tombs excavated so far contained dozens of mummies in a perfect state of preservation, many of which were prepared using a particular technique called *cartonnage*, in which the face of the mummy wore a mask made from linen bandages soaked in chalk, then covered with a thin layer of gilded paint. The final decoration – floral patterns in evocation of regeneration, or the figures of deities connected

213 CENTER RIGHT *THE PERFECT STATE OF PRESERVATION OF THE MUMMIES OF BAHARIYA IS PROBABLY DUE MORE TO THE FAVORABLE CLIMATIC CONDITIONS OF THE DESERT THAN THE EMBALMING PROCESS, WHICH WAS RATHER SIMPLER THAN THAT USED IN ANCIENT EGYPTIAN TIMES.*

213 BOTTOM RIGHT *THE CARTONNAGE TECHNIQUE, IN USE SINCE THE MIDDLE KINGDOM, GENERALLY REPLACED THE SARCOPHAGUS DURING THE GRAECO-ROMAN ERA. THE REFINEMENT OF THE DECORATIVE TECHNIQUES USED IS INDICATIVE OF THE ADVANCED ECONOMY OF THE OASIS.*

# The golden mummies of
# Bahariya Oasis

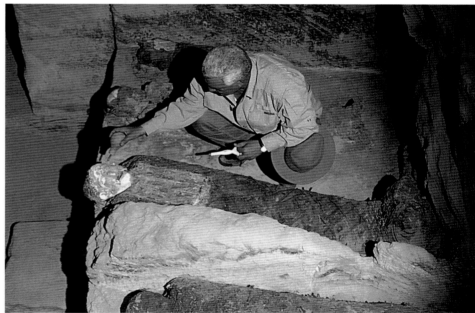

with the funerary world, or representations of protective amulets – was painted or modeled on the gold leaf. Eyes were painted in an attempt to reproduce the features of the deceased as realistically as possible.

Some of the mummies were placed in simple clay, anthropoid sarcophaguses devoid of inscription. They display decorative elements that were typical of the Roman era in Egypt, for example, motifs from the pharaonic age combined with classical designs, and gods from the Egyptian pantheon side by side with those from Roman mythology. The tombs so far studied at Bahariya were dug out of the rock like those from the 26th dynasty; they were, however, used as communal necropolises which was a common practice at the time and continued in Christian catacombs.

The most important tomb examined is number 54. A narrow staircase leads down to a first burial chamber, then a second chamber follows with entrances in the walls to a lateral room on either side. The tomb contained about forty mummies in perfect condition thanks to the lack of

*212 THE CARTONNAGE SHOWS THE FEATURES, HAIR, AND ORNAMENTS OF THE DECEASED. THE BACKGROUND COLOR OF GOLD REPRESENTED THE METAL WHICH, FOR THE EGYPTIANS, SIGNIFIED THE INCORRUPTIBLE FLESH OF THE GODS.*

*213 LEFT SOMETIMES THE BODIES OF THE MUMMIES WERE DECORATED WITH REPRESENTATIONS OF PROTECTIVE AMULETS CONNECTED WITH THE FUNERARY CULT.*

*213 TOP RIGHT THE DECORATION ON THE HEAD OF THIS MUMMY FAITHFULLY REPRODUCES HUMAN HAIR AND, ABOVE, THE TYPICAL REPRESENTATION OF THE GOD HORUS IN GRAECO-ROMAN TIMES IN THE FORM OF A HAWK.*

the final quality. Except in a few cases, the body of the deceased was no longer placed in a wooden anthropoid sarcophagus but simply wrapped in linen bandages. The mask of gilded plaster that covered the faces of many of the later mummies symbolized the sarcophagus and replaced it.

The discovery of the Roman necropolis at Bahariya and its famous "golden mummies" throws new light not only on the embalming techniques used during that period, but above all offers valuable information on the whole population of the oasis, in particular its eating habits and illnesses.

214 SOME BODIES IN TOMB 65, CLOSE TO TOMB 54, WERE BURIED IN SIMPLE CLAY SARCOPHAGUSES WITHOUT DECORATIONS OR INSCRIPTIONS.

215 TOP THIS PAINTING IN THE TOMB OF A RICH MERCHANT CALLED BANNENTIU DEPICTS RA'S SOLAR BARK SUPPORTED BY THE GOD SHU.

moisture, typical of the desert, that in many cases makes natural mummification possible.

By the Graeco-Roman age, mummification had become a fairly simple, rapid, and economic procedure which could be used on many of the dead rather than just the few rich members of society as was the case during the pharaonic era. The process of embalming had lost much of its magical and religious aspect, and the mummies were prepared in large numbers in enormous laboratories. These no longer belonged to the priests but to specialized workers who tried to use the minimum quantities of precious balsams, though of course to the detriment of

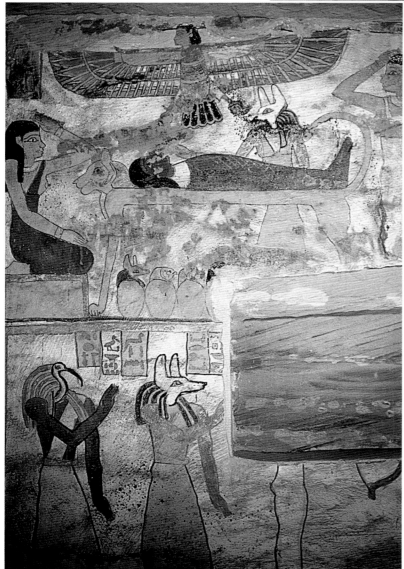

215 CENTER MANY TOMBS FROM THE 26TH DYNASTY, LIKE THAT OF BANNENTIU, WERE DECORATED WITH PICTURES SIMILAR TO THOSE IN THEBAN TOMBS.

215 BOTTOM LEFT DECORATIONS IN THE TOMBS FROM THE 26TH DYNASTY (664-525 BC) ILLUSTRATE THEMES TYPICAL OF CLASSICAL FUNERARY ICONOGRAPHY BUT WERE TREATED IN A VERY DIFFERENT STYLE.

215 BOTTOM RIGHT THIS PICTURE OF BANNENTIU'S TOMB SHOWS ANUBIS MUMMIFYING THE BODY OF THE DECEASED, WHO LIES ON A FUNERARY BED. HIS SOUL IS REPRESENTED BY THE BIRD BA WITH SPREAD WINGS.

# NEMRUD DAGH:

Nemrud Dagh:

Turkey ✦ NEMRUD DAGH

## Near the heavenly thrones

After defeat at the hands of the Romans at the battle of Magnesia ad Sipylum in 189 BC, the powerful Seleucid empire, inheritor of some of the conquests of Alexander the Great and then including much of the Anatolian peninsula and the Near East, began to fall apart as new kingdoms sprang up within its territories. The rulers of the new political entities were important local figures such as priests or generals who wished to establish their own royal power plus the independence and political autonomy of their states. One of these kingdoms was Commagene, a small mountainous region between the Euphrates and the Taurus mountains. The land was inhospitable due to the severe climate that prevailed for most of the year, but it was rich in natural resources and above all strategically important for its position as a corridor that had to be passed through by anyone wishing to travel between the East and West. This role shaped the entire history of the region, particularly during the final century BC when it was the target of the expansionist policies of the new rulers of the world: the Romans to the west and the Parthians to the east.

In spite of continuous pressures from its two great neighboring empires, the political skills of the kings of Commagene kept the small kingdom

independent for almost three centuries until it was finally annexed into the Roman empire in 72 AD by Emperor Vespasian.

The most important of the kings of Commagene was Antiochus I, who reigned from 62 to 38 BC, right in the middle of the civil wars that marked the end of the Roman Republic. Although Antiochus was allied to Pompey (who was defeated by Caesar), and despite having veiled sympathies for the Parthians and being defeated by Lucullus and Mark Anthony, Antiochus I maintained his power solidly for more than 30 years, in the course of which he launched a most unusual dynastic and religious program. The nature of the land on the borders of his kingdom, the coexistence of different cultures, and the desire to justify the absolute authority and prestige of himself and his heirs were the reasons why Antiochus established a new religion that included Greek and Persian deities but in which the king and his forefathers played a fundamental role.

The cult monuments dedicated to this new religion were the *hierothèsia*, i.e., the monumental tombs of the kings of Commagene, the most important of which was the tomb of Antiochus I. This was a funerary mound decorated with colossal statues build on the peak known today as Nemrud Dagh. The mountain stands 2150 meters high, relatively isolated in the Ankar Daglari chain, and for more than half the

*216 THE PHOTOGRAPH SHOWS THE HEADS OF TWO COLOSSAL STATUES (ZEUS OROSMADES AND ANTIOCHUS I) THAT DECORATED THE TOMB OF THE KING OF COMMAGENE BUILT ATOP MOUNT NEMRUD DAGH.*

*217 TOP THE ARTIFICIAL FUNERARY MOUND ON THE EAST TERRACE, 50 METERS HIGH, CONTAINS THE REMAINS OF ANTIOCHUS I, BUT THEY HAVE NEVER BEEN FOUND DESPITE SCIENTIFIC INVESTIGATIONS.*

*217 CENTER THE HEADS OF THE EAGLE AND LION ARE THE DIVINE SYMBOLS USED TO PROTECT THE TOMB OF ANTIOCHUS I, KING OF COMMAGENE.*

*217 BOTTOM LEFT THE PORTRAIT IN THE PHOTOGRAPH WAS LONG MISTAKENLY IDENTIFIED AS BEING OF APOLLON MITHRA HELIOS HERMES; IT IS INSTEAD ANTIOCHUS I. THE TWO CAN BE DISTINGUISHED BY THEIR HEADDRESSES.*

year is covered in snow. It may not be the tallest mountain in the area, but it is visible from almost anywhere in the region; perhaps this was the reason Antiochus chose it as the location for his tomb. Compared to other monumental complexes in modern Turkey, Nemrud Dagh was discovered very late (in 1881) and quite by chance when Charles Sester, a German engineer charged with finding new communication routes with eastern Anatolia, wished to verify the stories of local shepherds of a mountain ringed by enormous statues. Due to the height of the mountain and the sheer size of the remains, the news of the find was initially greeted with skepticism and incredulity, but following expeditions led by German scholars (Karl Humann and Otto Puchstein in 1882-83) and Turkish experts (Hamdi Bey and Osgan Effendi in 1883), pictures and stories of this monument spread around the world. After an initial exploration in 1939, extensive archaeological

The paths were walked twice a year by the king's subjects on the festivals (December-January) that celebrated the king's birthday and his ascension to the throne (July), and twice a month by priests on the days the cult was celebrated. The third terrace, which faces north, was an intermediate stage of the road that ran around the base of the mound.

The complete religious program including all the details of the cult's celebrations (which required the priests to wear Persian costume and to have the resources to provide food and wine to the celebrants) is known from a long inscription carved on the back of the huge statues that stand on the two main terraces. In this long text, Antiochus advocated the new faith as a fundamental element in the happiness of his subjects and their descendants, and as a guarantee of hope and salvation in the face of dangers and desperate situations that the king himself had experienced. The eastern terrace seems to have played the more important role in the cult, as is

investigations and geophysical surveys were carried out from 1953 to 1973 under the direction of Theresa B. Goell with the aim of excavating and studying the site and of finding the burial chamber of Antiochus I himself, but this has remained undiscovered even to the modern day. The monument built by Antiochus I on the peak of Nemrud Dagh was a mound 50 meters high with a base diameter of roughly 150 meters. The base was created with 3 terraces partially dug out of the rock, and the stone and rubble produced by that work were used to create the mound above. The two largest terraces, located on the east and west sides, were the point of arrival for processional paths that wound up the mountain.

indicated by a large monumental altar in the form of a truncated pyramid on the east side. On the opposite side, the enormous statues were erected on a base over 6 meters higher than the surface of the terrace; at either end, two bases bore the images of an eagle and a lion (now fallen) which respectively symbolized the heavens and monarchy.

The statues of seated gods between 8 and 10 meters high still dominate the scene. Zeus Oromasdes sits in the center, flanked on the left by the personification of Commagene with the features of Tyche, and to the right by Apollon Mithra Helios Hermes. To the sides of these three figures sit the deified King Antiochus and

Herakles Artagnes Ares. The statues were made from blocks of local limestone, but today all are missing their heads and suffer from cracks due to the weather and the extremes of temperature. At one time the statues were completely smooth as their enormous size, sculpted to be seen from afar, made detailed facial features and clothing unnecessary as can be seen in the beards of Zeus Orosmades and Herakles Artagnes Ares and in the treatment of the clothes.

There is an intermediate step between the level of the largest statues and the terrace on which a green sandstone cycle of reliefs of *dexiosis* (i.e., acceptance) shows Antiochus I greeting and being accepted by each deity. There is also the astrological

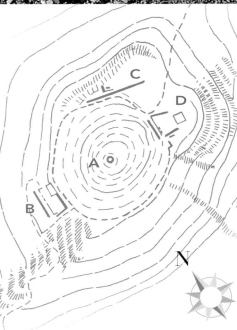

*219 BOTTOM  NOTE THE REPRESENTATION OF THE HOROSCOPE OF ANTIOCHUS I ON THE RELIEFS OF THE LOWER PLATFORM MADE FROM GREEN SANDSTONE; THE HOROSCOPE IS ONE OF THE EARLIEST KNOWN AND REPRESENTS THE DATE, 7 JULY, 61 BC.*

## LEGEND

**A** THE FUNERARY MOUND

**B** THE WEST TERRACE

**C** THE NORTH TERRACE

**D** THE EAST TERRACE

which incense was burned on the occasion of each religious festival.

The terrace on the west side of the mound was set up slightly differently: the rear was also lined with enormous statues, while the king's ancestors were arranged on the south and west sides (respectively representing his Persian and Macedonian sides) so that the sculptures formed a court enclosed on three sides. When discovered, the statues had almost all collapsed on the ground as a result of earthquakes, erosion of the mound, and perhaps the efforts of treasure hunters attempting to reach the burial chamber. This has meant that some of the reliefs of the king's ancestors have been preserved in excellent condition, particularly those in which the gods

relief of the lion which has survived almost intact on the opposite terrace. The north and south sides of the terrace are bounded by low walls made from blocks of stone that form two platforms on which slabs showing reliefs were placed. Today they are mostly in pieces, but they showed the representations of Antiochus's forefathers (whether real or presumed), each accompanied by explanatory inscriptions on the back. The north platform shows 15 of Antiochus's forefathers on his father's side including the kings of Commagene and Persia as far back as Darius the Great, while on the south side his ancestors on his mother's side are represented. These comprise 4 queens and 13 kings, among which Alexander the Great was in all likelihood included. A rectangular altar stood in front of each image on

show their acceptance of Antiochus I. The king and a god are shown in profile greeting one another in each scene of this colossal cycle. Antiochus wears a crown and carries a scepter but is shown wearing Eastern dress. The same gods are shown but are represented with different iconographies; Apollon Mithra Helios Hermes is also shown wearing Eastern dress; he also holds a *barsom* (bundle of twigs) and has a radiating halo. Herakles Artagnes Ares is shown as the classical version of Hercules, naked with a lion skin and a club. The series is completed by a very famous relief known as the "astrological lion relief." It shows the front view of a lion with its jaws wide open; on its neck it carries a crescent moon while in the background and on its body 19 stars with 8 rays form the constellation of Leo. In the top left, 3 larger stars with 16 rays represent, as indicated in the inscriptions, the planets Jupiter, Mercury, and Mars. The precision of the representation clearly refers to a horoscope (perhaps the oldest yet discovered) representing a day associated with personal events in the king's life. Identification of this day has long been a topic of debate among scholars. The elements in the relief show that Antiochus's horoscope was under

the constellation of Leo with the three planets in conjunction with the moon. The most probable date is therefore 7 July, 61 BC, the day that corresponds to the official concession of the kingdom to Antiochus by Pompey following the provisory granting by Lucullus in 69 BC.

The desire to build such a massive and costly tomb in such an improbable place may seem the bizarre whim of an extravagant monarch, but the text in the long inscription and the interpretation of the sculptures make the king's intention clear. This project of Antiochus I, part religious, part propaganda, was based on his desire to have his tomb "near to the heavenly thrones," almost as if to justify his close links with the gods.

The ambitious religious project to unite utterly diverse traditions and religious concepts only survived for a few generations, in the course of which the king's successors had their own *hierothèsia* built, though on a much smaller scale than Nemrud Dagh.

All that remains of the cult is the unique appeal of the time-defying monument that still holds the remains of Antiochus I despite twenty years of scientific research.

222-223 *ALTHOUGH NOW IN RUINS, THE HIEROTHESION OF ANTIOCHUS I STILL EVOKES A SENSATION OF POWER IN THE OBSERVER. THE GRANDEUR OF THE HUGE FALLEN HEADS — IN THIS CASE ZEUS AND AN EAGLE WITH A PROTECTIVE FUNCTION — IS FURTHER EMPHASIZED BY THE SOLITUDE AND RUGGEDNESS OF THE SITE.*

# The great rock tombs of PETRA

Jordan

PETRA

Petra

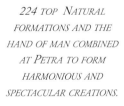

224 TOP NATURAL FORMATIONS AND THE HAND OF MAN COMBINED AT PETRA TO FORM HARMONIOUS AND SPECTACULAR CREATIONS.

224 CENTER THE STEEP ROCK FACES IN THE VALLEY OF PETRA FORMED A NATURAL DEFENCE BUT THEY WERE DUG OUT TO FORM HUNDREDS OF TOMBS OVER THE COURSE OF THREE CENTURIES.

Petra was the capital of the Nabataeans, a people historically attested from the fourth century BC that originated in the desert between modern Jordan and Saudi Arabia. Nomadic for a long time, the Nabataeans settled during the first century BC in sites that they had previously used on a seasonal basis. Of these, the most important was Petra (Reqem in the Nabataean language) that lies almost midway on the only road that connects the Red Sea with the Dead Sea. Sited in a valley hidden between steep mountains and only accessible through a few natural entrances, it was an ideal refuge for merchants who were not too proud also to steal and plunder. Their wealth and power resulted from two factors: their trade in the exotic goods in heaviest demand (especially oriental spices) and the progressive pacification of the Mediterranean. Based on a monarchical society and with their

own language and religion, they founded cities and conquered territories that included Damascus and part of Syria. The independence of the Nabataean kingdom lasted until 106 AD when the region was conquered by the Roman emperor, Trajan, and turned into the province of Arabia, but even under Roman domination, the capital remained Petra. It continued to prosper by maintaining its role as a caravan centre and an obligatory stop for all merchants passing by the Red Sea on their way from India or the East to the ports of the Mediterranean. The city declined with the collapse of the Roman Empire during the late-ancient era

*224 BOTTOM THE EFFECTS OF WIND EROSION CREATE ATTRACTIVE FORMS AND HIGHLIGHT THE COLORS OF THE SOFT SANDSTONE. NOTE THE CORINTHIAN TOMB IN THE BACKGROUND.*

*224-225 ED-DEIR IS DECENTRALIZED IN RESPECT TO THE OTHER MONUMENTS OF PETRA. THIS FINE VIEW, TAKEN FROM THE WEST, SHOWS ITS AUSTERE, BARE FAÇADE THAT LOOKS OUT OVER THE EMPTY DESERT.*

*226 AND 227 THE ELABORATE FAÇADE OF EL-KHAZNEH (LEFT) AND THE AREA OF THE THEATER (RIGHT) BECOME EVEN MORE EVOCATIVE IN THE DETAILED WORKS OF DAVID ROBERTS.*

and was at one stage temporarily occupied by the Crusades but was then remained inaccessible to Europeans for centuries. Its location was forgotten and its name passed into legend as a mythical city of inestimable treasures. Petra was rediscovered in 1812 by the Swiss traveller J.L. Burckhardt who reached the city in the guise of an Arab pilgrim who wished to perform a sacrifice on the peak of the nearby Jebel Harun.

There are many reasons for Petra's uniqueness. The valley and the narrow gorges occupied by the ancient city were created over the centuries by the passage of the torrent known today as Wadi Musa; steep walls of sandstone were formed that display geological layers of rock colored grey, pale yellow and bright violet but predominantly pink. The hand of man has added to this extraordinary natural phenomenon with constructions but, most of all, by digging the tombs of the kings and most important figures in the history of the city out of the rock face. In addition to their excellent condition, abundance and remarkable size, the funerary monuments display unique stylistic and compositional elements in a combination of architectural traditions from ancient Egypt, the Hellenised world and the Near East. The tombs at Petra are also special for one more peculiarity: a cruel stroke of fate has left only three funerary buildings with their rock inscriptions as either the soft stone in which they were carved has been worn away by the action of the wind or they were painted on plaster which has since fallen off. This silence is added to by the fact that all the tombs have been entered and robbed of their grave goods so that we have no means with which to date them with precision and this has resulted in many scientific debates about the chronology and attribution of individual buildings.

The first tombs lie in the area in front of the main entrance to the city along the sides of the dry river bed of the Wadi Musa. Two of these stand out for the presence of completely different architectural traditions: the Obelisk Tomb and the Bab el-Siq Triclinium. The first is carved out of the rock directly above the second and though their burial chambers are almost perfectly parallel, their façades are differently aligned.

The façade of the Obelisk Tomb is unique among the funerary structures at Petra: four obelisks originally 7 meters high stand on the lower storey in which the entrance to the burial chamber opens. The chamber is framed by two pillars crowned by a Doric frieze decorated with metopes and triglyphs. A niche between the two middle obelisks has the same decoration and the almost completely eroded relief of a male figure in Greek dress. The mixture of different architectural styles is typical of Petra and in this case especially

*228 TOP THE DJINN BLOCKS ARE LOCATED CLOSE TO THE ENTRANCE TO THE SIQ AND ARE DIFFERENT FROM THE OTHER BUILDINGS AT PETRA. POPULAR LEGEND DESCRIBES THEM AS BEING THE HOUSES OF SPIRITS.*

———————

*228 CENTER AND 228-229 IT IS NOT KNOWN IF THERE WAS A CONNECTION BETWEEN THE OBELISK TOMB AND THE BAB EL-SIQ TRICLINIUM. THE TWO WERE BUILT ALMOST ONE ABOVE THE OTHER BUT IN UTTERLY DIFFERENT STYLES AND USING DIFFERENT ARCHITECTURAL FEATURES.*

*230-231 A SERIES OF ERODED MAUSOLEUMS DELINEATE THE ROCKY WALL IN THE AREA OF THE ROYAL TOMBS, FACING WEST. THE FAÇADE VISIBLE ON THE FAR LEFT BELONGS TO THE PALACE TOMB. AT CLOSE QUARTERS IT RESEMBLES A TYPICAL PEDIMENT OF A ROMAN THEATER.*

apparent: obelisks are a symbol from pharaonic and Ptolemaic Egyptian monumental architecture and they have been combined with elements from the classical world reworked in an original manner, i.e. the metopes and triglyphs which unusually are of equal length. However, the Obelisk Tomb also combines different traditions in the impersonation of the dead. On the one hand there is the imageless symbol of the East, expressed here by the obelisks, and on the other hand, the Greek inspired representation of the deceased. The tomb was created for five people (the number of locules inside the funerary chamber) of which the most important lies in the far wall in an *arcosolium* typology (i.e. with a niche above a sarcophagus embedded in the wall).

Below the Obelisk Tomb, the two-storey façade of the Bab el-Siq Triclinium is cut entirely out of the rock. The lower storey is marked by four central half-columns and two lateral pillars bearing Nabataean style capitals, in this case quite worn. The storey is topped by a split pediment in turn crowned by a low attic decorated with four short pilasters. The entrance to the burial chamber lies in the centre below a low-arched tympanum. Inside the chamber, a simple horseshoe-shaped bench is the triclinium itself. The upper storey of the façade is very low, decorated by four short half-pilasters and also topped by a broken pediment. The monument is completed by two chambers on either side of the architectural composition devoid of any special features

except for the graves dug out of the flooring.

Architectural façades in tombs are a frequent feature at Petra but, in the case of the Bab el-Siq Triclinium, the effect is of a rather squashed construction that visibly contrasts with the vertical thrust of the slender obelisks in the tomb above. Besides stylistic details that indicate the Obelisk Tomb was constructed earlier, it is evident that the upper tomb's prior existence was responsible for the squat, almost compressed appearance of the Triclinium. No information exists about either of the two tombs, not even to date them with any certainty, though usually a funerary inscription engraved in Nabataean and Greek on the other side of the *wadi* is connected with the two buildings. The reason for the association, despite the distance

# The great rock tombs of Petra

## LEGEND

**A** REST HOUSE

**B** INSCRIPTION IN
NABATAEAN AND
ANCIENT GREEK

**C** TOMB OF THE
OBELISKS– BAB-EL-
SIQ TRICLINIUM

**D** EL-KHAZNEH-EL-
FAROUN

**E** TOMB OF 'UNAISHU

**F** ROYAL TOMBS

**G** TOMB OF SEXTUS
FLORENTINUS

**H** URBAN AREA

**I** UNFINISHED TOMB

**J** ED-DEIR

**K** TURKMANIYA TOMB

**L** TOMB OF THE
ROMAN SOLDIER

**M** RENAISSANCE TOMB

**N** TOMB OF THE SPLIT
PEDIMENT

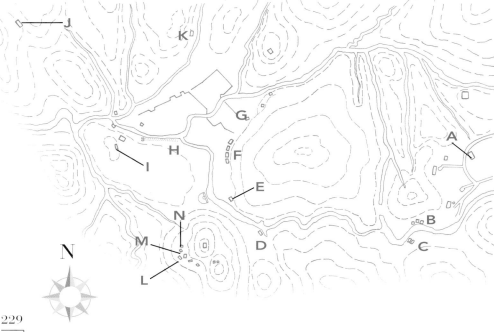

of the inscription from the tombs, is that there are no other tombs near the epigraph. The carving was made around the time of King Malichos (62-30 BC or, less probably, between 40-70 AD) which could be considered an indication of the date of the Obelisk Tomb if the connection really exists.

The location of the two tombs is on the extreme eastern edge of Petra. To reach the city, it is necessary to pass through the gorge, today known as the Siq, that has walls up to 80 meters high. Niches have been cut in the walls of the rock, sometimes empty, but some of which contain stylised figures, obelisks or pillars. Often these representations have a religious meaning (anthropomorphic or aniconic images of the gods) but often they are *nefesh*, i.e. monuments that represent and commemorate the dead. *Nefesh* means "vital breath" and represents the soul of the deceased and therefore it cannot be placed with the tomb itself as is made explicit in an inscription in the Siq which commemorates an inhabitant of Petra who died in the city of Gerasa where he was also buried.

At the end of the first section of the Siq, the walls close together almost preventing the light from entering, then it opens into a vast natural arena at the far end of which is the most celebrated of Petra's

buildings: the Khazneh el-Faroun. After preparing the rock wall in which the Khazneh was built, a huge rectangle was marked out and cut a few meters into the rock at which point a two-storey façade was carved measuring 25.30 x 39.1 meters.

As with most funerary monuments in Petra, the Khazneh was completely carved from the rock but its state of preservation is exceptional. Its isolated position and the fact that it was built inside the rock face meant that its outstanding, elaborate decorations and its sculptural work have been superbly conserved. There are many figures carved in the two orders: between the lateral intercolumns on the lower level, reliefs of Castor and Pollux (the Dioscuri) with horses have been carved on a base using classical iconography. On the upper level there are nine reliefs of female figures – three in the front niches, four in the niches inside and two in niches at the back. The latter two are winged and are therefore considered to represent Nike while the others (with the exception of the figure in the front niche of the *tholos* holding the cornucopia) wear a short tunic and brandish an axe in the personification of Amazons.

The inside of the tomb is equally elaborate. Three richly decorated doors in the vestibule lead into separate chambers of which the middle one, the largest measuring 11.97 x 12.53 meters, has three niches intended to hold sarcophaguses. The contrast of the darkness of the Siq and the light that illuminates the façade of the Khazneh is very powerful and must have been one of the reasons for the building's location, but what is truly exceptional is the elaborate variety of sculptural and decorative themes, quite different from those in the other tombs in Petra. They include numerous elements influenced by the world outside of Nabataean civilisation and many of these are derived from Alexandria, for example, the originality of the capitals and in particular the central acroter bearing the solar disc which was originally the symbol of the Egyptian goddess Hathor and later Isis. The Khazneh el-Faroun was not supposed to be simply the tomb of a man but also a place of worship for a man that had been deified. This is denoted by the symbol of Hathor-Isis and the central image on the pediment interpreted as Agathe Tyche or "good fortune".

The splendid overall effect and the richness of the details is countered by the total absence of epigraphic data which has led to widely differing chronological attributions (from the Greek period to the principate of emperor Hadrian, i.e. nearly three centuries of difference) based on more or less circumstantial evidence, including the resemblance between the "fantastic architectural features" and the second Pompeian pictorial style. Detailed analysis of architectural details have recently shown that the chronology of the Khazneh should be placed between the second half of the first century BC and the start of the first century

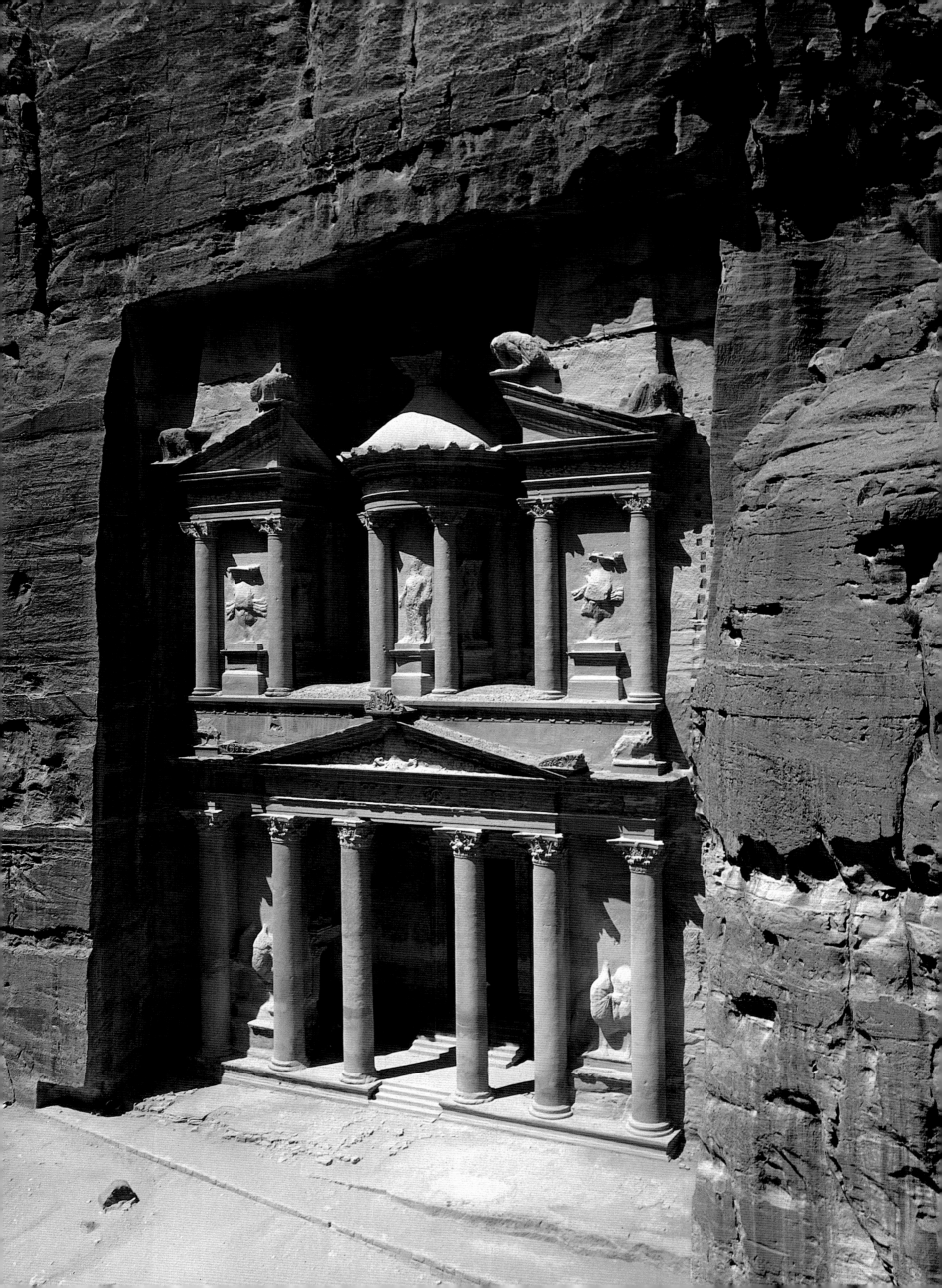

*234-235  THE END OF THE
SIQ NEAR THE THEATRE
BECOMES A TRUE "WAY OF
THE TOMBS" FROM WHICH
THE NAME STREET OF*

*FAÇADES IS DERIVED. TO
THE RIGHT, THE TOMB OF
UNAISHU, A HIGH
NABATAEAN DIGNITARY
CAN BE SEEN.*

*234 BOTTOM LEFT, 235 TOP
AND BOTTOM  MOST OF
THE TOMBS AT PETRA WERE
BUILT WITH FAÇADES OF
DIFFERENT DESIGNS, MOTIFS
AND STYLES RESULTING IN
ALL KINDS OF*

*COMBINATIONS. MANY
WERE CROWNED WITH
CRENELLATIONS, A MOTIF
THAT WAS VERY COMMON
IN HOLY AND FUNERARY
BUILDINGS IN THE NEAR
EAST.*

AD. However, it will be a long and difficult task to establish to which Nabataean king the building was dedicated.

Most of the other tombs at Petra are of another type, built one above the other as seen in the final section of the Siq and along the rock walls of the various *wadis* that flow into the valley. Their linear façades are in the shape of a tower, crowned by one or two attics decorated with sloping or stepped merlons, motifs inspired by Assyria and Persia. The presence of human figures in this typology is rare and classical elements are limited to the occasional architectural decoration. Most of the tombs have features peculiar to Nabataean architecture such as the capitals, the form of which resembles the Corinthian order but its body is trimmed down to a smooth block with the volutes limited to straight projections and the customary abacus flower stylised in a simple cube. The tower-style tombs (also known as pylon tombs) were also built by adapting the rock face and then sculpting the façade, starting from the top and gradually filling in the major features. This formula can be seen in the Unfinished Tomb located on the western slope of the inhabited area.

Tower-tombs are the real expression of Nabataean funerary architecture. They were built for court dignitaries and the merchants who made Petra a rich and powerful city. The inscriptions in the Nabataean language on two tombs are dedicated to such merchants: Unaishu and Turkmaniya. Unaishu is described as being the brother of Queen Shaqilat but this is meant in the sense that he was her minister. He was referred to by historical sources as having represented the Nabataean kingdom on several diplomatic missions including one that took him into the presence of emperor Augustus.

Although the text in the inscription on the tomb of Turkmaniya has been partially destroyed by flooding of the *wadi* and does not offer any information on the owner of the mausoleum, it is particularly important for the explicit mention of the layout of the funerary complex. The epigraph records not just the internal layout of the tomb (a vestibule and a burial chamber with locules) but also the external features (a courtyard, porticoes, a banqueting room and a water tank) that were used for the funerary rituals but which are no longer to be seen.

The abundance of tower-tombs (more than 600) does not mean that there was a monotonous repetition of the same typology: there were many different compositions and layouts of the façades but what distinguishes every one of them is the color of the rock from which they were cut. The polychrome effects of each are unique, for example, the differently colored veins of sandstone in the Silk Tomb make it seem as though it were wrapped in a sheet of silk. Attempts to date the tombs by the complexity of their compositions have been shown to be misguided. Confirmation of this error is given by comparison with similar tombs from other Nabataean sites (like Medain es-Saleh in present-day Saudi Arabia) which still bear dated inscriptions. The different types of

architectural decorations were therefore used indiscriminately (above all during the first century AD) and their choice was probably a simple matter of taste or financial resources.

One group that differs markedly from most of the other tombs is known as the "Royal Tombs". The name is given not just by the splendor of the façades but also by their position; they stand on the west side of Jebel el-Kubtha where they overlook the residential centre of Petra and form the backdrop to the city's main roadway. To the south is the Tomb of the Urn, easily identified even from a distance by a series of arches added in the fifth century AD

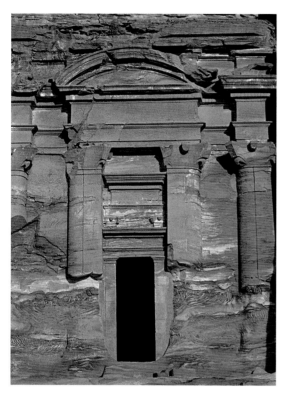

when the tomb was transformed into a church. The tomb is unique for the courtyard in front of the entrance with porticoes of Doric columns on two sides, carved – as usual – from the rock bed.

The frontage is especially tall and has two lateral half-pilasters linked to quarter-columns and two central half-columns with Nabataean capitals. These frame the entrance to the largest chamber which is decorated with a Doric frieze and crowned by a tympanum. Between the semi-columns, three apertures can be seen high up used for deposition of the bodies; the one in the centre still has its closure slab depicting a male bust. The columns are topped by the trabeation (on which the frieze is decorated by four busts,

today very worn), an attic and then the triangular tympanum crowned by a large urn. Although the general layout follows that of the more common façades, the numerous busts give this tomb a particularly distinguished character and this is emphasised by the anomalous but not unique presence of the three funerary cells, seemingly unviolated, at the top. The transformation of the tomb into a church has made understanding of other details impossible but it is very probable that the Tomb of the Urn was built to accommodate the remains of a king, perhaps Aretas IV.

Nearby, the Corinthian Tomb has a façade that at first glance resembles the Khazneh despite its poorer condition as a result of exposure to the weather. The similarity of the two buildings is, however, only apparent, due mainly to the common presence of a *tholos* on the second storey, but the two in fact display substantial differences. As it does not have a vestibule, the Corinthian Tomb lacks the depth of the Khazneh and its lower floor columns are connected to the surface of the frontage. The lower storey is typical of Nabataean style and taste whereas the upper order, even if it has Corinthian capitals, is similar in composition to the Khazneh but lacks the latter's extremely elaborate decoration. The internal layout is quite different with four independent and variously sized funerary chambers . These features, however, do not diminish the importance and size of the tomb which was also probably built to hold the remains of a member of the royal family but the absence of sculptural work

reveals a change in either taste or requirements.

Next to the Corinthian Tomb stands the Palace Tomb. This has a colossal façade split into three floors. Four niches on the first floor are crowned alternately by triangular gables and tympana with basket-handle arches, each niche framing the door of a funerary chamber. On the second floor, nine pairs of Ionic half-columns are crowned by a trabeation and an attic. The third floor also has half-columns but only on the south part of the building. The architectural model is once again very different; in all probability it was based on a Hellenistic palace decorated with

porticoed galleries on the upper floors. In spite of the almost monotonous architectural features devoid of figurative elements, the imposing dimensions of the Palace Tomb make it one of the most impressive buildings at Petra.

Smaller but equally important for their decoration and figurative elements are other tombs with architectural façades. One of these is the two-storey tomb of Sextius Florentinus located on the northern slopes of Jebel el-Kubtha topped by a pediment decorated with plants and crowned by an urn. The name of this tomb is given by a Latin inscription that records

that this man, the governor of the province of Arabia in 127 AD, was buried in Petra. As architectural details seem to conflict with that date, it has been suggested that the inscription referred to a second use of the tomb. Another particularly splendid tomb is that of the Roman Soldier, situated in the ravine of the Wadi Farasa. The tomb takes its name from an armored figure standing in front of a niche above the entrance door to the tomb flanked by two other very eroded reliefs. In addition to the tomb itself, the layout of the structure includes a central porticoed courtyard with a wide triclinium on the opposite side known as the "Polychrome Room" for the colored veins of

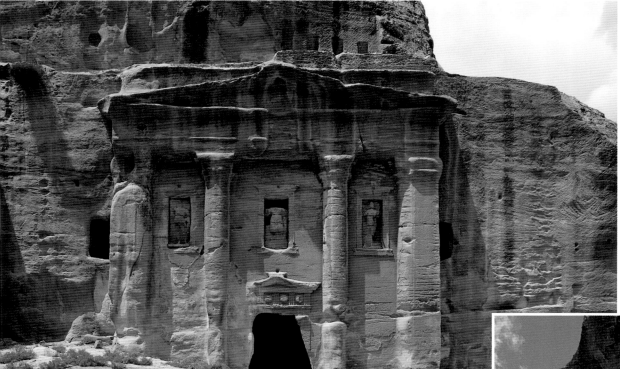

241 THE FAÇADE OF ED-
DEIR IS COMPLETELY BARE
OF ALL FIGURATIVE MOTIFS,
IN ACCORDANCE WITH THE
TRUEST NABATEAN
ARCHITECTURAL
TRADITION.

242-243 FAR AWAY FROM
THE CITY, ALMOST IN
MYSTICAL SOLITUDE, ED-
DEIR WAS OCCUPIED BY A
SMALL CHRISTIAN
COMMUNITY DURING THE
BYZANTINE PERIOD, HENCE
ITS NAME OF "THE
MONASTERY."

rock from which it was cut.

The largest tomb at Petra stands on a hill to the west of the city and is known as ed-Deir (the Monastery) as it was frequented by monks during the Middle Ages. The façade measures 50 meters wide by roughly 40 tall; it is similar to the Khazneh and the Corinthian Tomb in composition with half-columns on the lower storey and a central *tholos*, central niches with half-pediments and lateral pilasters on the upper level. Compared to the Khazneh, the lack of depth and chiaroscuro effects of the Deir are particularly noticeable, especially on the lower storey, and seem emphasised by the greater size of the façade and the type of decoration. There is no figured motif in the large façade of the Deir and the architectural decoration is typically local, for instance, the Nabataean capitals and the frieze of discs that appear flat and austere. The position of the building far from the city, the absence of figured reliefs, the evident disassociation from Hellenistic taste and the intentional choice of local architectural motifs are all elements that have suggested this is the tomb of Rabbel II, the last king of Petra before the Roman conquest of 106 AD, known for his proud attachment to local traditions and the Nabataean people.

# PALMYRA

Palmyra

The first indirect reference to a settlement in the oasis of Palmyra (ancient Tadmor) was made in the 19th century BC. The oasis, with its one fresh water and one sulfurous water springs, was at first just a stopping-off point for Semitic nomads who later settled. Its position in the Syrian desert on a crossroads of one of the most important communication routes between Mesopotamia and Syria, the Arabian Gulf and the Mediterranean, meant that Palmyra had developed into a "caravan city" by the first century AD, in which there was both a concentration and a diffusion of different cultural elements. A Greek influence was already significant during the Seleucid period (third to first century BC), and elements of the Roman culture spread from the end of the Republican period (first century BC) throughout the Imperial period (first to third century AD).

Information regarding the religious aspects of life in Palmyra is derived from the archaeological remains of tombs, sanctuaries, inscriptions, and monuments that portrayed figures: for example, reliefs, sculptures of the dead, frescoes found inside tombs, and depictions of Palmyrean deities. Our understanding of their ideology of death is therefore derived from a fusion of these sources.

In Palmyra, as elsewhere in Syria and Palestine, a tomb is called a "house of eternity": the home is the safe place where one enjoys the love inherent in a family circle and the well-being that follows from it. Funerary banquets

organized on a regular basis by relations on behalf of the deceased are indicative of the practice in which the dead were maintained as part of everyday life.

In Syrian areas a grave was marked by a single stone from remotest times. This stone is considered as the origin of all later funerary monuments, whether simple stelae or elaborate structures. The Aramaic and Palmyrean name of a funerary stele is *nefesh*, literally "breath" meaning "vital breath," and consequently "person." Use of the term with the meaning of

"funerary monument" demonstrates the identification of the tomb with the deceased in the sense that the tomb is the seat of the dead person's vital essence.

Palmyrean tombs are spread in various areas around the city in several necropolises. The most important are to the southeast, southwest, and north in what is known as the Valley of the Tombs.

The tomb structures found in Palmyra are "tower tombs" and "hypogean (underground) tombs." Very few examples remain of a third type, known as "temple" or "house" tombs.

Tower tombs were built almost exclusively in the Valley of the Tombs, with the earliest dating from between the first century BC and first century AD. The vertical nature of the monuments meant that they were first thought of as towers. Built using local stone, they have a square base and stand on molded steps that taper as they get higher, which give them an aspect of great elegance. A niche is usually found several meters above the entrance door showing reliefs and inscriptions that refer to the builder of the tomb. Rows of niches in the ground-floor

244 BOTTOM *Steppe-like and mountainous desert surrounds the oasis of Palmyra. The famous Valley of the Tombs lies among these*

*hills to the west of the city. The defensive walls known as the "Customs Walls" can be seen in the background.*

245 TOP *The tower-tomb of Giamblico, one of the best preserved, stands in the Valley of the Tombs.*

244-245 *Halfway up the side of the hill Umm Belqīs, at the foot of which the city of Palmyra lies, several tower-type tombs stand in alignment. The effects of the weather and neglect have been responsible for their poor condition. The last "tower tomb" on the right is that of Giamblico.*

245 BOTTOM *At the western end of the Great Colonnade, Palmyra's main road, stands what is known as the Funerary Temple. It is one of the very rare examples of a "temple tomb." The picture shows the rear view of the entrance to the underground tomb.*

room of the more elaborate tombs are separated by half-columns, pilasters, capitals, and friezes, while caisson ceilings are carved with floral or geometric patterns. Bays for four columns of six niches lying above one another are arranged from the height of the ceiling – which might reach 7 meters – to below the level of the floor. The stairway leading to the upper floors was placed either to the right or left of the entrance. The rooms on the other floors had the same divisions but were not so high as the ground floor and were decorated with less splendor. Tower tombs sometimes had as many as five stories and might hold as many as 300 funerary niches.

The most representative examples of this type of tomb are those of Elahbel and Giamblico. Elahbel was the eldest of the four brothers who built the tomb and who played an important role in Palmyra; his tomb was completed in 103 AD. On the north side stands the entrance to an underground chamber that lies separate from the central body of the tomb but which made use of the central foundations for several depositions. The main entrance is located on the south side and has the tomb's foundation date carved on the door. The main chamber measures 7.5 by 3 meters and is over 6 meters high and the tiers of niches are separated by pilaster strips with

Corinthian capitals. White rosettes stand out against the blue background on the caisson ceiling, and in the center there are sculpted busts of four figures with traces of red for clothes and white, blue, or black for jewelry. On the far wall two half-columns support a molded architrave, above and below which stand two rows of five female busts. A funerary bed colored with traces of red and from which the principal sculpture has disappeared completes the decoration of the wall. The tomb has four stories and is topped by a terraced covering.

Giamblico's tomb dates from 83 AD. The entrance door has a finely decorated architrave

246-247 THE VIEW OF
THE VALLEY OF THE
TOMBS IS VERY LOVELY AT
DAWN AND SUNSET WHEN
THE LIGHT INTENSIFIES
THE COLORS OF THE
STONE USED TO BUILD THE
FUNERARY BUILDINGS.
TRACES OF FIRES LIT BY
GOATHERDERS WHO
GRAZED THEIR FLOCKS IN
THE AREA CAN BE SEEN IN
THE TOMBS IN THE WORST
CONDITION.

247 TOP ELAHBEL'S
TOWER TOMB WAS
RESTORED IN 1973-76.
THE INSCRIPTION WITH
THE NAME OF THE OWNER
AND THE BUILDER OF THE
TOMB LIES OVER THE
ENTRANCE DOOR AND THE
MOLDINGS THAT NARROW
TOWARDS THE TOP. THE
FUNERARY BED ON WHICH
ELAHBEL'S SCULPTURE
WAS CARRIED STANDS
BELOW THE ARCH.

with floral-patterned gable resting on two gryphons. A second gable supported by two pilasters with Corinthian capitals forms the decoration of the façade on the third story; it used to protect a full-relief representation of the tomb's builder, but this is no longer present. Below are two projecting supports in the form of eagles and, lower still, the heads of lions. The interior is more sombre than that of Elahbel's tomb with the space between each column of niches framed by simple molded cornices and the ceiling decorated with diamond patterns.

The oldest tomb found in Palmyra has a hypogean structure and has been dated to the

247 CENTER THE BACK
WALL IN THE GROUND-
FLOOR ROOM OF
ELAHBEL'S TOMB CONTAINS
TEN BUSTS OF WOMEN IN
TWO ROWS, ONE ABOVE
THE OTHER. THE FACES OF
THE BUSTS WERE
DELIBERATELY DISFIGURED
BY THE ICONOCLASTIC
ANGER OF ARABS WHO
VISITED THE TOMBS. THE
PILASTERS TOPPED BY
CORINTHIAN CAPITALS ON
EITHER SIDE SEPARATE THE
AREAS RESERVED FOR
DEPOSITION OF THE DEAD.

247 BOTTOM
THE INTERIOR OF THE
MAIN ROOM IN
ELAHBEL'S "TOWER-
TOMB" HAS A SUPERB
AND RICHLY DECORATED
CAISSON CEILING. THE
SQUARE TILES ARE
DECORATED WITH
ENGRAVED FLORAL
MOTIFS IN WHICH WHITE
ROSETTES STAND OUT
AGAINST A BLUE
BACKGROUND; THEY
SURROUND FOUR BUSTS
WHICH STILL SHOW
TRACES OF THEIR
ORIGINAL COLOR.
UNFORTUNATELY THERE
ARE NO IDENTIFYING
INSCRIPTIONS SO IT IS
IMPOSSIBLE TO KNOW
THE IDENTITY OF THE
FIGURES PORTRAYED.

248 TOP LEFT
AN EXAMPLE OF A
PAINTED CORINTHIAN
CAPITAL IN THE "TOMB
OF THE 3 BROTHERS."

248 TOP RIGHT  THE FAR
WALL OF THE CENTRAL
CORRIDOR OF YARHAI'S
HYPOGEAN TOMB INCLUDES
TWO EXHEDRAS ON A HIGH
PLINTH WITH A HALF-DOME
ROOF THAT HAS BEEN
PARTLY REBUILT. A
SCULPTED GROUP OF
FIGURES STANDS BELOW.

second half of the second century BC. It lies below the temple of Baalshamin that was completed in the east of the city in 131 AD. Originally, this tomb probably also had an external structure, but this was a characteristic that later underground tombs discontinued, having no symbol above ground. The many hypogean tombs at Palmyra lie in the southwest and southeast necropolises and at the feet of the Arab castle that stands over the city. The most representative underground tombs are the "tomb of the three brothers," "Yarhai's tomb" and "tomb F."

In the "tomb of the three brothers" to the southwest of the city, a corridor with a slope of roughly 2 meters leads to an entrance of two enormous monolithic doors that turn on heavy hinges. The doors are decorated with geometric patterns, and the architrave and jambs bear five inscriptions in the Palmyrean dialect of the Aramaic language: the first commemorates the foundation of the tomb, the others are sales deeds of parts of the tomb and are dated between 160 and 241 AD.

Six steps descend into the tomb, which has a ground plan like an upturned T. Three 9-meter galleries (called exhedras in the inscriptions) lead away from the entrance to the right, to the left, and directly in front. They are all divided into vertical sections 3 or 4 meters high, each of which can accommodate six dead. Each niche is closed by a slab with a half-bust in relief of the deceased and a short epigraph giving his or her name and patronymic.

The central gallery is the most important of the three: immediately visible from the entrance is the full-relief sculpture of the founder of the tomb surrounded by his family. The deceased was shown lying on a triclinium in the typical banqueting position, suited to the periodic celebrations when the family honored their dead with a banquet. In this way, the dead seemed to be participating, at least symbolically, in the ceremonies arranged on their behalf.

The end of the central exhedra is especially richly decorated with columns, capitals, and

trabeations that support a splendidly frescoed false vault. Full-figure or half-length representations of the dead in their original vivid colors are shown on the walls in circular panels held up by images of winged victory. The arch below the vault shows scenes from classical mythology, although the faces of the deceased and the victories did not escape the iconoclastic vandalism of the first Arabs to visit the tombs.

The "tomb of the three brothers" contains 300 niches. Such a high number certainly would have exceeded the requirements of a single family, even considering later generations, but explanation is given by inscriptions generally carved on the trabeations of the entrance doors to both tower

248 BOTTOM THE ONLY EXAMPLE OF FRESCOES COMES FROM THE "TOMB OF THE 3 BROTHERS," IN WHICH GEOMETRIC MOTIFS AND VINE VOLUTES FRAME A MYTHOLOGICAL SCENE. IN THE CIRCULAR SPACES BELOW, THE IMAGES OF THE DEAD ARE SUPPORTED BY WINGED VICTORIES.

248-249 YARHAI'S TOMB WAS EXCAVATED IN 1934-35 AND PARTLY REBUILT IN THE DAMASCUS MUSEUM.

THE WEST EXHEDRA CONTAINS THE MAIN SCULPTURAL GROUP IN A PURPOSE-BUILT NICHE.

249 BOTTOM THE CEILING OF THE EXHEDRA IN THE "TOMB OF THE 3 BROTHERS" IS DECORATED WITH A GEOMETRIC PATTERN BASED ON OCTAGONS. IN THE CENTER, A MYTHOLOGICAL SCENE IS SHOWN IN A MEDALLION: GANYMEDE ABDUCTED BY ZEUS IN THE FORM OF AN EAGLE.

and hypogean tombs. These inform us that the builders of the tombs were able to cede part of them to others who to all effects became their owners. This fact allows us to deduce that business activities in Palmyra were not limited simply to trade but included more complex transactions such as the purchase and sale of land or buildings, including tombs.

Yarhai's tomb, today reconstructed in Damascus Museum, has a longitudinal plan. The tomb was dug out in 108 AD in the central part of the Valley of the Tombs and has its entrance to the north. A stairway 3 meters wide leads to the monolithic entrance door with a finely sculpted architrave. Two side exhedras were added to the

central corridor, measuring 14 x 3 meters, at the end of the second century AD. The east exhedra was left uncompleted while that to the west was given a stepped entrance, stone paving slabs, and was framed by a round arch. The walls of the room thus created were lined with full-relief representations: at the end, two priests, recognizable by their low cylindrical caps, recline on a triclinium with other figures in the same garb in the middle ground behind; on the left there is a cloaked woman. A series of male and female busts are positioned below the triclinium; two columns of niches with other busts in relief frame this scene and cover the other two walls of the exhedra.

The corridor leading to the south exhedra is divided by two arches at regular intervals with the space for the niches framed by moldings – six on one side and four on the other. The end wall is divided into two exhedras to the sides of which pilaster strips with composite capitals support an architrave decorated with listels overlaid with engravings of acanthus volutes. Each exhedra has pilasters at the sides topped by composite capitals and a molded architrave on which a half-dome in the form of a shell is placed. Each exhedra contains three niches with a half-dome in the form of a shell. Below, two sculpted groups of figures depict funerary banqueting scenes of the two families involved.

250-251 HIGH RELIEF
OF MALE AND HIS SISTER
BOLAŸA IN THE TOMB
OF TAI IN THE
SOUTHEAST NECROPOLIS.
A CASKET TO THE LEFT
OF THE TWO FIGURES
SYMBOLIZES WEALTH.

251 BOTTOM LEFT THIS
RELIEF FROM THE CAMP
OF DIOCLETIAN SHOWS
A MAN WEARING A
TUNIC, SOFT TROUSERS,
A CLOAK ATTACHED BY
A CLASP AT THE
SHOULDER, AND A PAIR
OF ANKLE BOOTS.

251 BOTTOM RIGHT
HIGH RELIEF FROM THE
TOMB OF SHALMALLAT.
AFTER 200 AD, WOMEN
WERE REPRESENTED
WEARING INCREASINGLY
ELABORATE ORNAMENTS.

# Tomb "F" at Palmyra

The underground "tomb F" in the southeast necropolis is one of the tombs excavated during the 1990s by the Nara archaeological institute (for the Research Center for Silk Roadology) under the direction of Takayasu Higuchi. Unfortunately, the ceiling collapsed, thus depriving the tomb of all its decoration, but it has made viewing of the tomb possible from above.

The tomb is laid out in the shape of a Latin cross. The entrance stairway to the south is a good 9 meters long, the central corridor to the north measures almost 18 meters, the east corridor more than 8 meters, and the western corridor less than 5 meters. These side corridors

## LEGEND

**A** ACCESS STAIRWAY
**B** EAST SIDE
**C** WEST SIDE
**D** CENTRAL CHAMBER
**E** BURIAL CHAMBER
**F** NICHES
**G** SARCOPHAGUSES

were not finished, which seems to have been because cedar wood – now missing – was used to line the walls, a fact we have learned from an inscription.

This particularly magnificent tomb was dug out in 128 AD by two brothers, Borrofa and Bolha. The monolithic entrance has an architrave made up of smooth laths overlaid by rounded moldings and dentils. Inside, the passages between sections are covered by a barrel vault and decorated with molded arches. The keystones showing heads of the Medusa have a protective purpose. Smooth listels, acanthus volutes, rounded moldings, and dentils decorate the surfaces on which the arches are

253 TOP  THE SIDES OF
THE PRINCIPAL EXHEDRA
IN "TOMB F" ARE LINED
WITH A HIGH PLINTH
WITH MOLDINGS AT THE
BASE. THE BASES OF THE
COLUMNS SEPARATING THE
NICHES STAND ON THE
PLINTH.

252 RIGHT  THE
MONOLITHIC ENTRANCE
TO "TOMB F" IS
DECORATED WITH A SERIES
OF RECTANGULAR AND
SQUARE MOTIFS THAT GET
SMALLER TOWARDS THE

CENTER  THE DOOR TURNS
ON A SINGLE HINGE. THE
ARCHITRAVE WITH
DENTILS IS SUPPORTED BY
TWO BRACKETS
DECORATED WITH
ACANTHUS LEAVES.

252-253 AERIAL VIEW
FROM THE NORTHWEST OF
THE EXCAVATIONS IN
"TOMB F." THE ENTRANCE
STAIRWAY TO THE TOMB,
THE PASSAGE ARCHES, AND

THE TWO EXHEDRAS TO
THE EAST, TO THE WEST,
AND THE NORTHSOUTH
FACING CENTRAL
EXHEDRA ARE ALL
CLEARLY VISIBLE.

# Tomb "F" at Palmyra

based and the strips that run along the walls at mid-height from the floor.

Immediately after entering the main corridor, two molded arch niches to the left and right contain full relief sculptures of sarcophaguses with figures lying on beds. The far exhedra contains, as is usual, the most important sculpture in the tomb, in this case the figure of a priest reclining on a triclinium with his left elbow resting on a cushion, a cup in his hand, his right leg bent over the left. He wears a mid-thigh-length tunic and floral-patterned Parthian-style trousers. Behind him there are four other figures and a child, headless except for one.

The Japanese archaeologists have counted the deposition of 82 bodies: 11 in the sarcophaguses and 8, for children, in trenches buried directly in the ground. There are few tomb goods, although these were placed near the head or feet of the deceased. There are rings, pendants, earrings, beads from a gold necklace, and pieces of silver and bronze which mostly came from the clothing in which the dead were dressed at the time of their deposition.

The richness of the funerary monuments and the decoration of the Palmyrean tombs in part reveal the conception of death in the city. Palmyreans wanted to show off their wealth, well-being, power, and happiness. Death for them was not a negative experience; the afterlife was part of an ordered world in which death did not signify destruction but simply the completion of terrestrial life.

Iraq
Ur

258 TOP
THE REPRESENTATION OF
THE IMDUGUD, A MYTHICAL
AND DIVINE BIRD WITH THE
HEAD OF A LION, FOUND AT
MARI WITH OTHER OBJECTS
CONFIRMS THAT
RELATIONSHIPS WITH
OTHER COUNTRIES EXISTED.

258 CENTER
THIS PHOTOGRAPH WAS
TAKEN IN 1930 DURING
EXCAVATIONS OF THE
ROYAL CEMETERY (SHOWN
IN THE BOX). TODAY
THERE IS ONLY AN
ENORMOUS HOLE IN THE
GROUND. THE ZIGGURAT
OF UR-NAMMU CAN BE
SEEN ABOVE.

The traveler passing through the vast, often desolate, plain of Mesopotamia in search of traces of the ancient Sumerians, Assyrians, or Babylonians does not come across tombs, epitaphs, tumuli, or large mausoleums, and certainly nothing like what might be found in Egypt, at Marathon, Palmyra, on the Appian Way, in Rome, or even European cemeteries. For ancient peoples, the world of the dead, at the end of the "road from which there is no return," was the "house whose inhabitants are deprived of light, where dust and mud are their food, where they are dressed like birds, they do not see the light and remain in darkness, cooing like doves." The dead lived below ground and were placed there, often without any visible signs, although sometimes we may be sure there were masonry structures (such as in the mausoleums of the third Dynasty at Ur), or we may suspect the existence of memorial stones. Those not fortunate enough to be buried were considered to suffer, while those who enjoyed funeral ceremonies were indeed lucky. Those buried with the objects of their everyday life were also privileged, such as ladies with their jewelry, a soldier with his weapons, a craftsmen with his tools, and other grave goods.

258 BOTTOM FEW FINDS
REMAIN FROM THE
BUILDINGS EXCAVATED
AT THE SITE OF UR,
EVEN FROM THOSE FROM
THE PERIODS THAT
FOLLOWED THE ROYAL
CEMETERY.

259 TOP THE LOVELY
HELMET FOUND IN TOMB
PG/755 THAT BELONGED
TO MESKALAMDUG IS KEPT
IN BAGHDAD. IT IS MADE
OF SOLID GOLD AND
MEASURES 24.8 CM IN
DIAMETER.

In most cases, the presence was not documented of "human" property such as slaves or wives, not even for the great and powerful sovereigns who ruled over vast territories, especially towards the end of the history of Mesopotamia. There was, however, one exception. Curiously, this exception is the set of tombs that has given up some of the most precious and interesting treasure from the whole of Mesopotamia. The kings buried in these tombs lived in very ancient times and ruled over a kingdom that was probably not very large. They were the kings of Ur, a city destined to prosper over time. Around 2000 BC during the third Dynasty, Ur would become the capital of a huge empire and mark the Sumerian renaissance, after the fall of the Semitic Akkadian dominion founded by the legendary Sargon of Akkad. The construction of the mausoleums mentioned above dates back to this second period, as well as the famous ziggurat, the best-preserved stepped pyramid, which was built by king Ur-Nammu, the earliest known legislator in the history of mankind. It would also seem from the Bible that Ur was the homeland of the patriarch Abraham, if it were not for the fact that the city was referred to as "Ur of the Chaldees," and the Chaldees were at Ur more than a thousand years after the presumed age in which Abraham lived. The tombs in which the magnificent treasure of Ur was discovered were from

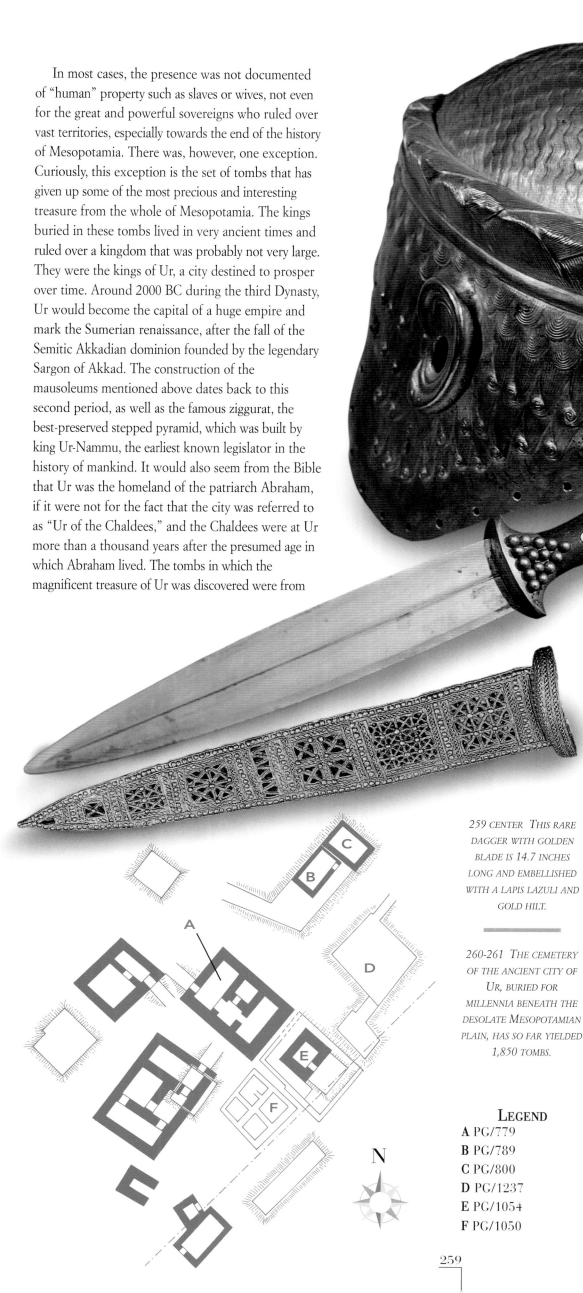

259 CENTER  THIS RARE
DAGGER WITH GOLDEN
BLADE IS 14.7 INCHES
LONG AND EMBELLISHED
WITH A LAPIS LAZULI AND
GOLD HILT.

260-261  THE CEMETERY
OF THE ANCIENT CITY OF
UR, BURIED FOR
MILLENNIA BENEATH THE
DESOLATE MESOPOTAMIAN
PLAIN, HAS SO FAR YIELDED
1,850 TOMBS.

### LEGEND

A PG/779
B PG/789
C PG/800
D PG/1237
E PG/1054
F PG/1050

before this period and belong to the middle of the third millennium BC (2500-2450 BC), during the last phase of what is known as the Protodynastic Era. The Sumerian kings buried there, whose names we know from inscribed seals, are not included in the famous "King List" that gives the names of the earliest rulers (antediluvian and postdiluvian) of the various cities in Sumerian Mesopotamia.

As far as Ur is concerned, the King List gives the names of rulers that followed immediately after those found in the cemetery, and as Mesannepada (the presumed founder of the first Dynasty) also proclaimed himself king of Kish, we may suppose that the rulers were only listed from when the kingdom was in its first phase of expansion. Kish is far to the north of Ur and not far from Babylonia. The kings buried in this royal cemetery were simply "kings of Ur," including a certain Meskalamdug, cited in other sources as the father of Mesannepada.

The tombs were situated just outside the temple and sacred area. Although interesting from the point of view of their tomb goods, they bear no similarity to the magnificence of the many underground rooms in Egypt and are far simpler. Each tomb was either a single chamber or a set of small chambers created by digging out the soil, lining it with stone or brick, and covering it with projecting ashlars or a barrel vault. The tomb was reached via a steeply sloping passageway. Their discover, Leonard Woolley, recounts in his diaries that excavation began at the start of 1927. He shortly became aware that there were two cemeteries belonging to two different epochs, one on top of the other.

The one below was what for them became the "Royal Cemetery." There were two types of burial: the tombs of the common citizens and the tombs of the kings. They cleared about two thousand of the first type, and about sixteen of the second were more or less conserved, since the sacrilegious hands of ancient tomb robbers had not refrained even here. Sometimes the chambers were unrecognizable, sometimes completely destroyed. Still, what the cemetery revealed was both overwhelming and disconcerting: on the one hand, it gave a number of indications about funeral ceremonies which had until then not been discovered in other areas of Mesopotamia; on the other, there was an incredible quantity of precious objects which displayed considerable artistic and technical skills and which can now be seen in the British Museum in London, the Iraq Museum in Baghdad, and the University of Pennsylvania Museum in Philadelphia.

It is worth describing at least one of the most complete, magnificent, and important tombs. The one known as PG/779 was one of the largest, with four chambers separated by arched passages. It seems that the dead were placed here in chests

below baldachins. Jewelry and plate were found here together with the body of a man whose head was wrapped in headgear decorated with thousands of beads of lapis lazuli. Next to him lay one of the most important objects to be found, the "Standard of Ur." Woolley describes the moment of the precious discovery, after they had lost all hope of discovering anything: the chief worker found a fragment of a shell inlay and, a minute later, uncovered the corner of a lapis lazuli and shell mosaic. Woolley recounts that they had to limit their work to half a square centimeter at a time to recover the standard. Wax-soaked cloth was applied to the back of the tiles, then each side was placed face down on a sheet of glass to which it adhered.

When the cloth was removed, every bit of dirt came off with it so that the pieces could then be fitted together perfectly: two main panels, each of which was a rectangle measuring 55 cm by 22 cm, and two triangular pieces. The panels were arranged in the form of an upside-down tent and the triangular parts closed off the ends. The whole was fixed to the end of a rod and was apparently carried in procession. Soon it was possible to recognize the motifs of war and peace on the two faces (each made up of three registers). Curiously, the scenes seem to follow reverse chronological order, so that the beginning is found in the lower registers. The purpose of the "standard" must have been to commemorate a victory that ended

with the capture of booty and a celebration. The lower register of the face depicting "war" shows four chariots, each pulled by two onagers, that urgently press into an attack on the enemy who is eventually overcome. Each chariot has four solid wheels and carries a charioteer and a lancer who wear helmets and the traditional Sumerian battle-dress of a fringed woolen skirt with a short cloak to cover the upper body. The charioteer holds the reins that pass through two rings at the height of the animals' backs, and the lancer makes use of a quiver full of spears at the front of the chariot. The middle register depicts the infantry with soldiers armed with axes and wearing helmets similar to those in the chariot but with more

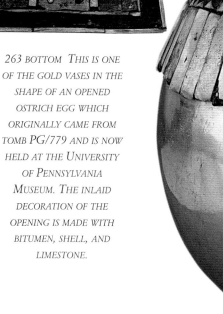

*263 CENTER RIGHT
TAKEN FROM THE
SKETCHES MADE BY
WOOLLEY, THIS DRAWING
SHOWS A SECTION OF
TOMB PG/779 WITH ITS
FOUR FUNERARY
CHAMBERS SEPARATED BY
CORRIDORS.*

N

*263 BOTTOM THIS IS ONE
OF THE GOLD VASES IN THE
SHAPE OF AN OPENED
OSTRICH EGG WHICH
ORIGINALLY CAME FROM
TOMB PG/779 AND IS NOW
HELD AT THE UNIVERSITY
OF PENNSYLVANIA
MUSEUM. THE INLAID
DECORATION OF THE
OPENING IS MADE WITH
BITUMEN, SHELL, AND
LIMESTONE.*

elaborate dress: over the customary undergarment, they wear a long covering that presumably acted as protection. It may have been made from leather (Woolley thought it was made from felt) and was the heavy infantry's means of defense. In the center of the register, a scene shows two soldiers fighting the enemy, immediately followed by a procession of prisoners escorted, it appears, by light infantry dressed almost like the charioteers.

At the right side of the standard, the procession of prisoners effectively does a U-turn into the upper register and marches escorted towards the center, where there stands an important figure in long dress: this is the king with the royal scepter in his hand. Behind him stand three dignitaries holding long sticks, the royal chariot driven by a dwarf (or maybe a child or a young prince) and, behind, a charioteer who holds the reins. The scene portraying peace shows a procession of people at the bottom who carry heavy bundles on their shoulders or who lead onagers. Their clothes differ from those of two Sumerian dignitaries who lead the procession; the scene may therefore depict a deportation or a line of prisoners carrying booty captured by the Ur army to the king. No one carries bundles in the middle register, but goats and oxen are led and a single person holds two fish. It seems clear that the procession is an offering to the king of animals for a banquet. The figures are dressed in the usual short skirt, are bare-chested, and wear the same headgear as the figures in the upper register. The figure of the king stands out for the splendor of his clothing and his greater stature. Six figures are seated before him, each holding a cup, while servants are busy to the right and left of the king. A woman, presumably a singer, accompanies a lyre-player on the extreme right. The front of the lyre is decorated with a bull's head just like real lyres found in the cemetery.

264 TOP AND BOTTOM, 265
BOTTOM  THE TOMB OF PU-
ABI (PG/800), A
NOBLEWOMAN WHO LIVED
ALMOST 5,000 YEARS AGO
(POSSIBLY A QUEEN OR
PRINCESS), HAS YIELDED A

RICH COLLECTION OF
GRAVE GOODS. THE
ADMIRABLY SIMPLE OBJECTS
PORTRAYED HERE CONSIST
OF A SHELL PLAQUE
DEPICTING TWO GOATS AND
A PAIR OF GOLDEN CUPS.

265 TOP  IN THIS
RECONSTRUCTION, THE
MEN OF PU-ABI'S RETINUE
ARE GATHERED IN THE
BURIAL PIT, WHERE MANY,
IF NOT ALL, WOULD HAVE
BEEN SACRIFICED.

PG/800 was the tomb of a woman named Pu-abi (previously read as Shubad or Shudab). This tomb contained the skeleton of a harp player, whose fingers were still on the strings of the harp, close to the bones of nine other women. Nearby were the remains of a coffer measuring more than a meter wide and two meters long, and a sled. The sled, dragged by two onagers, was unusual in that it must have been very fragile and suitable only for short journeys. Perhaps it was used on precious surfaces that the wheels of the chariots would have damaged. Two steps at the back aided access onto the sled and were decorated with inlaid shells and lapis lazuli in the same manner as the edges. The sides of the sled were decorated with the heads of bulls, lions, and lionesses. The reins were embellished with silver beads and the onagers wore collars made from copper. The lady, maybe a queen, was laid in a chamber that had no doors, so the vaulted ceiling must have been constructed after burial. Pu-abi had her hands joined and wore a splendid headdress ornamented with various gold diadems, semiprecious stones, and a gold comb adorned with rosettes. She wore crescent-shaped earrings, a bodice ornamented with long rows of pearls, and a belt. Necklaces, bracelets, brooches, rings, a dressed wig, and two attendants also wearing jewels were all found beside the body of the noble lady. It was calculated that she was no taller than 1 meter 50 and aged around 40, a respectable age for those times. Woolley later reconstructed her head using the skull of an attendant and the original and restored headdress.

Tomb PG/1054 produced two gold daggers and a seal bearing the inscription "Meskalamdug the king," which contrasted with the fact that the most important body of the five dead in the burial chamber seemed to be that of a woman, judging by the huge quantity of jewelry. Meskalamdug's actual tomb was the one known as PG/755 in which were found three yellow amber axes, bronze and gold daggers (with grips made from silver and gold and from lapis lazuli with gilded

*266 TOP  THIS GOLD CUP IS 15.2 CM HIGH AND WAS FOUND IN TOMB PG/800. TODAY IT IS HELD IN PHILADELPHIA. ANOTHER, SLIGHTLY SHORTER, WAS FOUND IN TOMB PG/1054 AND CAN BE SEEN IN BAGHDAD.*

*266 CENTER  THIS CUP, 9.4 CM HIGH, WAS FOUND IN TOMB PG/800 AND IS ALSO KEPT IN PHILADELPHIA. AN IDENTICAL CUP BUT WITH A HANDLE MADE FROM LAPIS LAZULI CAN BE SEEN IN THE MUSEUM IN BAGHDAD.*

*266 BOTTOM  THE "BELT" IN PHILADELPHIA IS A MASTERWORK OF THE GOLDSMITH'S ART. IT SHOWS A SERIES OF DIFFERENT ANIMALS SEPARATED BY A TREE TOGETHER WITH LEAVES AND ROSES. IT ALSO WAS FOUND IN TOMB PG/800, THE TOMB OF PRINCESS PU-ABI.*

267 PRINCESS PU-ABI'S
MAGNIFICENT GOLD
HEADDRESS, WITH COMB
AND EARRINGS, IS HELD IN
PHILADELPHIA. IT IS ONE
EXAMPLE, THOUGH A
VERY ELABORATE ONE, OF
TYPICAL WOMEN'S
HAIRSTYLES OF THE DAY.

The Royal cemetery of Ur

decorations), and the famous helmet, a masterpiece of the goldsmith's art. The helmet has holes at the edge to allow padding to be inserted, is molded in the form of a head of hair, encircled by a band that ends in a *chignon*, while the "hair" at the sides leaves the ears uncovered.

A large number of bodies were found in the long passageway outside the sepulchral chambers: 40 in tomb PG/1050-1051, which a seal indicated as the last resting place of king Akalamdug; at least 63 (of which 12 were women) in tomb PG/789; and 6 men and 68 women, some in rows, others surrounding 4 lyres, in tomb PG/1237. This last tomb is particularly important for the find of two stupendous sculptures made from gold, lapis lazuli, and shells of rampant goats resting against a small tree. The decorations of the lyres are also very beautiful and not just because of the representations of the bulls' heads with lapis lazuli beards that portray the Sun god (bull) who journeys across the sky each day; the bulls' heads may, in this sense, be the forerunners of the figure of Apollo, the lyre-player. The inlay work on the front of the instruments is also very interesting with its use of mother-of-pearl and pitch on wood showing the customary scene of a hero killing a bull with the head of a man or of the same bull dominating wild beasts. There are also animals acting like humans, taking drinks, carrying parts of other animals as food, or dancing and playing harps and sistrums; this last scene was also to be repeated in medieval bas-reliefs.

The different types of objects found in the Cemetery of Ur vary greatly: there were blades, the points of spears made from bronze or yellow amber (some of which were engraved), beauty cases and their contents, whetstones for sharpening blades,

swords and sheaths, plate made from gold, silver, and copper (cups, jugs, trays), more than 100 types of stone container, jewel boxes, shields, chests, and so on. Beadwork of at least 20 different typologies and materials were found: gold, silver, gold-plated copper, lapis lazuli, cornelian, agate, soapstone, hematite, rock crystal, shell, and paste made from glass and other materials, including wood. At other sites, beads have been found that belonged to armbands, bracelets, or necklaces, but in Ur they had a much wider use in the decoration of wigs, bodices and other clothes, belts, and even reins with some designs having originated in India and Anatolia. Beads were also, of course, elements in the composition of necklaces of different types.

Jewelry found included pendants in the shape of leaves, a design recently taken up by modern jewelers, and "dog collars" made from triangular parts joined together alternating the position of the corners. Also unusual were the chess sets made from shell and lapis lazuli that held the pieces inside. Recent studies have shown that these were "magical" or "semi-magical" boards of squares based on perfect arithmetical relationships. Model boats made from silver seem to evoke the cult of

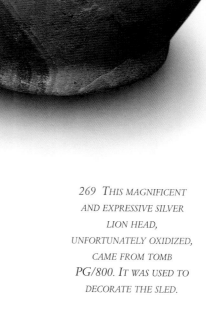

*268 THESE TWO VASES ALSO COME FROM TOMB PG/800. THE FIRST, 6.7 CM HIGH, IS MADE FROM LAPIS LAZULI AND THE SECOND, 16.5 CM HIGH, IS MADE FROM CALCITE.*

*269 THIS MAGNIFICENT AND EXPRESSIVE SILVER LION HEAD, UNFORTUNATELY OXIDIZED, CAME FROM TOMB PG/800. IT WAS USED TO DECORATE THE SLED.*

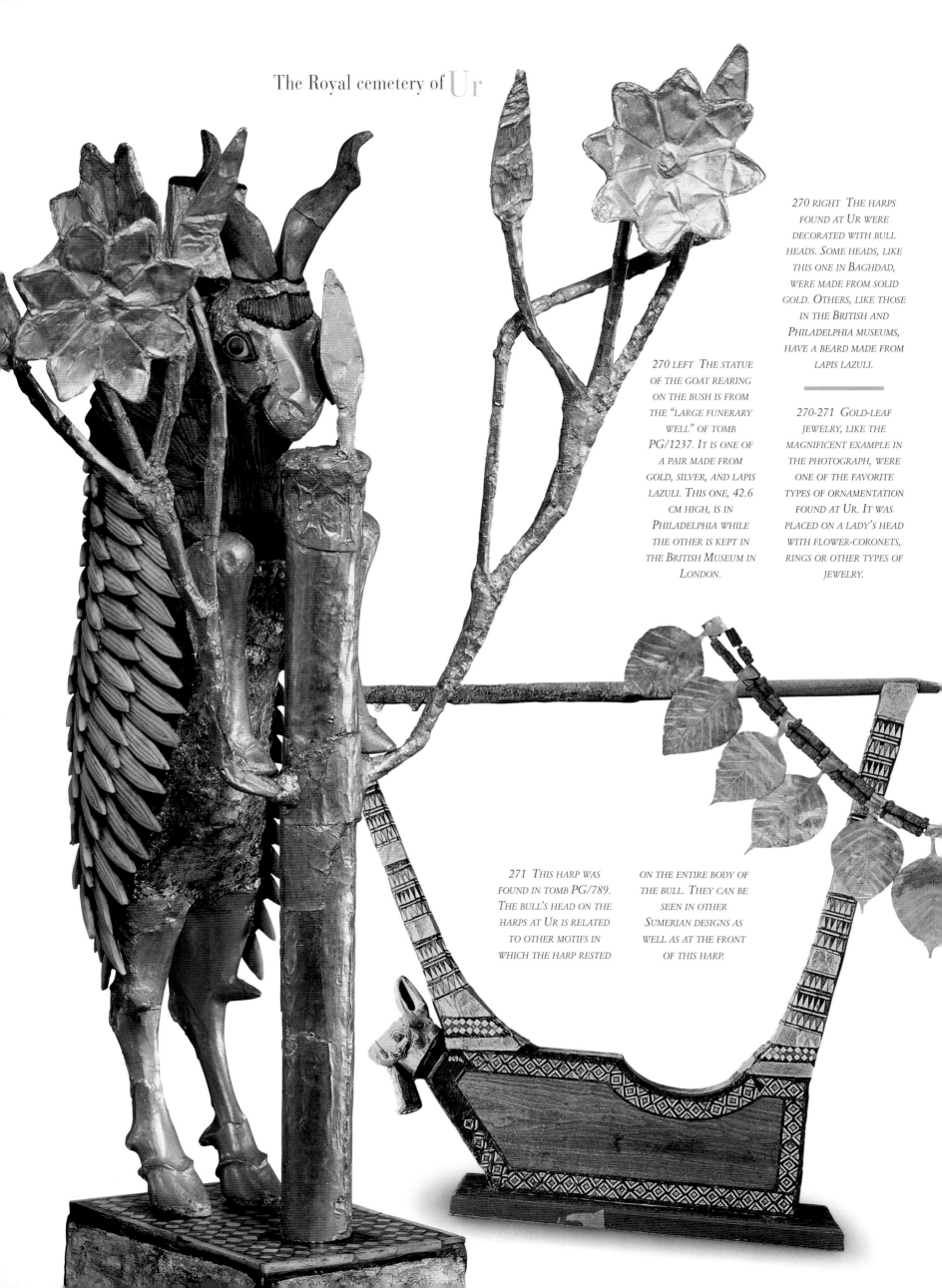

*270 right  The harps found at Ur were decorated with bull heads. Some heads, like this one in Baghdad, were made from solid gold. Others, like those in the British and Philadelphia museums, have a beard made from lapis lazuli.*

*270 left  The statue of the goat rearing on the bush is from the "large funerary well" of tomb PG/1237. It is one of a pair made from gold, silver, and lapis lazuli. This one, 42.6 cm high, is in Philadelphia while the other is kept in the British Museum in London.*

*270-271  Gold-leaf jewelry, like the magnificent example in the photograph, were one of the favorite types of ornamentation found at Ur. It was placed on a lady's head with flower-coronets, rings or other types of jewelry.*

*271  This harp was found in tomb PG/789. The bull's head on the harps at Ur is related to other motifs in which the harp rested on the entire body of the bull. They can be seen in other Sumerian designs as well as at the front of this harp.*

the Moon god, Nanna, who was especially venerated at Ur, as well as referring to the funerary cults and beliefs related to the world beyond the grave. The boat may have served to ferry the deceased without difficulty to the "land from which there is no return." The belief that a world beyond the grave existed is proven by the valuable tomb goods which the dead were expected to use to recreate as near as possible their terrestrial life. There were, among other things, also offerings of food above the burial chamber (e.g., PG/1054). Even so, the most striking aspect of the royal tombs at Ur was the presence of the human "tomb goods." It is clear that many, if not all, of the retinue of the king and queen were buried with their monarchs, including guards, courtesans, maidservants, ladies-in-waiting, musicians and singers. The transition from this world to the next seems to have been voluntary and untraumatic. A copper cauldron was found in tomb PG/1237 with the 74 dead all holding copper or limestone cups. It therefore seems that they all drew some drug or potion from the cauldron that made them sleep or that was, more probably, poison. The position of their bodies indicates that they had not moved and were, perhaps, singing up until the end while the musicians kept playing the lyres. The corpse of the monarch was therefore placed in the tomb and his retinue, whether few or many, followed him in; then the door was walled up and the sacrifice took place in front of the entrance. Finally, the tomb was covered over accompanied by various libations and food-offerings.

The Royal Cemetery of Ur

does not just reveal the existence of an unusual funeral ceremony and an enduring conception of an afterlife. It also tells us of the first chariot battle and represents the first known examples of vaults, domes, and apses. The degree of civilization Ur achieved must have been the result of remarkable experiences and abilities, for example, the knowledge of written language, metallurgy, technical skill in various crafts, a huge trading empire, a successful military organization, and a system of government seemingly free from conflict. This implies that there must have been great prosperity in stock-breeding and agriculture which for the Sumerians, who had no stone, metals, or wood, formed the basis of everything.

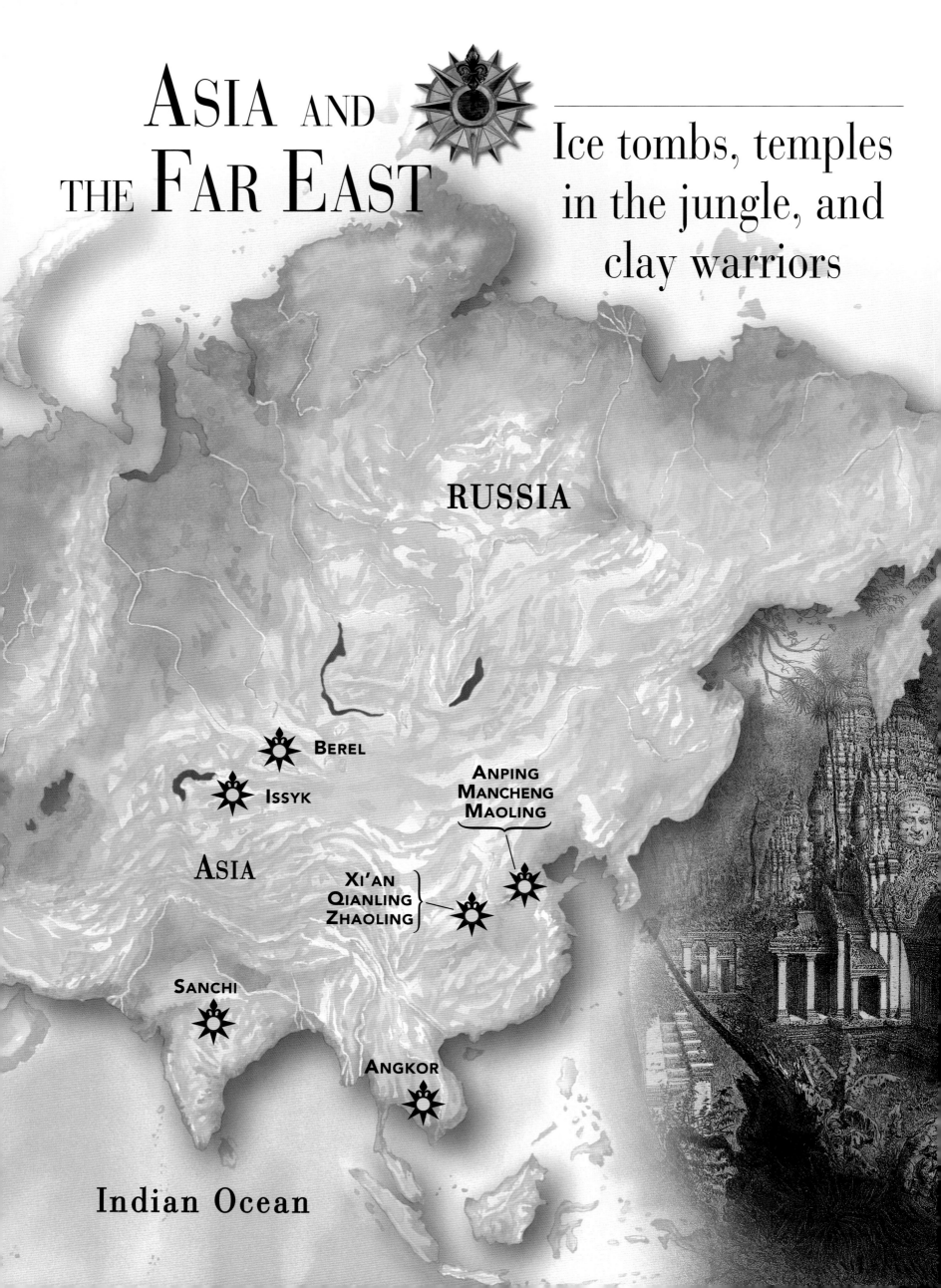

# ASIA AND THE FAR EAST

## Ice tombs, temples in the jungle, and clay warriors

RUSSIA

BEREL

ISSYK

ASIA

ANPING
MANCHENG
MAOLING

XI'AN
QIANLING
ZHAOLING

SANCHI

ANGKOR

Indian Ocean

Analogous to what happened in Europe and the Near and Middle East around the seventh millennium BC, populations of hunter-gatherers in Asia in lands that are now part of China, Japan, Korea, India, Pakistan and southeast Asia began to practice agriculture and settle on a permanent basis.

The communities living in the Yangtze valley in the center of China had already developed the cultivation of rice by the sixth millennium BC as well as practicing several forms of stock breeding.

It was here during the second half of the fourth century BC that one of the oldest cultures in Asia evolved, the Liangzhu, from which many tombs have been found. The dead were interred with large sets of grave goods, which included not only tools and ornaments made from jade (axes, blades, awls, and necklaces) but also two types of objects, also jade, called *bi* and *cong*; these were symbolic representations of the heaven and the earth and served as signs of distinction conferred by kings or heads of clans to the most deserving or important members of the tribe.

During the second millennium BC, when Neolithic peoples in the area began to use bronze and organized themselves in a proper

state ruled by the first kings of the Shang dynasty, large monumental tombs appeared in the form of upside-down pyramids.

However, not all the peoples in Asia had followed the development from a hunter-gatherer existence to an agricultural lifestyle. Some groups on the Siberian and Caucasian steppes in the regions of the Altai and around the Aral Sea continued an economy based on stock-breeding; this choice obliged them to remain nomadic as it was the only way they could exploit all the grazing areas in their territory on a rotational basis.

These peoples, of uncertain origin, were called by various names but were known most of all as Scythians. They created their own culture known for the extreme refinement of their arts and crafts, especially metal and goldworking, the construction of large tumulus tombs known as *kurgan*, and a complex funerary ritual that included the sacrifice not only of animals but also of human beings. The leaders of these peoples, based on a tribal type of organization, were buried with magnificent sets of grave goods as well as with servants and horses that were supposed to serve them in the life beyond the grave.

The oldest of these steppe peoples date from the middle of the third millennium BC, but those buried with the richest grave goods lived between the seventh and the fifth century BC. This was the period to which the tumulus tombs of the Saka people of Kazakhstan, other nomads, also belong. A distinguishing feature of their funerary ritual was the abundant use of gold in the clothing of the dead.

In the meantime, in China the Shang dynasty had been succeeded by the Zhou and the Qin dynasties. The first ruler of the latter, Qin Shihuangdi, founded the first Chinese empire in 221 BC when he united other peoples under his control. His gigantic tomb, located in Lintong near the modern city of Xi'an, was designed as a scale model of the country he had reigned over and of his court. Emperor Shihuangdi's tomb also contained members of his family, his concubines, and his servants, as well as several animals, bronze chariots, and numerous statuettes of members of his personal service.

The construction of this extraordinary burial complex, known to the world as the "tomb of the terracotta army," required thousands of artists who worked, it is calculated, for decades to finish it. Without doubt it is one of the largest and most impressive dwellings of eternity in the history of man. Inside there are three huge trenches that contained a multitude of terracotta statues – a proper army – numbering 7000 soldiers, 600 horses, and 100 battle chariots.

The huge tombs of the Qin rulers, particularly that of Shihuangdi, also inspired those of the dynasty that followed, the Han, who governed China at the beginning of the second century AD. The Han tombs were covered by huge earthen mounds and were in reality perfect underground replicas of earthly palaces, often decorated with splendid wall-paintings, many of which illustrated the world beyond the grave where, according to the metaphysical beliefs of the day, the *xian* lived, immortal creatures who were part man, part bird. These tombs were reached via approaches lined with stone sculptures called "Spirit Roads." The dead were buried dressed and wearing death masks made from jade, the stone attributed with extraordinary properties including that of preserving the bodies from physical corruption.

Tombs comparable to those of the Qin and Han dynasties, though with different characteristics, were built by the Tang dynasty that ruled China from the seventh to the tenth century AD, considered the country's Golden Age. The most magnificent example is the tomb at Qianling some tens of miles from Xi'an. It belonged to the Emperor Gaozong and his consort Wu Zetian, whose burial chambers were dug deep into the ground. They were decorated with realistic paintings of the earthly existence of the deceased and filled with a host of statuettes of the imperial court.

The dwellings of eternity of imperial China up until the Tang dynasty were the greatest examples of funerary architecture in Asia.

Other monuments that approach their scale are the great *stupa* at Sanchi near Bhopal in India, and the temple of Angkor Wat in Cambodia. Although neither were tombs, both were monuments used for funerary purposes and an expression of Buddhism.

The *stupa* at Sanchi – an important place of pilgrimage and devotion between the 3rd-13th century AD – was built during the second century BC. It is the most important of this type of construction, which was originally no more than a funerary mound raised to hold the reliquaries of the Buddha, but it developed into an allegorical representation in stone of the universe and its origin.

Finally, the temple complex at Angkor Wat at Angkor, the capital of the Khmer empire 240 kilometers northwest of Phnom Penh, was built by King Suryavarman II during the first half of the 12th century. It is embellished with splendid bas-reliefs and represents the materialization in stone of the god Vishnu and the deified king himself.

*275 BEAUTIFUL WALL-PAINTINGS DECORATE THE TOMB OF THE CHINESE PRINCESS, XINCHENG, FROM THE TANG DYNASTY. GRACIOUS LADIES-IN-WAITING AND MAIDS CAN BE SEEN IN HER BURIAL CHAMBER WEARING ELEGANT CLOTHES AND ELABORATE HAIRSTYLES AS THEY PAY TRIBUTE TO THE PRINCESS IN HER DWELLING OF ETERNITY.*

*276-277 QIN SHIH HUANGDI'S TERRACOTTA ARMY IS POSSIBLY THE MOST EXTRAORDINARY COLLECTION OF GRAVE GOODS EVER DISCOVERED, FOR THE THOUSANDS OF WARRIORS ALREADY UNEARTHED REPRESENT JUST A SMALL PORTION OF THE WHOLE AND MUCH MORE REMAINS TO BE DISCOVERED.*

# PEOPLES OF THE

Peoples of the Steppes

# STEPPES

*278 LEFT THE MIRROR FOUND IN THE KELERMES TUMULUS SHOWS THE ARTISTIC INFLUENCE OF THE NEAR EAST AND THE AEGEAN ON THE ART OF THE STEPPES. THIS IS EVIDENT IN THE HERALDIC FIGURES CONNECTED WITH THE CULT OF THE LADY OF*

*THE ANIMALS. THE MAN'S BREAST-PLATE FOUND AT TOLSTAJA MOGILA IN THE UKRAINE (MID FOURTH CENTURY BC) IS DECORATED WITH SCENES FROM DAILY LIFE AND MYTHOLOGY THAT ATTEST TO THE IMPORTANCE OF THE GRYPHON IN THE RELIGION OF THE SCYTHS.*

*278-279 THE COMB FOUND AT SOLOKHA IS A FINE EXAMPLE OF GRAECO-SCYTHIAN ART FROM THE 4TH CENTURY BC. IT DEMONSTRATES THAT THE GREEK WORKSHOPS ON THE BLACK SEA WORKED FOR THE SCYTHIAN ARISTOCRACY.*

Kazakhstan

BEREL

ISSYK

Since the earliest periods in the northern regions of Eurasia, groups of nomads whose lives were based on stock-breeding moved from place to place in search of new pastures. These nomads were referred to in Oriental, classical, and Chinese sources and belonged to the Saka people that created the "culture of the steppes." The name Saka was probably Iranian in origin and may be derived from the root *sak-* (to go, to wander). The Saka group numbered several tribal groups such as the Scyths, the Sauromatians (or Royal Sarmations), the Haumavarga Scyths, the Tigrakauda Scyths, the Issedonians, and others.

We know nothing of the origin of these tribes. Herodotus dedicated Book IV of his *Histories* to the customs of these nomads (common use of the women, euthanasia of the old, ritual endo-cannibalism, the cult of the sun to which horses

were sacrificed, the cult of gold connected with royalty, and many others) which he learned of during a stay in the trading center Olbia on the Black Sea. He describes a highly stratified nomadic society, and this account is corroborated by the imposing tombs of the aristocracy composed of elaborate underground funerary chambers that contained grave goods such as weapons, Greek vases, clothing, and headdresses lined with gold plaques depicting animals. The funerary rites required nobles to be accompanied to the world beyond the grave by their servants, concubines, and a large retinue of horses and chariots, and that their burial ceremonies be concluded by opulent commemorative banquets. When the leader of one of the tribes in the confederation died, the heads of the other communities would often sacrifice a representative of their own tribe, and the most beautiful horses were buried with their decorative trappings in the same tomb (Tuva necropolis).

The first examples of art from the culture of the steppes appeared in Europe in the 18th

century when numerous gold objects from Siberia (known as the "Siberian Treasure") were donated to Tsar Peter the Great. The interest aroused by these articles, made from precious metals with new stylistic and compositional features, stirred the greed of adventurers and treasure hunters who explored the steppes between the Caucasus and the Altai (the Mountain of Gold) where most of the *kurgan* (Turkish term for the funerary mounds of the nomads) were located. However, the new adventurers found that most of the tombs had already been plundered in ancient times.

Study of the structure of the tombs and of the materials used in the manufacture of the grave goods provides important information on the social organization, economy, crafts, art, and cults that the nomadic peoples practiced. Yet although the *kurgan* offer a fairly precise picture of the burial rites used, little information is provided on their beliefs about the afterlife, which were perhaps linked to Indo-Iranian cosmological rites.

The nomadic aristocrats cremated in the

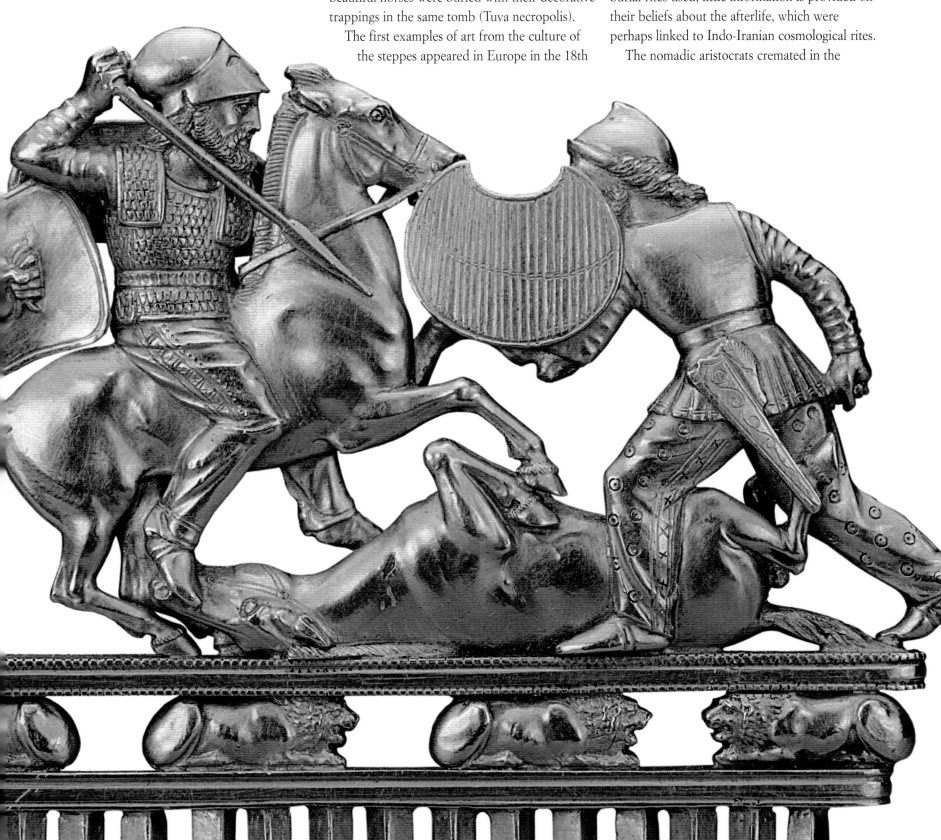

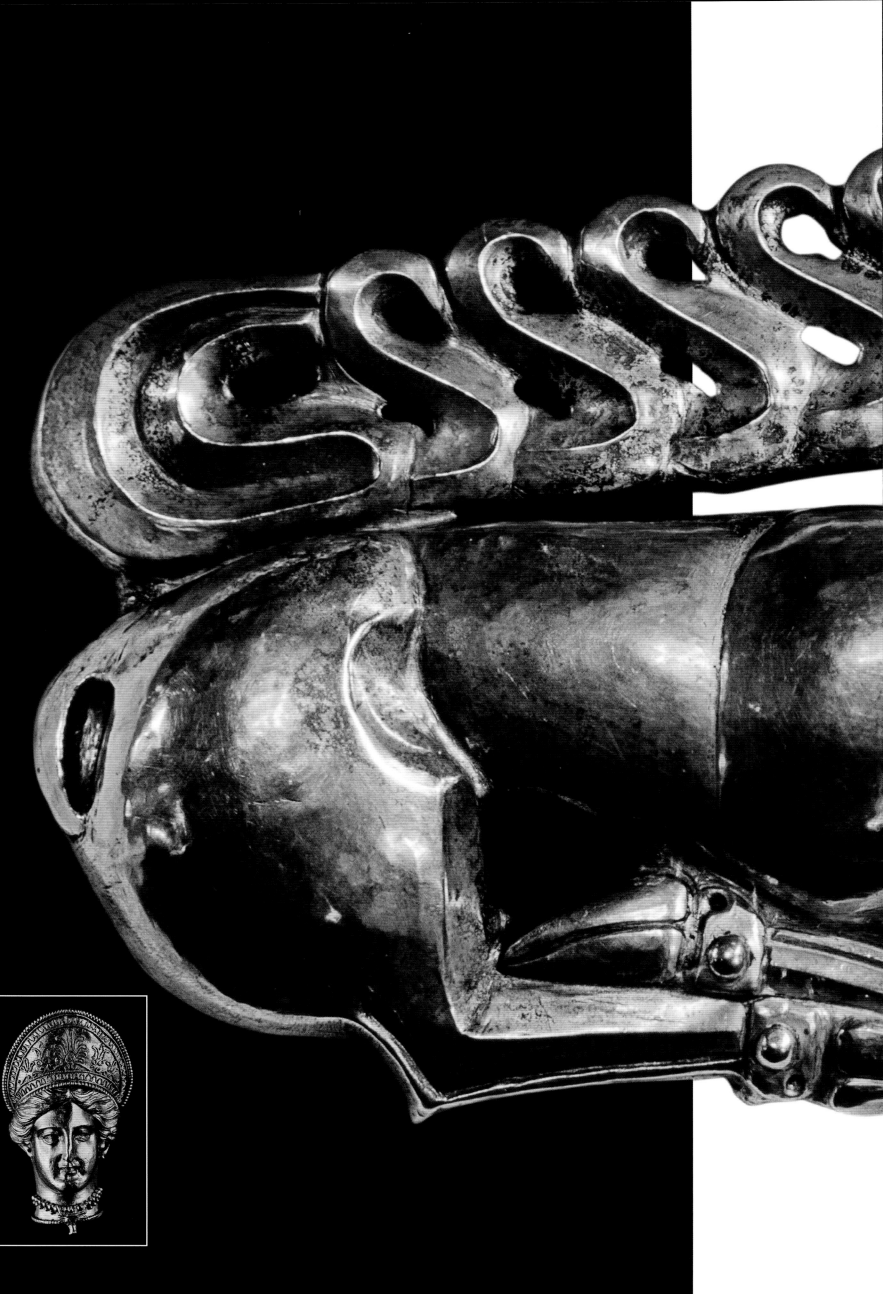

280-281 *This stag from Kostromskaya, in Russia, dating back to the 7th-8th century BC is characterized by a surprising abstract design. The magnificent pieces of Scythian jewelry often had a practical function, as in the case of buckles, buttons and harnesses. However, in the case of the death of important figures, they were buried with their owners.*

280 bottom *The Greek influence is clearly visible in this delicate Scythian pendant. The "barbarian" art of these nomads combined central Asian – and especially Persian – influences with Western ones.*

281 *Some Scythian artifacts evoke scenes of everyday life, such as this vase showing people interacting.*

282 top left Trading
links with the Near East
are demonstrated by this
plaque taken from a
quiver found in the

treasure at Ziwiyeh in
west Iran. It is decorated
with crouching
herbivores and front
views of lion heads.

*kurgan* of west Kazakhstan were probably
considered on a level with the Indian god Yama,
king of the dead, and the Iranian god Yima, son of
the Sun, who had given fire to man and whom
religious texts related to Chorasmia to the south of
the Aral Sea. Their wooden tombs were deformed
by rituals connected with incineration that were
perhaps linked to ritual purification.

Generally, there were three categories of
materials: objects manufactured in animalistic style,
horse trappings, and weapons (which were also
found in the grave goods in women's tombs). As
the various ethnic groups lived in different regions,
some tombs might contain goods made from a
material not found in other regions but, taken as a
whole, these elements formed the culture of the
steppes and were marked by an undoubted artistic
homogeneity. The most richly worked grave goods
were found in the northern Caucasian region of
Kuban. They were an expression of the Meoto-Scyth
culture, which was responsible for the the most
important tombs during the seventh to sixth
century BC. (Kelermes, Ul'skj, Tumulus of the
Seven Brothers, Elizavetinskaya). Many objects
discovered in the tumulus at Kelermes display
decorative motifs derived from both the Near

282 top right
The subject of this
plaque seems linked to
obscure underworld
rituals linked to the
afterlife as indicated by
the snake; the scene is
embellished by the
honeycomb pattern with
inlays of semiprecious
stones.

Eastern and Ionic repertoires of figurative elements, though they were executed in a local style. They are especially evident on a silver mirror lined in molded gold leaf: decoration of the mirror is divided into 8 sections and includes mythological motifs (*Potnia Theron* lifting two rampant lions by the front feet, sphinxes, heroes in combat with an animal) alternated with animalistic motifs (rampant lions, passing animals, animal fights). The Greek influence is also shown in the tumulus at Tolstaja Mogila in Ukraine where gold breastplates are decorated with scenes of animals and nomadic life

alternated with mythological scenes in which gryphons are widely featured. Gryphons were totemic animals and symbols of the sun and royalty. Local style is revealed in decorative effects created by the movement of the animals and the blurring and hiding of any natural features, as can be seen in the plaques, buckles, and decorative elements of parade chariots. The tumulus at Ul'skj revealed the end plate of a chariot on which images of birds were composed primarily of their beaks as their bodies were represented by no more than simple decorative volutes.

Generally, the *kurgan* consisted of a trench, often lined with wooden planks and covered with reed matting, in which the burial chamber lay. The tumulus was raised above the trench using earth and stones. The tumuli were rarely reopened to add a new body, though the practice occurred at Solokha: here the oldest tomb consisted of a shallow rectangular hole containing two burial chambers, one of which had been plundered. The second contained a cauldron with the remains of a funerary meal based on meat. The more recent tomb had been created in a peripheral area of the tumulus

*282-283 TOP THE ANIMALISTIC STYLE ON THIS PLAQUE FROM THE ORDOS DESERT REGION (THIRD CENTURY BC) HAS*

*REACHED ITS MAXIMUM EXPRESSION IN THE DYNAMIC DEPICTION OF FABULOUS ANIMALS AND TORTOISES IN COMBAT.*

*282-283 BOTTOM ANIMALISTIC ART WAS TYPICAL OF THE STEPPE PEOPLES. ON THIS DAGGER SHEATH, IT IS*

*HARMONIOUSLY COMBINED WITH ELEMENTS THAT ARE TYPICAL OF THE GREEK WORLD (END FOURTH CENTURY BC).*

and was still intact. It was composed of another shallow hole containing a number of rooms connected by a corridor. The largest room contained three niches of different sizes, the biggest of which held the body of a man with his arms adorned with ornaments and his head covered by a Greek-style helmet. Next to the body was found a fine example of Graeco-Scythian art, a comb, decorated with a battle scene between nomads. In the center, a rider has just unseated his enemy from his wounded horse lying on the ground between the two warriors. A third nomad is armed with a short sword, a shield, and *gorytus* – the sack that contained his bow and arrows. The entire scene takes place on five squatting lions arranged in heraldic pairs. Not far from the main chamber lay the tomb for the horses, buried with their groom.

From the beginning of the fourth century BC, this practice became standard, and the tumuli were each used by a single family unit. The presence of Greek articles in the grave goods is evidence of the strong Hellenization of the Scythian aristocracy, who were interred in richly decorated and painted wooden sarcophaguses (on the Kerch peninsula). The number of Greek articles, however, later tended to diminish in favor of items of local

manufacture free from all foreign influences.

During the first millennium BC, southern Kazakhstan was inhabited by the Tigrakhauda Saka people, whose funerary tumuli were built using alternating layers of stones and earth and were often surrounded by a ring of stones. The necropolis at Bassatyr contains 31 *kurgan* of various sizes, with the "Great *Kurgan*" in the shape of a truncated cone and surrounded by 94 rings in a spiral.

The necropolises of the ordinary Saka people, as opposed to the aristocrats, were structurally different in that the bodies were interred in wooden sarcophaguses placed in trenches and covered transversally with tree trunks (Kargaly necropolis). The necropolises of the late Saka period (fifth-fourth century BC) are better known; the tumulus was often completed by concentric stone circles fixed in the earth at the top of the mound. The grave goods included cauldrons, altars, and incense burners decorated with zoomorphic and anthropomorphic figures. The remains of the boiled meat of sacrificed animals eaten by the participants in the funerary rites have been found on the altars.

Although our knowledge of the funerary customs of the steppe nomads comes mostly from Caucasian and Ukrainian tumuli, it is to the east in southern and eastern Kazakhstan that the most recent discoveries have shed light on the Saka tribes, whose *kurgan*, today as in the past, mirror the history of a powerful, warlike people.

284 TOP RIGHT CHARIOTS
WERE OFTEN DECORATED
WITH BRONZE INSIGNIA
PORTRAYING ANIMAL
HEADS. IN THIS EXAMPLE
FROM THE 7TH-6TH
CENTURY BC TUMULUS AT
UL', THE DECORATIVE
VOLUTES WERE CREATED
USING THE "ALL BEAK"
BIRD MOTIF.

284 TOP LEFT THIS
SMALL PLAQUE SHOWS
THE TYPICAL TWO-
WHEELED CART USED BY
NOMADS TO MOVE ACROSS
THE EURO-ASIATIC
STEPPES.

285 TOP
THIS BRIGHTLY POLISHED
PLAQUE COMES FROM THE
STEPPES OF THE ORDOS
DESERT REGION (3RD
CENTURY BC). IT SHOWS
TWO CAMELS ON EITHER
SIDE OF A TREE, AND THE
HONEYCOMB PATTERN
THAT DECORATES THE
FRAME ORIGINALLY HELD
SEMIPRECIOUS STONES.

284-285 BOTTOM THIS
LOVELY BRONZE BUCKLE
FROM THE 5TH CENTURY
BC SHOWS AN ELK
ATTACKED BY A WILD CAT
AND A SNAKE ATTACKING
A HERBIVORE (IN THE
VOLUTE OF THE HORNS).
THE ANIMALISTIC STYLE
SIMPLIFIES AND UNIFIES
THE TWO SCENES IN A
MUCH LARGER
COMPOSITION.

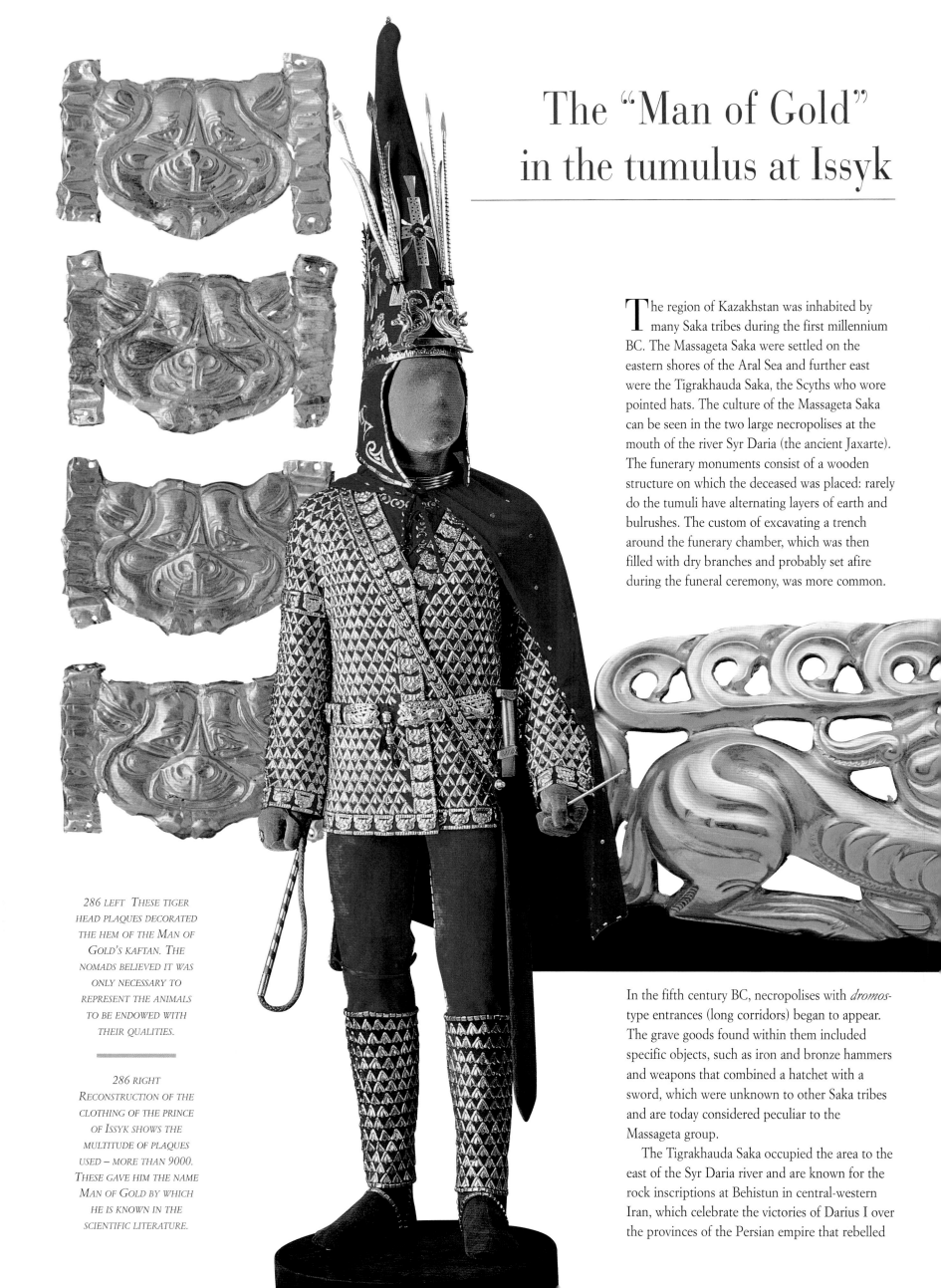

# The "Man of Gold" in the tumulus at Issyk

The region of Kazakhstan was inhabited by many Saka tribes during the first millennium BC. The Massageta Saka were settled on the eastern shores of the Aral Sea and further east were the Tigrakhauda Saka, the Scyths who wore pointed hats. The culture of the Massageta Saka can be seen in the two large necropolises at the mouth of the river Syr Daria (the ancient Jaxarte). The funerary monuments consist of a wooden structure on which the deceased was placed: rarely do the tumuli have alternating layers of earth and bulrushes. The custom of excavating a trench around the funerary chamber, which was then filled with dry branches and probably set afire during the funeral ceremony, was more common.

In the fifth century BC, necropolises with *dromos*-type entrances (long corridors) began to appear. The grave goods found within them included specific objects, such as iron and bronze hammers and weapons that combined a hatchet with a sword, which were unknown to other Saka tribes and are today considered peculiar to the Massageta group.

The Tigrakhauda Saka occupied the area to the east of the Syr Daria river and are known for the rock inscriptions at Behistun in central-western Iran, which celebrate the victories of Darius I over the provinces of the Persian empire that rebelled

*286 LEFT  THESE TIGER HEAD PLAQUES DECORATED THE HEM OF THE MAN OF GOLD'S KAFTAN. THE NOMADS BELIEVED IT WAS ONLY NECESSARY TO REPRESENT THE ANIMALS TO BE ENDOWED WITH THEIR QUALITIES.*

*286 RIGHT RECONSTRUCTION OF THE CLOTHING OF THE PRINCE OF ISSYK SHOWS THE MULTITUDE OF PLAQUES USED – MORE THAN 9000. THESE GAVE HIM THE NAME MAN OF GOLD BY WHICH HE IS KNOWN IN THE SCIENTIFIC LITERATURE.*

when he ascended the throne. In the first year of his reign, the Scythian tribes moved west, taking advantage of the disorder that had broken out in Assyria, Babylonia, and Elam. After clamping down on the troubles, Darius I moved into the eastern territories to push the nomadic tribes back into their own lands and to re-establish the royal right to exact tributes. Having arrived at a marsh, probably the Aral Sea, which has a low water level most of the year due to the many canals that drain off water from the rivers Amu Daria and Syr Daria for irrigation purposes, the Persian king realized he had not come into contact with the Massageta tribe (or the Haumavarga Saka as described in Persian

sources) but with a new tribe distinguished by their particular pointed hats. Archaeological research has shown that the plains in the southern and western regions of Kazakhstan were densely populated from the eighth century BC; it was here that concentrations of immense tumulus-type necropolises contained grave goods of such splendor that archaeologists call the tumuli "royal *kurgan.*"

The tumuli attributed to the Tigrakhauda Saka have a deep central trench that contains the funerary chamber lined with wooden planks. Once the funeral ceremony had been completed, the tumulus was constructed using alternate layers of stones and earth.

One of the most important discoveries of recent years, the necropolis of Issyk near the capital Almaty, occupies an important place in the history of archaeological discoveries. Excavated by Kazakhi archaeologists, it contains more than 40 tumuli of different dimensions; a large *kurgan* of roughly 60 meters diameter in the southern sector was built with layers of gravel alternated with stone and clay, using a technique that was typical of the necropolises in the region of Semirec'e and also seen in Zuantobe. The trench with the funerary chamber was placed in the center. Entered in ancient times, the chamber was found empty. Further excavation revealed a second chamber dated to the fifth-third century BC on the south side of the tumulus. It was built using

*286-287 The two buckles that adorned the belt of his kaftan depict elks with huge horns along their backs. A gryphon's head on the back suggests this is a fight illustrated according to the canons of animalistic art.*

*287 top This plaque adorned the knob of the dagger. It shows a galloping horse with a contorted body.*

*287 bottom The prince of Issyk wore two gold rings; one was decorated with a male head with radiating crown, which may have been a solar image linked to the cult of Mithras.*

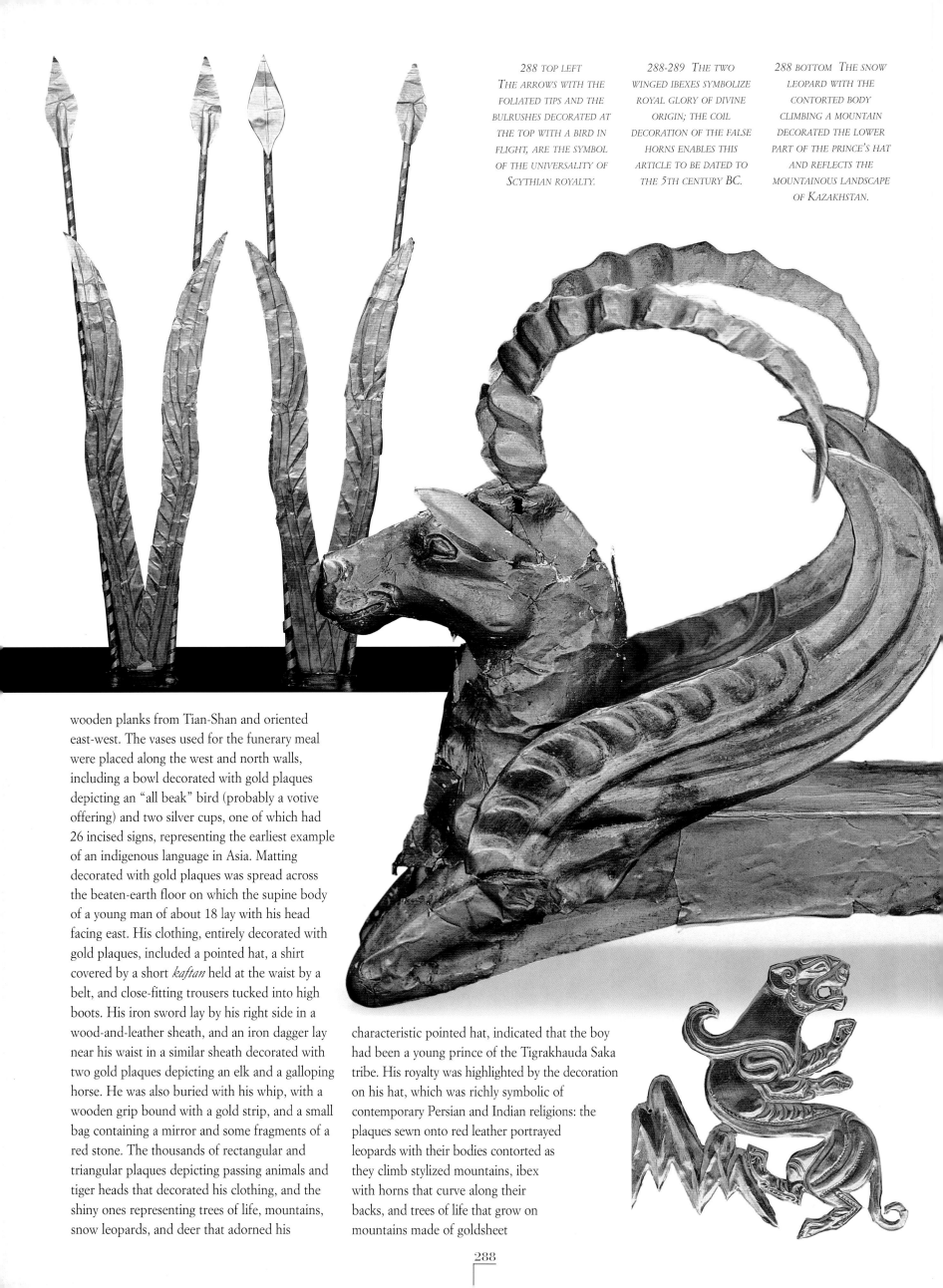

wooden planks from Tian-Shan and oriented east-west. The vases used for the funerary meal were placed along the west and north walls, including a bowl decorated with gold plaques depicting an "all beak" bird (probably a votive offering) and two silver cups, one of which had 26 incised signs, representing the earliest example of an indigenous language in Asia. Matting decorated with gold plaques was spread across the beaten-earth floor on which the supine body of a young man of about 18 lay with his head facing east. His clothing, entirely decorated with gold plaques, included a pointed hat, a shirt covered by a short *kaftan* held at the waist by a belt, and close-fitting trousers tucked into high boots. His iron sword lay by his right side in a wood-and-leather sheath, and an iron dagger lay near his waist in a similar sheath decorated with two gold plaques depicting an elk and a galloping horse. He was also buried with his whip, with a wooden grip bound with a gold strip, and a small bag containing a mirror and some fragments of a red stone. The thousands of rectangular and triangular plaques depicting passing animals and tiger heads that decorated his clothing, and the shiny ones representing trees of life, mountains, snow leopards, and deer that adorned his

characteristic pointed hat, indicated that the boy had been a young prince of the Tigrakhauda Saka tribe. His royalty was highlighted by the decoration on his hat, which was richly symbolic of contemporary Persian and Indian religions: the plaques sewn onto red leather portrayed leopards with their bodies contorted as they climb stylized mountains, ibex with horns that curve along their backs, and trees of life that grow on mountains made of goldsheet

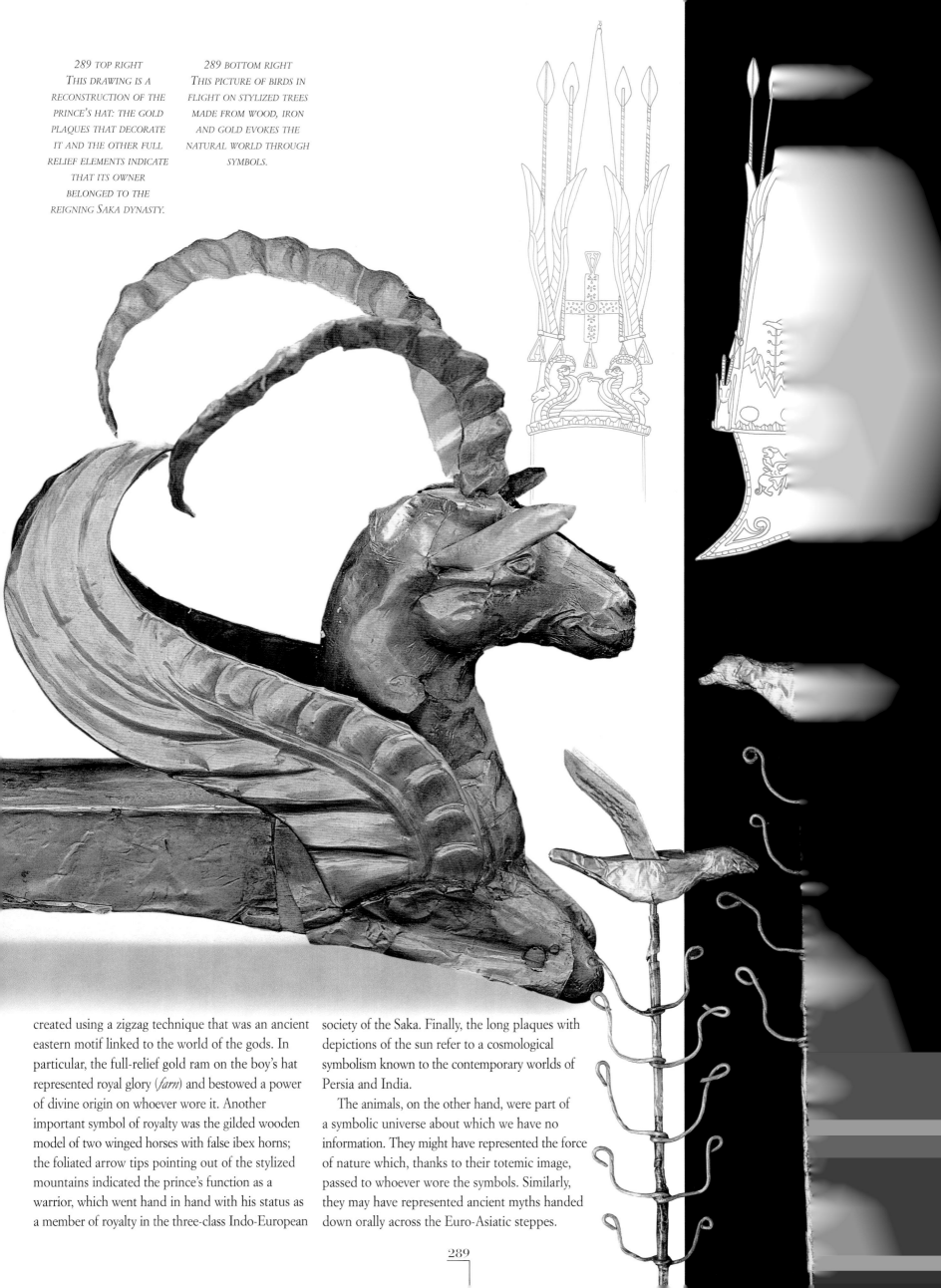

289 TOP RIGHT
THIS DRAWING IS A RECONSTRUCTION OF THE PRINCE'S HAT: THE GOLD PLAQUES THAT DECORATE IT AND THE OTHER FULL RELIEF ELEMENTS INDICATE THAT ITS OWNER BELONGED TO THE REIGNING SAKA DYNASTY.

289 BOTTOM RIGHT
THIS PICTURE OF BIRDS IN FLIGHT ON STYLIZED TREES MADE FROM WOOD, IRON AND GOLD EVOKES THE NATURAL WORLD THROUGH SYMBOLS.

created using a zigzag technique that was an ancient eastern motif linked to the world of the gods. In particular, the full-relief gold ram on the boy's hat represented royal glory (*farn*) and bestowed a power of divine origin on whoever wore it. Another important symbol of royalty was the gilded wooden model of two winged horses with false ibex horns; the foliated arrow tips pointing out of the stylized mountains indicated the prince's function as a warrior, which went hand in hand with his status as a member of royalty in the three-class Indo-European society of the Saka. Finally, the long plaques with depictions of the sun refer to a cosmological symbolism known to the contemporary worlds of Persia and India.

The animals, on the other hand, were part of a symbolic universe about which we have no information. They might have represented the force of nature which, thanks to their totemic image, passed to whoever wore the symbols. Similarly, they may have represented ancient myths handed down orally across the Euro-Asiatic steppes.

# The Prince who came from ice

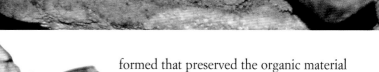

ost Saka necropolises are located in eastern Kazakhstan on the south- and east-facing slopes of Mount Kalbin, along the river Irtys and along the river Buchtarma as far as the Altai mountains. This is where the "royal *kurgan*" have been found, many of which are today known as "frozen *kurgan*." Scientists have identified three cultural phases in this region: the oldest is represented in the necropolis of Majemir (seventh-sixth century BC); the intermediate period is exemplified by Berel necropolis (fifth-fourth century BC), in which funerary chambers were built using wooden planks and horses were also interred; and the most recent phase corresponds to Kulazorga necropolis (third century BC) where the dead were interred in sarcophaguses made from stone slabs thrust into the ground. The cold winters, the depth of the burial trench (up to 7 meters below the level of the ground) and the sealing of the air in the tumulus by the vast quantity of stones used to build it, meant that a deep layer of permafrost

formed that preserved the organic material from decomposition.

The activity of tomb robbers prevalent in the region since ancient times often initiated the decomposition process, thus obliterating trace of organic remains. This occurred, for example, in the necropolises of Tuekta, Barshadar, Katanda, and Shibe and in the first *kurgan* at Berel that was excavated in 1865, where the trench was lined with wooden planks and contained a large sarcophagus hollowed from the trunk of a larch tree and covered with beech bark. In the necropolises of ordinary Saka people, the plank-lined trenches were replaced by a low wood building and sarcophaguses were not used. In many of the tombs, horses were buried in the

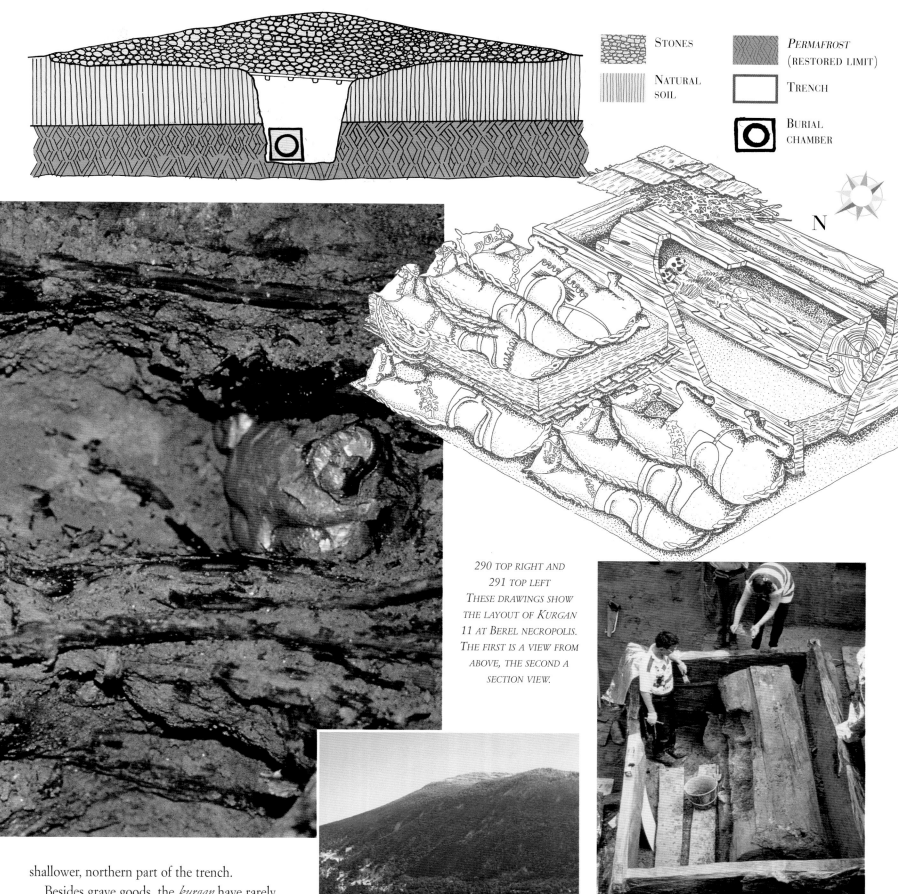

N

shallower, northern part of the trench.

Besides grave goods, the *kurgan* have rarely contained human remains and organic materials but this was the case of the *kurgan* of the priestess of Ak-Alakha on the Ulok plateau in the royal necropolis of Pazyryk, excavated in 1929 and 1950, and also in *kurgan* 11 in Berel necropolis. Berel necropolis was built on a natural terrace of the Bukhtarma river where excavation of *kurgan* 11, the first in a line of four tumuli, was begun in August 1998 by an international archaeological mission promoted by the Ligabue Research and Study Center of Venice, the National Scientific Reseach Center of Paris, and the Margulan Institute of Kazakhstan under the direction of H.P. Francfort and Z. Samishev with the support of E. Barinova.

*290 TOP RIGHT AND 291 TOP LEFT THESE DRAWINGS SHOW THE LAYOUT OF KURGAN 11 AT BEREL NECROPOLIS. THE FIRST IS A VIEW FROM ABOVE, THE SECOND A SECTION VIEW.*

*290 BOTTOM LEFT THIS BRIDLE RING IS DECORATED WITH A TIGER'S HEAD; THE VOLUTES OF THE EARS SOFTEN THE ALARMING IMAGE.*

*290-291 THIS PHOTOGRAPH SHOWS THE TIGER-HEAD BRIDLE RINGS MADE FROM WOOD AND GOLD LEAF AT THE MOMENT THEY WERE DISCOVERED IN THE PERMAFROST.*

*291 CENTER THIS DRAWING RECONSTRUCTS THE FUNERARY TRENCH OF KURGAN 11 IN BEREL NECROPOLIS. TO THE NORTH WE SEE THE BURIAL CHAMBER WITH THE SARCOPHAGUS MADE FROM A HOLLOWED LARCH TREE, AND TO THE SOUTH THE BURIAL OF THE 12 HORSES ON TWO LEVELS, COMPLETE WITH TRAPPINGS.*

*291 BOTTOM LEFT A VIEW OF BEREL NECROPOLIS IN NORTHEAST KAZAKHSTAN.*

*291 BOTTOM RIGHT INSIDE THE BURIAL CHAMBER, ARCHAEOLOGISTS CARRY OUT THE PRELIMINARY OPERATIONS FOR TRANSPORTATION OF THE SARCOPHAGUS TO ALMATY.*

Concluded in June 1999, the dig led to the
exceptional discovery of a royal tomb from the
fourth century BC that had been preserved in the
permafrost. Although the tumulus had been
plundered in ancient times, the layer of
permafrost was in good condition at a depth of
four meters and boded well for the condition of
the trench that was discovered lying east/west six
meters below ground level. The funerary
chamber occupied the northern section of the
trench and was built with planks of larch. The
southern part of the trench held the remains of
12 horses covered with richly worked trappings;
they were arranged in lines of six on two layers
divided by sheets of bark and twigs. The tomb
robbers had damaged the upper layer but the
lower was in good condition, with their coats well
preserved despite a certain degree of
decomposition and the fact that the weight of the
tumulus had flattened the animals.

The funerary chamber was built with planks of
pine and larch and covered inside with sheets of

*293 TOP THIS IS HOW THE BRIDLE RINGS IN THE FORM OF STYLIZED MOUNTAIN SHEEP APPEARED WHEN DISCOVERED IN THE PERMAFROST.*

*293 BOTTOM THIS SMALL SIXTH CENTURY BC PLAQUE REPRODUCES A CONTEST BETWEEN A GRYPHON AND A*

*HERBIVORE. ITS GRAECO-PERSIAN STYLE ATTESTS TO THE TRADE THAT TOOK PLACE BETWEEN THE NEAR EAST AND CENTRAL ASIA.*

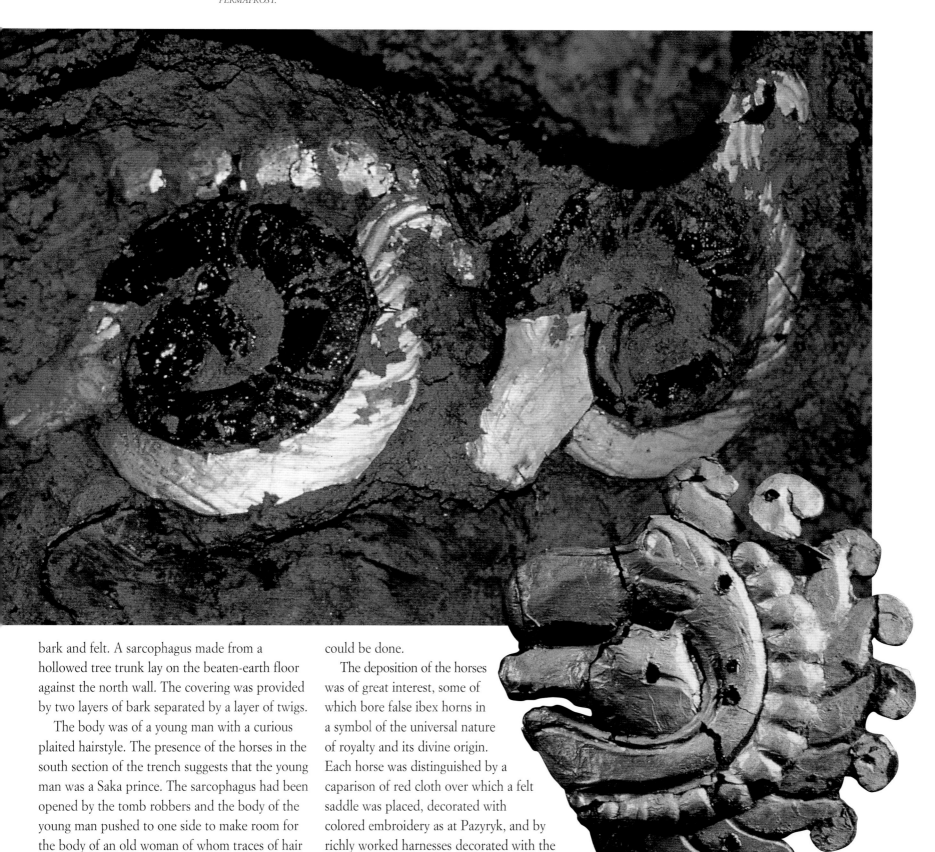

bark and felt. A sarcophagus made from a hollowed tree trunk lay on the beaten-earth floor against the north wall. The covering was provided by two layers of bark separated by a layer of twigs.

The body was of a young man with a curious plaited hairstyle. The presence of the horses in the south section of the trench suggests that the young man was a Saka prince. The sarcophagus had been opened by the tomb robbers and the body of the young man pushed to one side to make room for the body of an old woman of whom traces of hair and clothing still remained. Although neither of the two bodies had been mummified, the thickness of the permafrost had protected the bodies to the extent that many botanical tests could be made.

The difficulty of excavating a frozen *kurgan* lies in maintaining the conditions of the find exactly the same. It was therefore necessary to cut the permafrost into numbered blocks and transport them in refrigerator trucks to Almaty where analysis, inventory, and descriptions of the finds

could be done.

The deposition of the horses was of great interest, some of which bore false ibex horns in a symbol of the universal nature of royalty and its divine origin. Each horse was distinguished by a caparison of red cloth over which a felt saddle was placed, decorated with colored embroidery as at Pazyryk, and by richly worked harnesses decorated with the images of animals. In addition, each horse was identified by an animal (tiger, mountain sheep, elk, gryphon, etc.) for totemic reasons. The elaborate trappings were decorated with gilded wooden plaques engraved with the heads of wild animals, passing elks, scenes of animals fighting, and bridle rings decorated with elegant volutes of stylized mountain sheep, all of which were executed in the animalistic style typical of the culture of the steppes.

A sheet of gilded wood depicted a deer being

hunted by a gryphon, but the portrayal was reduced simply to the heads of the two animals. The image was based on a Graeco-Persian composition that could be identified by the streaked mane of the gryphon but, more importantly, attested to the long-distance commercial links of the flourishing Saka trading centers of the steppes.

# The Stupa at SANCHI

## IN THE MADHYA PRADESH

294 THE NORTH TORANA OF THE GREAT STUPA AT SANCHI IS ONE OF THE FOUR ENTRANCES TO THE BALUSTRADE THAT SURROUNDS THE CENTRAL BODY OF THE STUPA. TORANA ARE ELABORATE GATEWAYS DATING FROM THE 1ST CENTURY AD ALIGNED WITH THE FOUR POINTS OF THE COMPASS.

295 TOP THE TORANA WERE DECORATED WITH SCENES FROM THE LIFE OF BUDDHA USING SYMBOLS.

THE TREE REFERS TO HIS ENLIGHTENMENT AND SPIRITUAL SUPREMACY AND IS THEREFORE AN OBJECT OF WORSHIP, AS IN THIS TILE ON THE WEST TORANA.

295 BOTTOM THE REPRODUCTION ON THIS DETAIL OF THE FIRST ARCHITRAVE ON THE NORTH TORANA COMMEMORATES THE DEPARTURE OF THE BUDDHA FROM THIS WORLD.

The cultural world of India, filled with splendid works of art, devoted little effort to funerary architecture. It was only with the arrival of the Moslem invaders in the 12th century that mausoleums were developed, and it was probably this influence that prompted the rulers of the Rajput (Hindu warriors settled in what is today the state of Rajasthan) to build *chattri* (colonnaded pavilions topped by cupolas) on the cremation sites of their royal families. Disinterest in funerary monuments is consequent upon the fundamental belief in Indian culture that existence is not exhausted in a single life but slowly unravels throughout innumerable rebirths in different bodies. This reduces the value placed on the body of the dead person, who was not unique but is always reproduced in a different form each time he returns to life. The theory of *samsara* relates to the chain of rebirths and is rooted in the notion that the sum of the individual's personal actions during life initiates a series of effects which can only be partially enjoyed during the life in which they were generated. A sizable portion of the results of these deeds – known as *karma* – matures over a long period and determines the destiny of the individual in the next stage of his existence: it is therefore possible for the individual to create for himself a better future life by virtuous behavior in his current condition. The ultimate goal is not, however, to

improve one's condition of *samsara* but to interrupt it by means of personal conduct that does not result in further consequences. The conception of *karma* and, consequently, *samsara* is typical of the Hindu world and was the basis of the beliefs of Siddhartha Gautama who became the Buddha, the "Enlightened One," in the sixth century. Gautama had attained the Truth that lies hidden in the depths of every human being and had therefore reached the condition of enlightenment. Recognizing the suffering that

afflicts humanity and the universe, both consisting of unending series of ephemeral, painful, and meaningless phenomena, the Buddha had discovered that the root of suffering lies in attachment and preached the detached existence of the wandering ascetic as its antidote. In accordance with the Buddha's wishes, the ashes from his cremation were divided between eight of the most important rulers of the time, who had been present at his funeral, with the injunction to construct tombs over the reliquaries. Tradition tells us that this was the origin of the *stupa*, the most important monument in Buddhist architecture; the *stupa* is clearly the descendant of the ancient mounds of earth and brick that were used to cover the remains of important individuals during the second and first millennia

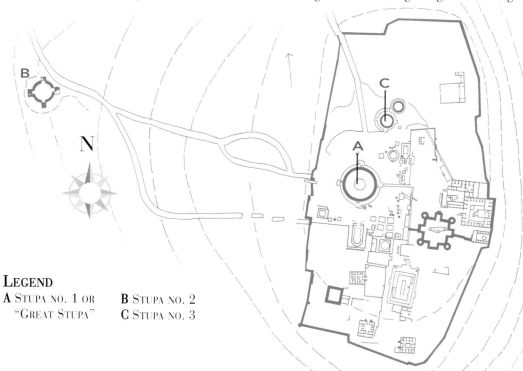

LEGEND
A STUPA NO. 1 OR "GREAT STUPA"
B STUPA NO. 2
C STUPA NO. 3

296 TOP LEFT THE PANEL ON THE EAST TORANA THAT SHOWS PART OF A ROYAL PROCESSION IS SO PERFECTLY DETAILED THAT WE ARE ABLE TO FORMULATE HYPOTHESES ON URBAN ARCHITECTURE IN WHICH MULTI-STORIED HOUSES WERE TOPPED BY WOODEN BALCONIES.

296 BOTTOM LEFT ANIMAL AND FLORAL IMAGES ARE WIDELY USED IN DECORATIVE PANELS; THIS ONE, ON THE WEST TORANA, SHOWS A CHARACTER WEARING THE TURBAN THAT WAS TYPICAL OF THE MAURYA PERIOD.

BC regardless, it seems, of whether they were buried or cremated. Cremation came to predominate, but Buddhism endowed the *stupa* with the meaning of the funeral tomb and transformed it into the tangible evocation of the presence of the Buddha and the venerable masters that followed him in the Buddhist monastic community. As a reliquary, the *stupa* took on many symbolic meanings, alluding not just to the Buddha but also to the *Dharma* – his doctrine – and representing the universe and

296 RIGHT THIS TILE ON THE EAST TORANA SHOWS HOW THE FIRST HOLY BUDDHIST SITES AROSE AROUND THE PIPAL TREE, THE SYMBOL OF ENLIGHTENMENT. THEY WERE ENCLOSED BY A WOODEN FENCE WITH A PORTICOED PAVILION FOR THE RITUAL CIRCUMAMBULATION.

referring to its cosmogony.

The "Great Stupa" was built at Sanchi, 70 kilometers from Bhopal, the capital of the state of Madhya Pradesh, and is the most complete and representative example of this type of monument. Its position on a rise at the confluence of two rivers offered many advantages: its natural and isolated setting favored monasticism, while its proximity to what at one time was the prosperous caravan city of Vidisha (today Besnagar) promoted relations with communities of merchants, the principal supporters of Buddhism. The many votive inscriptions on the *stupa* are direct indications of the generosity of the local merchants towards the construction of the various parts of the monument.

Sanchi continued to be an important place of devotion from its probable date of foundation in the third century BC until the 13th century AD, when Buddhism suffered a great decline in India, and the many monuments built during those centuries constitute a valuable archive for study of the evolution of Buddhist art.

297 BETWEEN THE JAMB AND THE ARCHITRAVE OF THE EAST TORANA, WE SEE THE OPULENT SHALABHANJIKA, THE DRYAD THAT GATHERS SHALA'S FLOWERS. SHE IS THE INCARNATION OF THE FERTILITY OF NATURE, WHICH IN TURN IS REPRESENTED BY THE YAKSHI, FEMALE SPIRITS THAT LIVE IN TREES.

The Stupa at
Sanchi

298 THE NORTHERN
TORANA OF THE GREAT
STUPA IS RICHLY
DECORATED WITH
WORSHIPING FIGURES AND
SURMOUNTED BY GREAT
SCULPTED DRUMS.

298-299 ELEPHANTS PLAY A
VERY IMPORTANT ROLE IN
THE DECORATIVE SCHEME OF
THE GREAT STUPA,
FOR BUDDHA HIMSELF IS
BELIEVED TO BE INCARNATED
IN THIS ANIMAL.

300 TOP A DOUBLE FLIGHT OF STEPS ALLOWS THE VISITOR TO CLIMB UP ON THE PLINTH OF THE GREAT STUPA TO PERFORM PRADAKSHINA, THE RITUAL CLOCKWISE CIRCUMAMBULATION.

300-301 THE IMAGE OF BUDDHA ON THE BASE OF THE STUPA DATES FROM THE 5TH CENTURY AD DURING THE GUPTA DYNASTY. IMAGES OF THE BUDDHA BEGAN TO APPEAR IN HUMAN FORM ONLY AFTER THE 2ND-3RD CENTURY AD, WHEN BUDDHISM STARTED TO ATTRIBUTE ITS FOUNDER WITH THE STATURE ACCORDED TO A DIVINITY.

Sanchi's fame is not linked to any episode in the life of the Buddha but is owed to the fact that one of the queens of Ashoka, the great emperor of the Maurya dynasty who embraced the Buddhist doctrine in the third century, came from a family of rich merchants from Vidisha. Buddhist chronicles recorded the visit that prince Mahendra, the person responsible for the diffusion of the message of the Enlightened One in Sri Lanka, made to his mother, and it was probably on this occasion that the oldest nucleus of the Great Stupa was built in baked brick and mortar.

Forgotten for centuries, the site was rediscovered by chance in 1818 by General Taylor and became a destination for amateur archaeologists and treasure hunters. Restoration work began in 1851 but it was not for another 30 years that systematic excavation of more than 50 buildings began under Major Cole and was completed by John Marshall, superintendent of the Archaeological Department from 1912-19. The main *stupa*, known as the "Great Stupa" or *stupa* no.1, has a diameter of 36.6 meters and is 16.46 meters high excluding the part at the top. The current monument dates from the second century BC, when a smaller construction attributed to Ashoka was incorporated within a body built from local sandstone blocks covered by a thick layer of plaster and expanded with new structures. The *stupa* stands inside an enclosure – the *vedika* – whose original construction from jointed laths can still be seen. The *vedika* has 4 gates, or *torana*, built in the first century AD, with two pillars topped by three curved architraves separated from one another by square blocks and by processions of riders on elephants and horses. The sinuous figures of *shalabhanjika* or *yakshi* (tree-spirits) stretch from the abacus of the jamb to the spiral volute on the first architrave while a great number of bas-reliefs decorate the surfaces of the *torana*. The *stupa* is in

300 BOTTOM THE PARASOL DEPICTED IN A TILE ON THE WEST TORANA WAS NOT SIMPLY A FUNCTIONAL OBJECT, IT WAS ALSO A SYMBOL OF EXCELLENCE IN BOTH A ROYAL AND SPIRITUAL CONTEXT.

302-303 THE SPIRALS THAT APPEAR AT THE ENDS OF THE ARCHITRAVES ON THE WEST TORANA ARE DECORATIVE ELEMENTS OF PARTICULAR IMPORTANCE: THEY SYMBOLIZE THE EXPANSION AND CONTRACTION OF THE COSMOS AND ALSO ALLUDE TO THE ESTRANGEMENT AND RETURN OF MAN TO HIS DEEPEST CENTER.

three sections: the high circular base, or *medhi*, that represents the earth; the dome-shaped body which stands on the base and alludes to the sky and, given its name of *anda*, also refers to the cosmic "egg" that floats on the primordial waters from which the universe was born; and the square railing – the *harmika*, on which the mast, or *yasti*, stands that symbolizes the center around which *stupa* winds, "compressing itself" in an ideal three-dimensional spiral made from a concentric series of bricks alternated with filling material – is finished with a sheath of stones. As a link between the underworld, the world and the sky, the *yasti* is a symbol of the *axis mundi* which is expressed in the Indian world as either a mountain or cosmic tree. And indeed the *harmika* and *yasti* refer to both, even if the Buddhist world seems to prefer the image of the tree given that Siddhartha's

enlightenment was attained below a pipal tree (*ficus religiosa*). The tree itself became an object of devotion and so was enclosed by a wooden fence that came to be symbolized by the *harmika* and was later transformed into a pavilion of worship.

Three parasols on the *yasti* symbolize the three jewels of Buddhism: the Buddha himself, the *Sangha,* and the *Dharma,* i.e., the Enlightened One, the Community, and the Doctrine. Although no reliquary has been found in a special chamber below the *yasti*, this remains the heart of the monument in its allusion to the immanent presence of the Buddha. At the same time, the *stupa* renders cosmogonic and metaphysical meanings explicit; for example, the circular form of the *anda* refers to the cyclical nature of existence, i.e., to the uninterrupted train of lives of *samsara* and, at the same time, it reproduces the

mythical structure of the world in a concentric series of continents that lie within rings of ocean. Similarly, the *vedika* not only separates the sacred space from the profane world, it also symbolizes the mountains that surround the universe. The *torana* also evoke the initiatory symbolism of the doorway, a place of communication between the profane and the sacred worlds, a cipher of spiritual transformation that occurs when entering the temple perimeter. The arms of the ideal cross that determine the sacred space project from the center and end at the four points of the compass. The right-to-left layout of the 4 *torana* transforms the cross into a *svastika*, the symbol of the sun and time. But the central point from which the cross extends is none other than the Buddha in the sense that he is Absolute, the First Principle, and the origin of space and time.

# The Stupa at Sanci

The cross in the form of the *svastika* stretches towards the periphery, symbolizing the concepts of cosmogonic and doctrinal irradiation in the sense that the doctrine of the Buddha – the *Dharma* – spreads equally towards all regions of the universe. The corridor between the *stupa* and the enclosure is for the ritual of *pradakshina*, or circumambulation, which consists of walking clockwise around the building following the path of the sun. And, as the *stupa* is a closed monument, the devotions of the initiate can only be practiced from the outside. There are no pictures of Siddhartha (the historical Buddha) on the gateways of Sanchi. At the time the *torana* were built, the more ancient and traditional school of Buddhist thought, the Theravada or "Way of the Elders," also known as the Hinayana or "Lesser Vehicle (of salvation)," was predominant, which placed more importance on the Buddha as the incarnation of the doctrine than on his human dimension as the Master. Consequently, the presence of the Buddha in the

bas-reliefs is evidenced by symbols, such as the footprints, connected with his presence: the tree symbolizes the moment of his enlightenment, the throne and the parasol emphasize his prominence among the members of the monastic communities, the wheel signifies diffusion of his doctrine, and the *stupa* is the celebration of his attainment of *nirvana* (the state of extinction from the incessant and painful earthly existence). However, the creative urge of the artists found ample material for expression in the "Jataka," the writings describing the previous lives of the Buddha in various guises.

The nearby *stupa* no. 3 is much smaller and simpler. It was built at the same time as the larger *stupa* but is preceded by a single portal like the others of the first century AD. Although of a lesser artistic value, this *stupa* has great religious importance, as it contains two sarcophaguses with the remains of Shariputra and Maugdalyayana, famous disciples of the Buddha.

Also the more distant *stupa* no. 2, standing on an artificial terrace at a height of 320 meters below the

summit of the hill, houses the remains of at least three generations of illustrious Buddhist masters in the reliquary chamber, which is strangely off-center. It is similar to *stupa* no. 3, and probably dates back to the second century BC as well, but without *torana* although its balustrade is decorated with simple, archaic scenes and splendid images of flowers and animals.

There are many other *stupa* in different states of preservation all around Sanchi hill: they do not contain reliquaries but are the votive offerings of pilgrims. Built in brick or stone depending on their size, on square or round ground plans, and once lined with stucco and painted, they demonstrate that the traditional funerary purpose of such structures slowly gave way to a celebratory function. The *stupa* represents the totality of the Buddhist world, which has its Supreme Guide in the Enlightened One, the message that leads to salvation in the Doctrine, and the Community of the faithful in monks and laymen.

*304-305 TOP AND BOTTOM STUPA 3 HAS JUST ONE TORANA, SUPPORTED BY FOUR YAKSHAS ON EACH JAMB (BOTTOM). IT WAS GREATLY VENERATED BECAUSE IT HOUSED THE RELICS OF TWO DIRECT DISCIPLES OF BUDDHA.*

*217 BOTTOM INFERIOR IN THE QUALITY OF THEIR MANUFACTURE, THE PANELS ON THE TORANA OF STUPA NO. 3 STILL OFFER INTERESTING SYMBOLIC IMAGES LIKE THIS REPRODUCTION OF A FIGHT WITH A SEA SERPENT.*

*306-307 A SUCCESSION OF HORSEMEN DECORATES THE BLOCKS THAT SEPARATE THE THREE ARCHITRAVES OF THE NORTHERN TORANA OF THE GREAT STUPA. THE PORTALS OF THE MONUMENT MARKED THE THRESHOLD BETWEEN PROFANE AND SACRED WORLDS.*

# The ANGKOR WAT complex

Angkor Wat

*Cambodia*
**ANGKOR**

The remains of the greatest and most interesting empire in Indochina flourished from the 9th-14th century AD in Cambodia. It was profoundly influenced by Indian culture, which had been diffused as early as the first centuries of the Christian era by Brahmans – the Hindu caste of priests – who arrived in Indochina in the retinue of merchants and were invited to stay at local courts as a result of their esoteric knowledge.

The Khmer rulers built their monuments following the rules of traditional Hindu architecture in a symbolic expression of profound cosmic and metaphysical themes. The many temples that still remain in Cambodia, particularly in the area of Siemréab, are evidence of a fertile fusion of native and imported elements. The local Khmer worship of ancestors and of the sacred mountain was merged with the Hindu ideal of the universal ruler and the myths of Mount Meru: the cosmic mountain, the center of the world and its regulating axis.

A grandiose Brahman ceremony celebrated on the sacred mountain of Phnom Kulen in the 11th century sanctioned the cult of the *devaraja* or "god-king" for the first time. It recounts that Shiva, one of the most important of Hindu gods, appeared to king Jayavarman II and invested him with the function of protector of the universe and as his representative on earth. As evidence of that power, Shiva conferred on the king the *linga*, or phallic-shaped stone, which was the god's symbol, and from that moment the sacred object became the tabernacle of the regal essence of the *devaraja*.

Consequently, during his reign each ruler built his own temple to hold the *linga* as a sign of his sovereignty and his divine essence, or to hold the image of the divinity with which he identified himself.

*308 TOP  WINDOWS WITH TURNED COLUMNS, POSSIBLY DERIVED FROM ANCIENT BAMBOO MODELS, LIGHTENED THE WALLS OF THE GALLERIES OF ANGKOR WAT.*

*308 BOTTOM  ANGKOR WAT IS THE SYMBOL OF THE MYTHICAL MOUNT MERU, WHICH RISES FROM THE COSMIC OCEAN, AND IS ARRANGED IN THREE TERRACES.*

*308-309  THE MAIN ENTRANCE TO ANGKOR WAT (BUILT DURING THE FIRST HALF OF THE 12TH CENTURY) IS INCORPORATED THE WESTERN FAÇADE, BEARING OUT THE THEORY THAT THE COMPLEX SERVED A FUNERARY PURPOSE.*

*309 BOTTOM  THE LIVELY SCENES DECORATING THE PEDIMENTS OF ANGKOR WAT, FRAMED BY MANY-HEADED NAGA SNAKES, DRAW ON HINDU MYTHOLOGY.*

## LEGEND

**A** PAVED ROAD THAT CONNECTS THE TEMPLE TO THE OUTER ENCLOSURE
**B** CROSS-SHAPED PLATFORM
**C** FIRST ENCLOSURE (PORTICO OF BAS-RELIEFS)
**D** CROSS-SHAPED CLOISTER
**E** LIBRARIES
**F** FIRST TERRACE
**G** SECOND TERRACE
**H** THIRD TERRACE
**I** MAIN SANCTUARY

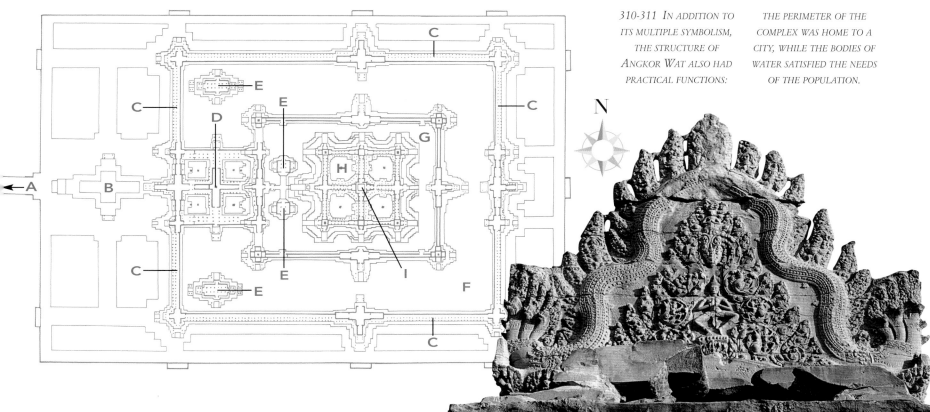

310-311 IN ADDITION TO ITS MULTIPLE SYMBOLISM, THE STRUCTURE OF ANGKOR WAT ALSO HAD PRACTICAL FUNCTIONS: THE PERIMETER OF THE COMPLEX WAS HOME TO A CITY, WHILE THE BODIES OF WATER SATISFIED THE NEEDS OF THE POPULATION.

N

On the king's death, his temple also assumed the additional function of a royal mausoleum. The most powerful *devaraja* also had mortuary temples built for their relatives in clear adherence to the local worship of ancestors in which the holy place also served as a link between generations. The majority of Khmer shrines therefore had a funerary function and, above all, rendered explicit the apotheosis of the king, who in life was the vicar of the god and, in death, identified himself with him. The symbolism incorporated in the temples was inspired by Hindu cosmogonic myths, especially that of the "churning of the milky ocean" in which the universe emerged from liquid, primordial chaos thanks to the joint action of the gods and devils who agitated the waters, using the cosmic mountain as a churning stick. The temple-mountain was therefore built in the center of a pool that symbolized the primordial waters in which life was hidden waiting to be made manifest. It was also the *devaraja* who gave and guaranteed existence to human beings: by constructing the *baray*

*312 AND 313 LOUIS DELAPORTE, A MEMBER OF THE 1866 "MEKONG EXPLORATION COMMISSION" EXPEDITION, MADE EXOTIC DRAWINGS OF ANGKOR WAT (TOP,*

*GENERAL VIEW; BOTTOM RIGHT, THE PAVED AVENUE AND THE MAIN ENTRANCE) AND THE BAYON, THE TEMPLE MOUNTAIN BUILT IN THE 13TH CENTURY (BOTTOM LEFT).*

*314-315 THE HEART OF THE KHMER CITY WAS CONSTITUTED BY THE RESERVOIRS (BARAYS), WHICH WERE BUILT BY ORDER OF THE KING FOR THE IRRIGATION, ALLOWING THREE ANNUAL RICE HARVESTS.*

(the pool that formed the heart of the Khmer cities and their religious structures) and the network of canals connected to it, the king both tamed and exploited water, quenching the thirst of man and animals, nourishing the rice-fields and the crops, and increasing trade. In this way, the myth of the churning of the milky ocean and the birth of the world was represented in a practical and functional way that justified the power of the *devaraja*.

Formerly, the more ancient *prasat* (the square tower-sanctuary on a stepped pyramidal base) had represented Mount Meru but soon evolved into the scenographic five-towered temple-mountain. The five towers reflected the five peaks of Mount Meru; four were placed at the corners of the temple and one in the center, all connected by colonnaded galleries. Just as the gods lived in celestial palaces on the peaks of the sacred mountain, so the king built

magnificent pavilions on the top of the temple; the result, as well as being a mausoleum, was the creation of a theatre of esoteric rites barred to the people.

The most famous funerary monument stands on the plain of Angkor, the "capital" of the Khmer empire, and was built by Suryavarman II between 1113 and 1150. It used to be called Brah or Vrah Vishnuloka, the "Sacred abode of Vishnu," the deity with whom Suryavarman identified himself and whose name he took, but is now known as Angkor Wat ("the royal monastery city"); the change of name resulted from the religious revolution initiated by Jayavarman VII in the 13th century, when the Khmer empire embraced Buddhism and Angkor Wat was transformed from a settlement dedicated to Vishnu into a Buddhist monastery that was never completely abandoned.

Angkor Wat complex is situated in the

southeast quadrant of what was the ancient capital of Yashodharapura, built in the 11th century. The temple perimeter measures 1500x1300 meters so that the internal space is about 2 square kilometers. There is a moat about 200 meters in width with terraces that lead down to the water. As the remaining buildings occupy only about 100,000 square meters, it is supposed that there used to be a series of buildings made from wood and other perishable materials for the priests, the temple staff, and very probably also for the nobility and court, as it seems that the king himself lived at Angkor Wat. The number of people that could be accommodated within the external walls could reach 20,000.

The fact that the complex faces west has caused bafflement and dispute, because temples in Hindu architecture and in the Khmer architecture that was derived from it traditionally open to the east.

316-317 THE FIRST TERRACE IS BOUNDED BY AN OPEN PORTICO DECORATED WITH GOPURA (THE ENTRANCES AT THE FOUR POINTS OF THE COMPASS) AND BY CROSS-SHAPED PAVILIONS AT THE CORNERS LIKE THE ONE IN THE FOREGROUND.

316 BOTTOM FIVE- AND SEVEN-HEADED NAGA ADORN THE BALUSTRADES THAT LINE THE AVENUES AND THE CROSS-SHAPED PLATFORM THAT OVERLOOKS THE MAIN ENTRANCE. THE NAGA SYMBOLIZE THE RAINBOW AND ARE CONSIDERED BRINGERS OF RAIN.

317 TOP TWO "LIBRARIES" STAND ON EITHER SIDE OF THE AVENUE IN THE OUTER ENCLOSURE, REACHED THROUGH THREE GOPURA.

317 BOTTOM THE PHOTOGRAPH SHOWS THE NORTHWEST WING OF THE PORTICO OF THE EXTERNAL ENCLOSURE WITH THE CROSS-SHAPED PAVILION AT THE CORNER.

318-319 ALTHOUGH GENERALLY DEFINED A "LIBRARY," THE FUNCTION OF THE ISOLATED STRUCTURE VISIBLE ON THE LEFT OF THIS PICTURE IS UNKNOWN. THE PHOTOGRAPH WAS TAKEN FACING WEST, LOOKING TOWARDS THE BREATHTAKING FIRST ENCLOSURE – THE GALLERY CONTAINING THE FAMOUS LOW RELIEFS OF ANGKOR WAT.

vaulted gallery with a double aisle closed by a solid wall on the inside and by columns on the outside. The main entrance is through a long raised open gallery with three cross-shaped entrances, each crowned by *gopura* (tall, tower-shaped structures borrowed from the architecture of southern India), while two further passages for animals and carts continue horizontally from the ends of the galleries. There are three more *gopura*-crowned openings, one for each side of the first boundary, though less elegant. The doors that open towards the four points of the compass in special pavilions, one within the other, celebrate the extension of royal power across the universe.

Once the visitor is inside the sacred city, the temple-mountain with its five peaks rises majestically before him. Another raised and paved avenue, almost 10 meters wide and flanked by *naga*, leads towards the temple. At regular intervals, six flights of steps per side lead to ground level, where housing and other lay

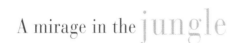

A mirage in the jungle

Suryavarman's decision may be justified by the fact that the funeral and related ceremonies were directed to the west, which would have emphasized the mausoleum aspect of Angkor Wat from the start of its construction. Furthermore, if the new city and its temple had been built facing east in the ancient capital of Yashodharapura, they would have faced away from the existing settlement, which would have been most ominous.

A masterpiece of proportions and balance, Angkor Wat rises 65 meters over the plain of Angkor. To enter the site, one crosses the moat

on a wide avenue 250 meters long and 12 meters wide paved with sandstone slabs on an embankment. The avenue is lined by a splendid *naga* balustrade and leads to the first enclosure wall, built from laterite. *Naga* are five- or six-headed snakes and, though a Hindu motif, they incorporate the local figure of the dragon of the waters, the bringer of rain and symbol of the rainbow that connects the heavens and the earth: it is quite deliberate, therefore, that they were chosen to embellish the avenue that connects the world of the profane to that of the sacred.

The front of the outer enclosure consists of a

buildings once stood. About halfway along the avenue, one comes across two buildings of uncertain purpose, but conventionally called "libraries," each about 40 meters long. They are built in the shape of a cross with three aisles and a vaulted ceiling, and hypostyle porticoes on the four sides that can be reached only via steps. Two rectangular pools lie further along; just before the entrance to the temple proper, the avenue opens into a cross-shaped platform on two levels, the lower of which stands on short round columns that resemble piles, an architectural feature that is fundamental to Cambodian construction.

*320 TOP LEFT THE FACES OF THE GODDESSES OF ANGKOR WAT ILLUMINATED BY AN INNER SMILE WERE ALL PORTRAYED WITH ELABORATE HAIRSTYLES OR, IF MALE, WITH CROWNS.*

*320 CENTER LEFT THE SECOND TERRACE STANDS ON A MOULDED PLINTH CROWNED BY A PORTICO WITH BLIND WINDOWS. THE LATERAL FLIGHTS OF STEPS LEAD TO ENTRANCE PAVILIONS WITH OVERLAID ROOFS.*

# The mountain of the gods

*320 BOTTOM LEFT VIEW OF THE PORTICO, WITH WINDOWS IN THE SHAPE OF SMALL TOWERS, AND OF THE CORNER TOWER ON THE SECOND TERRACE AS SEEN FROM THE CENTRAL BLOCK.*

*320 RIGHT THE VERTICAL THRUST OF THE SANCTUARY'S CROSS-SHAPED CENTRAL TOWER IS EMPHASIZED BY THE BUTTRESSES OF THE FOUR PORTICOES, WHICH CORRESPOND TO THE FOUR POINTS OF THE COMPASS.*

*321 ONE OF THE FOUR CORNER TOWERS (PRASAT) ON THE THIRD TERRACE. THE SURFACE OF THE PRASAT IS MARKED BY CONTINUOUS PROTUBERANCES AND RECESSES.*

The platform leads to the gallery's main entrance, formed by an avant-corps with one portico within another, surrounding the first of the three terraces on which Angkor Wat stands. Built on a high and richly moulded plinth, the gallery is made up of covered pillar porticoes that flank vaulted corridors supported by a blind wall. The gallery forms a rectangle measuring 187x215 meters and supports an incredible train of bas-reliefs 500 meters long. At the sides of the main entrance pavilion, two flights of steps lead up to the entrances from the ground, and the same structure is repeated symmetrically on the back of the first terrace. Two other, cross-shaped pavilions and steps open into the two side walls. The expedient of the cross-shaped pavilion with lateral steps is ingeniously used at the corners of the perimeter gallery as well, thus interrupting the horizontal sweep with the verticality of the roofs above.

One of the most original elements of the entire construction of Angkor Wat lies between the first and second levels: the cross-shaped cloister. Three parallel corridors, leading from the three entrances in the first gallery to the steps of the three *gopura* on the

# A mirage in the jungle

322-323 AND 323 TOP LEFT  The enigmatically smiling devata of Angkor Wat, beautiful female deities with complex hairstyles, wear skirts knotted at the front, with a wide panel on the right and a narrower band on the left.

322 BOTTOM  The many statues of the Buddha at Angkor Wat attest to the transformation of the Hindu sanctuary into a place of Buddhist worship which began in the 13th century.

323 TOP RIGHT  The main gallery in the cross-shaped portico once had a gilded wooden ceiling that hid the vault.

by the quincunx, stands in this enclosure measuring 100x115 meters. Twelve very steep stairways lead up to the third terrace, 60 meters long on each side. It is surrounded by a gallery with colonnaded windows that open both on the inside and the outside; the gallery has cross-shaped pavilions at the corners and *gopura* above the entrances facing the four points of the compass. The third terrace also has the cross-shaped ground plan of the cloister, which is achieved

floor above, are crossed at right angles by a fourth gallery with three aisles, thus creating four small internal courtyards. The fact that they are laid out on a high plinth and that there are steps leading down to the ground identifies the courtyards as pools of holy water which were indispensable to temple ceremonies. Beyond the cross-shaped cloister, the large first terrace also houses two "libraries."

The second terrace, 6 meters above the first and 10 meters from the ground, can be reached either from the front cloister or from steps on the other three sides and in the corner towers. Prohibited to the public, the terrace has no openings in the external wall of the gallery, but this is made attractive by the addition of blind windows with small columns. Emerging from the central stairway of the cross-shaped portico, one encounters two more small interconnected "libraries" joined to the entrance by a raised platform standing on short piles.

The 13-meter-high podium, forcefully moulded

by connecting the central *prasat* to the *gopura* with four galleries. But while the cloister extends horizontally, here the structure is imbued with a strong vertical thrust, with the central tower 42 meters high surrounded by four others that look like tiaras. This third floor represented the palace of the gods on Mount Meru and was open only to the high priest and the king; where they came into contact with the god portrayed by the statue in the central *prasat*.

## And the king became Vishnu

326 TOP  THE BAS-RELIEFS IN THE PORTICO OF THE FIRST LEVEL TERRACE PORTRAY THE DEIFICATION OF SURYAVARMAN II. THIS IS A DETAIL OF THE "JUDGMENT OF THE DEAD" ON THE SOUTH WING, SHOWING THE KING AS YAMA, THE SUPREME JUDGE.

326 BOTTOM  THE BATTLE OF KURUKSHETRA BETWEEN DIVINE AND INFERNAL POWERS AS DESCRIBED IN THE POEM THE MAHABHARATA IS PORTRAYED ON THE WEST WING.

The decoration admirably completes the monument: the multi-sided columns are divided into ten or twelve rings to make them lighter and resonant; the flat carvings of interwoven plants on the walls create a tapestry effect, and more than 1500 *apsaras* (heavenly nymphs) and *devata* (deities with complicated hairstyles) look on from every corner; sea monsters and *naga* frame the mythological scenes in the gables and pediments and are repeated in the gallery bas-reliefs, which unwind endlessly like illuminated manuscripts in the stone.

It is these bas-reliefs that underline the funerary purpose of Angkor Wat, as they are to be read, not in the customary manner of having them on one's right, but instead with them on one's left. The subjects all relate to the mythology of Vishnu, with whom the king identified himself, and appear to refer symbolically to the ruler's career. They begin with the depiction of the "churning of the milky ocean" and continue with episodes from the great Indian epics, the *Mahabharata* and the *Ramayana*, in which Vishnu, in the guises of Rama and Krishna, struggles against demonic forces, and ends with images of the judgment of the dead by Yama, lord of the afterlife, portrayed with the features of the king.

Deification of Suryavarman transformed Angkor Wat from a mausoleum into a palace of the gods with a rarefied and magical atmosphere.

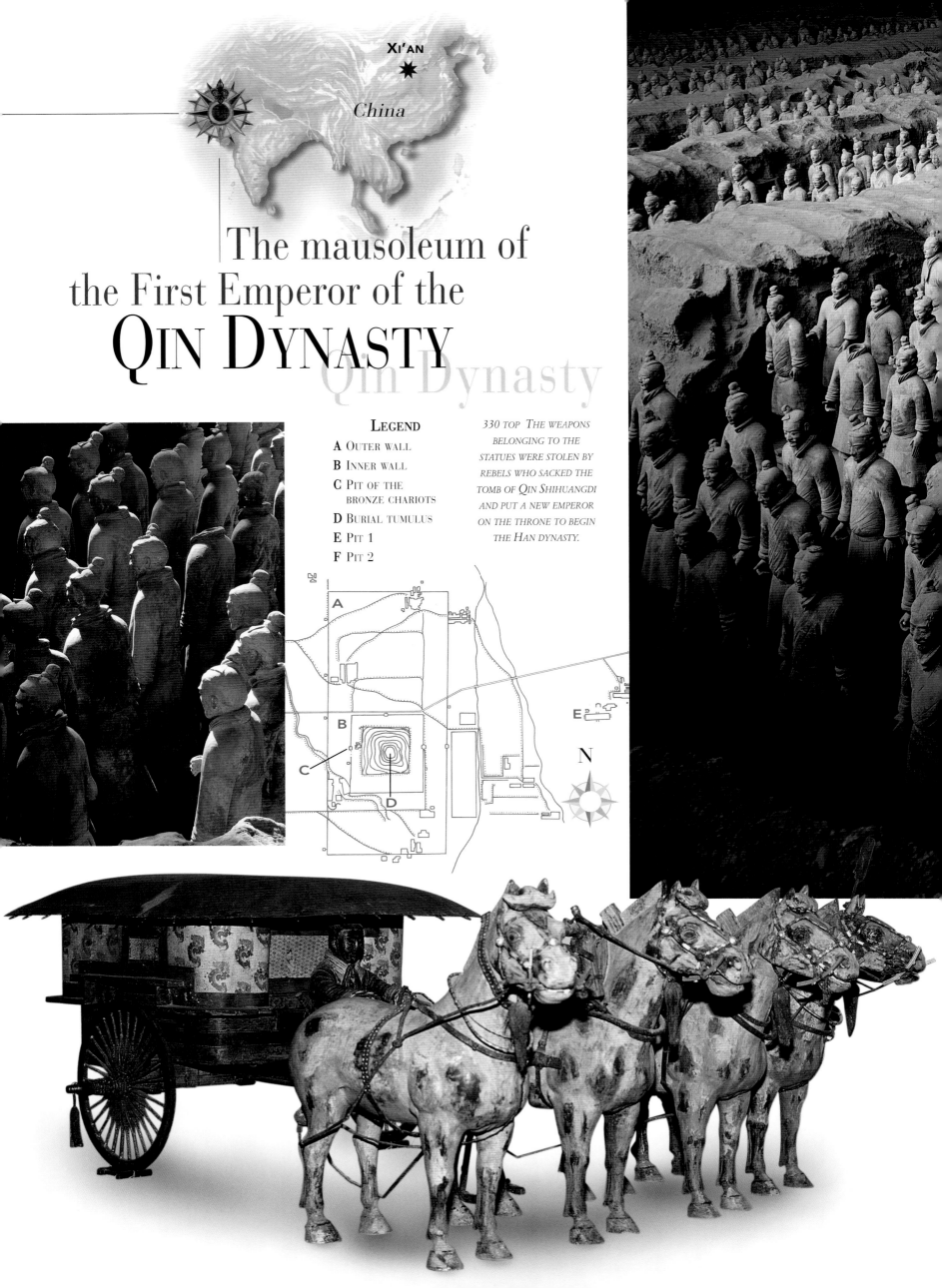

# The mausoleum of the First Emperor of the QIN DYNASTY

Xi'an

*China*

### LEGEND
**A** OUTER WALL
**B** INNER WALL
**C** PIT OF THE BRONZE CHARIOTS
**D** BURIAL TUMULUS
**E** PIT 1
**F** PIT 2

*330 TOP THE WEAPONS BELONGING TO THE STATUES WERE STOLEN BY REBELS WHO SACKED THE TOMB OF QIN SHIHUANGDI AND PUT A NEW EMPEROR ON THE THRONE TO BEGIN THE HAN DYNASTY.*

N

M uch of what we know today of the life, art, religion and culture of ancient China has been learned from the study of tombs and the splendid grave goods placed inside to accompany the eternal sleep of the dead. If it had not been for the continual preoccupation with the afterlife that deeply characterized the entire Chinese civilization from its beginnings until recent history, many pages of the history of ancient China would have remained blank to us. A very great amount of energy and money and a considerable percentage of the work force was always dedicated to the construction of monuments and mausoleums, which often featured the best artistic traditions of the various periods: they were designed to commemorate rulers, emperors, and members of the imperial household and the aristocracy forever,

almost as if the creation of long-lasting monuments could defeat the transitoriness of earthly existence. The Chinese tombs built with so much effort and expense for the wealthy well deserve the label "eternal," as they were designed right from the start to last much longer than their contemporaries, and to remain imperishable monuments that today, many centuries later, still impress us with their size. It is the very visibility of a funerary monument that gives the dead person it celebrates a continued and tangible presence in the world of the living, and the higher the social status of the person buried inside the tomb, the more the external dimensions and the magnificence of the grave goods had to reflect that status and the place he or she occupied in an organized, pyramidal society.

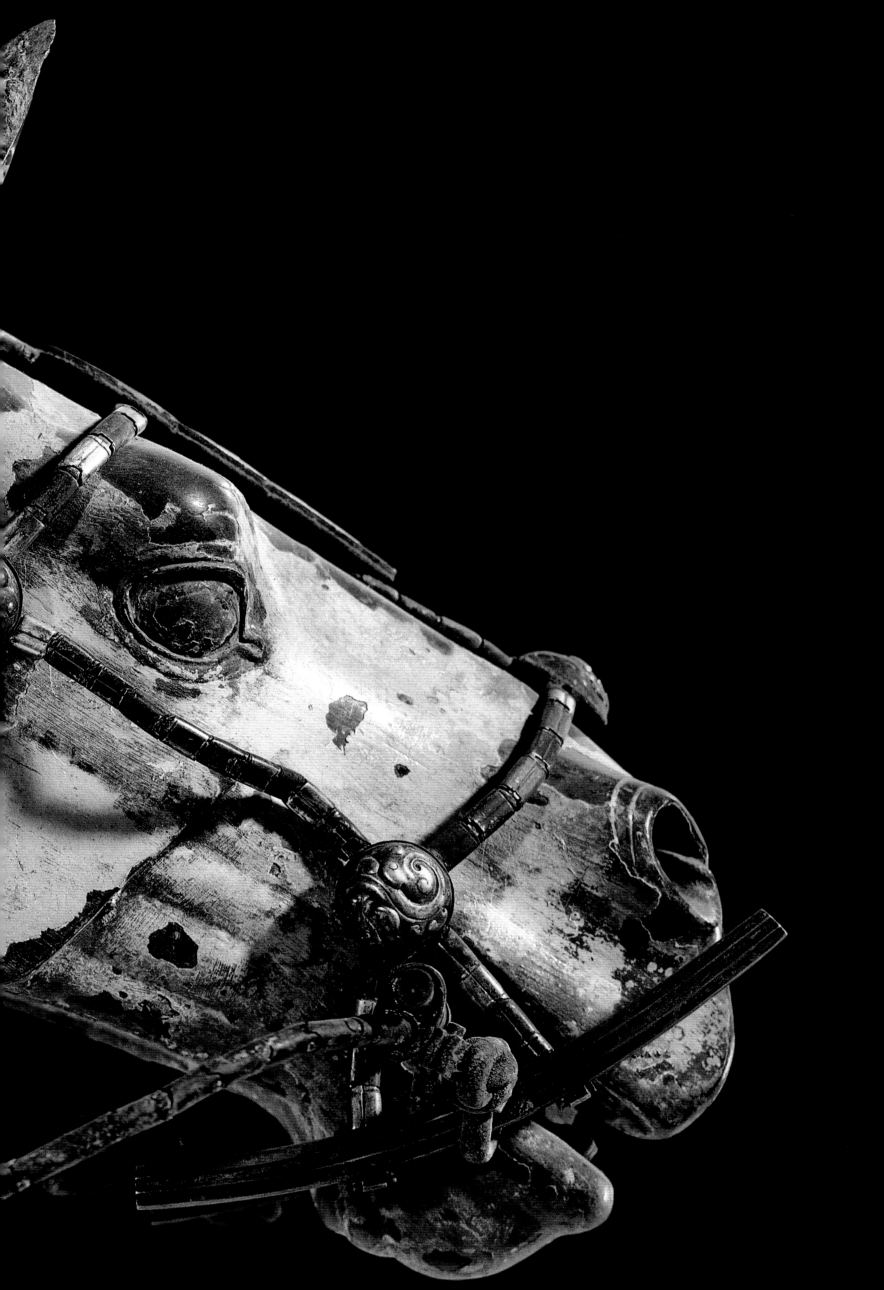

But besides this desire to make the social status of the dead perennially visible to all by means of the "ostentation" and size of the tomb, Chinese concern for the dead and for what we might call their "well-being" was the consequence of a form of religiousness that formed one of the cornerstones of Chinese culture: ancestor worship. This was not just a simple, obsequious respect for the previous members of one's family but one of the reasons for the existence of the living: the dead represented links in a chain of descendants that reinforced the identity of the individual within the family and clan. Being part of a lineage with its roots set in antiquity was in some way equal to breaking the law of transitory existence imposed on mortals by time. Widespread within all levels of Chinese society, ancestor worship assumed greater and monumental visibility the higher one's position in the social scale. This is the reason for

the magnificence of the tombs of the nobles and emperors, who were often surrounded in death by the graves of family members, individuals who, had demonstrated their loyalty to their ruler, or simply slaves to represent the same hierarchical scheme of mortal existence in the afterlife and demonstrate the strong continuity between the worlds of the living and the dead. This continuity was also emphasized by the burial of grave goods with their legitimate owners so that they might be used in the life beyond the grave in the same way they had been used in mortal existence. Right from the earliest times, this "cult of the dead" played a pivotal role in China: it was already fully in evidence among late Neolithic cultures (ca. 3500-2000 BC) in which a basic hierarchic structuring of society began to take place, which we see reflected in the tombs and funerary trappings of the élite. For example, in the Liangzhu culture, which flourished between 3300 and 2200 BC in the region of Lake Tai in eastern China, the tombs of those in the highest levels of society were profusely decorated with

ornaments and ritual objects made from jade. This material had strong symbolic value and was also to take on an important role in funerary practices in later periods of Chinese history. With the Bronze Age Shang dynasty (16th-11th century BC) and the emergence of the first form of a state in ancient China, the tombs of the kings and the aristocracy took on the form of monuments, as shown by the "royal" cemetery found near Anyang in Henan where the last of the Shang capitals was discovered. The large tombs in the shape of crosses or upside-down pyramids that penetrate deep into the ground demonstrate the past ability of the Shang rulers to manage an enormous work force and to procure the raw material, bronze, used to produce huge numbers of ceremonial containers for the preparation and consumption of food and drink. These "ritual bronze objects" were not only one of the principal components of the precious Shang grave goods but were also used by the living for the presentation of offerings to their ancestors. Despite

reflecting necessary alterations that took place in the funerary ritual and in the appearance of the tombs over time, the "dwellings of eternity" of the members of the Chinese aristocracy can be said to have assumed from this moment on the main characteristics that described them in later periods: a monumental nature, the huge expenditure of resources to construct them, and sumptuous funerary trappings. The culmination of this process in ancient China is unquestionably represented by the tomb of the First Emperor. The year 221 BC was a date of major importance in the history of China. After a long period of division and power struggles between the states into which China had separated following the decline of the central authority of the Zhou rulers, this was the year in which the Qin kingdom overcame its last adversaries

336 TOP THE FACES OF
THE TERRACOTTA SOLDIERS
WERE HAND-MODELED BY
SKILLED CRAFTSMEN AND
FAITHFULLY REPRODUCED
THE FEATURES OF EACH
INDIVIDUAL IN THE ARMY.

336 BOTTOM AND 336-337
THE ARMY COMPRISED
CAVALRY TROOPS AND WAR
CHARIOTS FOR THE HIGH-
RANKING OFFICERS. THE
ILLUSTRATIONS SHOW SOME
OF THE HORSES AND
CHARIOTS DURING
EXCAVATION.

337 BOTTOM THIS IS HOW
THE PIT CONTAINING THE
BRONZE IMPERIAL
CHARIOTS APPEARED AT
THE MOMENT IT WAS
DISCOVERED. RESTORATION
OF THESE MODELS
REQUIRED A LONG AND
DELICATE OPERATION.

338-339 IN PIT 1, TEN
WALLS OF BEATEN EARTH
SEPARATE THE ROWS OF
TERRACOTTA WARRIORS –
SIX THOUSAND IN ALL –
THAT ARE ARRANGED
ALONG A FRONT
MEASURING 755 BY 203
FEET.

and united the country under the leadership of a single man. Aware of the importance of his achievement and of the huge task of reunification he had performed, he dropped his title of *wang* (monarch), which had until then been used to designate the highest figure in the Chinese social scale, and proclaimed himself Qin Shihuangdi, "First Sovereign Emperor of the kingdom of Qin". This signaled the institution of the empire, whose very long history was only to be brought to an end in February 1912 when Pu Yi, the last emperor of the Qing dynasty (1644-1911), abdicated and the People's Republic of China was created 37 years later.

Construction of the funerary complex where the emperor was to rest for eternity began in 256 BC, the year of his ascent to the Qin throne, and was still in progress when Qin Shihuangdi died in 210 BC.

# The mausoleum of the First Emperor

Never completely finished, the immense monument was supposed to symbolize the greatness and magnificence of the First Emperor in Chinese history, and to record him for posterity with his other projects: unification and strengthening of sections of the Great Wall, engineering and hydraulic works, and standardisation of the writing script, weights and measures, and the gauge of carts for better and more efficient administration of the vast, newly created empire. The dynasty founded by the First Emperor was short-lived, although the intentions of Qin Shihuangdi were that it would continue for "ten thousand generations." Nevertheless, the country underwent profound, radical and enduring transformations between 221 and 206 BC, the years in which the dynasty flourished. The plain of Lintong was chosen as the site for the construction of the mausoleum. Not far from the modern city of Xi'an, near which the capital of the new empire was built, the large artificial tumulus stands out clearly against the Li range of mountains. Despite its much reduced size, it still plainly marks the exact spot where Qin Shihuangdi was buried. In common with the imperial tombs of the principal Chinese dynasties, the tomb of the First Emperor has not yet been excavated: the knowledge we have of the funeral ceremonies, religious practices, and contents of the grave goods of the highest levels of Chinese society has been derived from excavation of the tombs of nobles, or members of the imperial household, and from descriptions given in classical texts. This is the case with the tomb of Qin Shihuangdi, the internal structure and contents of which were described by the Chinese historian Si Maqian of the Han dynasty (206 BC – 220 AD). His reports form the basis of what we know of this important tomb while we wait for it to be opened and studied by modern archaeology. All of the First Emperor's funerary complex can be described as a gigantic "scale model" of the territories over which Qin Shihuangdi exercized his authority. The burial tumulus in this geographical microcosm is positioned off-center inside two rectangular enclosure walls where the remains of buildings, probably a series of temples for ancestor worship, have been found. Sacrificial pits have been discovered around the tumulus and near the enclosure walls in which the following objects, among others, have been unearthed: terracotta statues of servants, handmaidens of the court, and grooms; two scale models in bronze of chariots similar to those used by Qin Shihuangdi; sacrificial victims and many ditches containing the remains of animals that probably symbolized the Emperor's hunting lands; the imperial stalls and tombs of concubines and members of Qin Shihuangdi's family. The Emperor's body, according to Si Maqian's description, lies inside the tumulus in an elaborate sarcophagus in the center of a model of his conquered territories, featuring rivers of mercury kept in movement by complex mechanisms. The vault is made from bronze and studded with gems representing stars in a symbolic depiction of Heaven.

*340 THIS CHARIOTEER, WITH HIS HANDS HELD FORWARD TO HOLD THE REINS OF HIS HORSES, WAS FOUND BEHIND THE REMAINS OF A LIGHT, TWO-WHEELED CHARIOT IN PIT NO.1.*

*341 THE EXPRESSION ON THE FACE OF THIS TERRACOTTA INFANTRYMAN SHOWS PRIDE AND FEARLESSNESS. HIS LONG HAIR IS PLAITED AND HELD IN A BUN ON THE SIDE OF HIS HEAD.*

*342-343 THE FEATURES OF A YOUNG CIVIL SERVANT HAVE BEEN REPRODUCED WITH THE UTMOST SENSITIVITY IN THIS STATUE. VARIOUS TOOLS WERE USED TO MODEL THE FIGURES: WOODEN STICKS FOR LARGE SURFACES, CUTTING TOOLS FOR THE FACIAL FEATURES, AND EVEN THE ARTISTS' FINGERS FOR CERTAIN DETAILS.*

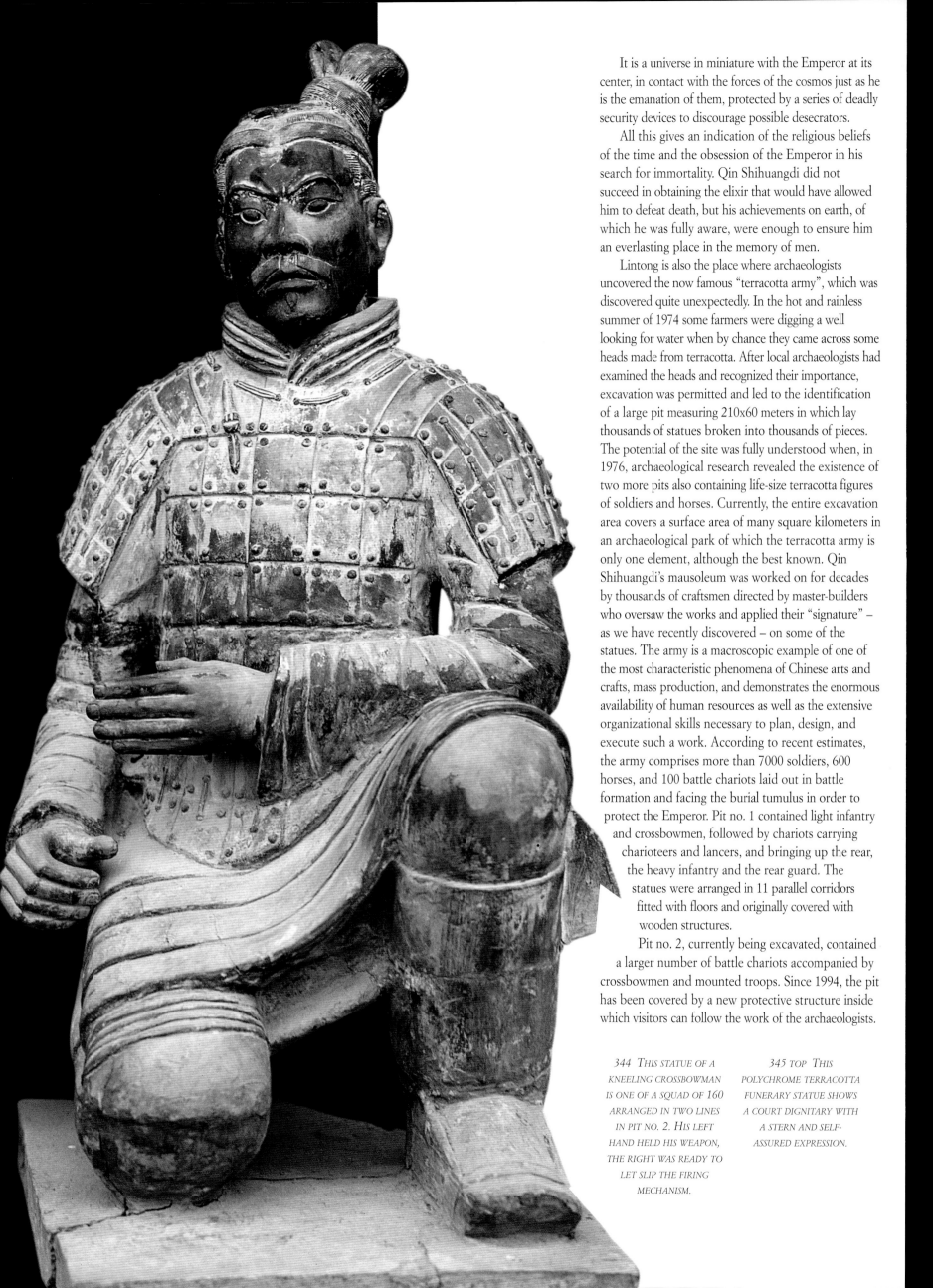

It is a universe in miniature with the Emperor at its center, in contact with the forces of the cosmos just as he is the emanation of them, protected by a series of deadly security devices to discourage possible desecrators.

All this gives an indication of the religious beliefs of the time and the obsession of the Emperor in his search for immortality. Qin Shihuangdi did not succeed in obtaining the elixir that would have allowed him to defeat death, but his achievements on earth, of which he was fully aware, were enough to ensure him an everlasting place in the memory of men.

Lintong is also the place where archaeologists uncovered the now famous "terracotta army", which was discovered quite unexpectedly. In the hot and rainless summer of 1974 some farmers were digging a well looking for water when by chance they came across some heads made from terracotta. After local archaeologists had examined the heads and recognized their importance, excavation was permitted and led to the identification of a large pit measuring 210x60 meters in which lay thousands of statues broken into thousands of pieces. The potential of the site was fully understood when, in 1976, archaeological research revealed the existence of two more pits also containing life-size terracotta figures of soldiers and horses. Currently, the entire excavation area covers a surface area of many square kilometers in an archaeological park of which the terracotta army is only one element, although the best known. Qin Shihuangdi's mausoleum was worked on for decades by thousands of craftsmen directed by master-builders who oversaw the works and applied their "signature" – as we have recently discovered – on some of the statues. The army is a macroscopic example of one of the most characteristic phenomena of Chinese arts and crafts, mass production, and demonstrates the enormous availability of human resources as well as the extensive organizational skills necessary to plan, design, and execute such a work. According to recent estimates, the army comprises more than 7000 soldiers, 600 horses, and 100 battle chariots laid out in battle formation and facing the burial tumulus in order to protect the Emperor. Pit no. 1 contained light infantry and crossbowmen, followed by chariots carrying charioteers and lancers, and bringing up the rear, the heavy infantry and the rear guard. The statues were arranged in 11 parallel corridors fitted with floors and originally covered with wooden structures.

Pit no. 2, currently being excavated, contained a larger number of battle chariots accompanied by crossbowmen and mounted troops. Since 1994, the pit has been covered by a new protective structure inside which visitors can follow the work of the archaeologists.

344 THIS STATUE OF A
KNEELING CROSSBOWMAN
IS ONE OF A SQUAD OF 160
ARRANGED IN TWO LINES
IN PIT NO. 2. HIS LEFT
HAND HELD HIS WEAPON,
THE RIGHT WAS READY TO
LET SLIP THE FIRING
MECHANISM.

345 TOP THIS
POLYCHROME TERRACOTTA
FUNERARY STATUE SHOWS
A COURT DIGNITARY WITH
A STERN AND SELF-
ASSURED EXPRESSION.

Pit no. 3, on the other hand, contains the HQ of the imperial army with statues of NCO's arranged around a chariot on which a figure that may represent the commander-in-chief of the entire army stands. Production of the terracotta soldiers was split into two distinct phases: in the first, standardized phase, the clay was extracted from nearby Mount Li, the raw material was prepared, and the basic bodies of the statues constructed. Their hollow bodies were created by the application and compacting of layers of clay in a standardized phase. In phase two, the details of the armor were delineated and the statues were painted with bright colors with great care. However, the soldiers only received individual facial features and a "personality" when the heads, produced separately and each one unique, were attached to the bodies. The individuality of every soldier suggests that each member of the army was a separate portrait.

The mausoleum of the
First
Emperor

*345 BOTTOM THE RIDER WITH HIS HORSE SADDLED AND READY WAS FOUND IN PIT NO. 2. THE SOLDIER WAS ORIGINALLY ARMED WITH A CROSSBOW HELD IN HIS RIGHT HAND.*

*346-347 A PLATOON OF ARMORED INFANTRY IS ARRAYED INSIDE THE PIT. IT IS BELIEVED THAT THE HEADDRESSES OF THE INDIVIDUAL WARRIORS REFLECTED THEIR RANK. THE FRAGMENTS OF STATUES IN AN AREA STILL BEING EXCAVATED CAN BE SEEN ON THE RIGHT.*

# Tombs and funerary practices of the HAN DYNASTY

Han Dynasty

*349 TOP LEFT THIS PHOTOGRAPH SHOWS A DETAIL OF ONE OF THE TOMB WALLS AT ANPING, WHICH WERE MOSTLY DECORATED WITH LONG LINES OF CARTS IN ROW AFTER ROW.*

*349 TOP RIGHT THE USE OF BRICK AND VAULTS WAS ONLY ADOPTED IN HAN CHINA TO BUILD TOMBS. EVERYDAY BUILDINGS WERE MAINLY BUILT FROM WOOD.*

*348-349
REPRESENTATIONS OF TRAINS OF CARTS ARE VERY COMMON IN THE HAN TOMBS. THEY SYMBOLIZE BOTH THE JOURNEY THE SOUL HAS TO MAKE AND, AS AT ANPING, THE SOCIAL STATUS OF THE DECEASED.*

*348 BOTTOM
THIS PHOTOGRAPH SHOWS THE PORTRAIT OF THE DECEASED, AN OFFICIAL IN THE HAN COURT, WEARING A LARGE RED ROBE AND A BLACK HEADDRESS.*

The mausoleum of the First Emperor served as the "model" which inspired the magnificent imperial tombs of later dynasties, starting with those of the Han dynasty (206 BC – 220 AD), founded by Liu Bang, the chief of the rebel troops who led the revolt against the Qin dynasty. Han period tombs are characterized by a broad typological diversity and a variety of construction techniques, reflecting changes which occurred over the centuries, regional traditions, and, of course, the social status of the deceased. Frequently the deceased were portrayed inside the tombs, alongside other images forming cycles of murals adorning many of the Han dynasty tombs, especially those discovered in the vicinity

of Luoyang, the second capital of the Han. An example of a tomb decorated with murals is the one excavated in 1971 at Lujiazhuang, a small village in the district of Anping, Hebei province, which was dated to AD 176, the late Han period, by means of inscriptions found inside the tomb. Built entirely in bricks – a material that was used in China almost exclusively in the architecture of tombs and rarely in other types of buildings, for which wood was preferred – the tomb of Anping is divided into ten sections or halls, the main one being the funerary chamber. Here we find the mural portraying the deceased, an official of the Han court dressed in a formal robe and sitting in a dignified pose. He

is accompanied by almost unending rows of light chariots pulled by horses and painted in regular, superimposed rows distributed over the walls of the funerary chamber: the chariots symbolize both the high rank of the deceased and the journey of the soul to the afterlife.

Besides being built of bricks, Han period tombs were also cut inside the rock of hills, like those in the southwestern province of Sichuan or, on a more monumental scale, like those discovered in Shangdong in eastern China. Internally, Han tombs are often subdivided into various rooms, thus assuming the shape of underground houses if not actual palaces, as in the case, for example, of the large tomb

discovered in the region of Xuzhou, dating to the first decades of the dynasty. Motifs and images used to decorate the tombs show an obvious preference for subjects related to the afterlife, to a world populated by deities and mythical creatures such as the *xian* or "immortals", anthropomorphic beings which had human features but a body covered with feathers, when not provided with actual wings. From as early as the 5th century BC, it was believed that the *xian* dwelled on mythical islands located off the East China coast: these islands were paradisiacal places populated by other mythical creatures, where the *xian* jealously guarded the "elixir of immortality" so

of these funerary objects – had a strong magical and symbolic power, since they represented the substitutes for the actual things and beings portrayed in them, which accompanied the deceased in their eternal sleep.

Many of the elements characterizing the Han funerary complexes became part of the Chinese mortuary tradition of later centuries, such as that of complementing the burial area with the so-called "Spirit Road," two rows of stone sculptures lined up along a route leading directly to the tomb. The origin of this practice is still obscure, though literary souces mention that during the Spring and Autumn period (770-476 BC) some of the feudal lords had their tumulus graves marked by large stone slabs on which protective images, clan emblems, or scenes from the afterlife were either engraved or carved in relief. However, the earliest documented use of stone sculptures as part of the "program" of a funerary monument dates to the early Han dynasty and is found at the tomb of Huo Qubing, who died in 117 BC. Huo Qubing was a general who led a series of victorious military campaigns against the Xiongnu, one of the main Central Asian nomadic tribes that regularly threatened the northern borders of the Chinese empire. The victories of Huo Qubing over the Xiongnu were so important that emperor Wudi (who reigned between 140 and 87 BC) to honor the memory of his valorous soldier, wanted the general to be buried in a large funerary tumulus constructed at Maoling, the burial ground of Han emperors. The shape of the tumulus which marks Huo Qubing's tomb is traditionally meant to recall Mount Qilian, a site where the general had triumphed in one of the most important victories over the Xiongnu. A group of

assiduously sought after by mortals, including the First Emperor of Qin. Beliefs related to the attainment of "immortality" are echoed in the use, typical of the Han period, of jade "shrouds" used to encase the corpse of the deceased. These jade shrouds, made for Han princes and members of the aristocracy, were "tailored" using thousands of jade plaques sewn together by means of gold or silver threads. Jade was preferred because religious-magical beliefs of the period held that this material preserved the body from decay and therefore ensured the preservation of the corpse. One of the most notable instances of this funerary practice is seen in the jade shrouds in which prince Liu Sheng and his consort Dou Wan were encased when they were buried in their tomb discovered at Mancheng, Hebei province. The tomb was cut into the rock of a hill and resembles an underground palace; in it were found some superb burial goods including inlaid bronze incense burners, precious containers for ritual offerings, and several metal lamps.

Han funerary art abounds in subjects related to the world of the supernatural, as can be seen in the murals and in the stone bas-reliefs discovered in Han period tombs of central and eastern China. Figures to ward off evil, deities, mythical beings, depictions of immortals and their universe predominated over subjects inspired by terrestrial life, such as portraits of the deceased, processions of carts, and scenes from daily life. However, an element of great importance in the tombs of the Han period is represented by the presence of objects connected to everyday life. These are painted terracotta statuettes reproducing people (attendants, dancers, cooks, soldiers), animals, and objects such as houses and carts. They provide an invaluable source of information on the architecture, clothing, and many other aspects of the Han world which would otherwise have remained unknown. Having come into use with the decrease in human and animal sacrifices practiced until the death of the First Emperor, the *mingqi* – the traditional name

enormous stone sculptures was positioned on and around the tumulus: they are carved with motifs of good omen alluding to the mythical realms of the immortals or celebrating the heroic deeds of the general. The most important of these sculptures is the one representing a horse trampling over a "barbarian," an allegory of the Chinese victory over their nomadic adversaries. At the beginning of the 20th century, it was this sculpture that allowed French explorer and archaeologist Victor Segalen (1878-1919) to identify this tomb as that of Huo Qubing.

By the end of the Han dynasty, the "Spirit Road" had become one of the main elements in important cemeteries, whose layout included a pair of stone pillars marking the limit of the burial area, stone sculptures on either side of the "Spirit Road,"and, at the end of this route, the tomb itself marked by a funerary tumulus in front of which might stand a commemorative stele and a small temple for the presentation of offerings to the deceased.

*350 TOP  THE STRIPES ON THE COAT OF THIS STONE SCULPTURE FOUND NEAR THE TOMB OF GENERAL HUO QUBING SUGGEST IT WAS PROBABLY A TIGER.*

*350-351 THE EXTRAORDINARY FUNERARY ROBE OF DOU WAN, CONSORT OF PRINCE LIU SHENG, APPEARS PERFECT IN EVERY ANATOMICAL DETAIL. IT WAS MADE FROM THOUSANDS OF JADE PLATES.*

*351 TOP  THIS GILDED BRONZE LAMP SHOWING A YOUNG ATTENDANT ON HIS KNEES WAS PART OF THE GRAVE GOODS FOUND IN THE TOMB OF MANCHENG.*

*351 CENTER THE RECONSTRUCTION OF MANCHENG'S TOMB SHOWS THE BURIAL CHAMBER, IN FRONT OF WHICH IS A ROOM CONTAINING FUNERARY OFFERINGS AND A TRANSVERSAL PASSAGEWAY WHERE CARTS AND HORSES WERE FOUND.*

# The imperial mausoleums of the TANG DYNASTY

QIANLING
ZHAOLING ⟩ ✦

*China*

With the dissolution of the Han empire, China entered a long phase of political disunion lasting more than three centuries during which many dynasties flourished contemporaneously. These were founded by noble Chinese families but also by members of the aristocracy of foreign peoples that controlled the northern part of the country. In the long term, the synthesis produced by this coexistence of different cultures paved the way for the great artistic, cultural, political and economic flourishing of the Tang empire (618-907 AD) which is considered the "Golden Age" of Chinese history and was unquestionably one of the greatest periods of cosmopolitanism and opening of the Far Eastern country to influences and cultural elements from abroad. This process of synthesis is also evident in the tombs of the Tang period, whose appearance, layout, internal decoration, and type of funerary trappings closely follow the models of imperial tombs of the northern Qi dynasty (550-577 AD).

The structure of these underground tombs centers on the deeply buried mortuary chamber, which is revealed to the outside world by an artificial tumulus and reached by a long descending walkway. The walls of the chamber and corridor are richly decorated with cycles of murals celebrating the deceased and his social status. Naturally there are also religious subjects, and guards were painted at the entrance to the tomb to protect the grave. Continuing the Han tradition, small funerary statues reproduced a

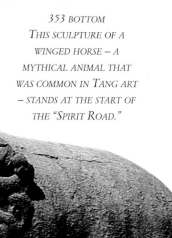

354 TOP A HORSE FLANKS THE "WAY OF THE SPIRITS" THAT LEADS TO THE IMPERIAL TOMBS. THIS ANIMAL WAS ONE OF THE FAVORITE SUBJECTS OF TANG ART, IN BOTH MYTHICAL AND REAL FORM.

354 BOTTOM DESPITE HAVING LITTLE DETAIL, THE STATUES OF THE FUNCTIONARIES THAT LINE THE "WAY OF THE SPIRITS" OF QIANLING EXUDE A COMPOSED DIGNITY THAT IMPOSES RESPECT.

354-355 A "GUARDIAN" LION PRECEDES A GROUP OF HEADLESS STATUES, WHICH ORIGINALLY DEPICTED AMBASSADORS AND FOREIGN GUESTS GATHERED AT THE FUNERAL OF THE EMPRESS WU.

scaled-down version of a world populated by women, horsemen, attendants, and soldiers, while the forms and decorations of the grave goods were an expression of the immensity of the contacts and cultural relationships of the Chinese with foreign peoples and countries, even distant ones, and of the taste for exoticism that characterized much of the art of the Tang dynasty.

Many of these characteristics are evident in the Tang funerary complex at Qianling, about 85 kilometers from the modern city of Xi'an, which used to be the capital at the time of the Tang under the name Chang'an, "Everlasting Peace." The complex is striking for its size, since it holds the largest of the imperial tombs from this dynasty. The gigantic mausoleum was built to hold the remains of the third Tang emperor, Gaozong (who reigned between 649 and 683) and his consort Wu Zetian. Close to the tumulus that indicates the burial place of the imperial couple, there are other, smaller, excavated tombs that were built for the Princes Yide and Zhanghuai and the Princess Yongtai.

The imperial couple, Gaozong and Wu Zetian, are buried in a tomb, as yet unexcavated, dug inside a natural rise that was artificially increased in size. The burial tumulus is visible from afar and is reached along a "Spirit Road" 3 kilometers long lined at the start by statues of real and mythical animals – winged horses, a pair of curious birds similar to ostriches, and pairs of horses – followed by statues of human figures. At the end of the "Spirit Road" stand two commemorative stele: a eulogy to the emperor Gaozong is engraved on the one on the left, while the one on the right is known as the "stele without inscription," as it was supposed to have been dedicated to Wu Zetian but was never completed. The right side of the "Spirit Road" is also the location of a group of headless statues representing foreign

*356-357 The practice of protecting the entrances of funerary complexes with large sculptures of lions began at Qianling. This custom replaced the mythical animals that had performed the same function during the preceding Han dynasty.*

guests and ambassadors that were present at Gaozong's funeral. Although the heads of the faithful portraits are missing, inscriptions on the back of the statues record the countries the personages came from and thus attest to the enormity of the Tang empire, the contacts maintained with other countries, and the profound political and cultural influence that China exerted over all the peoples of Asia at that time.

Although we are well aware of the external appearance of this monumental burial ground, we will not know exactly how the interior is laid out or what it might contain until it is opened by archaeologists. Excavation of many other tombs of the members of the Tang aristocracy have yielded important finds and entire cycles of murals depicting the sumptuous and cosmopolitan life at the Tang court. They show maidservants, attendants, maids of honor, musicians, dancers, military parades, guards of honor, exotic animals, foreigners, hunting scenes, and games of polo (which originated in central Asia and was actively practiced by the Tang aristocracy).

Predominant over supernatural and magical elements in Tang funerary art was the propensity for realism in the faithful reproduction of the world and society in which the dead person had lived. This realism can be seen in the many terracotta funerary statuettes (painted, or glazed in the famous "three colors" method, called *sancai*, of the Tang dynasty) of common subjects: loaded camels that alluded to the thriving trade along the "Silk Road," or horses from Ferghana, a particular breed that originated in Afghanistan and was very popular with Chinese emperors from the Han dynasty on. These figurines reflect the varied and cosmopolitan world of Tang society whose capital, Chang'an, was at the time Asia's largest and most populous city, where peoples from all places converged and met. The cultural openness of Tang society is shown in its arts and iconography, above all in those objects produced for the aristocracy that are often found in grave goods: gold and silver pots in shapes similar to Sassanid metalwork and decorated with Late-Ancient motifs combined with typically Chinese images and symbols.

*358-359 CENTER FRIGHTENING IMAGES OF MONSTERS, CALLED SHENMUSHOU, WERE PLACED INSIDE TANG TOMBS AND IN THE BURIAL CHAMBER TO PROTECT THE DEAD FROM MALEFICENT SPIRITS.*

*359 RIGHT THIS MALE HORSEBACK FIGURE IS WEARING CLOTHES IN CENTRAL ASIAN STYLE. THE TANG EMPERORS IMPORTED A PARTICULAR BREED OF HORSES THEY CALLED "HORSES FROM HEAVEN" FROM THE DISTANT STATE OF FERGHANA IN WHAT IS NOW NORTHERN AFGHANISTAN.*

*359 BOTTOM THIS SMALL STATUE PROBABLY PORTRAYS A MUSICIAN OR STORYTELLER. HE IS WEARING AN ELABORATE HEADDRESS COVERING THAT SOURCES DESCRIBE AS "PARROT-SHAPED"; THE PARROT WAS AN EXOTIC CREATURE KNOWN FROM CONTACTS WITH INDIA. DANCERS, MUSICIANS FROM CENTRAL ASIA, ACROBATS, AND ENTERTAINERS WERE MUCH APPRECIATED AT THE IMPERIAL COURT AND ARE ONE OF THE MOST POPULAR SUBJECTS IN TANG FUNERARY STATUES.*

Funerary objects from the
# Tang dynasty

# The Tomb of Princess Xincheng

To the modern world, the rich pictorial cycles that adorn the inner walls of the imperial Tang tombs represent a window on ancient China: thanks to their pictorial realism, the animated expressions of the figures, and the details of the clothes and objects, the China of the Tang dynasty comes back to life before our eyes each time a new tomb is excavated. Inspired by the real world, this was the exact function of the wall paintings together with all the other objects that made up the tomb's funerary trappings: their purpose was the faithful and vital reproduction of the world the dead individual had inhabited so that it would all be available

again once death had claimed his or her earthly existence. A tomb in the China of the Tang dynasty constituted the "house" of the dead and transferred the dead person's home to a level beyond this world, so that entering a Tang tomb means invading the "private" space of the dead occupant. Many graves of the Tang aristocracy have now been investigated by archaeologists, but each new occasion is like entering a private space. One of those opened recently is that of Princess Xincheng, which was excavated in 1994-95. Hers is one of the many satellite tombs in the funeral complex called Zhaoling located to the west of the other large group of Tang tombs at Qianling in the modern district of Liquan. Zhaoling is dominated by the large tumulus that marks the burial spot of Li Shimin, the founder of the dynasty and better known by the name of Taizong, who reigned from 626 to 649 AD. The structure and iconography of the tomb of Princess Xincheng are exactly the same as those of other tombs from the second half of the 7th and the start of the 8th centuries. It is entered through a descending corridor with walls containing niches at regular intervals on either side in which small funerary statues stand. Vertical ducts were needed to ventilate the tomb during its construction, but they were also the means by which tomb-robbers were able to plunder the tomb of its most valuable treasures. As in many other cases, a long train of attendants, servants, soldiers, ox-drawn carts, grooms, horses, and a litter (in which it is easy to imagine Princess Xincheng being carried) are painted on the walls of this long corridor on a base of dried straw mixed with mud, then plastered. It is almost certainly a funeral procession but also

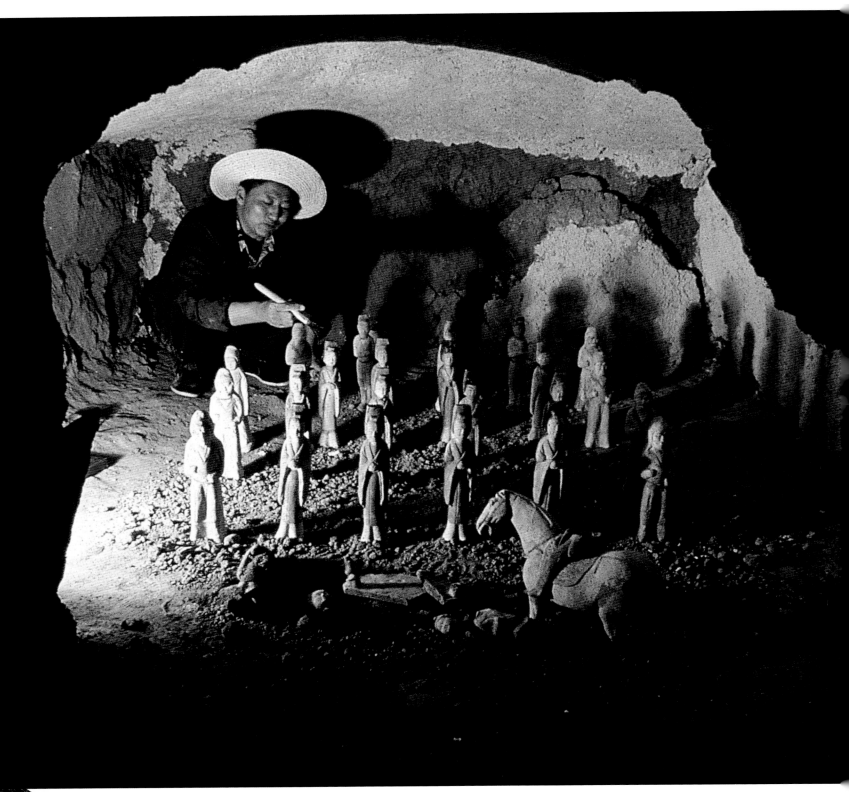

362-363
An archaeologist analyzes some small statues placed in one of the niches along the sides of the long sloping passageway. The statuettes are known as mingqi and formed an integral part of Chinese tomb goods from the Han dynasty on.

362 bottom Two details of the paintings in the tomb of Princess Xincheng show a group of ladies in the costume of the period, with long sleeves that cover their hands and elaborate hairstyles.

# The Tomb of Princess
## Xincheng

*363 TOP RIGHT A STONE SLAB ENGRAVED WITH A LONG EPITAPH ALLOWED THE PRINCESS BURIED IN THIS TOMB TO BE IDENTIFIED.*

*364 AND 365 THE SIMPLICITY AND ELEGANCE OF THE FEATURES OF THESE TWO FACES PAINTED IN THE TOMB OF THE PRINCESS ARE CHARACTERISTICS SHARED BY ALL CHINESE PICTORIAL ART AND CONVEY AN AMAZINGLY LIVELY PICTURE OF COURT LIFE, AS DO THE HIGHLY SUBTLE EXPRESSIONS OF THE VARIOUS FIGURES, DIGNITARIES AND MAIDSERVANTS WHO WOULD HAVE ACCOMPANIED THE DECEASED IN THE AFTERLIFE.*

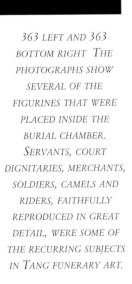

*363 LEFT AND 363 BOTTOM RIGHT THE PHOTOGRAPHS SHOW SEVERAL OF THE FIGURINES THAT WERE PLACED INSIDE THE BURIAL CHAMBER. SERVANTS, COURT DIGNITARIES, MERCHANTS, SOLDIERS, CAMELS AND RIDERS, FAITHFULLY REPRODUCED IN GREAT DETAIL, WERE SOME OF THE RECURRING SUBJECTS IN TANG FUNERARY ART.*

a representation of the last stretch of the princess's journey to another world; the portrayal is lively, dynamic, and symbolic of the continuity between the worlds of the living and the dead. This continuity is even more noticeable in the chamber that held the remains of Princess Xincheng: here the figures framed by representations of simple architectural structures on the walls express the gaiety and liveliness of the court (we are, after all, in the "private apartment" of the princess). Ladies in elegant clothes and long hair set in elaborate styles chat in a friendly manner; maidservants bear flowers, musical instruments, lights, beautiful containers, and make-up boxes in a final, perpetual homage to life and to Xincheng in her dwelling of eternity.

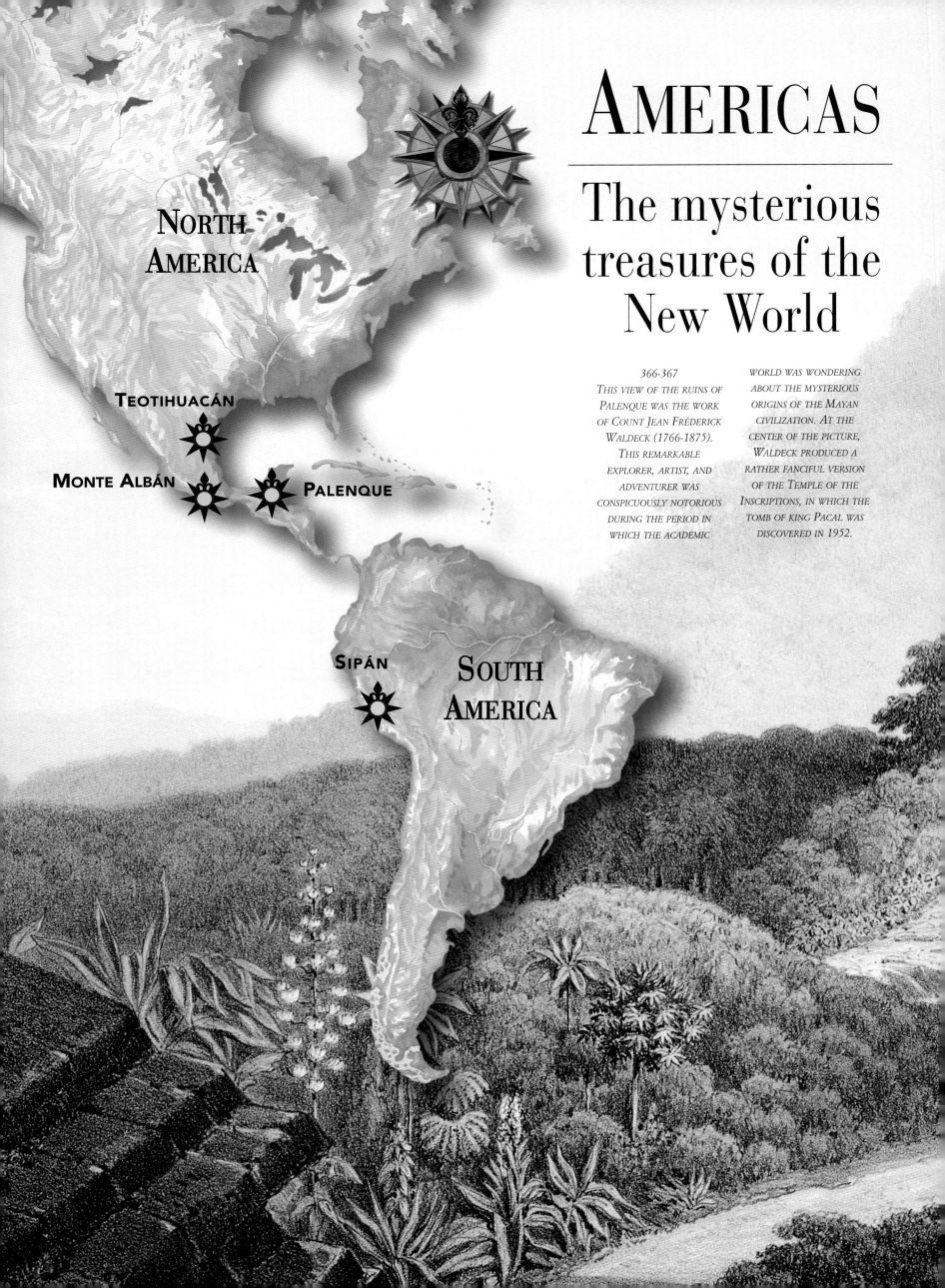

# AMERICAS

## The mysterious treasures of the New World

NORTH AMERICA

TEOTIHUACÁN

MONTE ALBÁN

PALENQUE

SIPÁN

SOUTH AMERICA

*366-367*
*THIS VIEW OF THE RUINS OF PALENQUE WAS THE WORK OF COUNT JEAN FRÉDERICK WALDECK (1766-1875). THIS REMARKABLE EXPLORER, ARTIST, AND ADVENTURER WAS CONSPICUOUSLY NOTORIOUS DURING THE PERIOD IN WHICH THE ACADEMIC WORLD WAS WONDERING ABOUT THE MYSTERIOUS ORIGINS OF THE MAYAN CIVILIZATION. AT THE CENTER OF THE PICTURE, WALDECK PRODUCED A RATHER FANCIFUL VERSION OF THE TEMPLE OF THE INSCRIPTIONS, IN WHICH THE TOMB OF KING PACAL WAS DISCOVERED IN 1952.*

Death is an irrefutable and inescapable condition that all living creatures will eventually attain. Nonetheless, man tries in every way to obviate the insecurity death causes him by presaging places he will visit after death and by creating heavens and hells, infraworlds, and final destinations. Depending on the type of society one lives in and its beliefs, one's afterlife will always follow a particular type. Christian society, for example, holds that the individual's existence after death is conditioned by a scale of moral values: if the deceased behaved well during earthly life, he will enjoy the delights of Paradise; if he did not, he will be obliged to suffer the eternal flames of Hell. The determining factor of the individual's destination after death in pre-Hispanic Mexico was the manner in which he died. Thus, warriors who fell in battle or who were sacrificed were destined to enjoy the light of the sun from dawn till midday, while women who died in childbirth enjoyed the same privilege – since giving birth was considered a battle – but from midday to dusk. For those whose death was caused in some manner by water (drowning, dropsy, etc.), the deceased would converge on Tlalocan, a place of eternal summer presided over by the god Tlaloc. Any other type of death meant the deceased was obliged to make a long journey filled with danger to Mictlan, where the couple, Mictlantecuhtli and Mictecacíhuatl, represented the duality of death that presided over the infraworld.

It is a simply stated fact that all peoples of the earth have burial practices that vary according to their beliefs. Archaeology has allowed us to discover and study the funerary practices customarily carried out by the huge number of different peoples throughout the continent of America with their different levels of development. However, we must point out the distinction between methods used in common burials and those performed for specific ceremonial purposes. In the former, i.e., when death was natural or accidental, burial did not follow a particular ritual; in the second, the individuals were killed for precise purposes and their burial had a particular ceremonial function, whether the individuals concerned were sacrificed to accompany a recently deceased member of the higher social ranks or whether they were killed in a propitiatory ritual or as part of an offering to the gods, a temple, etc.

From the funerary practices known to have taken place in America, three examples have been chosen that illustrate the ritual of inhumation reserved for high-ranking individuals, and one based on common burials with a propitiatory purpose. The four cultures examined were all founded on a clearly hierarchical and class structured society, at the top of which an élite governed a population dedicated to various productive activities such as pottery, sculpting, building, and agriculture. The four contemporaneous, civilizations flourished within the modern borders of Mexico and Peru: three in Mexico and one in Peru. This concentration should not cause surprise, as it was the Mesoamerican and Andean regions that formed the cradles for the more advanced civilizations that flourished before the arrival of the European conquerors; similar development did not occur in other regions.

The three cities selected from Mesoamerica all played a role of primary importance during their era: Teotihuacán, Palenque, and Monte Albán. The first was situated in the heart of Mexico, 35 kilometers north of Mexico City, and reached such a level of power and development that its influence can be seen in many other parts of Mesoamerica. Construction of the city began a little before the Christian era, and archaeology tells us that its oldest buildings are the Pyramids of the Sun and the Moon. From that moment the city grew in size until it covered 22 square kilometers and its population reached an estimated total of 125,000. The city was divided into four vast sections, or quadrants, by two large perpendicular roads, the Avenue of the Dead that ran north-south, and the other that crossed it east-west. Their junction is known as Ciudadela ("Citadel"), which became the center of the city from about 250 AD.

The importance of Teotihuacán was felt not only at the city's apogee but also by the peoples that came after the city had been destroyed. It can be confidently stated that the influence of Teotihuacán on these peoples was predominant in many of their customs, rituals, type of economy, and even in the layout of their towns.

Palenque rose and developed in the forests of Chiapas in a different natural environment from the one that surrounded Teotihuacán. This Maya culture reached its peak between 300 and 600 AD. The magnificence of its architecture and skilful stucco decorations is considered unique and of such

importance that the expression "Palenque style" has been coined. It was here that during excavation work carried out in 1951, an extraordinary tomb was discovered inside the building known as the Temple of the Inscriptions which provided a broad, though not complete, knowledge of the funerary practices used in ritual inhumation of important Mayan dignitaries. The tomb belonged to a ruler, Pacal, of about 65 years of age on whose face a jade mask had been placed. Many years later, another sensational find was made, this time in Building 13 next to Pacal's tomb: it was the tomb of a high-ranking woman who, according to studies still in progress, may have been a relative of Pacal.

Monte Albán stands in the central valley of Oaxaca in a region between the plateau where Teotihuacán lies and the area inhabited by the Maya. The city was first built several centuries before the birth of Christ on the top of a *cerro* (hill) that was later transformed to suit construction of the city. The main plaza was large in size and bordered by various buildings. The research undertaken by Alfonso Caso and his team during the 1930s and 40s in a number of tombs provided information on architecture, sculpture, pottery, the chronology and origin of hieroglyphic writing, and, naturally, inhumation practices. An important fact regarding the tombs at Monte Albán was that the city was occupied by two cultural groups: the Zapotecs and the Mixtecs. The first built the city and the second, who arrived some centuries later around 1000 AD, occupied the site and used some of the Zapotec tombs. An important example of this type of occupation is the famous Tomb 7, which provided archaeologists with a huge amount of valuable information regarding funerary practices and the offerings that were deposited with the dead.

It is interesting to know that these three pre-Hispanic cities are numbered among the World Heritage sites by UNESCO for their importance and unusual characteristics.

Peru, on the other hand, can boast one of the most surprising discoveries in pre-Hispanic archaeology from recent years: the royal tombs of Sipán, a site on the country's north coast near the river Lambayeque. This was the region inhabited by the Moche, whose culture never ceases to amaze students of the Andean civilizations.

This farming and military culture developed

between 100-800 AD and was already known to archaeologists for the quantity and high quality of its pottery.

This valuable legacy has been enhanced by a wave of information provided by the excavation of a series of tombs inside one of several buildings that had been subject to continual looting. The aim of the widespread practice of raiding tombs is to rob them of gold objects so that they may be sold to unscrupulous individuals, but the result is that untold damage is caused to archaeological sites like Sipán. In this case, the scientists were fortunate and part of the legacy was saved, thus enabling the study of the burial practices of Moche dignitaries as well as of the many rituals represented on ornaments made from gold, silver, copper, and other materials found during the excavations.

All these examples are evidence of human reluctance to face death. Man searches for any way to lengthen his life, to survive over time. Such behavior is well summed up in an ancient *Nahua* poem:

"Do we perhaps really live in the ground?
Not forever above ground
Only a little time here!
Although jade is crushed
Although gold too is cleaved
And the feathers of the quetzal are broken
Not forever above ground
Only for a little time here!"

*369 THIS FUNERAL MASK MADE FROM GREEN STONE BELONGED TO THE TEOTIHUACÁN CIVILIZATION. IT WAS PLACED ON THE FACE OF THE DECEASED WITH OTHER ORNAMENTS TO ACCOMPANY HIM ON HIS JOURNEY BEYOND THE GRAVE.*

*370-371 THE TEMPLE OF THE SUN, LEFT, AND THE TEMPLE OF THE INSCRIPTIONS, RIGHT, ARE TWO OF THE PRINCIPAL MONUMENTS OF THE CITY OF PALENQUE, WHICH FLOURISHED BETWEEN AD 300 AND 900.*

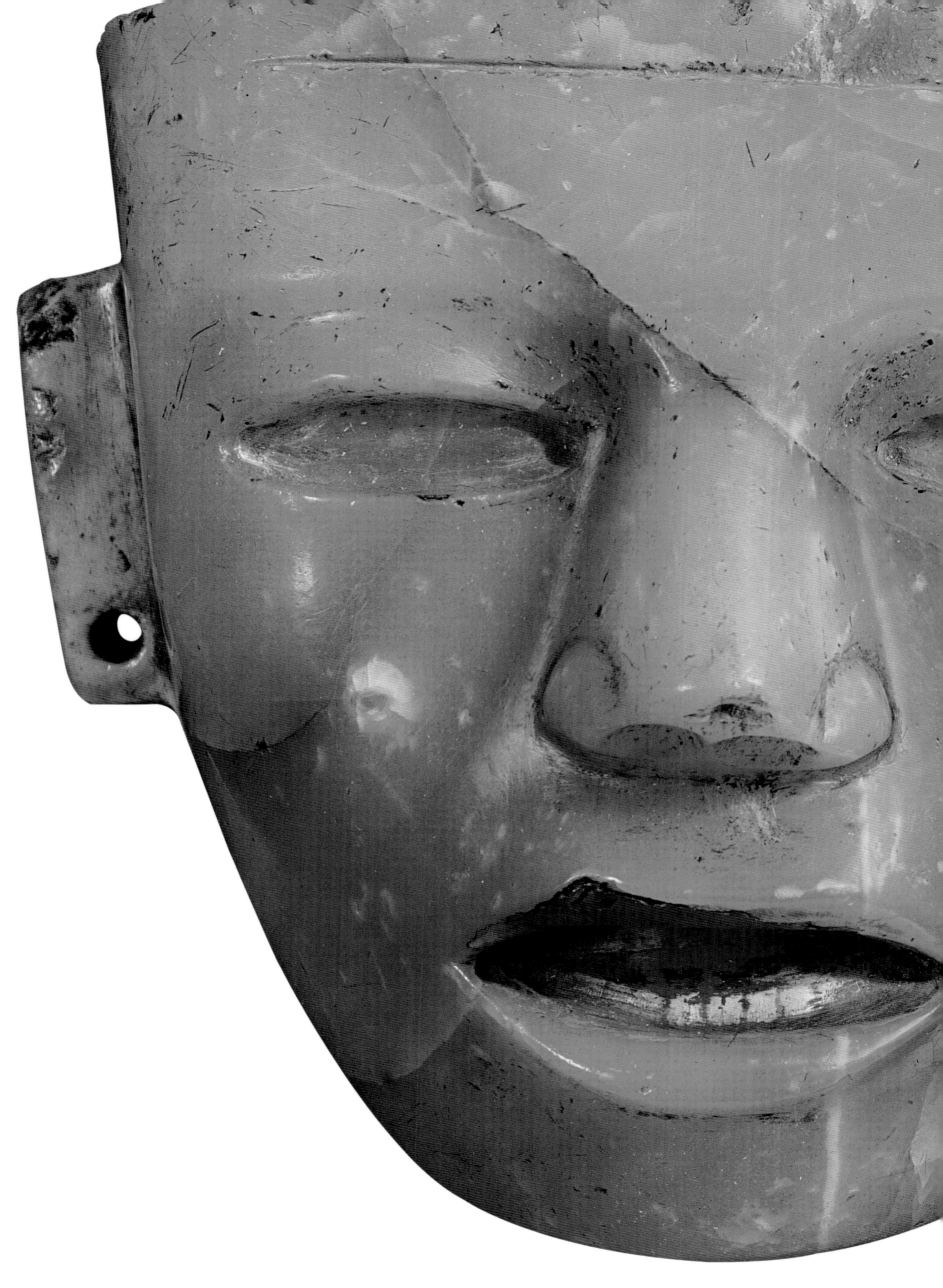

372 TOP THIS STONE
MASK ENCRUSTED WITH
SMALL STONE TILES AND
EYES MADE FROM SHELL

AND OBSIDIAN IS ONE OF
THE LOVELIEST EXAMPLES
OF THESE FUNERARY
ITEMS.

# The city of the gods: TEOTIHUACÁN

Teotihuacán

372 BOTTOM A CAVE
DECORATED WITH THE
SYMBOLS OF LIFE AND
DEATH WAS DISCOVERED
BELOW THE PYRAMID OF
THE SUN, THE MAIN
FAÇADE OF WHICH IS
SHOWN IN THE PICTURE.

372-373 THE PHOTOGRAPH
SHOWS THE AVENUE OF THE
DEAD, AT THE END OF
WHICH STANDS THE
PYRAMID OF THE MOON.

The Teotihuacán culture flourished between the first and the eighth century AD; during this period the city reached a population of 120,000 inhabitants and covered a surface area of 20 square kilometers. Contemporaneous with settlements like Monte Albán, Cholula, and others further away such as Copán in Honduras and Kaminaljuyú in Guatemala, its influence was fairly important. Recent excavations at Copán have shown that a ruler, who had perhaps come from Teotihuacán, directed the administration of the city for a certain time and that he was later buried there. The prestige of the city in central Mexico was so great that even after it had been burned and devastated, peoples who later settled in this region – including the Aztecs – recognized its importance. In 1325 AD, when the Aztecs founded Tenochtitlan, Teotihuacán had already been destroyed for centuries, but it was still easy to guess that under the layers of rubble and vegetation lay the remains of a great city: not knowing who had built it, the Aztecs considered it had been the work of the gods. In the *Nahua* language, Teotihuacán means "city where men became gods" and the *Nahua* groups, of which the Aztecs were one, thought that the gods had met in the city to make the Fifth Sun rise, which would enlighten humanity. It is also known that the

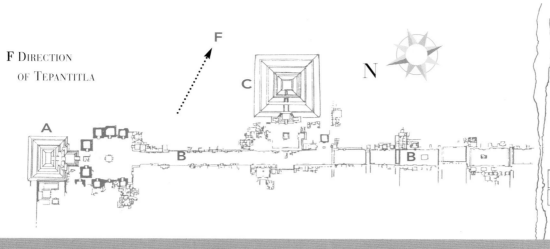

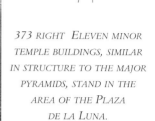

*373 RIGHT ELEVEN MINOR TEMPLE BUILDINGS, SIMILAR IN STRUCTURE TO THE MAJOR PYRAMIDS, STAND IN THE AREA OF THE PLAZA DE LA LUNA.*

*374-375 THE IMPOSING PYRAMID OF THE MOON CLOSES THE NORTHERN END OF THE AVENUE OF THE DEAD AT TEOTIHUACAN (1ST-8TH CENTURY AD).*

*376-377 IMPRESSIVE SCULTURES REPRESENTING QUETZALCOATL ADORN THE FEATHERED SNAKE'S TEMPLE.*

Aztecs went to Teotihuacán where they dug through the rubble to discover what the gods had created. This fact explains the discovery of more than 40 Teotihuacán items (ceramic and stone masks) among the offerings found when we excavated the Great Temple in Tenochtitlan in present-day Mexico City.

The proximity of Teotihuacán to Mexico's capital and the huge mounds that hid temples and palaces always acted as powerful spurs to researchers. The first excavations were made during the 17th century, and from that moment the site became a destination for both scholars and interested travelers. After nearly three centuries of examination, Teotihuacán is perhaps the Mesoamerican city about which most has been written.

Numerous tombs have been found over the years, but it is important to distinguish between the common practices of inhumation and those that had a ceremonial or ritual nature. Our knowledge of both, however, has increased over recent years.

In common burial practices, the dead were placed with offerings below the floors of houses, as has been shown in recent digs in the area of Ventilla to the southwest of the Avenue of the Dead. About 300 graves of adults and children have been found; their bodies were placed directly in the ground and were usually accompanied by offerings such as pottery containers, stone (especially obsidian) objects, shells, and occasionally masks placed over the face of the dead. Many of the offerings were closely linked to the activity that the dead had performed in life. It is

thought that Ventilla used to be a district where the inhabitants were mostly craftsmen and stone offerings have been found in the graves of carvers and sculptors who specialized in working with stone. Most of the bodies were hunched up, and tests have shown that they had been wrapped in material or covered so that they formed the funerary *bulto*, on which a stone mask was sometimes placed. The practice with children was different, especially if they were babies or particularly young: children were laid on a flat piece of ceramic and covered with another.

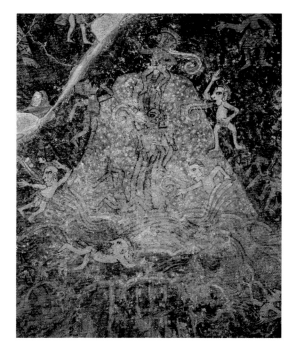

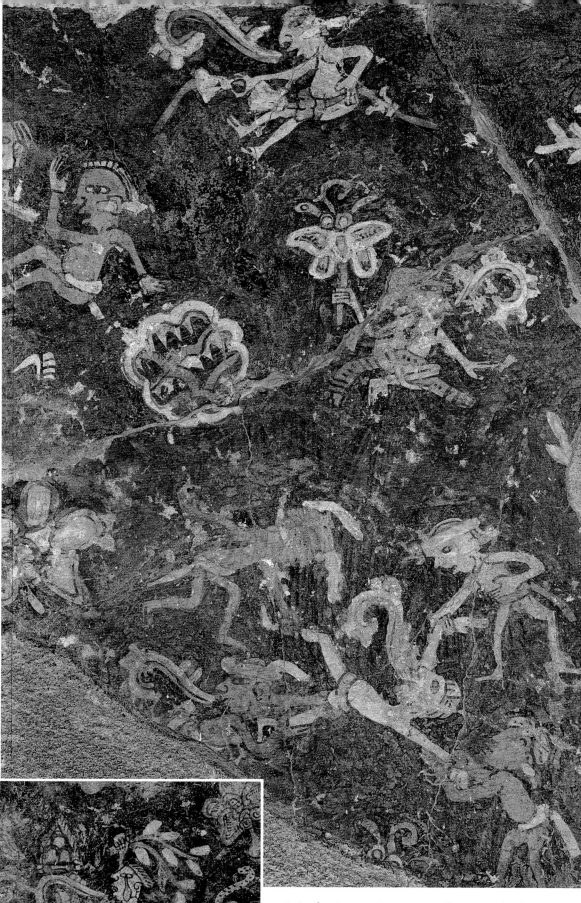

Ritual burial practices differed according to the circumstances, some of which should be described. A first example is given by the burial of children in the Pyramid of the Sun: Batres recounts that during excavations of this enormous structure from 1905-08, he found the skeletons of infants seated in the four corners of each of the four sections of the pyramid. Their presence had an important symbolic value, as children were usually dedicated to Tláloc, the god of water. This fact, together with the discovery by archaeologist Jorge Acosta during the 1970s of a cave below the pyramid, inside which a channel had been dug out, leads one to suppose that the pyramid was in fact dedicated to the gods of water; indeed, the name by which it is known today was only given to the structure during the colonial era.

It is also interesting to note that caves had a double nature in the pre-Hispanic world: they represented the origin from which all peoples came and at the same time one of the paths that led to the infraworld, the place of the dead.

A similar argument is valid for the Avenue of the Dead, *Miccaotli* in the *Nahua* language, which is one of the two main cross-streets that divide the city into four sections. At one time it was thought that the avenue was lined with tombs on both sides, but archaeology has disproved this hypothesis and shown that the structures were mostly temples and the entrances to palaces inhabited by the Teotihuacán nobility.

Another example of ritual inhumation with

379 RIGHT THIS
MURAL AT TEPANTITLA
SHOWS A WELL-DRESSED
PRIEST PRESIDING OVER
THE RITE PERFORMED
AT SOWING TIME.

The expansion and authority of Teotihuacán would be difficult to explain without the existence of a distinct military outlook, particularly given the city's influence over distant regions of Mesoamerica. Detailed examination of the skeletons will tell us whether the individuals were of Teotihuacán origin or not. If the hypothesis that they were from another Mesoamerican culture is true, there would be no doubts that they were sacrificed enemies; it would thus follow that Teotihuacán based its expansion on military campaigns and forced the conquered peoples to pay tributes in the same way as other pre-Columbian peoples did, for example, the Toltecs, Maya, and Aztecs.

A funerary tumulus was found in the center of the temple of Quetzalcóatl that contained 20 bodies buried in ritual fashion. Such a discovery in so important a temple points to the hypothesis that human remains strictly linked to the symbolism of the constructions themselves might be found in analogous buildings. Recently a tunnel was dug into the Pyramid of the Moon where a grave was found containing a number of offerings including the remains of animals and fragments of stone and pottery.

Both the Pyramid of the Moon and the Ciudadela (the Citadel, i.e., the plaza where the Temple of Quetzalcóatl stands) were

propitiatory aims was discovered inside the temple of Quetzalcóatl, the Feathered Serpent. In the 1980s and between 1992 and 1994, during work carried out under my direction in the "Special Teotihuacán Project," archaeologist Rubén Cabrera found graves containing 2, 4, 8, 9, and 18 individuals whose bodies were arranged in alignment with the four cardinal points of the compass. They seemed to have been sacrificed, as their hands had been tied behind their backs and they had all been placed hunched up alongside one another. Some wore forged collars in the shape of human jaws, and obsidian arrowheads were found near to the heads of some. Other objects lay next to the bodies, including ornaments for ear lobes (*orejeras*) and the nose

(*narigueras*). Shale discs were found aligned with the spines of the bodies that probably formed part of some sort of clothing. Studies so far show that the groups were either all female or all male. The men were aged between 16 and 45, and some had artificially deformed skulls. The unusual nature of these burials has led specialists to believe that they were ritual inhumations related to astronomy and the calendar and associated with fertility. The pyramid in which they were found stood in the very center of the city – the *axis mundi* – and was thus imbued with the maximum degree of holiness.

These findings call attention to the fact that Teotihuacán was essentially a warrior culture and not theocratic as was long thought.

The presence of Tlaloc has induced scholars to think that the place depicted is *Tlalocan*, the paradise of the god of water, in which there was an eternal summer with plants in perennial bloom, and which was inhabited by all those who died from causes related to water (drowning, dropsy, etc.).

As far as the theme of death is concerned, there are stone sculptures of skulls at Teotihuacán that refer to the god of death and the infraworld. Perhaps one of the most interesting figures is a sculpture that was found in front of the Pyramid of the Sun in 1964: the head faces forward and bears a circle of radiating rays still colored their original red which has been interpreted as the setting sun on its way to illuminate the world of the dead. In fact, certain Mesoamerican cultures believed that, having set, the Sun was devoured by the Earth and went to illuminate the beyond before being brought back the following morning in the east. This cycle symbolized the constant conflict between the forces of the day and the forces of the night in accordance with a belief

important centers of the city. That fact is important because these buildings were considered part of the "center of the universe" and were the means by which it was possible to ascend to the heavens or descend into the infraworld.

Information that scholars consider of special interest has been gathered regarding the "journey to the beyond." One example is a wall-painting found during the 1940s in a residential complex in the district of Tepantitla, northeast of the ancient city. The walls were profusely decorated, and one scene portrayed a nude figure, crying, holding a green branch in one hand and presenting the symbol of speech. This figure appears in the lower right section of the wall a little above a spring whose water runs across the whole of the lower part of the scene. The rest of the scene shows a range of people busy in various activities but all cheerful: they sing, play, chase butterflies, and swim while the god of water and fertility, Tlaloc, presides over the scene.

that was present in many myths and philosophies of pre-Hispanic Mexico. A paradigm of this type of belief was seen in the ball game, which simulated the daily struggle between opposite forces.

Teotihuacán was destroyed around 700 AD, and in many parts of the city the remains of fires and holes have been found in the floors of houses where looters have searched for graves in the hope of robbing them of their offerings. The reasons for the city's destruction are still far from clear: some scholars believe that there was a revolt by a group of workers against the ruling élite; others favor the breakdown of trading with other peoples, which would have brought about the gradual suffocation of the city. Still others consider that a climatic change took place due to deforestation of the area which caused a reduction in rain and led to a violent revolt by famine-struck farmers, but none of these hypotheses yet has enough evidence for it to be accepted without reserve. For my part, I believe that the key lies in the Teotihuacán socio-economic system, which required the subjected peoples in the expanding empire to contribute different products as tributes to the conquerors; as happened in other civilizations, that the conquerors were overwhelmed by the combined forces of the retaliatory subjected peoples. This socio-economic system was prevalent among societies that rose in central Mexico after the fall of Teotihuacán and ended in the same results.

Whatever the real reasons, at a certain point the greatness of Teotihuacán went into eclipse, but even so its influence was still felt by the cultures that followed it in the heart of Mexico. Today, archaeology has enabled us to probe the secrets that the great city has kept for centuries; even if what has so far been recovered already dazzles visitors, the work continues.

382 TOP  THE PICTURE SHOWS THE MAIN, NORTH-FACING, FAÇADE OF THE TEMPLE OF THE INSCRIPTIONS AT PALENQUE. WE SEE THE WIDE STAIRWAY THAT LEADS TO THE SQUARE IN THE HIGH PART OF THE TEMPLE. THE BUILDING CONSISTS OF NINE SECTIONS BUILT ON TOP OF ONE ANOTHER AND A SANCTUARY ON THE TOP, IN WHICH THE STEPS THAT LEAD TO THE BURIAL CHAMBER WERE DISCOVERED.

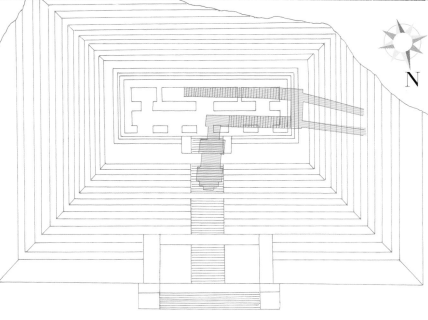

382-383  THE TEMPLE OF THE INSCRIPTIONS HELD THE REMAINS OF PACAL. IT IS A TYPICAL MESOAMERICAN PYRAMID WITH STUCCO RELIEFS ON THE FAÇADE OF THE SANCTUARY THAT DEMONSTRATE THE HIGH AESTHETIC LEVEL REACHED IN PALENQUE ARCHITECTURE.

N

# PALENQUE
## and Pacal's hidden tomb

T he Mayan city of Palenque lies in the north of Chiapas where the mountain forest gives way to a vast plain that stretches as far as the Gulf of Mexico. This large city developed during the same era as the equally important Mayan settlements of Tikal, Uaxactún, Copán, Quiringuá, Yaxchilán, and Bonampak, all sites that rose during the Classic period, defined as between 250 and 950 AD. This was a period of great splendor during which the great cities reached their zenith and artistic expression flourished. It was not easy to survive in an environment as exacting as the forest, considering that agriculture, the basis of the Mayan economy, was practiced using methods that contributed little to the constant enrichment of the soil.

It is now known that frequent violent clashes took place between these cities for control of increasingly large arable areas. Stele, glyphic inscriptions, and figurative representations that have survived to the present day show individuals bound with cords who, defeated, were at the mercy of the victor. As part of this scenario, Palenque played an important role in relation to the other Mayan cities. The site was studied and the object of deep researches since the 19th century: no one would have imagined that in 1952, after many digs in the Temple of the Inscriptions, a royal tomb with all its grave goods would have been found just as they had been buried there around 750 AD. The discovery of these tombs makes fascinating reading even today: "The last perforated stone slab was removed in the sanctuary. Previous investigations had revealed the purpose of this slab as being to close off the steps inside. The large stones that obstructed the stairwell had been taken out so that it was now possible to confirm that the first flight consisted of 45 steps." With these words, archaeologist Alberto Ruz described the start of the exploration of the stairway that led to the burial chamber from the upper section of the Temple of the Inscriptions.

The second flight, whose existence was deduced from a bend where descending steps were visible was soon found to contain 27 steps. Investigation of the stairway brought to light various offerings and the remains of 5 bodies that had been buried together, one of which was female. The bones, which had traces of red paint on them, were in very poor condition as they had been covered with lime. The skeletons were found next to a

triangular stone measuring 162 cm across the base and 236 cm in height. This slab was the entrance door to the burial chamber.

On 13 June 1952, Ruz wrote: "The rocks and detritus that sealed the door were removed so that, with the aid of a flashlight, I was able to see through a crack beyond the triangular slab. A large chamber decorated with plaster wall-reliefs was almost totally occupied by an enormous carved sarcophagus." Two days later it was possible to enter the room.

Four small steps led into the burial chamber: most of the space was filled by the limestone sarcophagus closed with a lid of the same material and decorated with various figurative bas-reliefs. The room measured 7 meters long

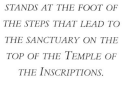

384-385 THE MAYAN
CITY OF PALENQUE WAS
KNOWN TO THE WEST
FROM THE 18TH
CENTURY. CAPTAIN

ANTONIO DEL RÍO WAS
THE FIRST TO BEGIN
EXCAVATIONS OF THE SITE.
THIS LITHOGRAPH BY
JOHN STEPHENS IN THE

19TH CENTURY INCLUDES
THE PALACIO (ON THE
LEFT) AND THE TEMPLE
OF THE INSCRIPTIONS (ON
THE RIGHT).

384 BOTTOM
THE DRAWING BY
FREDERICK CATHERWOOD
SHOWS THE ARRANGEMENT
OF THE BUILDINGS AT
PALENQUE, INCLUDING THE
PALACIO AND THE TEMPLE
OF THE INSCRIPTIONS.

385 LEFT THIS STUCCO
REPRESENTATION BY
CATHERWOOD OF A FIGURE
HOLDING A CHILD WAS
FOUND ON THE MAIN
FAÇADE OF THE SANCTUARY
OF THE TEMPLE OF THE
INSCRIPTIONS.

GENERAL PLAN
of the Ruins of
PALENQUE.

This Plan is not to be regarded
as perfectly correct. No means
existed of cutting down the dense
Forest which surrounds the
Monuments and consequently
the bearings and ... must
be considered on ...
approximation

north-south and 3.75 meters wide east-west. The ceiling was the typical false Mayan vault. The sarcophagus measured 3 m long, 2.10 m wide and 1.10 m high. The interior of the block was dug out in the shape of a uterus with the sides colored red. A perfectly fitting stone cover in the same shape closed the cavity. The enormous slab that closed the sarcophagus measured 380 cm long, 220 cm wide, and was 25 cm thick. In the

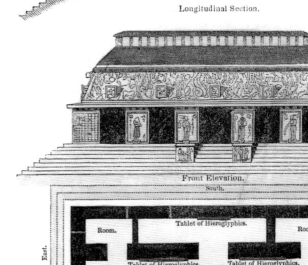

385 BOTTOM RIGHT
THESE DRAWINGS BY
CATHERWOOD MADE
DURING THE 19TH
CENTURY SHOW
ELEVATIONS OF THE
TEMPLE OF THE
INSCRIPTIONS, AND A
FLOOR PLAN OF THE
SANCTUARY AT THE TOP
OF THE TEMPLE, WITH ITS
FIVE ENTRANCES AND
INTERNAL LAYOUT OF THE
ROOMS.

center of the bas-reliefs that decorated the upper surface there was a young man reclining with his head tilted back. He wore a short and richly ornamented loincloth, a waistband with the representation of a flayed head at its center a collar, and armbands. A tree in the form of a cross decorated with fertility symbols (water, rain, etc.), and around which a two-headed snake was twisted, rose above the young man. At the top of the tree there was a bird with long feathers – a quetzal – and two shields depicting the sun. Three designs associated with fertility appeared below the young man: a flower, a shell, and a grain of corn. Lower down, the skeletal face of the Lord of the Earth appears once more. A strip of glyphs frames the scene including part of the firmament with symbols of the sun, moon, and Venus as well as human heads and hieroglyphs. This may be considered one of the most impressive examples of Mayan art, in

385 TOP RIGHT
THIS OVAL RELIEF OF
THE PALACIO SHOWS
KING PACAL RECEIVING
THE ROYAL HEAD-DRESS
FROM THE HANDS OF HIS
MOTHER ZAC KUK IN
625 AD.

Elevation showing the Building, and the Pyramid on which it stands.
10 5 0   10   20   30   40   50   60 ft.

Tablet of Hieroglyphics.   Tablet of Hieroglyphics.
Longitudinal Section.

Front Elevation.
South.

Room.   Tablet of Hieroglyphics.   Room.

Tablet of Hieroglyphics.   Tablet of Hieroglyphics.
Outer Corridor.

East.

North.

386-387 *At the end of the 19th century, Alfred Percival Maudslay posed at a window of the tower of the Palace complex, still partly overgrown by the vegetation.*

386 *bottom left The Temple of the Cross and the Temple of the Sun, in the southeastern area of Palenque, are depicted with a certain degree of naivety in this panel painted in the late 18th century.*

387 *top In 1839-1842, the architect-artist Frederick Catherwood scrupulously and precisely depicted the Mayan monuments. This drawing shows the patio of House C, in the Palace complex.*

*387 BOTTOM*
*THIS IMAGINATIVE*
*REPRODUCTION OF A RELIEF*
*IN PALENQUE WAS MADE BY*
*THE 19TH-CENTURY*
*EXPLORER FREDERICK*
*WALDECK, WHO ADDED*
*SEVERAL INCONGRUOUS*
*ELEMENTS TO THE FIGURE,*
*SUCH AS A PHRYGIAN CAP.*

which symbols of life and death appear in all their complexity.

Who, then, was the individual for whom such a magnificent tomb was prepared? The first physical anthropological studies showed it was a man lying with his head facing north. Although the remaining bone material was in very poor condition, it was possible to ascertain that when he died he was about 50 years old and 173 cm tall. Later it was discovered that the man was Pacal, the ruler of Palenque.

His face had been covered with a mask made of nearly 200 fragments of jade, with eyes made from shell, the irises from obsidian, and the pupils created with a touch of black pigment. The mask had been placed directly on the face of the deceased, whose skin had first been covered with a thin layer of plaster – a mixture of lime and fine sand – to which the fragments had adhered. Death masks were quite common in pre-Hispanic Mexico and many examples have been found in recent years. The ears of the man were adorned with large *orejeras* of the same material; *narigueras* were also found.

A diadem made from 41 perforated pieces of jade, strung together and mostly round, was found on his forehead. It is thought that the central part of the diadem was made

*388 TOP LEFT*
*THE TRIANGULAR STONE DOOR CLOSED THE ENTRANCE TO THE BURIAL CHAMBER OF PALENQUE.*

*388 TOP RIGHT*
*THE PHOTOGRAPH SHOWS THE INTERNAL STEPS LEADING TO THE BURIAL CHAMBER. NOTE THE "PSYCHODUCT" ON THE LEFT THAT JOINED THE CHAMBER TO THE OUTSIDE.*

from an intense green jade plaque with a depiction of Zotz, the god-bat. This would seem correct, since the vampire bat had always been associated with death or the infraworld.

In addition to the jewelry that covered his head and face, other examples were found on various parts of Pacal's body. There was a collar made from 118 jade beads, and a large chest plate made from 9 concentric rows each of 21 tubular jade beads. He also wore jade jewelry on his arms and legs: two bands formed by 200 beads each around his forearms, and five rings – one on each finger – on either hand.

The tomb also contained shells, some of which lay on top of the lid. Some pearls were identified next to the jade beads of the diadem and ear jewellery. Other objects made from bone, flint, obsidian, stone, pyrite, and stucco also accompanied the body. Two anthropomorphic stucco heads in particular stand out, perhaps taken from sculptures so that they might be included in the grave goods. Both were placed on the floor of the burial chamber, one on either side of the stone sarcophagus. The quality of these two heads deserves a short digression. The larger of the two measures 43 cm high and has fine features with a small mouth and thin lips.

*388 BOTTOM THE DRAWING SHOWS THE RECONSTRUCTION OF THE TEMPLE OF THE INSCRIPTIONS AT PALENQUE, WHERE THE TOMB OF KING PACAL WAS FOUND.*

*389 LEFT THE BURIAL CHAMBER WAS MADE USING THE MAYAN ARCH. THE INTERIOR IS ALMOST COMPLETELY OCCUPIED BY THE ENORMOUS STONE SLAB THAT COVERED THE KING'S SARCOPHAGUS.*

*389 RIGHT THE DRAWING SHOWS THE BAS-RELIEF DECORATION ON THE SARCOPHAGUS'S SLAB. THE MAIN FIGURE APPEARS IN THE CENTER ABOVE THE*

*SYMBOL OF FERTILITY. BELOW WE SEE THE GOD OF THE INFRAWORLD AND, ABOVE, A CORN PLANT WITH A BIRD AS A SYMBOL OF THE SUN.*

The aquiline nose shows the artificial extension of the profile up to the middle of the forehead as was the fashion among Mayan nobility. According to Ruz, the face has a serene and distinguished expression. The hair, graduated at the level of the temples, is tied in a ponytail and then folded forwards; the earlobes are pierced so that jewelry can be attached.

The other head measures 29 cm high; the face, wider than the first, has a less delicate mouth while the nose is similar with the join that also originates at the forehead. The ears too are perforated. Both carvings are superb and there is no doubt that the artist was a true master.

An interesting aspect of the Temple of the Inscriptions containing Pacal's tomb is that it was constructed from nine separate sections laid on top of one another. Because successive levels diminished in size, the building assumed the shape of a pyramid. The topmost section was the temple itself, and its façade was decorated with richly worked stucco figures of humans. It was here that Ruz discovered the stone slab that covered the stairway leading to the tomb. The series of nine architectural sections may symbolize the nine steps that lead to the world of the dead in Mesoamerican mythology.

Another point of interest that has increased our knowledge of the funerary customs of the Maya was the discovery of a narrow duct from the burial chamber that runs along one side of

392 LEFT THIS STUCCO HEAD WITH TYPICAL MAYAN FACIAL FEATURES MEASURES 28 CM HIGH AND IS KEPT IN THE NATIONAL ANTHROPOLOGICAL MUSEUM IN MEXICO CITY. MAYAN ARTISTS WERE SURPRISINGLY ADVANCED IN THEIR TECHNIQUES FOR WORKING WITH STONE AND STUCCO.

392-393 THESE GREEN STONE NECKLACES FOUND IN PACAL'S TOMB ADORNED THE CHEST OF THE MONARCH. RINGS, OREJERAS, AND OTHER ORNAMENTS WERE ALSO PART OF THE KING'S GRAVE GOODS.

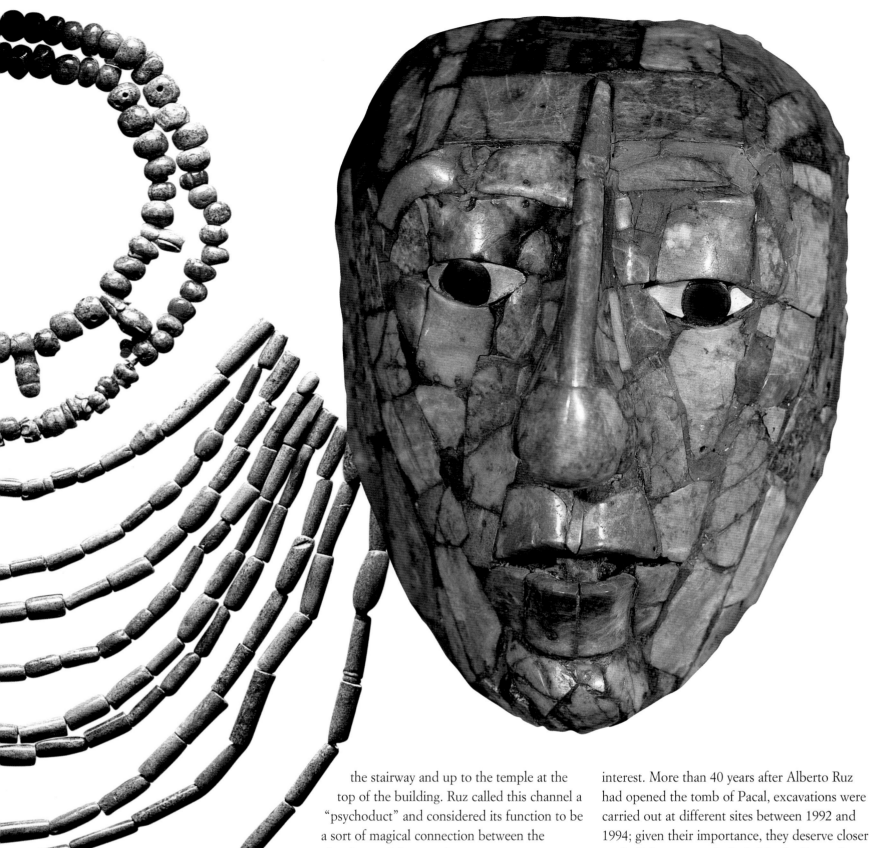

the stairway and up to the temple at the top of the building. Ruz called this channel a "psychoduct" and considered its function to be a sort of magical connection between the chamber and the temple.

The discovery of Pacal's tomb provides irrefutable evidence that some Mayan buildings were constructed primarily for funerary purposes, a point that had until then been in doubt because Mesoamerican pyramids usually existed simply as high bases for the temples at the top. On this point, Ruz had this to say: "We believe that only the Temple of the Inscriptions was built as a real pyramid-tomb: the funerary purpose had to have been fundamental since the entire architectural design of the structure seems centered on this function, as well as on its integration with the pyramid and its material and symbolic connection with the temple, with particular attention (being paid) to the solidity, stability, and durability of the building over time."

Considered in this light, the discovery of a new tomb can be said to be of exceptional

interest. More than 40 years after Alberto Ruz had opened the tomb of Pacal, excavations were carried out at different sites between 1992 and 1994; given their importance, they deserve closer study. Palenque was included in the list, and so new digs were begun in various architectural complexes. One of these was Building 13, which stands next to the Temple of the Inscriptions on the west side. It is a smaller building than the Temple but of great importance in the context of the ceremonial square at Palenque. One of the most surprising results of the research was the discovery of a tomb in which another female individual of the local dynasty had been buried. In 1994, a burial chamber measuring 3.80 m by 2.50 m was discovered that contained a rectangular stone sarcophagus painted red. The sarcophagus was closed by a single slab of rock measuring 2.40 m by 1.18 m. Unlike the lid over Pacal's sarcophagus, however, this one was undecorated. The chamber was reached via a door and 5 steps, on either side of which lay a body, doubtless sacrificed, to accompany the deceased on her journey to the afterlife. Inside the chamber, the body of a female adult lay face down along the east side of the sarcophagus, while the body of a young male child lay on his back on the other side.

A censer had been placed on the slab, and three clay whistles lay inside a niche in the east wall. On the steps were a huge ceramic plate, two orange-colored pots, and a skeleton whose bones were not anatomically connected. When the archaeologists had carefully salvaged all these objects, they proceeded to move the stone slab to see who had been buried in the sarcophagus. This is the description given by one of them: "Perhaps one of the most sensational moments in this find was when the stone lid of the sarcophagus was moved away. After 14 hours of work (due to lack of space) required to move it southwards, we came face to face with the remains of a tall, well-built female lying on the bottom of the sarcophagus with her head facing west. A collection of jade, pearls, obsidian knives, bone needles, and shells covered and surrounded the skeleton, which had been decorated with roughly 200 pieces of jade united to form a mask, collars, *orejeras*, headgear, armbands, and *tobilleras*."

Studies are still in progress, but the importance of how our knowledge of Mayan funerary customs has been furthered is clear.

# The sacred Zapotec city: MONTE ALBÁN

Monte Albán

*396 LEFT THIS POTTERY URN IS IN THE FORM OF AN OLD, SEATED GOD. MANY URNS OF THIS TYPE WERE FOUND IN ZAPOTEC TOMBS.*

*396 TOP RIGHT THIS HUMAN SKULL DECORATED WITH TURQUOISE TILES WAS FOUND IN TOMB 7 AT MONTE ALBÁN. THE RICHNESS OF THE DECORATIONS IN THIS TOMB, REUSED BY THE MIXTECS, IS INDICATIVE OF THE QUALITY OF THE GRAVE GOODS THAT ACCOMPANIED THE DECEASED TO THE AFTERLIFE.*

*396-397 THE AERIAL PHOTOGRAPH SHOWS THE MAIN SQUARE IN MONTE ALBÁN IN THE HIGH AREA OF THE HILL AROUND WHICH MOST OF THE TOMBS WERE DUG.*

*397 BOTTOM THE ALMOST INSIGNIFICANT ENTRANCE TO TOMB 7 GIVES NO INDICATION THAT ONE OF THE RICHEST SETS OF MIXTEC GRAVE GOODS WAS FOUND HERE. IT CONTAINED A LARGE NUMBER OF HIGH QUALITY PIECES OF JEWELLERY MADE FROM GOLD, ROCK CRYSTAL, JADE AND BONE.*

**LEGEND**

**A** SOUTH PLATFORM
**B** OBSERVATORY
**C** PLATFORM OF THE DANCERS
**D** GREAT SQUARE
**E** NORTH PLATFORM
**F** POSITION OF TOMB 7

The pre-Hispanic city of Monte Albán stands at the top of a *cerro* (hill) that overlooks the modern city of Oaxaca. In the central valleys of the state of Oaxaca, a mountainous region between the center of Mexico and the area of the Maya, many archaeological sites have been found, which attest to the site's importance and explain how it could be influenced by neighboring regions and influence them in turn. Various cultures developed in Oaxaca, including those of the Zapotec and Mixtec peoples, which are best

known today as a result of their archaeological sites. Both cultures are very ancient and have deep roots, but studies of various sites such as Monte Albán tell us that it was the Zapotecs who first occupied the main valleys and that not until around 1000 AD groups of Mixtecs did reach neighboring regions and settle in Zapotec centers. The site of Monte Albán, founded at the same time as Teotihuacán and Palenque, is a typical example.

Construction of Monte Albán was begun around 500 BC, the period from which one of its oldest monuments, the "Building of the Dancers" on the southwest side of the central Great Plaza, is dated. Around 500-600 AD, the city reached the peak of its splendor and its population of roughly 30,000 inhabitants is an indication of its development. After 800 AD, the city began a slow decline and, following the Spanish conquest, it fell into oblivion until the 20th century.

During the 1930s, Don Alfonso Caso directed various excavations on the site. Besides investigating the city's Great Plaza and many of its buildings, he discovered a large number of tombs, some of which were decorated with fine wall paintings. These investigations revealed an important fact: several of the Zapotec tombs had been reused during Mixtec occupation.

It should be pointed out that the Mixtecs created many calendarial, religious, and historical codices now exhibited in European museums. Only one of these documents remains in Mexico: the *Codex Colombino*. It was Mixtec craftsmen who produced wonderful creations in gold and silver as well as the loveliest pottery in Mesoamerica, characterized by unmatched polychrome coloring. However, pottery finds of the highest quality were made in Zapotec tombs reused by the Mixtecs. One of the most important finds, Tomb 7 at Monte Albán, fully merits description because the quality and richness of its grave goods and decoration equal those of more important discoveries made in the tombs of great lords throughout the Mesoamerican region.

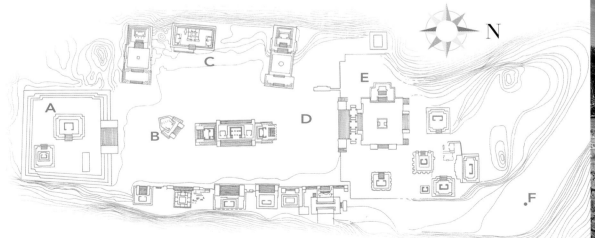

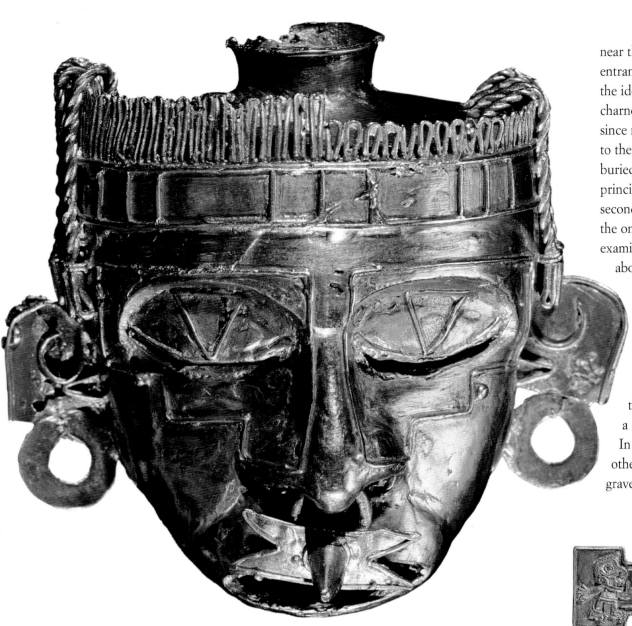

near the north wall, and four between the entrance and the antechamber. This gave them the idea that the tomb had been used as a charnel house, a theory that we do not support, since many of these bones must have belonged to the first body and its attendants that were buried there. The body that seems to be the principal Mixtec occupant (and therefore the second high-ranking body buried in the tomb) is the one at the end of the tomb. An osteological examination of the bones describes the man as about 60 years old, with the ritual deformation of the skull and tubercular excoriation of the left parietal bone. His deformed appearance might have been significant, because certain types of disease in the pre-Hispanic world were associated with divinity. Furthermore, some myths from the central regions of Mexico consider that a sick god will be transformed into a sun. In addition to the skeletons, the tomb held other human bones which formed part of the grave goods: these included a skull encrusted

The finding of Tomb 7 is documented as follows: "On 9 January 1932, we found at Monte Albán in Oaxaca the tomb that was given the number 7, being the seventh to be catalogued, and inside there was a large quantity of jewelry forged from precious materials." This was Alfonso Caso's description of the discovery of the tomb, which occurred during the first dig at the site. The tomb lies outside the perimeter of the Great Plaza towards the northeast side and was discovered on a Saturday afternoon. The excitement caused by initial recognition of the importance of the find was such that it was decided to continue work through the night. Zapotec tombs were built of real rooms with stucco-lined stone walls on which various scenes were painted and in which niches were sometimes created to hold grave goods. The ceilings were formed by huge stone slabs and were either flat or ridged with sloping sides. The large number of tombs excavated at Monte Albán has enabled the evolution of Zapotec tomb design to be reconstructed.

Tomb 7 has an antechamber that leads to the main room. The former measures 1.85 m long and 1.40 m wide and has a flat roof; the main room is 3.60 m long, 1.25 m wide, and 2 m tall. Despite being in poor condition, traces of wall paintings still remain. The tomb is aligned on an east-west axis below an architectural complex

and the entrance is situated on the east side. Although Tomb 7 is not one of the most magnificent, the Mixtecs decided to reuse it during their occupation of the city many centuries after its construction. The antechamber contained three pottery urns belonging to the first burial, two of which show effigies of the deity Cocijo, the Zapotec god of water. Studies of these urns have shown that they correspond to phase III-b of Monte Albán (500-600 BC) which was a period of great splendor during which the tomb was originally prepared. Reuse by the Mixtecs took place, according to Caso, during the 15th century AD or perhaps at the start of the 16th.

When first discovered, the entrance to the principal chamber was blocked, and so it was necessary to remove the mass of earth. It was discovered that the stone slab used by the Zapotecs to close the tomb had been taken out by the Mixtecs to close the open hole in the roof, which they used to exit the tomb after they had buried nine of their own dead.

Once they had succeeded in entering, the archaeologists began to retrieve the objects they found, including bones scattered all around, and marked down their exact positions. This enabled them to map the arrangement of the bodies: one was at the end of the tomb, three next to the wall of the main chamber, another

with turquoise mosaic tiles, three thighbones covered with engravings of figures, and five jaws painted red. The objects made from gold included true works of art; the ten breastplates are, in the words of Caso, "the most valuable for what they tell us from a scientific viewpoint." One of these portrays a figure wearing a helmet in the style of the head of a cat or snake, and a mouth mask in the form of a defleshed jaw while his chest bears several glyphs relating to dates.

Five other breastplates represent the god Tlaloc and animals like jaguars or maybe the *hacuache* ("opossum"). The tenth breastplate is of a rare beauty composed of various parts joined together: the upper plate represents a ball-court; the one below is a solar disc with a skull in the center; the third element depicts a

flint knife with animal jaws open downwards (a symbol of the moon); the fourth represents the Lord of the Earth, Tlaltecuhtli, whose task it was to devour corpses. Hung on this last part of the breastplate are four pendants, each of which supports a rattle. Taken as a whole, this ornament is truly impressive for the quality of its manufacture and for the symbolism of the decorations associated with Mixtec beliefs of the heavens and the infraworld.

Another exceptional gold decoration is the small head of the god Xipe Totec, the lord of goldsmiths, who is portrayed with his eyes half-shut and with an *orejera* as an ornament. Other pieces of special interest are in the style of a human or divine face with several pendants attached. Many are of gods made from gold, for example, Quetzalcóatl as well as those already

mentioned, but there are also many mythological animals such as pheasants and eagles. More rattles and other pendants hang from the beaks of the latter. There are also representations of stars: two of particular interest are a gold image of the sun and a silver one of the moon as symbols of day and night. In general, the jewelry was made using the "lost wax" technique, but in this case the pieces were embossed and the lack of welding between the different metals is particularly commendable.

The 11 rings found in the tomb deserve special mention: most of them are profusely decorated with a variety of images. The upper section of the rings worn to cover the fingers and referred to as "false nails," was fashioned in the shape of human nails. Together with other finds including the handle of a fan, an *orejera*, armbands, rattles, and a diadem with feathers they all combine to form an impressive collection.

In addition to the above-mentioned items, an additional 24 silver objects were found including rings, rattles, a small container, and false nails made from silver and copper. The only weapon found in the tomb was a copper hatchet, and this absence of warlike offerings suggested to Caso that the high-ranking man buried in Tomb 7 was a priest and not a soldier.

One of the materials used in the grave goods of the deceased was jade, a raw material that was highly prized in the pre-Hispanic world and used to manufacture rings, *orejeras*, and other objects. Rock crystal was also used despite

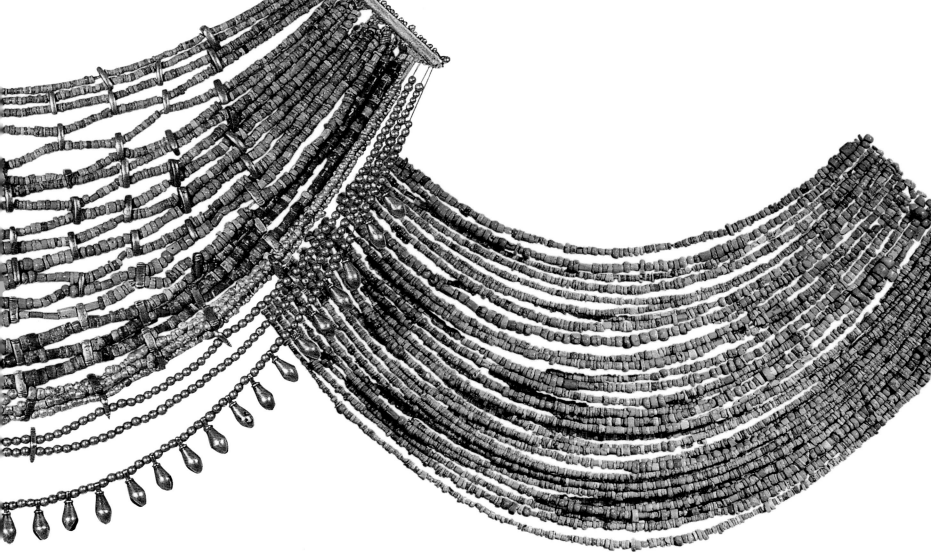

difficulty in manufacture caused by its hardness. Some of the objects made from rock crystal that have been found are a cup, an *orejera*, and various beads, which are of excellent quality due to the transparency of the material. Since alabaster was another popular material due to its milky coloring, it was used to produce several containers and a cup with a base displaying a series of carved animal heads. Referring to obsidian, widely used in ancient Mexico, there are *orejeras*, *navajas*, and a small *nariguera*. Only six weaving spools were found. Other pieces, such as collars and *orejeras*, were made from materials such as dark amber and yellow amber. Pearls were also used to make necklaces whereas shells were very popular in the manufacture of bracelets, armbands, *orejeras*, and necklaces, the latter being created from fragments of different types.

Examples of necklaces and other ornaments also exist that were made from a combination of different materials.

The skilful hands of the Mixtec artists also turned animal bones into two types of products: those used as jewelry or ornaments, and those carved to display mythical or historical scenes. The ornaments included necklaces and *orejeras*, while various figures and scenes were engraved on large bones. It should not be forgotten that animals were always imbued with a particular symbolism: the eagle was compared to the sun and used as its emblem; the jaguar represented night; the snake had a wider symbolism and was used as an element of fertility as well as being associated with the earth; snails and shells were linked to water and to fertility; and certain gods were linked with or represented by particular animals.

*400  THIS BREASTPLATE IS MADE FROM PRETTY GOLD PENDANTS AND WAS FOUND IN TOMB 7, WHICH CONTAINED ONE OF THE RICHEST SETS OF GRAVE GOODS YET FOUND.*

*400-401  THE CONTRAST OF THE RED AND GREEN STONES WITH THE GOLD BEADS AND PENDANTS ON THIS NECKLACE GIVE AN IDEA OF THE SPLENDOR OF THE ORNAMENTS FOUND IN TOMB 7.*

*401 TOP RIGHT THIS BREASTPLATE MADE FROM ROWS OF TURQUOISE BEADS IS ANOTHER EXAMPLE OF THE MAGNIFICENCE OF THE GRAVE GOODS IN TOMB 7.*

*401 bottom  THESE THREE PIECES OF BONE ARE ENGRAVED WITH REPRESENTATIONS OF BIRDS, SNAKES, AND HUMAN FIGURES. THIS TECHNIQUE REACHED A SURPRISING QUALITY AMONG MIXTEC CRAFTSMEN IN OAXACA.*

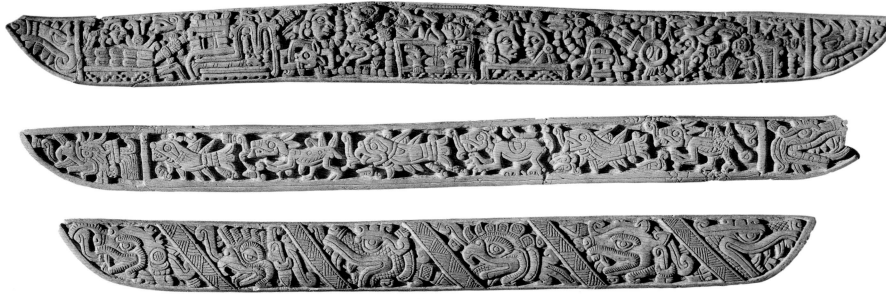

402 top  THREE SMALL STEPS LEAD TO THE BURIAL CHAMBER INSIDE ONE OF THE ZAPOTEC TOMBS AT HUIJAZOO DECORATED WITH WELL-PRESERVED POLYCHROME PAINTINGS.

402 bottom  THIS STONE RELIEF ADORNS A ZAPOTEC TOMB AT HUIJAZOO AND REPRESENTS A RICHLY DRESSED PRIEST WEARING AN ELABORATE HEADDRESS.

In general, all the objects lay either in the chamber or the antechamber and were found on the surface or mixed up in the earth and human bones. Some of them were clearly linked to a skeleton, like the six gold and four silver bracelets that lay among the bones of the forearm of one of the buried individuals.

One of the conclusions reached by Mr. Caso is that all the materials, save the three Zapotec pottery urns mentioned at the start, were from the Mixtec culture. He then referred to the codices drawn up by this people and analyzed the resemblance among images shown and the objects discovered at Monte Albán. The similarities were conspicuous.

An important aspect that should not be neglected is metalworking. In general terms, it can be stated that the use of precious metals – whether gold or silver – was not widespread during the Mesoamerican Classic period. Use and elaboration of these metals were developed later, and specialists believe that the techniques used may have been passed from the peoples of South America, where metalworking started in much earlier times, as was the case in Colombia, Peru, and Panama.

There is no doubt that the finds in the tombs of Monte Albán threw new light on the funerary practices of both the Zapotecs and the Mixtecs. They also provided a great deal of information on the objects that usually accompanied the dead and allowed specialists to expand their ideas on the use of metals and the various types of stones, shells, corals, and bones. Later investigations have increased that knowledge; for example, the tombs at Zaachila, not far from Monte Albán, revealed numerous gold and, in particular, ceramic objects during excavations in the 1960s.

A more recent discovery is the tomb at Huijazoo, a Zapotec site strategically located at the entrance to the central valleys of Oaxaca. A tomb was found in 1985 formed by two antechambers and a main burial chamber containing the best-preserved wall decoration. The paintings clearly show richly dressed individuals in procession, sometimes in groups of nine. This was an important number, as it mirrored the number of levels or infraworlds that the deceased had to cross (facing a series of traps and dangers on the way) to reach the deepest level where the dead were thought to reside. There were even nine steps descending to the heavy stone door that blocked the entrance to the tomb.

*403 BOTTOM THIS MURAL IN A TOMB AT HUIJAZOO SHOWS AN OLD PRIESTESS CARRYING A BAG. THE SYMBOL OF THE WORD COMES FROM HER MOUTH TO INDICATE SHE IS SPEAKING.*

*403 TOP LEFT THE OWL WAS ASSOCIATED WITH NIGHT AND DEATH; IT IS DEPICTED IN THIS RELIEF INSIDE A TOMB AT ZAACHILA IN OAXACA.*

*403 TOP RIGHT A SKELETON WITH A NECKLACE IS SHOWN IN A WALL RELIEF IN A ZAACHILA TOMB.*

Much remains to be investigated about the Mixtec and Zapotec peoples. The various 16th-century documents written by monks and chroniclers are of inestimable value; combined with data revealed by excavations, they provide vital historical information. To these can be added the Mixtec codices which supply an inexhaustible source of information relating to the histories of these peoples, their mythical and religious beliefs, and their customs, along with other data that allow us to understand who they really were.

When the Spanish arrived in the region of Oaxaca, the ancient burial practices slowly disappeared. The importance of this area to the Europeans is clear from the fact that the Spanish monarchs bestowed the title of Marquis of the Valley of Oaxaca on Hernán Cortés, the conqueror of Mexico. With natural resources of gold and semiprecious stones, the region had always been attractive to the ambitious *conquistadores*.

Archaeology will continue to uncover new tombs that will increase our knowledge and understanding of societies that have preceded us. Full knowledge of past societies helps us better to understand the present and to recognize that, since man has first existed, he has always tried to cheat death. The various myths relating to that survival and the ideas that man creates for himself about gods, life, and death reveal no more than the need to trascend and escape the fate he refuses to accept.

# SIPÁN:
## Magnificence and mystery of the Moche royal tombs

Sipán

Peru
**SIPÁN**

When Europeans reached the South American continent in the 16th century, they found themselves face to face with peoples of different origin that had been absorbed by one of the greatest empires of antiquity, the Inca empire. Chroniclers traveling with the conquerors sponsored by the Spanish monarchy left ample documentation of their amazement at the empire's advanced social and political organization, the Incas' developed technical exploitation of the territory, and the complex scheme of religious-cum-magical thought that attempted to resist the imposition of Christianity.

These peoples were closely linked to the natural world and adored the sun, rivers, mountains, lagoons, and sea. They spoke of mythical deities and practiced special worship of the dead, who they believed continued to exert a determining influence over the living. There was nothing more extraordinary than the attention the Inca people continued to pay to the bodies of the Inca emperors after their death, and they maintained lands and palaces, gave offerings and honors, and demonstrated their devotion to their former rulers during processions held every year. It was as if the power of the emperors continued to be exercized after death; so many resources,

including people, were dedicated to the cult of the ancestors.

Unfortunately, all the important graves and shrines belonging to either the Inca or other, earlier, populations and cultures were plundered by the *conquistadores* and, even more damaging, by tomb robbers during the 20th century who continued to feed the illicit trade in excavated objects.

In 1987, our small team of archaeologists was given the extraordinary opportunity to excavate the tomb, still intact, of a governor of the pre-Inca Moche (or Mochica) culture. The Moche kingdom flourished in the lee of the Andes between the first and the seventh century AD, a thousand years before the Incas annexed this region of Peru. They built large pyramidal structures from adobe (unbaked bricks) and developed sophisticated methods of working metals for the production of weapons, tools, and jewelry. Moche pottery was distinguished by a surprising realism and was one of the most sophisticated among the ancient American civilizations.

The tomb of the illustrious individual we called the "Lord of Sipán" was situated in the central section of a stepped platform 12 m high made from adobe that stood in front of two colossal pyramids roughly 40 m in height and covering more than 100 square meters at the base. Probably it had been the most important place of worship in the Lambayeque

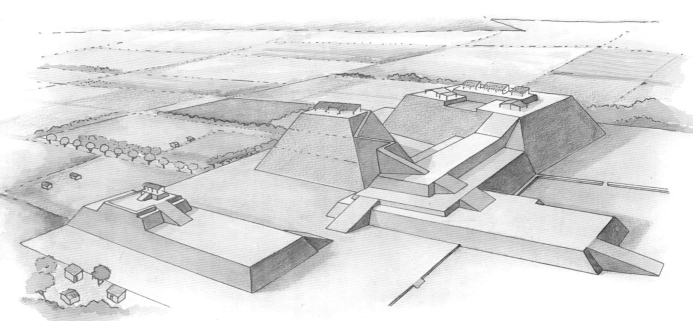

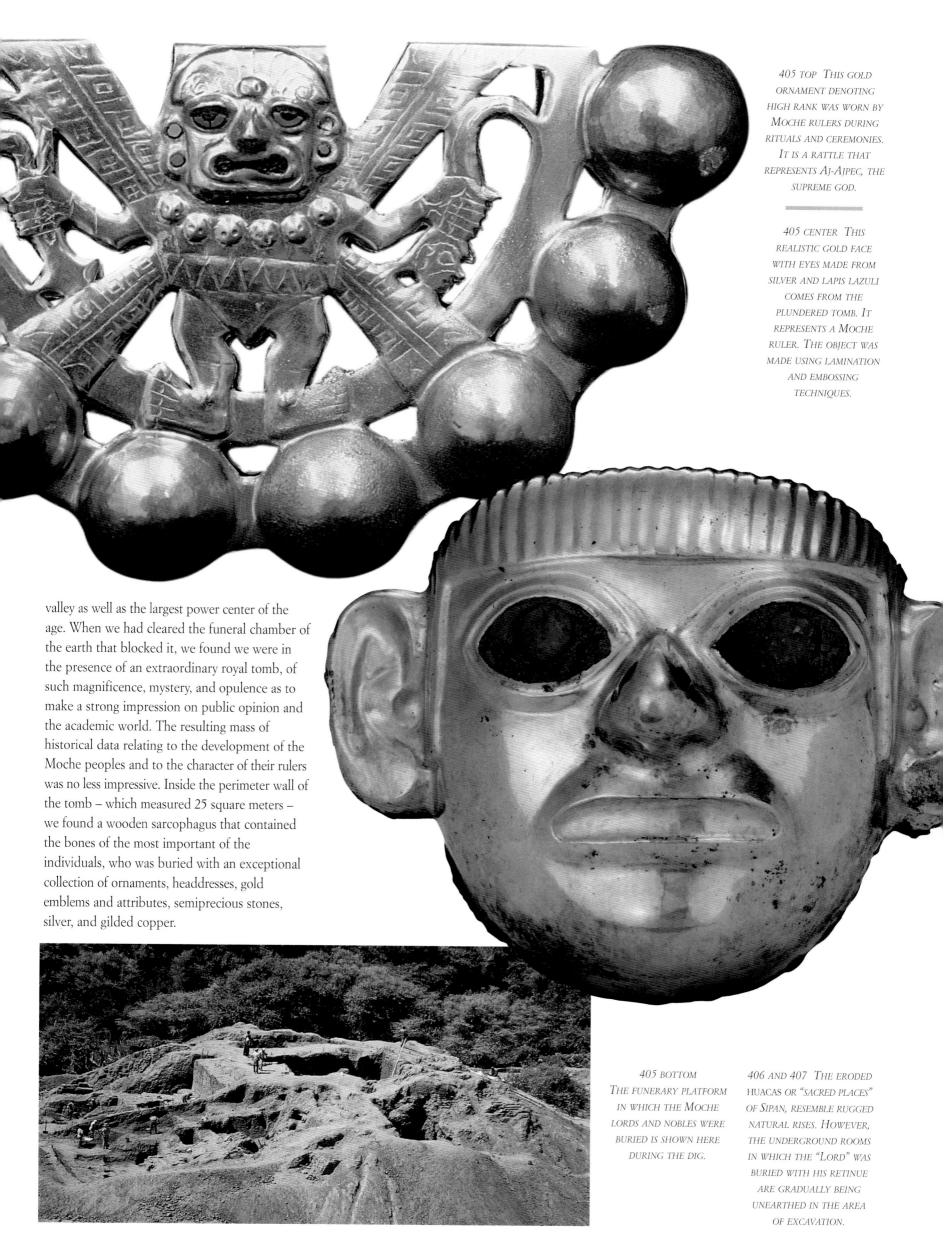

405 TOP THIS GOLD
ORNAMENT DENOTING
HIGH RANK WAS WORN BY
MOCHE RULERS DURING
RITUALS AND CEREMONIES.
IT IS A RATTLE THAT
REPRESENTS AJ-AJPEC, THE
SUPREME GOD.

405 CENTER THIS
REALISTIC GOLD FACE
WITH EYES MADE FROM
SILVER AND LAPIS LAZULI
COMES FROM THE
PLUNDERED TOMB. IT
REPRESENTS A MOCHE
RULER. THE OBJECT WAS
MADE USING LAMINATION
AND EMBOSSING
TECHNIQUES.

valley as well as the largest power center of the
age. When we had cleared the funeral chamber of
the earth that blocked it, we found we were in
the presence of an extraordinary royal tomb, of
such magnificence, mystery, and opulence as to
make a strong impression on public opinion and
the academic world. The resulting mass of
historical data relating to the development of the
Moche peoples and to the character of their rulers
was no less impressive. Inside the perimeter wall of
the tomb – which measured 25 square meters –
we found a wooden sarcophagus that contained
the bones of the most important of the
individuals, who was buried with an exceptional
collection of ornaments, headdresses, gold
emblems and attributes, semiprecious stones,
silver, and gilded copper.

405 BOTTOM
THE FUNERARY PLATFORM
IN WHICH THE MOCHE
LORDS AND NOBLES WERE
BURIED IS SHOWN HERE
DURING THE DIG.

406 AND 407 THE ERODED
HUACAS OR "SACRED PLACES"
OF SIPAN, RESEMBLE RUGGED
NATURAL RISES. HOWEVER,
THE UNDERGROUND ROOMS
IN WHICH THE "LORD" WAS
BURIED WITH HIS RETINUE
ARE GRADUALLY BEING
UNEARTHED IN THE AREA
OF EXCAVATION.

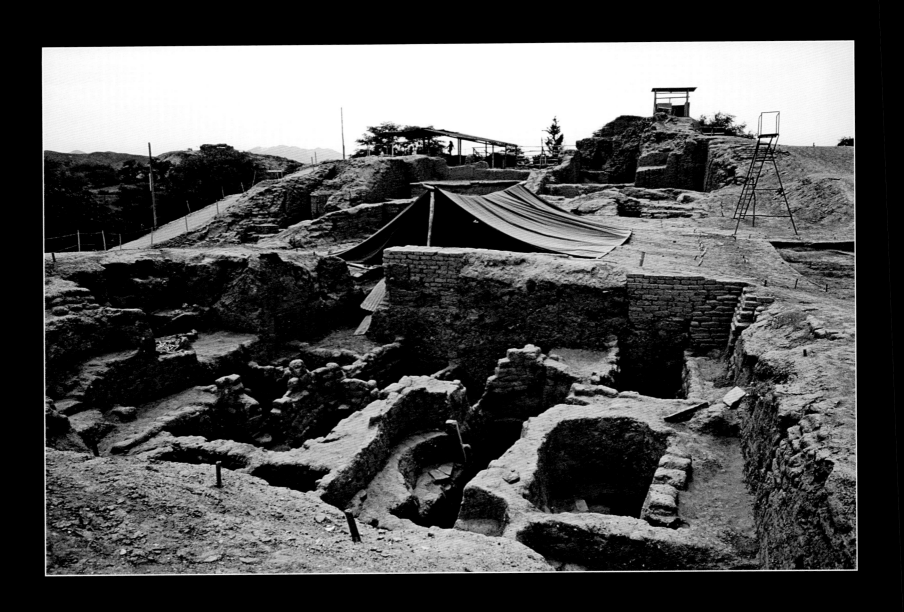

408 TOP AMONG THE ALMOST CRUSHED VOTIVE OFFERINGS AND REMAINS OF THE LORD OF SIPÁN, NOTE THE MORE IMPORTANT SYMBOLS OF COMMAND SUCH AS THE GOLD AND TURQUOISE OREJERAS AND THE NARIGUERAS.

408 CENTER THIS BREATHTAKING VIEW OF THE BURIAL CHAMBER SHOWS THE DISPOSITION OF THE LORD'S SARCOPHAGUS, SURROUNDED BY SIX COMPANIONS (ONLY FOUR OF WHICH ARE VISIBLE), TWO LLAMAS AND A DOG. A GUARD WAS FOUND LYING AT ROOF LEVEL, WHILE A SECOND "SENTINEL" WAS DISCOVERED SITTING IN THE SOUTHERN WALL, AT THE TOP OF THE PICTURE.

This opulent collection of funerary trappings, including exquisite works of art made using advanced gold-working techniques, constituted the symbols of power of the "Lord of Sipán," a man who had been dead for 1600 years and buried with all the personal effects he had used in life. Around the main sarcophagus we found eight skeletons of the closest members of the royal entourage, plus the remains of sacrificed animals and many offerings arranged with extreme care to accompany the deceased on his journey to eternity.

This find is undoubtedly the richest tomb in the New World, and it seem to have turned page in the great book of the study of pre-Columbian American cultures. Based on the evidence before us, it was our task to explain who this distinguished personage and his attendants were and what the meaning of his numerous possessions was, as well as to reconstruct the funerary ritual that had preserved the interment until our intrusion. Before investigation of the royal tomb itself took place, it was necessary to document a small bay in the upper section of a side wall filled with offerings. We found 1137 items of earthenware containing the remains of food, some copper crowns, the remains of sacrificed llamas, and the skeleton of a man; he too

was a ceremonial offering following the definitive closure of the main tomb. Before entering the funeral chamber – the roof of which had originally been made with large wooden beams that had crumbled to dust – we found the skeleton of a soldier holding a copper helmet and carrying a shield on his left forearm. The feet of the soldier had been amputated, an unequivocal symbol of immobility and of his duty to remain

eternally at his post guarding the holy tomb of his king. In a wall niche slightly higher than the lord, the skeleton of another man was seated in an attitude of watchfulness. In the center of the chamber, the wooden sarcophagus, measuring 2.20 m by 1.25 m and made with planks held together by metal strips, held the funeral bundle containing the remains of the "Lord of Sipán" and all the various vestments, clothes, ornaments, and symbols he had used in the various ceremonies over which he had presided in life. The hypothesis that the Moche had conceived the existence of another world in which their rulers continued to exercize their functions was borne out by the sumptuousness of the funerary trappings and by the fact that they contained some of the most important symbols of rank and authority yet identified in the art of this culture. The attributes of power were always buried with the ruler and were never inherited: each ruler had to have his own ornaments and emblems manufactured. Before our discovery, scholars of this pre-Inca civilization had identified various scenes in pottery, woven items, and wall paintings in which mythological beings or individuals of rank appeared. The main character in these scenes – i.e., the figure who received offerings, was honored or presided

408 BOTTOM  THE GOSLING
SHOWN ON THIS PAIR OF
GOLD AND TURQUOISE
MOSAIC OREJERAS WAS A
SACRED CREATURE LINKED
TO THE CULT OF FERTILITY.

409  THE SPLENDID EFFIGY
THAT ADORNS THIS OREJERA
(ONE OF THE LORD'S MOST
IMPORTANT PAIR) SHOWS
THE MONARCH HIMSELF
MAGNIFICENTLY DRESSED AS
A WARRIOR CHIEF.

410-411 THE SPECTACULAR
CRESCENT DIADEM MADE
FROM A SINGLE SHEET OF
GOLD WAS THE MOST
IMPORTANT SYMBOL OF THE
SUPREME AUTHORITY OF
THE LORD OF SIPÁN.

410 BOTTOM PARTIALLY
HIDDEN BY THE
DISINTEGRATED REMAINS
OF FEATHER ORNAMENTS,
THE SPLENDID CRESCENT
CROWN MEASURES 62.7 CM
ACROSS.

## The treasure in the tombs of
### Sipán

over ceremonies – wore ornaments or emblems that resembled those we found in the tomb. Consequently, the character represented in the works of art was not mythological and the individual that we were looking at had to have been the most important man of his age, the man that occupied the apex of military, religious, and civil power. We never ceased to be surprised by the association of each set of his attributes or vestments with a particular ritual, parade or ceremony illustrated in the iconography, and by the association of the symbology of his emblems and ornaments with gods, a sure indication that he was the Moche's representative of divine power on earth.

The objects found in the sarcophagus included several whose use was purely funerary, like the impressive gold pieces depicting two eyes, a sort of covering for the teeth, a nose bearing religious symbols, and a chin-cover which together formed a type of funerary mask that would protect and replace the vital sense organs of the dead man. In a magical transformation at the moment of his death, the lord symbolically

assumed a new face, a face made from gold that was incorruptible, divine, and eternal. The skull of the skeleton rested on a large gold plate and its facial section had originally been colored using cinnabar, the vermilion pigment used in the most important ceremonies. Three pairs of gold and turquoise *orejeras* lay at the sides of the head. This type of ornament, attached through a hole in either earlobe, was worn by men of high social caste, and there are many examples that might be included among the finest works of pre-Columbian South American goldsmiths. The first pair found in the tomb is distinguished by a miniature sculpture that appears to represent the lord himself with weapons and attributes that represent battle: a crescent crown, a collar of owls' heads, and bells that hang from his belt; a warrior made from turquoise mosaic is represented on both sides of the effigy. Corresponding items are found elsewhere in the tomb, analogous to the skeletons that lay at the sides of the ruler. A second pair of *orejeras* is made in a

*411 TOP THIS GOLD FUNERARY MASK WITH EYES, NOSE COVER, AND TEETH WAS PLACED ON THE FACE OF THE LORD WHEN HE WAS BURIED.*

*411 BOTTOM CRESCENT NARIGUERAS LIKE THE ONE IN THE PHOTOGRAPH WERE A TYPICAL ORNAMENT OF HIGH-RANKING MOCHE MEN.*

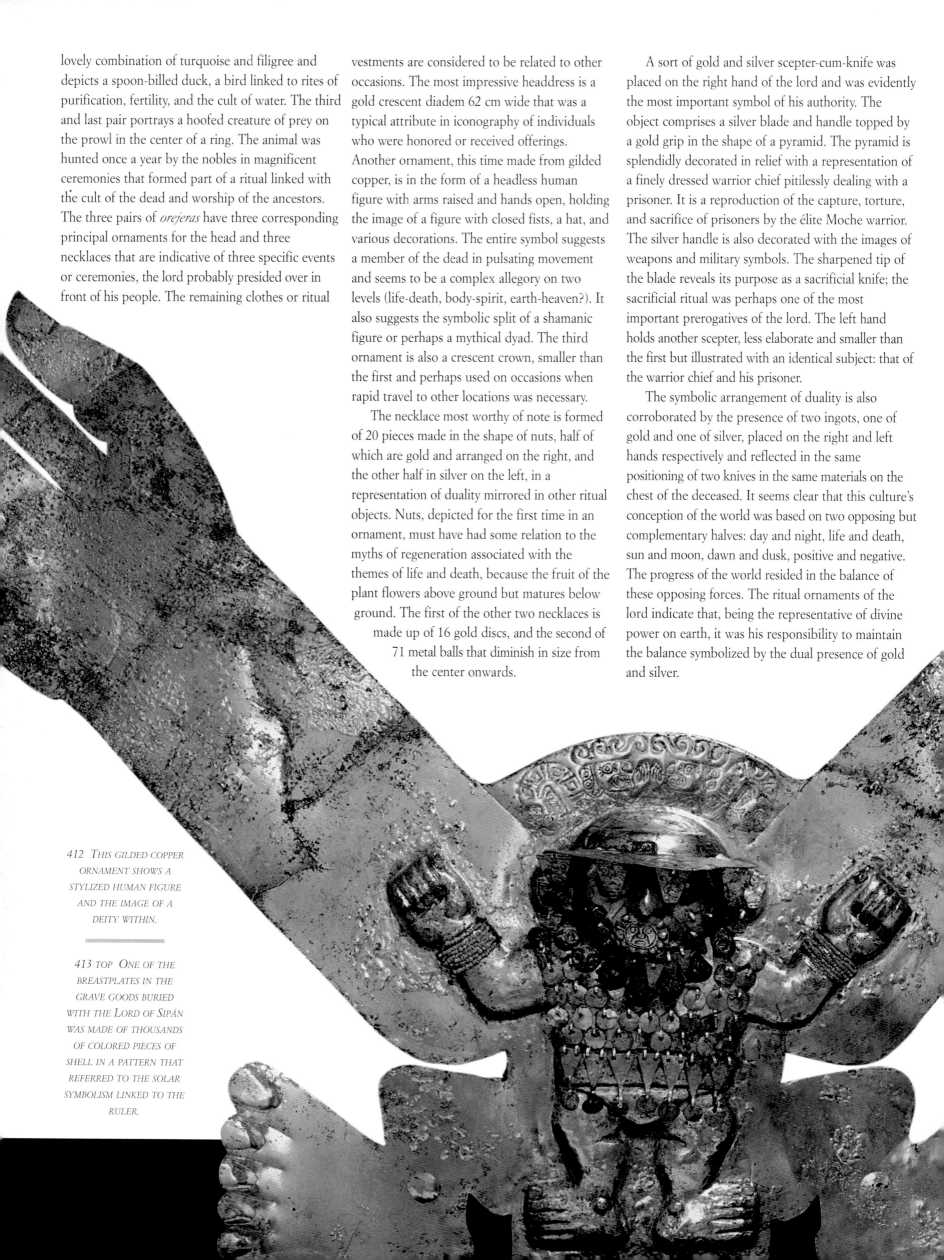

lovely combination of turquoise and filigree and depicts a spoon-billed duck, a bird linked to rites of purification, fertility, and the cult of water. The third and last pair portrays a hoofed creature of prey on the prowl in the center of a ring. The animal was hunted once a year by the nobles in magnificent ceremonies that formed part of a ritual linked with the cult of the dead and worship of the ancestors. The three pairs of *orejeras* have three corresponding principal ornaments for the head and three necklaces that are indicative of three specific events or ceremonies, the lord probably presided over in front of his people. The remaining clothes or ritual

vestments are considered to be related to other occasions. The most impressive headdress is a gold crescent diadem 62 cm wide that was a typical attribute in iconography of individuals who were honored or received offerings. Another ornament, this time made from gilded copper, is in the form of a headless human figure with arms raised and hands open, holding the image of a figure with closed fists, a hat, and various decorations. The entire symbol suggests a member of the dead in pulsating movement and seems to be a complex allegory on two levels (life-death, body-spirit, earth-heaven?). It also suggests the symbolic split of a shamanic figure or perhaps a mythical dyad. The third ornament is also a crescent crown, smaller than the first and perhaps used on occasions when rapid travel to other locations was necessary.

The necklace most worthy of note is formed of 20 pieces made in the shape of nuts, half of which are gold and arranged on the right, and the other half in silver on the left, in a representation of duality mirrored in other ritual objects. Nuts, depicted for the first time in an ornament, must have had some relation to the myths of regeneration associated with the themes of life and death, because the fruit of the plant flowers above ground but matures below ground. The first of the other two necklaces is made up of 16 gold discs, and the second of 71 metal balls that diminish in size from the center onwards.

A sort of gold and silver scepter-cum-knife was placed on the right hand of the lord and was evidently the most important symbol of his authority. The object comprises a silver blade and handle topped by a gold grip in the shape of a pyramid. The pyramid is splendidly decorated in relief with a representation of a finely dressed warrior chief pitilessly dealing with a prisoner. It is a reproduction of the capture, torture, and sacrifice of prisoners by the élite Moche warrior. The silver handle is also decorated with the images of weapons and military symbols. The sharpened tip of the blade reveals its purpose as a sacrificial knife; the sacrificial ritual was perhaps one of the most important prerogatives of the lord. The left hand holds another scepter, less elaborate and smaller than the first but illustrated with an identical subject: that of the warrior chief and his prisoner.

The symbolic arrangement of duality is also corroborated by the presence of two ingots, one of gold and one of silver, placed on the right and left hands respectively and reflected in the same positioning of two knives in the same materials on the chest of the deceased. It seems clear that this culture's conception of the world was based on two opposing but complementary halves: day and night, life and death, sun and moon, dawn and dusk, positive and negative. The progress of the world resided in the balance of these opposing forces. The ritual ornaments of the lord indicate that, being the representative of divine power on earth, it was his responsibility to maintain the balance symbolized by the dual presence of gold and silver.

*412 This gilded copper ornament shows a stylized human figure and the image of a deity within.*

*413 top One of the breastplates in the grave goods buried with the Lord of Sipán was made of thousands of colored pieces of shell in a pattern that referred to the solar symbolism linked to the ruler.*

# The treasure in the tombs of
## Sipán

*413 BOTTOM LEFT*
*THE PAINSTAKING PROCESS*
*OF CLEANING THE GOODS*
*DURING THE DIG*
*INCLUDED THE USE OF A*
*GENTLE AIR SPRAY THAT*
*HELPED BRING THE GOLD*
*AND SILVER ORNAMENTS*
*BACK TO THEIR ORIGINAL*
*SPLENDOR.*

*413 BOTTOM RIGHT*
*THIS SUPERB EMBLEM*
*PORTRAYS AJ-AJPEC, "THE*
*DECAPITATOR," AND WAS*
*MADE FROM A SINGLE*
*SHEET OF GOLD. IT*
*MEASURES 45 CM IN*
*HEIGHT.*

Another of the more remarkable emblems found in the lord's tomb is what is referred to as his thigh protector, a gold piece 45 cm in height and weighing about a kilogram. It was made in the form of a crescent axe decorated on the upper part with the image of Aj-Ajpec, "the Decapitator." This god, the most important of that era, holds a human head in one hand and a knife in the other to symbolize his power over human life. Found in a tomb for the first time, this ornament was probably worn hanging from the belt and perhaps was supposed to represent the tail of sacred birds, from which it was believed most of the kings of ancient

Peru were descended. A second "thigh-piece," identical but made of silver, reiterates the theme of duality. Two gold bells showing the same god form part of the emblems. A small gold ingot was placed in the lord's mouth and a series of *spondylus* shells, a crustacean from the waters of present-day Ecuador much valued as a votive offering, lay around the *fardo* or mummy bundle.

The grave goods include ten chest plates made from rows of small pieces of shell. Some are white, others red, and some are formed by beads of both colors, all assembled to create complex designs. One of these chest plates shows

a triangular motif in which the tip points downwards; it represents the shining sun, one of the mythical incarnations of the lord as a sun god. Then there are vestments of a military stamp such as the copper headpiece showing the image of a fox head, the tips of spears, arrows, and a dagger.

The principal item of sacred clothing to have survived is a cotton tunic covered with small plates made of gilded copper. Other tunics, all made of cotton, had crumbled to dust. Also found for the first time were metal emblems in the form of standards or metal icons suitable for transportation in which a recurring religious, or perhaps heraldic,

414-415 *A GOD CAN BE SEEN IN THE CENTER OF THIS STANDARD MADE FROM GILDED COPPER PLAQUES ORIGINALLY SEWN ONTO A SHEET OF COTTON. THE EDGES ARE DECORATED WITH PICTURES OF A MYTHICAL FRUIT.*

415 RIGHT *A TRUE WORK OF MOCHE ART, THE RULER'S MAIN SCEPTER-CUM-KNIFE BEARS A GOLD PYRAMID ON THE TIP OF WHICH ARE REPRESENTATIONS OF HIS MILITARY SYMBOLS AND SCENES OF A WARRIOR CHIEF TORTURING HIS ENEMY PRISONERS.*

The treasure in the tombs of
# Sipán

415 LEFT *THE END SECTION OF THE SILVER SCEPTER FOUND IN THE LORD OF SIPÁN'S TOMB DEPICTS A PRISONER PROSTRATING HIMSELF BEFORE A RICHLY DRESSED MILITARY CHIEF.*

image appeared of a god with his arms raised. These emblems would have been used for worship during processions and ceremonies. There were probably other ornaments made from organic materials, now disintegrated, such as cloaks, fabrics, or headdresses made of feathers whose former existence is attested to by the remaining metal supports. The collection of ornaments, emblems, vestments, and clothing is also evidence of the progress achieved by the craftsmen and goldsmiths of the era and their ability to obtain exotic materials originating in places far away from the kingdom. Priest, warrior, and ruler, the Lord of Sipán was the head of the social pyramid and had to be buried with the very greatest honors.

The remains of the attendants surrounding the body of the lord lay in reed sarcophaguses. On the right side lay the bones of a military chief covered with weapons, headdresses, and copper chestplates; on the left and facing in the other direction, another adult man acted as a standard-bearer or master of ceremonies. Lying beside the smaller limbs of the latter we found the remains of a dog, the lord's faithful companion during ritual hunts; according to ancient myths, he would have led his master on the journey towards the world of the dead.

Three women younger than 20 years of age at the time of their sacrifice lay at his feet and head; with them was a young child in a corner, whose presence was perhaps linked to beliefs of cyclical regeneration. There were also the remains of two llamas, the first of the sacrifices made during the funeral ceremony. A set of five niches, or *hornacinas*, set out along three sides of the burial chamber held 212 small anthropomorphic pottery containers portraying prisoners, warriors, or figures at prayer. The careful arrangement of these effigies created a setting that suggests there was a symbolic transposition of the real people to the figures in the clay pots (which also contained food

and death, and a crown in the style of an owl with wings spread. This priest was in charge of the cult of the mythical man-bird and occupied the second position in the Moche élite.

The third tomb explored was at the bottom of the oldest section of the platform and was a simple trench measuring 3 by 2 meters containing a mummy bundle originally wrapped in cotton. Like the lord, the body was surrounded by all its property, ornaments, emblems, and vestments, the variety and richness of which suggested a member of a high social caste similar to that of his successor three or four generations later. Many of the ornaments and symbols of command were analogous, which suggested the two had performed the same social role; other objects were indicative of important cultural changes that had taken place. There were three gold and three silver collars; the most remarkable (placed on the chest in the first layer of material wrapped around the body) and a

true work of art is an assembly of ten gold pieces to form a sort of spider, each of which is itself an assembly of smaller parts. The body of the creature bears a human head and sits in the center of a web. The reverse sides of the pieces are decorated to form three snakes with birds' heads alternated with three strips that rotate clockwise. They probably represent the god of the wind and of water in movement, the principle of life.

Two other necklaces, both also composed of ten pieces, were placed near the body. One of them is a realistic representation of the head and chest of a ferocious puma or jaguar with fangs made of shell. The reverse side is decorated in a similar fashion to the previous necklaces with a spiral motif, but in two parts instead of three. Curiously, in both cases the realistic designs would have been visible to observers, but the symbolic decorations would only have been seen by their user.

The third necklace is formed by natural representations of the thin, withered face of an old man. The counterpart is composed of 3 silver

The treasure in the tombs of Sipán

offerings). As this was supposed to be a dwelling to last for eternity, all the order and symbology of the world and the deeds and majesty of the lord were reproduced inside the burial area.

Continued archaeological investigation of the inside of the platform disclosed 12 tombs belonging to different hierarchies and epochs, which made the platform a mausoleum containing members of the very highest nobility and their court. The tombs faithfully mirror the role and social placement of each individual: two were royal, one was a priest, another two were military commanders, four were soldiers, and the other three were various individuals.

The tomb of the priest had a chamber similar to that of the lord, in which there were five attendants: two women, a man, a child with a dog, and a guardian to watch over the grave. The grave goods were far less magnificent than those of the lord but included ornaments and vestments closely related to his religious activities; for example, a votive cup for sacrifices held in his right hand, two copper necklaces of anthropomorphic heads representing life

*416 TOP THE RELIEF IMAGE OF THE MAN-CRAB (THE GOD OF THE SEA) WAS MADE USING ROUGH SHEETS OF GILDED COPPER WHICH WERE ORIGINALLY SEWN ONTO A COTTON CLOTH.*

*416 BOTTOM THIS SURPRISING MINIATURE MADE FROM GOLD, SILVER, AND TURQUOISE WAS FOUND IN THE TOMB OF THE OLD LORD. IT REPRESENTS A MOCHE MONARCH IN ARMS WEARING A DIADEM IN THE SHAPE OF AN OWL WITH SPREAD WINGS.*

*417 THE PHOTOGRAPH SHOWS THE IMAGE OF A POWERFUL ANTHROPOMORPHIZED CAT LIKE DEITY, MADE USING FRAGMENTS OF SHELL AND TURQUOISE SET IN GOLD-PLATED COPPER.*

necklaces formed by anthropomorphic heads: the first portrays a young man, the second an individual with pronounced teeth, and the third is an anthropomorphic deity with the fangs and eyes of a cat.

The old lord had originally had his face covered with a full-size gilded copper funerary mask with a missing eye, and with five plates in the form of an owl's head and chest hung from the lower end. An assembly of gilded copper pieces on the man's chest formed a series of chestplates that culminated in eight thin sheets, each in the shape of a tentacle, to create an octopus; this creature may have been related to the journey of the soul to the bottom of the sea.

One of the most interesting symbols in these funerary trappings was the depiction in gilded copper of a mythical being with a human face and the fangs

of a wild cat which probably represented one of the most important gods. The ferocious face with teeth made from shell has three two-headed snakes on its forehead and head. The first snake bears the heads of fish, the second the heads of birds, and the third – the great feline snake associated with the Milky Way and the heavens – with the head and chest of wild cats. The whole is an incarnation of the sea, land, and sky, the three areas of the universe this god reigned over.

Another god with similar power and importance was the man-crab, the god of the sea that was often shown fighting the feline god. Other emblems found include standards illustrating gods with their arms open, resembling those found in the first tomb. The tomb of this earlier lord also

contained ten gold and ten silver bells depicting the image of Aj-Ajpec, other simpler bells made from silver-plated copper, a gold thigh-protector, several small silver thigh-pieces, and ten *narigueras* made in an exquisite combination of silver and gold and symbolic patterns. One of these is without doubt the loveliest of the dignitary's ornaments: it is a miniature sculpture in gold and silver of a ruler bearing weapons, wearing a tunic of miniature fragments of turquoise and an impressive crown in the form of an owl with oversized and open wings with artificial feathers that vibrate if moved. This marvelous ornament perhaps covered part of the lord's face on special occasions and at his burial.

Two pairs of round *orejeras*, one in gold and one in silver, with small hanging discs attached to the

*418 TOP TWO BREASTPLATES – ONE MADE FROM PARTS SHAPED LIKE AN OCTOPUS'S TENTACLES AND THE OTHER FROM ELEMENTS REPRESENTING SNAKES' HEADS – FRAME THE OLD LORD'S FUNERARY MASK.*

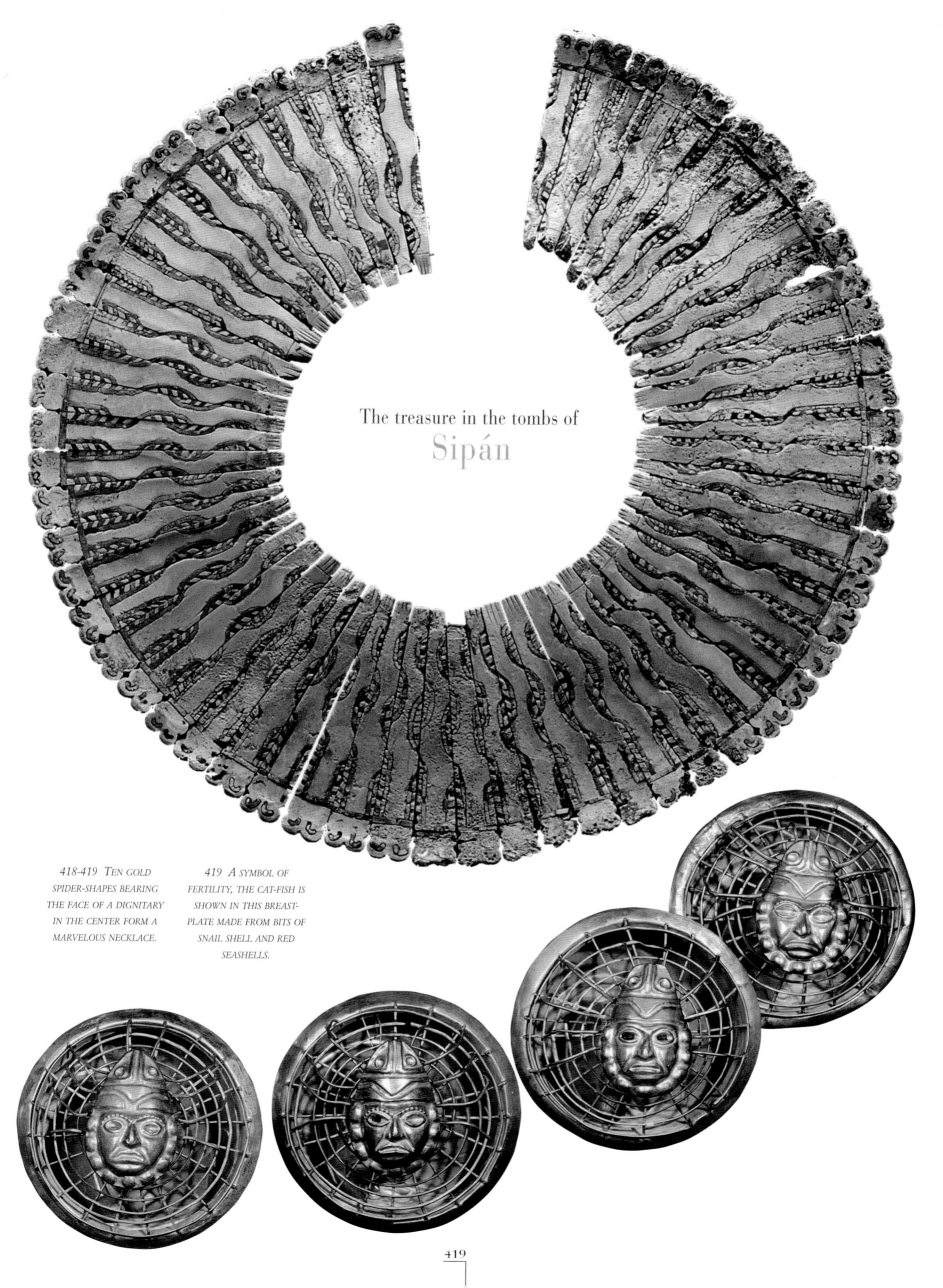

The treasure in the tombs of
**Sipán**

*418-419  Ten gold
spider-shapes bearing
the face of a dignitary
in the center form a
marvelous necklace.*

*419  A symbol of
fertility, the cat-fish is
shown in this breast-
plate made from bits of
snail shell and red
seashells.*

420 TOP  A FIGURE WITH HIS ARMS RAISED FORMS THE MAIN MOTIF IN THIS GILDED COPPER STANDARD. IT MAY HAVE BEEN A DYNASTIC EMBLEM OF THE RULERS OF SIPÁN.

420 BOTTOM THIS SCEPTER-CUM-KNIFE WAS CERTAINLY USED IN SACRIFICIAL CEREMONIES. IT ENDS IN A SORT OF RATTLE IN THE FORM OF A FRUIT.

421 TOP RIGHT THESE ORNAMENTS FOR THE EARLOBES BELONGED TO THE OLD LORD. THE TINY DISCS VIBRATE AT EVERY MOVEMENT.

421 CENTER A WARRIOR CHIEF IS REPRESENTED ON THIS GILDED COPPER ORNAMENT THAT WAS USED AS A SYMBOL OF RANK.

421 BOTTOM THE NECKLACE COMPOSED OF THE IMAGES OF THE FACE OF AN OLD MAN BELONGED TO THE OLD LORD AND HAD A SYMBOLIC VALUE.

surface of the main discs, complete the set of trappings. During the funeral ceremony, four chestplates composed of shaped fragments of snail and sea shells were placed on his chest and arms; the plates were decorated with designs of triangles and circles to form radiating images, fish, and geometrical patterns. The most beautiful is a work of art showing a series of catfish, a creature that was associated with the fertility that took the water of the Andean rivers to the desert.

A gold scepter-cum-knife and another in silver were two symbols of authority in the form of military garments and weapons. To the right of the mummy bundle lay ten metal spears, while other weapons intentionally crushed were perhaps placed there as symbols of the trophies of war.

Food and drinks were placed in 26 small containers set around the bundle. This type of votive offering depicted people, dogs, and owls, which probably represented the subjects and animals related to the night and the journey to the world of the dead.

The only attendants of this old dignitary were a girl of 16 and a llama that had been sacrificed and placed just above the height of the dead man's head. He probably held both military and religious power in the kingdom, but separated into distinct functions.

The royal tombs of Sipán, built as the eternal abodes of the men who ruled a complex and hierarchical society, reveal to the modern world the mystery, magnificence, religious concept, and knowledge of the ancient, pre-Columbian cultures.

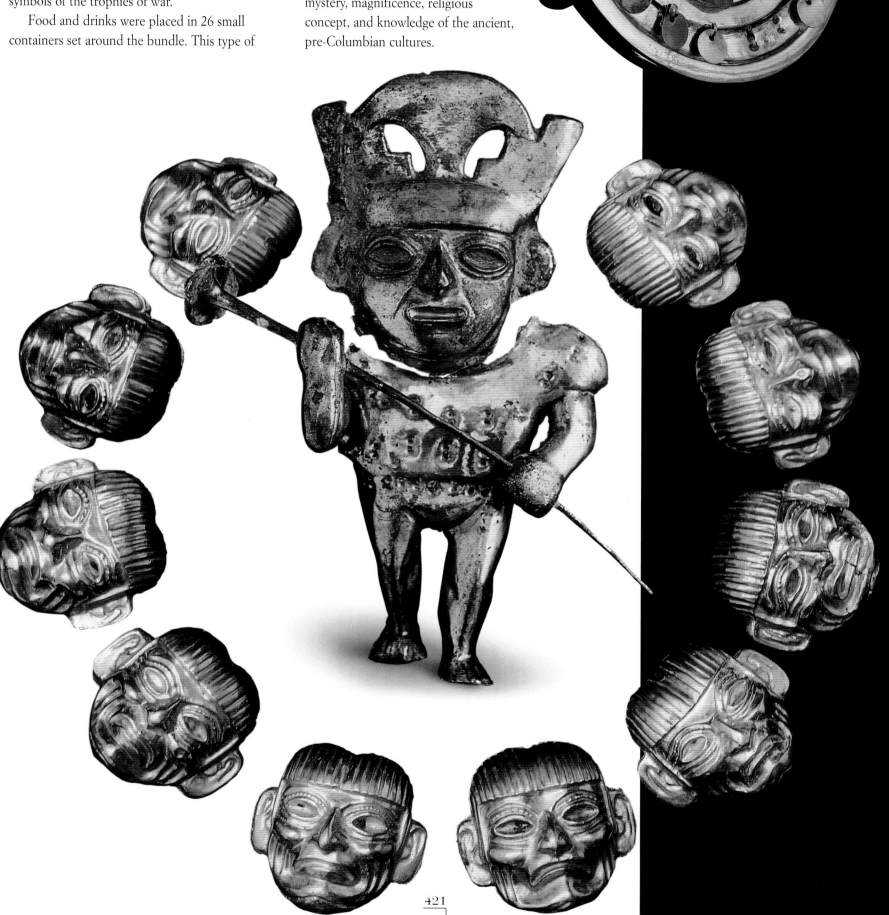

AEOLIAN: architectural order defined by a type of capital formed by two volutes divided by a palmette that increases in width; especially widespread in the northwestern area of Turkey (ancient Aeolia).

ALIGNMENTS: groups of menhirs arranged in parallel lines; the most important is at Carnac in Brittany.

AMAZONOMACHY: representation of a battle between Greeks and Amazons, the mythical women warriors descended from Aries and Aphrodite.

ANDA: mound-shaped body of the *stupa* that alludes to the heavenly vault and the cosmic egg.

APSARAS: heavenly nymph

ASHOKA: most important emperor of the Maurya dynasty.

ATTIC: the crown of the façade comprising a low wall, either smooth or decorated with reliefs.

AUGUR: priest who practised divinatory arts by observing the flight of birds or other natural phenomena.

BARAY: artificial basin for collecting water.

BETHEL: sacred stone considered to be the abode of a god or the god himself.

BRAH or VRAH: sacred, venerable.

BUCCHERO: a type of pottery produced in Etruria, created by firing in an atmosphere lacking oxygen so that the clay took on a shiny black appearance.

CENTAUROMACHY: representation of a battle between the Lapiths, a mythical people from Thessaly, and the Centaurs, creatures with the top half of a human body and the lower section of a horse.

CHAMBER TOMBS: chamber tombs were sometimes built above ground and sometimes dug out of the rock. They were mostly covered by a mound of earth or stones in order to recreate the underground setting of the world of the dead. There are 2 versions of chamber tombs: passage tombs and gallery tombs.

CHATTRI: pavilions supported by columns and a dome; they were built on places where rulers had been cremated.

CYST TOMB: small tomb dug out of the rock or underground and lined with stones.

CLIPEA: round shield.

COLUMEN: part of a roof corresponding to the main beam.

CRATERE: large cup made from clay or metal in which water
and wine were mixed.

CROMLECH or CIRCLES: derived from the Breton words *crom* = circle and *lech* = place; refers to a group of menhirs arranged in a circle or semicircle, the most important of which is Stonehenge (England).

DEVARAJA: the god-king or the divinized king.

DEVATA: female deity.

DHARMA : cosmic order in the Hindu world that governs the phenomena in the universe and the moral law that inspires mankind; for Buddhists, the *dharma* is the doctrine proclaimed by the Buddha himself.

DOLMEN: derived from the Breton words *dol* = table and *men* = stone (stone table); a structure created by placing a flat rock on vertical stones (uprights).

DROMOS: corridor.

ESCHATOLOGY: doctrine regarding the ultimate fate of man.

FICTILE: object made from terracotta or clay.

FRIEZE: architectural element placed above the architrave; in the Doric order it comprises alternating metopes and triglyphs.

GALLERY TOMBS: in gallery tombs there is no distinction between the gallery and the chamber, as the structure is a single corridor with walls and roof formed by large stone slabs.

GOPURA: entrance gateway with pyramidal superstructure.

HARMIKA: square balustrade on the top of a *stupa*.

HEROON: cult place connected with the burial of the heroized dead.

HINAYANA: the Lesser Vehicle (of salvation), name given to the older Buddhist school of thought by the one that followed, the Mahayana (Greater Vehicle).

HYDRI: large three-handled vase, normally used to hold liquids.

HYPOGEAN: term derived from the ancient Greek word *hypógeion* = underground; an underground place generally used for purposes of worship or burial.

HYPOGEAN TOMB: chamber tomb dug out of the rock.

ICONOCLASM: movement against any form of worship of images; such images were to be destroyed.
In this period, people began to live in fixed settlements and took up agriculture and worship. There was an important advance in the religious aspect of everyday life.

"JATAKA": stories of the previous lives of the Buddha said to have taken place between the 2nd c. BC and the 4th c. AD.

KANTHAROS: container for drinks having two vertical handles that sometimes rose above the lip.

KARMA: deed, cause and effect of action that links beings to *samsara*, the return to existence.

KLINE: bed much used in the Greek world with a headrest and sometimes a footrest; it was used for relaxation during a symposium.

KRISHNA: incarnation of the god Vishnu in the "Mahabharata."

KURUKSHETRA: site of the large eschatological conflict in the "Mahabharata."

LARNAX: funerary box.

LINGA: phallic symbol of Shiva.

LYRE: a stringed musical instrument comprising a sound box with two arms joined to a small board; the strings were stretched between the board and the harmonic box.

"MAHABHARATA": epic eschatological Indian poem composed between 4th c. BC and 4th c. AD.

MAHENDRA: name of the son – for some the grandson – of the emperor Ashoka.

MAUGDALYAYANA: a famous disciple of the Buddha.

MAURYA: dynasty that flourished in India in the 3rd and 2nd c. BC.

MEDHI: base of the *stupa* that alludes to the earth.

MEGALITH: derived from the ancient Greek words *mégas* = large and *lithos* = stone; refers to structures in various regions of the world (menhirs, alignments, cromlechs, dolmens, chamber tombs, passage tombs, hypogean tombs) made from large stones.

MEGARON: typical long, low Mycenaean house; it was essentially composed of a porticoed vestibule, a living room and chamber, but also included a number of internal courts and smaller rooms.

MENHIR: derived from the Breton words *men* = stone and *hir* = long; it stood vertically in the ground and generally measured between 1 and 6 meters in height.

MERU: mythical cosmic mountain at the center of the Hindu universe.

MESOLITHIC: term derived from the ancient Greek words *mesos* = middle and *lithos* = stone; refers to the transition period between the Paleolithic and the Neolithic epochs. It was characterized by the domestication of cereals, vegetables, and animals and by an intense lithic culture. It began around 10,000 BC and lasted for approximately a millennium.

METOPE: stone slabs (smooth or decorated with reliefs) that alternate with triglyphs in the Doric frieze.

MINGQI: funerary statues generally made from painted terracotta depicting animals and people; they were placed in Chinese tombs starting with the Han dynasty (206 BC – 220 AD).

MOULDING: straight or curved profiled architectural element.

NAGA: mythical being, part serpent.

NEOLITHIC: term derived from the ancient Greek words *néos* = new or recent, and *lithos* = stone. The start date of the period varies according to location: Jericho (ca. 9000 BC), Catal Hüyük (Anatolia, ca. 7500 BC), in other places ca. 4000-3500 BC.

NIRVANA: ineffable state of extinction of sorrowful existence.

PALEOLITHIC: derived from the ancient Greek words *palaiòs* = old and *lithos* = stone. The Paleolithic epoch is divided into the Early, Middle, and Late Paleolithic periods; it began approximately 1.8 million years ago and ended 10,000 years ago. During this period, man used stone tools, existed by hunting, and created art and the cult of the dead.

PANCRATIST: athlete in the discipline of pancration, which included wrestling and bare fist boxing.

PASSAGE TOMB: passage tombs in a round tumulus are formed by a passage lined with upright stones that leads to a larger sepulchral chamber. The walls of the chamber are made with large stone slabs; the roof is also covered with slabs of rock, sometimes to form a *thòlos* or "false vault".

PATERA: round wide cup often made from bronze that was used in the pouring of libations.

PATRONYMIC: name derived from that of the father.

PEDIMENT: crown of the façade (generally triangular) that rests on the trabeation.

PILASTER: grooved pillar that stands out from the surface of a wall.

PIPAL TREE: *ficus religiosa* or *ashvattha*; the tree that Buddha was sitting beneath when he achieved enlightenment.

POROS: limestone.

PORTA SCEA: gate that opened obliquely to the city walls at the end of a corridor lined by two parallel sections of the walls.

PRADAKSHINA: clockwise circumambulation around an object to be worshipped.

PRASAT: sanctuary with tower structure.

RAJPUT: warrior people from central Asia who settled in what is now the Indian state of Rajasthan during the early Christian era.

"RAMAYANA": epic Indian poem about Rama, the incarnation of the god Vishnu; composed between the 2nd c. BC and the 2nd c. AD.

RELIEVING TRIANGLE: empty triangular space over the architrave of Mycenaean gates.

SAMSARA: cycle of existences through which the soul will transmigrate.

SANGHA: community of Buddhist monks and laymen.

SARDONYX: semiprecious stone in the onyx family; generally brown but sometimes yellow.

SHALABHANJIKA: girls or nymphs who gather flowers from the *shala* tree.

SHARIPUTRA: a famous disciple of the Buddha.

SHIVA: third god of the Hindu trinity (the Absolute); the god of destruction of the universe, often considered the supreme god.

SYRINX: wind instrument made from reeds of different lengths; also known as pan-pipes.

STUPA: funerary mound transformed into a reliquary and place of worship.

SURYAVARMAN II: ruler and builder of Angkor Wat between 1113 and 1150.

SWASTIKA: cross with arms that alludes to the expansion of the cosmos from the First Principle.

TAPERING: gradual reduction in the thickness of a structure as it increases in height.

THERAVADA: the Doctrine of the Elders, a name that the followers of the older Buddhist school of thought (Hinayana) gave themselves.

THOLOS: derived the from ancient Greek word *thòlos* = round building or vaulted building.

THOLOS TOMBS: round tombs covered with a false dome.

TORANA: portals in the *vedika* that face the four points of the compass.

TRILITHIC SYSTEM: Mycenaean construction technique used to create openings in the walls. It was based on three stone blocks: two vertical (the uprights) and one horizontal (the architrave).

TRIGLYPH: stone slabs marked by three vertical grooves and used on Doric friezes in alternation with metopes.

TUMULUS: large earthen mound often used to cover dolmens. The tumulus marked the presence of dolmens and protected the tombs.

TYMPANUM: triangular space within the pediment; it can also refer to the highest section of the entrance walls and the back walls of a chamber tomb.

VEDIKA: enclosure around a *stupa*.

WAY OF THE SPIRITS: the name given to the approach to the most important tombs from the Han dynasty on (206 BC – 220 AD); it was completely lined by stone statues.

VISHNU: the second god of the Hindu trinity (the Absolute); his function was to conserve life and he was often considered the supreme god.

VISHNULOKA: abode or paradise of Vishnu.

WANAX: Mycenaean king.

YAKSHA: spirit of the trees.

YAKSHI: dryad, nymph of the trees.

YAMA: god of the dead.

YASHTI: imaginary point around which the *stupa* unfolds.

ZOOPHOROUS: frieze decorated with the figures of animals and, in a wider sense, living beings.

## PREFACE
### Text by Alberto Siliotti

**Alberto Siliotti** is a scientific journalist who specializes in Egyptology. He has spent many years studying and researching, taking part in archaeological trips, organizing exhibitions and publishing scholarly and general articles.
He is a member of the Egypt Exploration Society and co-ordinator of the digital catalogue of paintings in the Theban tombs. For White Star Publications he has written *Egypt - Temples, Men and Gods* (1994), *Guide to the Valley of the Kings, the temples and Theban necropolises* (1996), and *Guide to the Pyramids of Egypt* (1997).

### Photo credits:
Agenzia Luisa Ricciarini: page 16 bottom.
Stefano Amantini/Atlantide: pages 4-5.
Massimo Borchi/Archivio White Star: pages 2-3.
Livio Bourbon/Archivio White Star: pages 14-15, 24-25.
Giovanni Dagli Orti: pages 1, 10-11, 16-17, 22 top.
Araldo De Luca/Archivio White Star: pages 6-7, 12-13, 18 top, 20-21.
Michael Freeman: pages 22-23.
Bildarchiv Huber/Sime: page 9.
Andrea Jemolo: page 19.
Museo Archeologico Lambayeque, Sipan: page 8.
Photobank: page 23.
University of Pensylvania Museum/ Philadelphia: page 18 bottom.

## EUROPE
## FROM DOLMENS TO THE TREASURES OF VERGINA
### Text by Alberto Siliotti

### Photo credits:
Giovanni Dagli Orti: page 28.
Gianni Dagli Orti/Corbis/Contrasto: pages 30-31.
Roger Viollet: pages 26-27.

## MEGALITHIC TOMBS IN BRITTANY AND IRELAND
### Text by Emiliana Petroli

**Emiliana Petrioli** is a Professor in the Faculty of Literature and Philosophy at Florence University and gives courses at the Higher Institute of Religious Studies (Faculty of Theology for Central Italy). She has written numerous articles on religions from prehistory, the Near East in ancient times, and the Classical world.
She has given papers at many national and international conferences.

### Bibliography
Cipolloni Sampò M., *Dolmen*, De Luca Edizioni d'Arte, Rome, 1990.
Facchini F., Gimbutas M., Kozlowski J.K., Vandermeersch B., *La religiosità nella preistoria*, Jaca Book, Milan, 1991.
Guilaine J., *Sépultures d'Occident et Genéses des Mégalithismes (9.000 a.C.-3.500 a.C.)*, Editions Errance , Paris, 1998.

### Photo credits:
Antonio Attini/Archivio White Star: pages 40-41.
Philippe Beuzen/Scope: page 32.
Christophe Boisvieux: page 40 bottom.
Hervé Champollion/Ag. Top: pages 32-33, 33 center.
Giovanni Dagli Orti : pages 38 top and center, 39 bottom, 40 top, 42, 43.
Gilles Ehrmann/Ag. Top: pages 38-39.
Bernard Galeron/Scope: page 36 top.
Jacques Guillard/Scope: page 36 bottom.
Thomas Mayer/Das Fotoarchiv: page 33 bottom.
Morcrette/Wallis: page 35 top.
Photobank: page 35 bottom.
Martin Schulte: pages 33 top, 34-35, 35 bottom, 36 center, 36-37.
Senolf/Wallis: page 37 bottom.

## THE CULT OF THE DEAD IN THE ETRUSCAN TERRITORIES IN LAZIO
### Text by Alberto Trombetta

**Alberto Trombetta** was born in Perugia in 1966 and studied Estruscology and Italic Antiquities at the city university, completing his thesis on the topography of Perugia in Etruscan times. As an archaeologist he has worked for the Archaeological Superintendency for Umbria since 1990, for which he has carried out digs around Perugia, Orvieto, and Assisi.

### Bibliography
Filippo Coarelli (edited by), *Le città etrusche*, Milan, 1973, Mondadori.
Jacque Heurgon, *Vita quotidiana degli etruschi*, Milan, 1992, Mondadori.
Massimo Pallottino, *Etruscologia*, Milan, 1985, Hoepli Editore.
Mario Torelli, *L'Arte degli Etruschi*, Rome-Bari, 1985, Laterza.
Mario Torelli, *Etruria, guide archeologiche* Laterza, Rome-Bari, 1993.

### Photo credits:
Agenzia Luisa Ricciarini: pages 48, 49, 51.
Archivio Iconografico, S.A./Corbis/ Contrasto: pages 52, 53.
Archivio Scala: pages 45 top, 47 bottom, 50 center right, 64 bottom, 65 top, 66, 67, 76-77, 77 top.
Stefano Cellai: pages 54-55.
Stefano Chieppa/Il Dagherrotipo/ Realy Easy Star: page 74 bottom right.
Giovanni Dagli Orti: pages 44 center, 44-45, 54 bottom, 60, 61, 62, 63, 64-65, 65 bottom, 68-69, 69 bottom, 74 bottom left, 78, 79.
Gianni Dagli Orti/Corbis/Contrasto: pages 56-57, 57 top and bottom, 58 and 59.
G. Gasponi: pages 46 bottom, 69 top, 75 top, 76 bottom.
Andrea Getuli/Il Dagherrotipo/ Realy Easy Star: pages 70 top, 72-73.
Marco Mairani: pages 44 top, 70-71, 74-75, 75 bottom.
Luciano Pedicini/Archivio dell'Arte: pages 71 bottom, 77 bottom.
Stefania Servili/Il Dagherrotipo/ Realy Easy Star: page 71 top right.
The British Museum: pages 46-47, 50 top, 50 center left, 50-51 bottom.

## THE UNDERGROUND TOMB OF HAL SAFLIENI AND THE BROCHTORFF CIRCLE IN THE ISLANDS OF THE MALTESE ARCHIPELAGO
### Text by Emiliana Petrioli

### Bibliography
Bonanno A., *Maltese Megalithic Art. Fertility Cult or Sexual Representation?*, "Collected Papers" Published on the occasion of the Collegium Melitense, "Quatercentenary Celebrations" (1592-1992), pp.75-91.
Petrioli E., *Aspetti culturali dell'ipogeo di Hal Saflieni nell'isola di Malta*, "Studi Sardi",vol. XXIX (1990-91), pp. 163-213.
Stoddart S., Bonanno A., Gouder T., Malone C., Trump D., *Cult in an Island Society: Prehistoric Malta in the Tarxien Period*, "Cambridge Archaeological Journal" 3:1 (1993), pp. 3-19.

### Photo credits:
Daniel Cilia: pages 80, 81, 83 top and center, 84, 85.
Giovanni Dagli Orti: pages 80 bottom, 82-83.
Henri Stierlin: page 83 bottom.

## THE TOMBS AND TREASURES OF THE KINGS OF MYCENAE
### Text by Furio Durando

**Furio Durando** graduated in Classical Literature at the University of Milan and specialized in Archaeology at Bologna University. He is an archaeologist and a post-graduate lecturer. He has been a member of several digs and has published numerous articles and the volume *Ancient Greece, the Dawn of the West* (White Star, 1997).

### Bibliography
Chadwick J., *Il mondo miceneo*, Milan, 1980.
Mylonas G., *Mycenae and the Mycenaean Age*, Princeton, 1966.
Simpson R., *Mycenean Greece*, Park Ridge, 1981.
Taylour W., *I Micenei*, Florence, 1987.

### Photo credits:
Archivio Scala: page 87 bottom, 89.
Bettmann/Corbis/Contrasto: page 90.
Giovanni Dagli Orti: pages 92, 93, 94 top right and left, 96-97 bottom, 97 top and bottom, 98, 99 top right and left, 99 bottom right.
Kevin Fleming/Corbis/Contrasto: page 88.
Hulton-Deutsch Collection/Corbis/ Contrasto: pages 90-91.
Studio Kontos: pages 98-99 bottom.
Agenzia Luisa Ricciarini: pages 96-97 top.
Giulio Veggi/Archivio White Star: pages 86, 86-87, 94 center and bottom.

## THE TOMB OF PHILIP II OF MACEDONIA AT VERGINA
### Text by Furio Durando

### Bibliography
Andronicos M., *Vergina. The Royal Tombs*, Athens, 1991.
Ginouvès R. – I. Akamatis et al., *Macedonia, from Philip II to the Roman Conquest*, Athens, 1993.
Touratsoglou I., *Makedonia*, Athens, 1995.
Hatzopoulos M. – Loukopoulos L. (edd.), *Philip of Macedon*, Athens, 1992.

### Photo credits:
Giovanni Dagli Orti: pages 101 bottom, 104 bottom, 104-105, 105 top, 106 top right, 106 bottom, 107.
Alfio Garozzo/Archivio White Star: pages 102-103.
Studio Kontos: pages 100 bottom, 100-101 top, 104 top, 106 top left.

## AFRICA AND THE NEAR AND MIDDLE EAST
### Text by Alberto Siliotti

### Photo credits:
Araldo De Luca/Archivio White Star: pages 110, 112-113.
Library of Congress, Washington: pages 108-109.

## THE PYRAMID OF CHEOPS
### Text by Alberto Siliotti

### Bibliography
Goyon G., *Le secret des bâtisseurs des grandes pyramides, Khéops*, Paris, 1990.
Lauer J.-Ph, *Histoire monumentale des pyramides d'Egypte*, Le Caire, 1962.
Lauer J.-Ph, *Me mystère des pyramides*, Paris, 1988.
Lehner M., *The Complete Pyramids*, London, 1997.
Montet P., *Géographie de l'Egypte ancienne, I-II*, Paris, 1957-61.
Porter B., Moss R.L.B, *Topographical Bibliography of Ancient Egyptian Hieroglyphic Texts, Reliefs and Paintings*, Oxford, 1960.
Posener G., Sauneron S, Yoyotte J, *Dictionnaire de la civilisation égyptienne*, Paris, 1959.
Rinaldi C., Maragioglio V., *L'architettura della piramidi Menfite*, parti II, III, IV, V, VI, VII, VIII (fino alla quinta dinastia), Rapallo, 1963-1975.
Siliotti A., *EGITTO - Uomini, templi e dei*, Vercelli, 1994.
Siliotti A., *Guida alle piramidi d'Egitto*, Vercelli, 1997.
Stadelmann R., *Die Ägyptischen*

*Pyramiden - Von Ziegelbau zum Weltwunder*, Mainz am Rhein, 1991.
Vandier J., *Manuel d'archéologie égyptienne*, Paris, 1952-58.

**Photo credits:**
Archivio White Star: pages 115 top, 118, 119, 120-121, 122-123,129 top left.
Antonio Attini/Archivio White Star: pages 125 bottom left, 128-129.
Marcello Bertinetti/Archivio White Star: pages 116-117, 124-125, 130-131, 132 top, 134-135.
Araldo De Luca/Archivio White Star: pages 114, 125 top, 132 bottom, 132-133 bottom, 133 bottom, 136-137.
National Geographic Society: pages 132-133 top.
Alberto Siliotti/Archivio Image Service: pages 125 bottom right, 128 top, 129, 133 top right and left.
Giulio Veggi/Archivio White Star: pages 114-115, 126-127.

## THE VALLEY OF THE KINGS AND THE TREASURE OF TUTANKHAMUN
### Text by Alberto Siliotti

**Bibliography**
Belzoni G.B., *Viaggi in Egitto e in Nubia,* critical edition edited by A. Siliotti, Verona, 2000.
Carter H., Mace A.C., *The Tomb of Tut.Ankh.Amen*, London, 1922-1933
Desroches Noblecourt Ch., *Tutankhamon*, Paris, 1963.
Frankfort H., *La religione dell'Antico Egitto*, Torino 1957.
Goyon J.C., *Rituels funéraires de l'ancienne Égypte*, 1972.
Hornung E., *Tal der Könige*, Zurich / Munich 1982.
Montet P., *Géographie de l'Egypte ancienne*, I-II, Paris, 1957-61.
Porter B., Moss R.L.B, *Topographical Bibliography of Ancient Egyptian Hieroglyphic Texts, Reliefs and Paintings* , Oxford, 1960.
Posener G., Sauneron S, Yoyotte J., *Dictionnaire de la civilisation égyptienne*, Paris, 1959.
Reeves N. *The complete Tutankhamun*, London, 1990.
Reeves N., Wilkinson R. H., *The complete Valley of the Kings*, London, 1996.
Siliotti A., *EGITTO - Uomini, templi e dei*, Vercelli, 1994.
Siliotti A., *Guida alla Valle dei re, ai templi e alle necropoli tebane*, Vercelli, 1996.
Vandier J., *Manuel d'archéologie égyptienne*, Paris, 1952-58.

**Photo credits:**
Felipe Alcoceba: pages 140-141.
Giovanni Dagli Orti: pages 150 bottom, 151 bottom.
Araldo De Luca/Archivio White Star: pages 139 bottom, 142-143, 144 top, 144 bottom right, 145 bottom left, 146-147, 148, 149, 152-153, 158, 159, 160-161, 162, 163, 164, 165, 166, 167, 168-169, 170, 171, 172-173, 174, 175, 176, 177, 178, 179.
Kenneth Garrett: pages 138-139.
Griffith Institute/Asmolean Museum: pages 154, 155, 156, 157.
Alberto Siliotti/Archivio Image

Service: pages 145 top, 145 bottom right, 150-151.
Giulio Veggi/Archivio White Star: page 150 top.

## THE TOMB OF SENNEFER AND THE TOMBS OF THE NOBLES IN THEBES
### Text by Alberto Siliotti

**Bibliography**
AA.VV., *Reconstitution du caveau de Sennefer dit "Tombe aux Vignes"*, Paris, 1985.
Bruyère B., *Rapport sur les fouilles de Deir el Médineh*, Cairo, 1924 - 1953
Cerny J., *A Community of Workmen at Thebes in the Ramesside Period*, Cairo, 1973.
Porter B., Moss R.L.B, *Topographical Bibliography of Ancient Egyptian Hieroglyphic Texts, Reliefs and Paintings*, Oxford, 1960.
Schiapparelli E., *Relazione dei lavori della Missione archeologica italiana in Egitto: I, la tomba intatta dell'architetto Kha*, Turin, 1922.
Shedid A.G., Seidel M., *Das Grab der Nacht*, Mainz am Rhein, 1991.
Siliotti A., *EGITTO - Uomini, templi e dei*, Vercelli, 1994.
Siliotti A., *Guida alla Valle dei re, ai templi e alle necropoli tebane*, Vercelli, 1996.
Vandier J., *Manuel d'archéologie égyptienne*, Paris, 1952-58.

**Photo credits:**
Ag. Double's: pages 198 top, 198 bottom left, 197 bottom right.
Archivio White Star: pages 192-193.
Marcello Bertinetti/Archivio White Star: pages 184-185.
Damm/Bildarchiv Huber/Sime: pages 194 top left, 194 bottom, 195, 196.
Giovanni Dagli Orti: pages 183 bottom, 188 bottom, 188-189, 198-199.
Araldo De Luca/Archivio White Star: pages 180-181, 186-187, 188 top, 190-191, 202-203.
Charles Lenars: pages 194 top right, 199 bottom.
Alberto Siliotti/Archivio Image Service: pages 182-183, 183 top, 199 bottom left.

## THE GOLDEN MUMMIES OF BAHARIYA OASIS
### Text by Alberto Siliotti

**Bibliography**
Fakry A., *The Oasis of Egypt*, Cairo, 1974
Porter B., Moss R.L.B, *Topographical Bibliography of Ancient Egyptian Hieroglyphic Texts, Reliefs and Paintings*, Oxford, 1960.

**Photo credits:**
Marcello Bertinetti/Archivio White Star: pages 206-207.
Marc Deville/Ag. Gamma: pages 204 top right, 204-205, 208, 209, 210-211, 212, 213 top left, 213 bottom right.
Plailly/Eurelios: pages 205 top and bottom, 210 bottom, 211 top and bottom, 213 top right, 213 center right, 214, 215 top right, 215 bottom.
Alberto Siliotti/Archivio Image Service: pages 204 top left, 215 top left.

## NEMRUD DAGH: NEAR THE HEAVENLY THRONES
### Text by Marcello Spanu

**Marcello Spanu** (Rome 1961) is a Researcher of the ancient world at the Department of Sciences in the Faculty of Cultural Heritage, Tuscia University, in Viterbo. He has been a member of archaeological digs in Italy and Turkey.
He is the author of many scholarly articles on the art and architecture of Roman provinces, including the monograph Keramos of Caria.

**Bibliography**
Humann K., Puchstein O., *Reisen in Kleinasien und Nordsyrien*, Berlin, 1890.
Neugebauer O., van Hoesen H.B., *Greek Horoscopes*, Philadelphia, 1959.
*Nemrud Dagi. The* hierothesion *of Antiochus I of Commagene*. Winona Lake Indiana, 1996.

**Photo credits:**
Antonio Attini/Archivio White Star: page 224 top.
Massimo Borchi/Archivio White Star: pages 217, 218 basso, 218-219, 220 top, 220 bottom, 221.
Carteret/Hoa Qui/Ag. Franca Speranza: page 220 center.
Robert Frerck/Odyssey/Ag. Franca Speranza: pages 216, 218 top.
Alberto Siliotti/Archivio Image Service: page 219 bottom.
Adam Woolfitt/Corbis/Contrasto: pages 222-223.

## THE GREAT ROCK TOMBS OF PETRA
### Text by Marcello Spanu

**Bibliography**
Amadasi Guzzo M.G., Equini Schneider E., *Petra*, Milan; 1997.
Browning I., *Petra*, London, 1982.
Brünnow R., von Domaszewki A., *Die Provincia Arabia I*, Strasbourg, 1904.
MacKenzie J., *The Architecture of Petra*, Oxford, 1990.

**Photo credits:**
Archivio White Star: pages 226, 227.
Yann Arthus-Bertrand/Corbis/Contrasto: pages 230-231.
Antonio Attini/Archivio White Star: page 237 bottom right.
Massimo Borchi/Archivio White Star: pages 224 bottom, 224-225, 160 top and bottom left, 233, 240 top, 241 top, 242-243.
Giulio Veggi/Archivio White Star: pages 224 center, 228, 229, 232 top and bottom right, 234, 235, 236, 236-237, 237 bottom left, 238, 239, 240-241.

## THE NECROPOLIS AT PALMYRA
### Text by Danila Piacentini

**Danila Piacentini** is a specialist in Semitic philology and epigraphy. Under the guidance of Professor Amadasi Guzzo, she wrote a thesis on the spoken language in Palmyra (Syria).
She contributes to the teaching of Semitic epigraphy at "La Sapienza" University in Rome, with particular emphasis on Phoenician epigraphic finds in the sanctuary of Astarte at Tas Silg (Malta).

**Bibliography**
Amy R. - Seyrig H., *Recherches dans la nécropole de Palmyre*, Syria 7, 1936, 228-266.
Drijvers H.J.W., *Afterlife and Funerary Symbolism in Palmyrene Religion*, in *La soteriologia dei culti orientali nell'impero romano*, Bianchi U. - Vermaseren M.J. (ed.). Atti del colloquio internazionale, Rome 24-28 September 1979, *Études préliminaires aux religions orientales dans l'empire romain 92*, Leiden, 1982, 709-733.
Gawlikowski M., *Monuments funéraires de Palmyre*, Warsaw, 1970.
Schmidt-Colinet A., *Das Tempelgrab n° 36 in Palmyra. Studien zur palmyrenischen Grabarchitektur*, Mainz am Rhein, 1992.
Seyrig H., *Le repas des morts et le "banquet funèbre" à Palmyre*, Annales archéologiques de Syrie 1, 1951, 1-11.

**Photo credits:**
Tristan Blaise/Ag. Visa: pages 244-245.
Giovanni Dagli Orti: pages 248 top right, 248 bottom, 248-249, 249 bottom, 250, 251.
Renato Lievore/Ag. Focus Team: pages 246-247.
Nara International Foundation-commemorating the Silk Road Exposition (research centre for Silk Roadology): pages 247, 252, 253, 254, 255.
Richard T. Nowitz/Corbis/Contrasto: pages 256, 257.
Henri Stierlin: pages 244, 245 top and bottom, 248 top, 249 bottom.

## THE ROYAL CEMETERY OF UR
### Text by Claudio Saporetti

**Claudio Saporetti** was formerly the Research Director at the National Research Council and now teaches Assyriology at the University of Pisa. He also directs the Assyriology Workshop and is in charge of the "Eshnunna" project and the EAC project (Electronic analysis of cuneiform texts).

**Bibliography**
Frankfort H., *The Art and Architecture of the Ancient Orient*, Harmondsworth 1969; in italiano *Arte e Architettura dell'Antico Oriente*, Turin, 1970, 43 sg.
Giacardi L. - Boero S.C., *La matematica delle civiltà arcaiche*, Turin, 1979, 257 sg. (*Il mistero di un antichissimo gioco mesopotamico*).
Invernizzi A., *Dal Tigri all'Eufrate, I Sumeri e Accadi*, Florence 1992, 288 sg.
Nissen H.J., *Zur Datierung des Königsfriedhofes von Ur, unter besonderer Berücksichtigung der Stratigraphie der Privatgräber*, Bonn, 1966.
Parrot A., *Sumer*, Paris, 1960; in italiano *I Sumeri*, Milan, 1982, 175 sg.

Pinnock F., *Ur: la città del dio-luna*, Bari, 1955, 117 sg (*IV. Il Cimitero Reale*).
Pollock S., *Chronology of the Royal Cemetery of Ur*, "Iraq" 47 (1985), 129 sg.
Saporetti C., *Gilgameö e Minosse*, "Mesopotamia" 21 (1986), 243.
Woolley C.L., *Ur Excavations II. The Royal Cemetery*, London, 1934.
Woolley C.L., *Ur of the Chaldees*, London, 1930, ediz. 1942, 23 sg. (*II. The Graves of the Kings of Ur*).
Woolley C.L., *Excavations at Ur*, London 1954; in italiano *Ur dei Caldei*, Turin, 1958, 61 sg. (*III: La Necropoli Reale*).

**Photo credits:**
Archivio Scala: page 270 left bottom.
Giovanni Dagli Orti: page 258 top left.
Henri Stierlin: page 259.
The British Museum: pages 262, 262-263, 263 top and center.
The Trustees of The British Museum: pages 264 top and bottom, 265 top and bottom.
Robert Tixador/Ag. Top: page 258 bottom.
University of Pensylvania Museum, Philadelphia: pages 262 top right, 263 bottom, 266, 267, 268, 269, 270 left, 270-271, 271 right.
Nik Wheeler/Corbis/Contrasto: pages 260-261.

## ASIA AND THE FAR EAST
### Text by Alberto Siliotti

**Photo credits:**
Archivio White Star: pages 272-273.
Patrick Aventurier/Ag. Gamma: page 275.
Araldo De Luca/Archivio White Star: pages 276-277.

## THE FUNERARY RITES OF THE PEOPLES OF THE STEPPES
### Text by Paola D'Amore

**Paola D'Amore** is curator of the Near and Middle Eastern department of the National Museum of Oriental Art in Rome. She has taken part in several archaeological trips to Syria. She was the curator of the Italian leg of the exhibition "Kurgan treasures from the northern Caucasus" (Rome 1991) and scientific edition of the "Oxus" exhibition (Rome 1992). She has written many articles on Iranian art in the 1st millennium BC.

**Bibliography**
Artamanov M.I., *Treasure from Scythian Tombs*, London, 1969.
Briant P., *Etat et pasteurs au Moyen Orient ancien*, Paris, 1983.
D'Amore P., *Elementi scitici ed assiri nelle guaine iraniche del I millennio a.C.: Vicino Oriente 1*, 1978.
D'Amore P., Lombardo G., *Vicino Oriente e Caucaso*, Rome, 1991.
Greyson A.K., *Assyrian and Babylonian Chronicles*, New York, 1975.
Jettmar K., *Art of the Steppes*, New York, 1964.
Khazanov A.M., *Storia sociale degli Sciti*, Moscow, 1970.
Khazanov A.M., *The Dawn of Scythian History: Iranica Antiqua 17*, 1982.
Leskov A. et alii, *I tesori dei kurgani del Caucaso settentrionale*, Rome, 1991.
Marcenko K. - Vinogradov Y., *The Scythians in the Black Sea region: Antiquity 63*, 1989.
Minnns E.H., *The Art of the Northern Nomads*, Cambridge, 1942.
Erodoto, *Le storie* (edited by Annibaletto L. ), Milan, 1956.
Parlato S., *La cosiddetta campagna scitica di Dario: Annali dell'Istituto Orientale di Napoli 41*, 1981.
Piotrovsky B., *L'art scythe*, Leningrad, 1986.
Schiltz V., *Gli Sciti*, Milan, 1994.
Sulimirski T., *Prehistoric Russia*, London, 1970.
Talbot Rice T., *The Scythians*, London, 1957.

**Photo credits:**
Agenzia Luisa Ricciarini: page 284 top.
Archivio Iconografico, S.A./Corbis/Contrasto: page 281.
Camera Commercio Italo-Kazaka: pages 286-287, 288, 289.
Centro Studi Ligabue, Venezia: pages 282, 282-283 top, 284 top left, 286-287, 287 top, 290, 291, 292, 293.
Charles O'Rear/Corbis/Contrasto: pages 280, 280-281.

## THE STUPA AT SANCHI IN THE MADHYA PRADESH
### Text by Marilia Albanese

**Marilia Albanese** is a lecturer in Indian Culture at the Civic School of Oriental Languages and Cultures in Milan, of which she is also President. She is also director of the Lombard section of the Italian Institute for Africa and the Orient in Milan. She has made about twenty trips to India, Sri Lanka, Thailand, Cambodia, and Laos to deepen her knowledge of the Hindu and Buddhist worlds. She has written many articles and books.

**Bibliography**
Delahoutre M.: *ARTE INDIANA*, ed. Jaca Book, Milan, 1996.
Marshall Sir J. and Foucher A.: *The Monuments of Sanchi*, Delhi, 1955.
Mitra D.: *SANCHI, Archaeological Survey of India*, New Delhi, 1978.
Pant S.: *The Origin and Development of Stupa Architecture in India*, Varanasi, 1976.
Taddei M.: *INDIA ANTICA*, ed. Mondadori, Milan, 1982.
Sivaramamurti C.: *INDIA, CEYLON, NEPAL, TIBET*, 2 vol., ed. Utet, Torin, 1988.
Tadgell C.: *The History of Architecture in India*, Viking, New Delhi, 1990.

**Photo credits:**
Stefano Amantini/Atlantide: pages 303-304.
Patrick Aventurier/Ag. Gamma: page 303 bottom.
Marcello Bertinetti/Archivio White Star: page 295 top.
Massimo Borchi/Archivio White Star: pages 294, 295 bottom, 296, 297, 300 top and bottom, 300-301, 302-303, 304.

Chris Lisle/Corbis/Contrasto: pages 306-307.
Adam Woolfitt/Corbis/Contrasto: pages 298, 299, 298-299.

## THE ANGKOR WAT COMPLEX Text by Marilia Albanese

**Bibliography**
Boisselier J.: *Le Cambodge*, in "Manuel d'archéologie d'Extrême Orient, Asie du sud-est, Tome I", Picard, Paris, 1966.
Coedès G.: *Angkor, an introduction*, Oxford University Press, London, 1963.
Dagens B.: *Angkor la foresta di pietra*, ed. Electa/Gallimard, Trieste, 1995.
Mazzeo D. e Silvi Antonini C.: *Civiltà Khmer*, in "Le grandi civiltà" ed. Arnoldo Mondadori, Milan, 1972.
*Angkor et Dix Siecles d'Art Khmer*, Catalogue de l'exposition à la Galerie nationale du Grand Palais, Paris January/May 1997.
Stierlin H.: *Angkor, Architecture Universelle*, Office du Livre, 1970.

**Photo credits:**
Archivio White Star: pages 312, 313.
Christophe Boisivieux: pages 320 bottom, 326-327.
Livio Bourbon/Archivio White Star: pages 310-311, 324-325, 328-329.
Marco Casiraghi: pages 326 top, 326 bottom.
Michael Freeman: pages 314-315, 318-319.
Brian Harsford/Ffotograff: page 320 top left.
Suzanne Held: pages 316, 317 top, 320 bottom and top right, 320 center, 321, 322, 322-323, 323 top.
Friedrich Stark/Das Photoarchiv: page 327 bottom.
Henri Stierlin: page 323 center and bottom.
Alison Wright: pages 316-317, 317 bottom.

## THE MAUSOLEUM OF THE FIRST EMPEROR OF THE QIN DYNASTY
### Text by Filippo Salviati

**Filippo Salviati** (Florence 30/08/1961), has a Ph.D. from the School of Oriental and African Studies in London and is a Research Doctor in the art and architecture of ancient China at the University of Rome. He also writes for several newspapers and magazines (Giornale dell'Arte, Archeo, Minerva, The Asian Art Newspaper). He is the author of several volumes in Italian and English including China: land of heavenly emperors (1997) and Memories of the Orient, the catalogue of an exhibition at Rimini Museum in 1999.

**Bibliography**
AA.VV., *7000 anni di Cina. Arte e archeologia cinese dal neolitico alla dinastia degli Han*, Silvana Editoriale, Milan, 1983.
AA.VV., *Cina 220 a.C. I guerrieri di Xi'an*, Abitare Segesta Cataloghi, Milan, 1994.

Arthur Cotterell, *The First Emperor of China*, Penguin Books, London, 1981.
Filippo Salviati, *Cina, terra degli imperatori celesti*, Archeo-monografie, De Agostini-Rizzoli, Year VI, no. 2, April, 1997.

**Photo credits:**
Aschenbrenner/Bildarchiv Huber/Sime: pages 330 top, 330-331, 341.
Araldo De Luca/Archivio White Star: pages 332-333, 334-335, 338-339, 342, 343, 346-347.
Bertrand Gardel/Hemispheres: page 345 top left.
Photo Corc/Ag. Gamma: pages 336 top, 336-337, 337 bottom.
Scholz/Bildangentur Schuster/Farabola: page 330 bottom.
Summerfield/Index, Firenze: pages 336 bottom, 340.
Vogelsang/Zefa: page 344.

## TOMBS AND FUNERARY PRACTICES OF THE HAN DYNASTY
### Text by Filippo Salviati

**Bibliography**
AA.VV, *Stories from China's Past. Han Dynasty Pictorial Tomb Reliefs and Archaeological Objects from Sichuan Province, People's Republic of China*, Chinese Culture Foundation, San Francisco, 1987.
Edmund Capon and William MacQuitty, *Princes of Jade*, Sphere Books, London, 1973.
Wu Hung, *Monumentality in Early Chinese Art and Architecture*, Stanford University Press, Stanford, 1995.
Michèle Pirazzoli-t'Serstevens, *The Han Civilization of China*, Phaidon Press, Oxford, 1982.

**Photo credits:**
Art Exhibitions China: page 351 top.
Cultural Relics Publishing House for the photo of Anping: pages 348-349.
Francesco Salviati: pages 350 top.
Summerfield/Index, Firenze: pages 350-351.

## THE IMPERIAL MAUSOLEUMS OF THE TÁNG DYNASTY
### Text by Filippo Salviati

**Bibliography**
Lucia Caterina, "Dipinti murali in tombe di epoca Tang", China, vol.16, 1980, pp.317-359.
Edward Capon e Werner Forman, *La Cina dei Tang. Civiltà e splendori di un'età d'oro*, De Agostini, Novara, 1990.
Carol Michaelson, Gilded Dragons. *Buried Treasures from China's Golden Ages*, British Museum Press, London, 1999.
Shaanxi Provincial Museum, *Highlights of the Táng Dynasty Tomb Frescoes, Shaanxi People's Fine Arts Publishing House*, Xi'an, 1991.

**Photo credits:**
Patrick Aventurier/Ag. Gamma: pages 360, 361, 362, 363, 364, 365.
Courtesy of Eskenazi Ltd: pages 353 center, 358 left, 359 bottom.
Christie's Images: pages 358-359 center, 359 right.

Cultural Relics Publishing House, Pechino: pages 354-355.
Lowell Georgia/Corbis/Contrasto: page 354 top and bottom.
Suzanne Held: pages 352 bottom, 352-353, 353 bottom, 356-357.
Francesco Salviati: page 353 top.

## AMERICAS
### Text by Eduardo Matos Moctezuma

**Eduardo Matos Moctezuma** is the current director of the Templo Mayor in Mexico City. He studied in Mexico, specializing in History and Anthropology. During his long professional career since the 1960s, he has held positions of authority in the bodies (INAH and ENAH) responsible for the conservation and study of Mexico's archaeological heritage.

He has received awards from universities around the world (France, Venezuela, and Colorado) and has always combined his on-site research at Teotihuacan, Puebla, Tula, and Mexico City with his academic commitments. He has published more than fifty articles and twenty books including: "The Aztecs", Jaca Book 1989, and "The Great Temple of the Aztecs", Thames & Hudson, 1988.

**Photo credits:**
Archivio Scala: page 369.
Archivio White Star: pages 366-367.
Massimo Borchi/Archivio White Star: pages 370-371.

## THE CITY OF THE GODS: TEOTIHUACAN
### Text by Eduardo Matos Moctezuma

**Bibliography**
Cabrera Castro, Rubén, (Coord.), *Memoria del Proyecto Arqueológico Teotihuacan*, Colección Científica, no. 132, INAH, Mexico, 1982.
Cabrera Castro, Rubén, *Las excavaciones en la Ventilla, un barrio teotihuacano*, Revista Mexicana de Estudios Antropológicos, tomo XLII, Mexico, 1996, pp. 5-30.
Cabrera Castro, Rubén, *Últimas excavaciones (1980-1988)*, apéndice del libro de Eduardo Matos Moctezuma, *Teotihuacan, la metrópoli de los dioses*, Corpus Precolombino, sección Civilizaciones mesoamericanas, proyecto de Román Piña Chán, Matos Moctezuma, Eduardo (Coord.), La aventura Humana, de Carlo Demichelis, Lunwerg Editores, S.A., Barcelona, Madrid, 1990, pp. 187-220.
Sugiyama, Saburo, *Descubrimientos de entierros y ofrendas dedicadas al Templo Viejo de Quetzalcóatl, Teotihuacán 1980-1982*. Nuevas interpretaciones, Cabrera, Rubén, Noel Morelos e Ignacio Rodriguez (Coords.), INAH, Mexico, 1991, pp. 275-326.
Matos Moctezuma, Eduardo, *Teotihuacan, la metrópoli de los dioses*, Corpus Precolombino, sección Civilizaciones mesoamericanas, proyecto de Román Piña Chán, Matos Moctezuma, Eduardo (Coord.), *La aventura Humana*, de Carlo Demichelis, Lunwerg Editores, S.A., Barcelona, Madrid, 1990, 240 pp.
Matos Moctezuma, Eduardo, *Museo de la cultura teotihuacana. Gula*. Artes de México, Instituto Cultural Domecq, Mexico, 1995, 143 pp.
Matos Moctezuma, Eduardo, *Introducción*, p. 15; *La Pirámide del Sol en Teotihuacan*, pp. 16-23; *Excavaciones recientes en la Pirámide del Sol, 1993-1994*, pp. 312-329; *La Pirámide del Sol en Teotihuacan*, Antología, Artes de México, Instituto Cultural Domecq, Mexico, 1995.
Matos Moctezuma, Eduardo, *La Pirámide del Sol y el primer coatepantli conocido del centro de México*, Antropología e Interdisciplina, Ruz, Mario Humberto y Julieta Aréchiga (Eds.), XXIII Mesa Redonda de la Sociedad Mexicana de Antropología, *Homenaje a Pedro Carrasco*, Mexico, 1995, pp. 404-413.

**Photo credits:**
Yann Arthus-Bertrand/Corbis/Contrasto: pages 374-375.
Antonio Attini/Archivio White Star: pages 372 bottom, 372- 373, 373 right, 376, 376-377.
Giovanni Dagli Orti: pages 372 top, 380 bottom right.
Rafael Doniz: pages 378 top, 378-379, 379 right.
Werner Forman Archive/Index, Firenze: page 381.
Ignacio Guevara: page 380 top left.
Marco Pacheco: page 378 bottom.

## PALENQUE AND PACAL'S HIDDEN TOMB
### Text by Eduardo Matos Moctezuma

**Bibliography**
Templo de las Inscripciones
Ruz Lhuillier, Alberto, *Exploraciones arqueológicas en Palenque*: 1949, informe inédito, Archivio Técnico de la Dirección de Monumentos prehispánicos, vol. 17, INAH, Mexico, 1949.
Ruz Lhuillier, Alberto, *El Templo de las Inscripciones de Palenque*, Collección Cientifica, Serie Arqueología, no. 7, INAH, Mexico, 1973.
Green Robertson, Merle, *The Sculpture of Palenque, The Temple of the Inscriptions*, vol. 1, Princeton University Press, Princeton, 1983.
Gonzáles Cruz, Arnoldo, *Nuevos descubrimientos en Palenque, el Templo de la Cruz*, sobretiro de Arquelogía Mexicana, no. 2, CNCA/INAH/Editorial Raices, Mexico, 1993.
Gonzáles Cruz, Arnoldo, *El Templo de la Reina Roja, Palenque, Chiapas*, Arqueología Mexicana, vol. 5, no. 30, 1998, p. 61.

**Photo credits:**
Antonio Attini/Archivio White Star: pages 392-393 center, 393, 394.
Archivio White Star: pages 384, 385, 387 top, 389 right.
Biblioteque de l'Homme/BNP: pages 386-387.
Biblioteque Nazionale de France, Parigi: pages 386, 387.
Massimo Borchi/Archivio White Star: pages 382, 383, 385, 388 left.
Werner Forman Archive/Index, Firenze: page 392 left.
Henri Stierlin: pages 390 top and bottom, 391, 395.

## THE SACRED ZAPOTEC CITY: MONTE ALBÁN
### Text by Eduardo Matos Moctezuma

**Bibliography**
Caso, Alfonso e Ignacio Bernal, *Urnas de Oaxaca*, no. 2 de las Memorias del Instituto Nacional de Antropología e Historia, INAH-SEP, Mexico, 1952.
Caso, Alfonso, Ignacio Bernal y Jorge Acosta, *La cerámica de Monte Albán*, no. 13 de las Memorias del Instituto Nacional de Antropología e Historia, INAH-SEP, Mexico, 1967.
Caso, Alfonso, *El Tesoro de Monte Albán*, Insituto Nacional de Antropología e Historia, III, SEP, Mexico, 1969.
Caso, Alfonso; *Culturas Mixteca y Zapoteca*, Biblioteca del Maestro, Ediciones encuadernables de El Nacional, Mexico, 1942.

**Photo credits:**
Giovanni Dagli Orti: pages 396 top right, 398, 399, 401 bottom.
Rafael Doniz: pages 396 left, 397 bottom, 400 left, 402, 403.
Franck Lechenet/Hemispheres: pages 396-397.
Henri Stierlin: pages 400-401 center, 401 right top.

## SIPÁN: MAGNIFICENCE AND MYSTERY OF THE MOCHE ROYAL TOMBS
### Text by Walter Alva

**Walter Alva** studied archaeology at the University of Trujillo. He specialized in pre-Inca cultures at an early age and was supervisor of the archaeological monuments in the region of Lambayeque between 1975 and 1977. Since 1977 he has been the director of the Museo Arqueológico Nacional Brüning de Lambayeque. He has led many digs in Peru including the one that led to the discovery of the royal Moche tombs in Sipán. Today he is a member of various archaeological institutes and an honorary professor in many Peruvian universities. He has been awarded military and civil recognition by the government of Peru and is still the director of archaeological research at Sipán.

**Bibliography**
Alva, Walter. *Discovering the New World's Richest Unlooted Tomb*. National Geographic Society, 174 (4): 510-555. Washington, D.C. 1988.
Alva, Walter L. y Donnan, Christopher B. *Royal Tomb of Sipán*. Catálogo de Exhibición Fowler Museum of Cultural History. Los Angeles, California, 1993.
Cieza de León, Pedro de. *The travels of Pedro Cieza de León*, A.D. 1532-1550. London: Hakluyt Society, 1864.
Evans, Clifford. *Finding the Tomb of the Warrior-God*. National Geographic, 91 (4): 453-482. Washington, D.C. 1947.
Jonnes, Jiulie. *Mochica Works of art in Metal: A review*. Dumbarton Oaks Conference on Pre-Columbian Metallurgy of South America. (E.P. Benson, de.): 53-104. Washington D.C., 1975.
Kutscher, Gerdt. *Nordperuanische gefaf malereien des Moche-Stliss*. Germany: Materialien zur Allegemeinen und Vergleicheden Ärchaologie. Band 18. Verlag C.H. Beck. München. Bonn, 1983.
Lavalle Vigue, Daniéle France. *Les Représentations animales dans la céramique Mochica*. Paris: Université de Paris. Mémoires de L'Institut d'Ethnologie, IV. Institut d'Ethnologie, Musée de l'Homme, 1970.
Lechtman, Hearther Nan, *Style in technology-Some early thoughts*. Material Cultura, Styles, Organization and Dynamics of Technology, (H. Lechtman and R. Meorill, eds.) West Publishing. Co., St Paul. 1977.
Ruppert, Hans. *Geochemische Unter suchungen an Turkis und sodalith ans Lagerstatten und Prekolumbieschen Kulturem del Kordilleran*. Berliner Beitragen Zur Archäometrie Van 8: 101-210. 1983.
Uhle, Max. *Die Ruinen von Moche*. Journal de la Societé des Américanistes, n.s., Tomo X: 95-117. Paris: 1913.

**Photo credits:**
Nathan Benn/Corbis/Contrasto: page 407.
Araldo De Luca/Archivio White Star: page 432.
Museo Archeologico Lambayeque, Sipan: pages 404, 405, 408 top and bottom, 409, 410, 411, 412, 413, 414, 415, 416, 417, 418, 419, 420, 421.
Kevin Schafer/Corbis/Contrasto: pages 406, 408 center.

**The Spanish texts by Eduardo Matos Moctezuma and Walter Alva were translated by Bianca Filippone.**

*The Publisher wishes to thank the Chamber of Commerce Italo-Kazakha, the Centro Studi Ricerche Ligabue, Eskenazi Ltd, The Nara International Foundation - commemorating the Silk Road Exposition - and his Research Center for Silk Roadology.*